SO-EGI-721

The Democratic Ideal
and the Shoah

SUNY series in Contemporary Jewish Thought
Richard A. Cohen, editor

The Democratic Ideal and the Shoah

The Unthought in Political Modernity

SHMUEL TRIGANO

Translated by
GILA WALKER

SUNY
PRESS

First published as *L'idéal démocratique à l'epréuve de la Shoa*, by Shmuel Trigano.
Copyright © 1999 by Éditions Odile Jacob, 15, rue Soufflot, 75005 Paris,
http://www.odilejacob.fr

Published by
State University of New York Press, Albany

© 2009 State University of New York

All rights reserved

Printed in the United States of America

No part of this book may be used or reproduced in any manner whatsoever
without written permission. No part of this book may be stored in a retrieval
system or transmitted in any form or by any means including electronic,
electrostatic, magnetic tape, mechanical, photocopying, recording, or otherwise
without the prior permission in writing of the publisher.

For information, contact State University of New York Press, Albany, NY
www.sunypress.edu

Production by Eileen Meehan
Marketing by Fran Keneston

Library of Congress Cataloging-in-Publication Data

Trigano, Shmuel.
 [Idéal démocratique à l'épreuve de la Shoa. English]
 The democratic ideal and the Shoah : the unthought in political modernity /
Shmuel Trigano ; translated by Gila Walker.
     p. cm. — (SUNY series in contemporary Jewish thought)
 Includes bibliographical references and index.
 ISBN 978-1-4384-2629-7 (hardcover : alk. paper)
  1. Holocaust, Jewish (1939–1945)—Historiography. 2. Holocaust, Jewish (1939–
1945)—Moral and ethical aspects. 3. Holocaust, Jewish (1939–1945)—Causes.
4. Jews—Identity. 5. Philosophy, Jewish. 6. Democracy. 7. Jews—Politics and
government. 8. Jews—Intellectual life. I. Title.

 D804.348.T7513 2009
 940.53'18072—dc22   2009005427

10 9 8 7 6 5 4 3 2 1

There is hardly an aspect of contemporary history more irritating and mystifying than the fact that of all the great unsolved political questions of our century, it should have been this seemingly small and unimportant Jewish problem that had the dubious honor of setting the whole infernal machine in motion. Such discrepancies between cause and effect outrage our common sense [. . . and] gravely threaten our sense of proportion and our hope for sanity.

—Hannah Arendt, *Anti-Semitism*

Enemy of the Jews, the anti-Semite has need of them. Anti-democratic, he is a natural product of democracies and can only manifest himself within the framework of the Republic.

There may not be so much difference between the anti-Semite and the democrat. The former wishes to destroy him as a man and leave nothing in him but the Jew, the pariah, the untouchable; the latter wishes to destroy him as a Jew and leave nothing in him but the man, the abstract and universal subject of the rights of man and the rights of the citizen.

Does the Jew exist? And if he exists, what is he? Is he first a Jew or first a man?

—Jean-Paul Sartre, *Anti-Semite and Jew*

The deeper motives of anti-Semitism have their roots in times long past; they come from the unconscious.

—Sigmund Freud, *Moses and Monotheism*

Contents

INTRODUCTION

A Reversal in Perspective

A strange debate has been raging in Western democracies in recent years, one that raises a number of interrelated questions. Is the Shoah a unique event in the history of humanity, or is it just one out of the many genocides marking the bloody history of the twentieth century? Is this catastrophe to be understood in the sole light of the singular experience of the Jewish condition or in that of the universal experience of contemporary politics? What about the Armenians, the Gypsies, the Cambodians, and the Rwandans? Were they not struck by the same tragedy as the Jews? How much importance is to be given to the Jewish dimension of the genocide and how much to its universal thrust?

In this debate, at first sight academic, it is the assumption of the "singularity of the Shoah" that is on the hot seat. There are those who see the Shoah as an utterly unique event with the Jews at its center and consider comparisons to any other event a sacrilege. This thesis has been stated over and over again in the English-speaking world.[1] Among its advocates are Elie Wiesel, who regards the Holocaust as "the ultimate event, the ultimate mystery, never to be comprehended or transmitted";[2] Georges Steiner, who locates the "qualitative differences between the Shoah and innumerable other examples of mass murder" in the "symbolic and meta-physical-theological realm";[3] Claude Lanzmann, who refers to the "obscene effrontery" of those who "deny the specificity of the Holocaust and its impious character by diluting or burying an exorbitant crime, of another nature altogether, in a question of universal evil";[4] and Paul Ricœur, for whom the Shoah is a "uniquely unique event" and its victims "delegates to our memory of all the victims of history."[5] All of the theologies of the Shoah that see a divine mystery in it subscribe to this viewpoint. The others, their staunch opponents, hold this interpretation to be a self-serving ideological manipulation aimed at promoting the power, prestige, and identity of the Jews in particular and Western discourse in general. Western democracies, they claim, identify with Jewish martyrology in an attempt to wash away their own genocidal colonial sins. The extermination of the Jews would thus "mask" other genocides in the past and, worse still, in the present. Notwithstanding the revisionist tone of this argument, it is defended not so much by revisionists as by thinkers belonging to what used to be quali- fied as leftist circles, who criticize the "conservative liberal ideology"[6] in particular, and liberal democracy in general.

What they are denouncing in the invocation of the Shoah's uniqueness is the claim by a particular group to what Tzvetan Todorov calls "a permanent privilege." "Such-and-such a group has been a victim of injustice in the past," he explains. "This opens to it in the present an inexhaustible line of credit. Since society recognizes that groups, and not individuals, have rights, you might as well profit from it; and, the greater the offense in the past, the greater the rights in the present. Instead of struggling to obtain a privilege, you receive it automatically by belonging to a once-disfavored group."[7] Todorov also states that "[T]he group that does not manage to detach itself from persistent com- memoration of the past [. . .], or rather those who at the center of that group incite others to live thus, are less deserving of sympathy: in this case, the past serves to repress the present."[8] We can clearly see that the collective status of the Jews is very much at issue in this debate. According to Alain Brossat, the discourse on the singularity of the Shoah has ceased to focus on the singular monstrous nature of the crime "to harden into a narrowly sectarian-stance: the Shoah is us, its uniqueness is ours, it is our affair. It is not a surprise that the (historical) discourse of singularity easily joins up with the religious discourse of chosenness. Auschwitz becomes paradoxically intelligible as the sign or mark of the elective particularity of Jewish destiny." Brossat concludes that "Israel, defined as a payment for Auschwitz, becomes inseparable from the Shoah [. . . and] as insane and unimaginable as it might seem, the Shoah enters the sphere of calculations and interests" of "Jewish community leaders in the Diaspora" and "strategists in the State of Israel."[9]

Such an ideological outlook extends beyond the confines of the newly emerging Left to encompass coalitions more to the center Right of the political spectrum (Gaullist or "national republican") that readily join in the chorus. It is commonplace in these circles to hear criticism of Jewish "*communautarisme*."[10] And it is sometimes voiced with regard to the Shoah. Jean Mattéoli, chairman of the Study Mission on the Spoliation of Jews in France[11] and formerly a French resistance fighter, expressed his "hope that the Jews do not make this mistake. French Jews are Jews but they are French. To make a distinction between Jewish Frenchmen and Catholic Frenchmen, or what have you, for strictly comparable damages would create a truly disturbing precedent, to which the Jews themselves could ultimately fall victim. In France there is no difference at all between a Jew and a non- Jew [. . .]. The Germans were the ones who made this distinction [. . .]. It is sad to see the Jewish community declaring that it is satisfied with a sum of money from German firms. There is no cause and effect relationship between the damage and the compensation."[12] In short, French Jews were killed by the Germans because they were Jewish, but it was the Frenchmen in them who died. That such an ideological arc stretches from the Left to the Right underscores the structural rather than the conjunctural underpinnings of the debate on the uniqueness of the Shoah.

And what a strange debate it is! The "unique" character of an event (which is always singular, by definition) is seldom the subject of so much discussion. Who argues over the unique character of the French Revolution in 1789, an event peculiar to France yet of universal significance? What is being called into question in the current debate is the very substance of the event (be it absolutized or negated)—namely, the *Jewish* victims. As we will see, the question of singularity and universality is not just hollow verbosity; a good number of other issues are surfacing in this debate. We have reached a critical juncture: those who lived through the Shoah directly and their contemporaries are passing away, and the memory of the Shoah is about to be instituted for generations to come.

What, then, is the deep-seated, hidden meaning of this controversy? On the one hand, the thesis of absolute singularity safeguards the central phenomenon of the Shoah, namely, the identity of the victims, but at the same time it inevitably converts the Shoah into an absolute that compels silence and opens onto an aura of mystery whose sacredness is highly problematical. On the other hand, the thesis of absolute universality disregards the concrete reality of the extermination of the Jews and tends in the direction of the most simplistically disturbing interpretation possible, that of a "plot" on the part of Jews who are accused of symbolically manipulating the Shoah to serve their own interests.

I will start my analysis with the following hypothesis: If the Shoah indeed concerns everyone insofar as it addresses the question of the meaning and value of modernity, then it is solely because the singular experience of the Jews is at its center. The Shoah thus can be understood from the perspective of the many hecatombs that marked the twentieth century without its uniqueness being negated. If the Shoah is to serve as a "lesson" to us, then it is precisely this problematical superposition of the singular and the universal that must be understood. And by lesson I certainly do not mean the discovery of an intrinsic "meaning" to the Shoah or a utilitarian interpretation that turns it into an *exemplum*, a model for understanding a whole series of events, as Tzvetan Todorov would have it. The Shoah marks a major break in modernity, and it is a matter of comprehending its effects on those of us who live "after."

It is a break that lacerates us in all spheres of life and tears through the spaces of democratic politics. I will try to delineate its contours progressively, starting from the current controversy and delving deep down into its buried fundaments, to the "primal scene" of modern politics. What does it reveal to us about the modern world against the backdrop of the promises harbored by modernity and the expectations that it had awakened? My purpose in raising this question is neither moral nor psychological—terms in which it has been framed repeatedly before. Rather, it is ethical, for ethics concerns acts. And what better, more dignified, and vivifying way is there of memorializing the victims of the genocide than drawing a lesson from the Shoah insofar as our acts are concerned, which means comprehending the vices of modern politics to prevent such catastrophes from happening again.

Such an endeavor is premised upon a "comprehensive" approach embracing the singular and the universal, Jews and modern people, the unique Shoah, and the whole political modernity of the democratic nation-state. The point is not to judge on the basis of moral principles, as has been done so many times before, but to understand what happened in the past and what is happening today. There are those who try to delegitimate attempts to "think Auschwitz"[13] by asserting that all such efforts are sacrilegious. This is a purely rhetorical, self-contradictory stance, since the assertion is itself a product of thought. Filmmakers, writers, philosophers, or theologians who take up the Shoah obviously structure their ideas, arrange their effects, and select the elements that will be integrated into their works. Only through thought, and not mystery, can we prevent banalization and indifference. Only by questioning reality can we escape the grips of fate. Auschwitz did not take place at some indefinite time in some abstract realm of principles. It happened in the very heart of modern, democratic Europe. Masking this reality, prohibiting its intellectual grasp, amounts to condemning the "survivors' (and most particularly the Jews) to the eternal status of victims, bound forever to Nazism; it means letting an unresolved "mystery" sap democracy until it undermines or corrupts it totally. Moreover, such a taboo on an event can only lead to its eclipse in the long run. It becomes too heavy and too remote a burden for individual consciousness to bear.

These questions do not concern the number of angels on the head of a pin. They are not merely a matter of memory, nor do they concern the past only. They have acute, even dire, present-day relevance, and they prefigure the politics of tomorrow. The debate on the Shoah engages a subterranean and subjacent debate on the future of modern politics. The Second World War marked a break in the history of the modern world, and democracy has not been the same since. Its normative transcendence has been eroded, its abstract universality tempered. The rights of man have opened the doors to women, blacks, and cultural and sexual minorities. While multiculturalism was becoming a buzzword in Europe, President Clinton expressed his hope that the United States would be the world's first truly "multiracial democracy"; in the same country, "communitarianism" is being increasingly advocated in an attempt to bring individuals and social groups closer to politics. The collapse of communism announced even more drastic changes, including the inevitable decline of the parliamentary system of political representation based on a bipolar cleavage between the Left and the Right. In what way can the Shoah, as the culmination of a long process set in motion at the start of the modern era, elucidate current developments in democratic citizenship? In what way can the singular experience that the Jews had of democratic citizenship shed light on recent realities? The Jewish experience of absolute singularization within citizenship could serve as a litmus test for democracy in general. We need not delve very far into the experience that the Jews had of a radical loss of citizenship to see that the life they were forced to endure, outside the civilized democratic framework, as if in a state of civic weightlessness, casts by default a harsh light on political modernity, and the precious lesson to be learned from this concerns everybody. Both critics and advocates of the Shoah's singularity are implicitly referring to an order of things that is beyond them. Far from being a manipulation by Jews, as revisionists and neoleftists contend, the (often excessive) centrality of the Shoah in public debate may well express something of the fundamental democratic aspiration and deeply ingrained life instinct that has survived totalitarianism and the hecatombs of the twentieth century. Examining these perspectives, hidden behind all the rhetorical noise, is at the heart of my investigation.

To carry through such a task involves comprehending this "singularity" not as an exception to modernity but as a phenomenon inherent to it, and this requires a qualitative leap. Instead of raising the question of the singularity *of* the Shoah, it is the singularity *in* the Shoah that is at issue. It is the *singularization* of the Jews in the Shoah that needs to be analyzed. If the Shoah is to be understood as an intrinsic part of modernity of universal import, then the singularity lodged at its center assumes a different dimension. The focus is not so much on the event's unique, exceptional character as on the radical, absolute singularization to which the Jews were subjected in Europe and which culminated in their extermination. How did it come to pass that the Jews of Europe, individual citizens and nationals of their respective countries, were singled out from their fellow countrymen to be concentrated and destroyed en masse with no regard to nationality, to be demoted from a legal and political status to a racial and biological state? What makes for the unique, incomparable character of the Shoah is this experience of singularization of the Jews in the realm of democratic citizenship in particular and of political modernity in general, the experience of being excised from contemporary humanity. We must start from reality, that is, from the civic status of Jews and not from some mythical notion of an "eternal" Jew, dissociated and dissociable from his citizenship. We must start from modernity to understand totalitarianism rather than thinking of the latter as an exception in an attempt to preserve the moral and ideological integrity of the former. What were the foundations upon which Nazism leaned to isolate the Jew in the citizen?

This shift in focus from the Jew to the citizen is a complete reversal in the usual perspective. It runs counter to the contention made by advocates of the singularity *of* the Shoah that it is the Jew in the citizen who is to be considered firstly, and even exclusively, as if one could separate the singularity of the Jew from the rational, democratic universalism of the citizen, which would remain intact. In point of fact, the question concerns democracy first and foremost. How did it come to pass that the Jew subsisted in the citizen without being protected, to the point of overriding the citizen in him or her?

Rethinking the Shoah in conjunction with modernity raises, however, a number of moral and epistemological questions that must be addressed. Apprehending modernity as an integral whole, embracing the Enlightenment and the Shoah, human rights and anti-Semitism or racism, democracy and totalitarianism as all part of the same picture is tricky, perhaps even dangerous, business because of the confused thinking to which it may lead. It means using an approach that is basically sociological (whose foremost concern, therefore, is not morality, which does not mean that it is immoral). This approach aims at acquiring a *morphological* view of reality, from a position outside the subject of contemplation, in an attempt to grasp it in its formal objectivity without taking its "spirit" into consideration. If we were to frame the issue in the terms that oppose intentionalist and functionalist historians of the Shoah, then this approach would fall into the functionalist category, since it endeavors to understand what it was in the making of modernity that could produce firstly anti-Semitism and then a catastrophe such as the Shoah. The "intentionalist" school would be the one that asserts the integrity of modernity, understood as a value and an ultimate ideal, that the happenstance of Nazism or the specific project of Hitler as an individual man threatened in an extemporaneous, erratic manner. To this school, the Nazi phenomenon was a departure from the rationality of modernity, which, as a structure, an edifice, and a value, has survived intact.

The morphological view does not necessarily apprehend the whole truth of a phenomenon, but it does grasp its force of inertia. For this reason, the approach must be accompanied by a protocol specifying the limits and defining the aims. Democracy is not totalitarian; the Rights of Man run contrary to racism; the emancipation of the Jews was defeated by the Shoah. But they all belonged to the same period of time (modernity), to the same place (Europe), and to the same society (the democratic nation-state). And there is a pressing need to understand why this was so, particularly today in an era that abounds in genocides and human catastrophes. I am drawing therefore a very emphatic boundary between democracy and totalitarianism, knowing nonetheless that the line that divides brings together what it separates by setting them side by side.

It is this boundary that the revisionists cross when they see in democracy the mark of capitalism, Nazism, and colonialism. This is the case for Paul Rassinier, one of the foremost revisionists, for whom Nazi Germany, the capitalist bourgeois West, and the USSR are regimes of the same type, equally guilty of atrocities (the Gestapo, colonial wars, the Gulag and the KBG, etc.). It is also the case in neoleftist circles. Brossat sees a connection between recent crimes ("the Rwandan genocide, the ethnic purification by the Serbs and the urbicide practices in Grozny and Sarajevo") and "the distinctive dominant trait of our present-day history, namely the globalization of the democratic paradigm," and he wonders about the "link between the now-total domination of a single politico-cultural model—capitalist democracy—and the outpouring of extreme violence."[14] Louis Janover, an analyst of the intelligentsia, quotes leftists denouncing "the so-called revisionist historians, nostalgic for National Socialism, who [. . .] transform a partial *truth*[15]—the democratic, Zionist and Stalinist manipulation of the Nazis' genocidal enterprise—into a total lie,"[16] while he himself asserts that what are called "the mistakes and blunders of 'democracy' are usually massacres."[17] All these views bear the stamp of Marxism and its critique of "bourgeois democracy." In fact, this line of reasoning seems irresistibly drawn to the Marxist temptation to interpret the hiatus inherent in everyday life (the fact that an individual's experience seldom lives up to his or her hopes and expectations) in ideological terms, as a mystification.

This will not be my case. I will distinguish between democracy as a value and a yet-to-be attained ideal, and democracy as an accomplished reality, a reality that has been implemented for the past two centuries and that has demonstrated all its potentials, the best and the worst. Knowing the ambivalence of modern reality, I will not use the failings of democracies as a pretext to call into question the democratic ideal. All the same, one cannot fail to note that democracy gave rise to the rule of law, but also to what Jacob Talmon called "totalitarian democracies."[18] In his classic study, the Israeli historian observes that totalitarianism was grounded in the democratic ideal and notably in the fervor that characterized the French Revolution. The two viewpoints are not necessarily contradictory. Democracy, liberty, and modernity are vague concepts that can be invested with different meanings (Communist-period use of the expression "socialist democracies" is a notable case in point). We can therefore criticize the perversion of democracy by "totalitarian democracies" in the name of the democratic ideal while staying within the bounds of modern reason. It would be counterproductive to let ourselves be trapped by an ideological appropriation of words. On the ethical plane, my analysis will be guided by the spirit and promise of the democratic ideal, aptly summed up by the Republican motto "liberty, equality, fraternity." But one must understand how this passion for liberty, equality, and human community (which is the true sense of the term *fraternity*) could lead to such grave miscarriages and failures, due no doubt to human beings but perhaps also to defects intrinsic to the ideas themselves and their underlying framework. This is why, to understand the Shoah and other political catastrophes of the twentieth century, we must take the democratic citizen as the starting point, not the "eternal" Jew in his singularity. Concentrating primarily on the Jew without examining the history of political modernity, whose figurehead is democracy, safeguards its ideal integrity but condemns us to understanding nothing about its erratic history. This perspective tends to view the Jew as an archetype outside history, and it promotes more literature and theology on the Shoah than political philosophy. I do not mean to say that theology has nothing to say about the Shoah, but neither can it say all there is to be said on the subject. The genocide brings humans into question well before God.

There are vast areas of darkness in modernity that the dazzle of the Enlightenment should not lead us to ignore, especially after such a long series of recurrent human and political catastrophes. One of its greatest "mysteries" is without a doubt the anti-Semitic phenomenon (before the racist phenomenon), which has remained unexplained despite the wealth of publications on the subject. We still have not understood what could give rise to it in a culture that had broken with Christianity, and its historical animosity toward Judaism, and emancipated the Jews (who played along) by assimilating them (to all other human beings). We still have not understood how the racist mania of classification and, more generally, the socioeconomic hierarchization of people (the classes) were possible in an era that gave primacy to equality. And what about the invention of universal man just when colonialism was conquering the planet and destroying entire civilizations? Why did the distinctive identity of the nation come to disrupt the principle of universality that governed human rights? Why can only nationals be citizens? The least that can be said is that there is a gap between the promises of modernity and reality, a structural ambivalence of sorts. And there have been times when darkness prevailed over light. Thus the transition to Nazism and Vichy took place in compliance with the formal rules of parliamentary democracy. In the Weimar Republic in 1932, a majority of the electorate (51 percent) did not hesitate to vote into parliament two parties—the Nazis and the Communists—that militated in favor of dissolving the Republic, and the advantage given to the Nazi Party in these elections (37 percent in July and 33 percent in November) made it impossible to form a government without them. Setting aside the parliamentary intrigues of the Nazis and von Papen's conservative party, which can be put down to manipulation, the Nazi rise to power firstly expressed a deep-seated desire among the citizens of the Weimer Republic. In France, it was the National Assembly on July 10, 1940, that voted to confer absolute powers upon Marshal Pétain, who was thereby legally established as chief of state before he did away with the Republic.

To explore this equivocal area between democracy and totalitarianism, Tzvetan Todorov employs the concept of the "extreme." This topological metaphor fits the subject of analysis into a picture structured on the relationship between center and periphery, with the periphery characterized by its remoteness (at the extremity) from the source of all values (that is, from the center, which he maintains is "extreme" as well but by its intensity). The concentration camps are "the extreme manifestation of totalitarian regimes which are the extreme form of modern political life." As such, they serve as "an instrument, a magnifying glass" to get a better look at the ordinary morality and everyday reality of our world.[19] Todorov's system of measurement thus uses excess rather than normality as a yardstick. The idea that excess can provide insight into the norm implicitly signifies that the norm harbors the potential of excess, or, to put it otherwise, that Nazism is a potential development of democracy. I will not have recourse to such a metaphor in my analysis, all the more so in that it serves Todorov to subsume the singularity of the destruction of the Jews into a more general category that fails, in my opinion, to apprehend what needs to be understood—namely, the singularization of the Jews in the Shoah.

To consider political modernity as a whole, and hence to put it to the test of totalitarianism and of the Shoah as typically "modern" phenomena, I propose to adopt Freud's model of the relationship between the conscious and the unconscious. Just as there is a part of the mind that defies the individual's control, so democracy has an unconscious dimension. Irrationality, or rather prerationality, is lodged at the very heart of democratic rationality. It is a constituent part of its makeup. Repressed by the conscious mind (the emerged part of the iceberg), unconscious thoughts continue beneath the surface to exert an influence on the mind, to the point of submerging it in certain circumstances. The unconscious cannot be dissociated from the conscious. We can see in the latter democracy as a value and a potential prospect, and in the former, democracy as an accomplished history and an achieved reality. According to this model, everything that the self cannot accept in the real world is pushed into the unconscious, in particular, traumatic experiences, repressed to protect the development of the self. The conscious mind is like a frail craft floating on the sea of the unconscious, born from the sea and fighting to withstand its turmoil. When Freud set out to explain the conscious in light of the unconscious, which the psychoanalyst tries to bring to the surface, he by no means pretended that the conscious was an illusory simulacrum, as Marx said of ideology. Quite the opposite—it was to clarify and solidify the conscious mind that he took to exploring the subterranean waters of the unconscious. Freud saw the conscious mind as the seat of the ego, the most resistant part of the individual despite its frailty, the locus of compromise between interiority and exteriority whose purpose is to safeguard the individual. Whereas the ego strives to be moral, the unconscious is amoral and therefore potentially immoral. To fight against the impulses welling up from the unconscious, it creates a hyper-moral superego whose energy is derived from the unconscious (the process of "sublimation"). Freud thought that the greatest saints, those who embodied the highest moral standards, had had to struggle to overcome stronger immoral impulses than individuals with ordinary passions. To Freud, then, morality was commensurate with the propensity for sin. But it remained a principle of regulation of life and the conscious self and not a mystification, as Marx would have said. In a similar way, in setting out to examine the unconscious dimension of democracy, my purpose is not to turn it against the conscious dimension in an attempt to undermine the foundations and value of the democratic ideal but, on the contrary, to strengthen democratic reason and sharpen its defenses against the realm of darkness lurking inside. Just as the extremely moral superego is closely related to the submoral unconscious, so there is a relationship or a contiguity between democracy and its flip side within a single system—the human psyche for Freud and modernity, notably in its political dimension, for our purposes. There would be, then, a structural flaw in modernity, which has given rise over the past two centuries to the demons that have ravaged democracy—the frail tip of the modern iceberg.

I am proposing here a tentative explanatory model that offers the advantage of being framed in the psychoanalytical terms that have become common everyday parlance. It is not meant to be the "last word" on the subject, but it may useful insofar as it combines the qualities of a psycho-analytical approach with those of a more sociological methodology, providing a descriptive account of social reality. This model clearly demonstrates the "clinical" thrust of my undertaking, the aim of which is to probe the ins and outs of a strange phenomenon, prior to and as a foundation for the exercise of judgment. The sense of moral outrage that the Shoah elicits does not suffice; the haste with which moral judgment is passed all too often hides a refusal to undertake a considered examination of reality. This is a serious mistake when it comes to the analysis of totalitarianism, which is first and foremost a historical and political phenomenon. We can hardly hope to get rid of fascism simply by condemning it and holding it up to public ridicule. To look at the question from an analytical perspective, we have to understand the good along with the evil, the moral along with its opposite. I am aware that this approach may shock common opinion with its inclination to immediacy and pathos. I also am aware that it runs counter to the current, all-embracing ethical outlook that runs the risk of becoming a new form of metaphysics if it refuses to recognize and examine the historical nature of the human condition.

The problematic that will be discussed here unfolds on two stages: Jewish singularity and democratic universalism. It is this antinomy that I will set out to understand. Part 1 concentrates on the contemporary manifestations of this singularity; part 2 delves into its universal substratum, that is, into the fundaments of political modernity and its inhospitality to all forms of singularity, and understanding what constitutes this singularity will be the subject of part 3. In this method of exposition, the theory put forward cannot be fully stated at the outset, thus certain notions may assume a different meaning in the course of the analysis.

Part 1

The Jew-of-the-Citizen

CHAPTER 1

Naked Singularity in the Shoah

It is hard for us to picture what the singling out of Jews under the Nazi heel was like, how the surrounding world suddenly collapsed, the ground gave way, and we were sent hurtling into a bottomless pit. How, in the most familiar places, our compatriots turned away from us as if repelled by an invisible wall. How our points of reference were overturned and we were left in the nakedness of a world stripped of meaning. When the Gestapo (or Vichy's police) came to track them down one by one in their homes, the Jews were citizens who thought they were like all other individuals in the citizenship game. But arrested and deported, they were nothing but naked Jews, stripped literally (of their clothing for the bogus showers, but real gas chambers at the end of the train ride) and figuratively (of their legal status, their individual identity, and their humanity, reduced to numbers to be registered on the infamous account books of the total Reich). At Auschwitz—which I will take as a symbol of the camps—Jews were grouped together without distinction of origin and nationality. With their individuality and identity dissolved in a generic mass, were they still "Jews"? In the deportation, the Jew was singled out from the citizen, removed from civic normality, and isolated in a vacuum, but this singularity was so cut off from political and human universality that it was devoid of meaning, even for itself. Absolute uniqueness is tantamount to a dis-identification. It is in this respect that I say that it is "naked," because by being reduced to itself, to its own exteriority, it is stripped of meaning. Meaning is always a movement in the direction of others, a movement toward the future. Massification necessarily leads to "reification." The Nazis went so far as to imagine making lamp shades from the skin of their victims, soap from their fat, wigs from their hair, and ingots from the dental gold plundered from their corpses. Something in the way of a "mineralization" of the human had taken place in the camps. The human had become an inert object in a forsaken world, not merely exterminated.

The Model of the Individual Citizen

It is important to know something of the history of the admission of Jews to citizenship to understand the profound nature of such a subversion of order and its deep-seated impact on both the Jewish condition and the civic condition. The emancipation of the Jews in the French Revolution had totally transformed the identity of the Jews in Europe: from a "nation," in the ancien régime sense, tolerated but excluded from the official social order, they had become abstract individuals like all other citizens. This restructuring of their identity was the condition of admission to citizenship. The emancipation of the Jews went hand in hand with the suppression of all the orders, castes, and corporations that had been an integral part of the deeply inegalitarian aristocratic society. Before the Emancipation, the Jews had been identified as a "corporation"—a despised caste, to be sure, but nonetheless a full-fledged hereditary group that sometimes acted as a professional corporate entity in the economic sphere.

A representative of the Jews at the Convention put the spirit of revolutionary citizenship in the following terms: "There can be no equality where there are differences."[1] Thus Jewish citizenship was founded on the demise of the "Jewish nation," that is, of the collective status of Jews. The opinions expressed by two well-known advocates of the Emancipation, Comte de Clermont-Tonnerre and Abbé Grégoire, are straight to the point. "They say to me, the Jews have their own judges and laws. I respond that is your fault and you should not allow it. We must refuse everything to the Jews as a nation and accord everything to Jews as individuals," Paris deputy Clermont-Tonnerre famously declared, adding, "We must withdraw recognition from their judges [. . .] We must refuse legal protection to the maintenance of the so-called laws of their Judaic organization; they should not be allowed to form in the state either a political body or an order. They must be citizens individually. But, some will say to me, they do not want to be citizens. Well then! If they do not want to be citizens, they should say so, and then, we should banish them. It is repugnant to have in the state . . . a nation within the nation."[2] And Abbé Grégoire called for "an end to organizations that manage Jewish community civic affairs and an end to Jewish communities [. . .] they will be obliged to use the national language in all their documents and even in the practice of their religion."[3]

Upon these bases, the Jews undertook to recast and redefine themselves. Their "regeneration" (an idea to which I will return) was inherent in the project of their emancipation as the title of Abbé Grégoire's *Essay on the Political, Moral and Physical Regeneration of the Jews* (1789) explicitly states. The Jews were asked to formally renounce the historical bond that they had forged among themselves for thousands of years and to don the robes of individual citizens. The "Grand Sanhedrin," convoked by Napoleon I in 1807, pronounced in no uncertain terms the dissolution of the Jewish nation and its political bonds and restructured Jewishness around a denominational definition of Judaism: "Divine law [. . .] contains religious measures and political measures," they proclaimed. "Religious measures are by their nature absolute and independent of circumstance and time. This is not the case for political measures, which were intended to govern the people of Israel in Palestine when there were kings, priests, and judges. There are no further grounds for applying such political measures since the people of Israel no longer form a national body."[4]

From that point on Jews appeared in the public sphere as abstract individuals, whose Jewishness was no longer anything but a private affair. This new frame of mind was accompanied by the radiant promise of a universalism that espoused the progress of humanity and on the altar of which the Jews willingly sacrificed a particularity henceforth seen as closed, restricted, and ultimately meaningless. There in a nutshell is the structural principle of Jewish modernity, as much in its institution as in its ideology. With the Napoleonic conquests, which launched the signal of Jewish emancipation throughout despotic Europe, this model spread first to European Jewry before extending, in the colonial period, to Mediterranean Jewry, thereby leaving its hallmark on the two geographic worlds where the majority of Jews lived before the great migratory movements of the early twentieth century. Modern Jews cannot be considered from outside this prism. Modern consciousness cannot see Jews in any other light.

Admittedly, this was the destiny of all the peoples of Europe at the time, but it had an exceptional taste for the Jews because of the condition that was theirs before the Emancipation—that of an excluded people, that considered itself in exile, with a culture, language, and religion that differed from its surroundings, and no territory of its own. If the other peoples of Europe were recast by the alchemy of modernization to meet the criteria of citizenship, they nevertheless kept their lands, their traditions, their languages, and the fundaments of their culture—all of which was ineluctably lost to the Jews, who were no longer a people and who entered the homes of other cultures and other peoples. That is why their experience was paroxysmal, and that is why they were more modern than the moderns. It is in this sense that their singular destiny has meaning for modernity as a whole.

The "Racialization" of the Jews

This is the model that was brutally shaken by Auschwitz, where modern Jews found themselves, as if by force of fate, by some physical, generic necessity (call it the Jewish "species"), defined as a collective, as a sociohis-torical body, only to be thrust in the same breath outside history to an unimaginable no-man's-land. In the camps, there was a complete overturn-ing of the individual civic condition of modern Jews who were revealed to themselves and to others as a people, a collective formed by the necessity of the world, and even the necessity of nature (as if it were a biological or physical fact). Suddenly, belonging to the Jewish community was no longer a matter of choice, as it had been theoretically for the Jews in Western Europe, via religion, or in Eastern Europe, via political activism (Jews had already opted for a national and collective destiny in Bundism, a nationalist movement of the Diaspora in Poland, or in Zionism and its struggle to build a Jewish national state). Tragically confronted with this new situation, the Jews pursued by the Nazis seemed to have been struck with paralysis. They did not immediately understand what target was being attacked in them, and this is why they had such difficulty dodging the blow. The deportation took hold of the Jews in a place where they were no longer expecting it. It hit them in the "dark," repressed, and unresolved part of their identity and did so on the basis of a logic that was inconceivable to them and to modern consciousness. The deportation came to track down Jews who were no longer anything but individuals; it tracked them down because of their affiliation to a collective that modernity (and modern Jews to begin with) had repudiated or, at least, temporarily dismissed. Their citizenship had been founded, in fact, upon the ruins of this collective. Thus Auschwitz made an archaic relic surface from the unconscious of modern Jews and non-Jews alike, a cumbersome corpse that no one knew what to do with, a vestige of the past that *resembles* a "Jewish people" and that weighs upon them immeasurably.

But what I am defining here in the light of history as a "people" was a race to the Nazis, a generic population below the level of historical or political differentiation. If the "people" surged back again, then it found itself immediately invalidated as such and defined as a "race." It goes without saying that what seemed "obvious" to the Nazis was not at all so in reality. The Jews do not constitute a "race," the very concept of which is regarded as problematical today. When the Nazis isolated, objectively, a Jewish "collective" from a supposedly abstract, universal citizenry, and stripped it of its citizen status, they were acknowledging in acts this dimen-sion of "peoplehood" without being able to recognize it for what it was. We can read this ambiguity between the lines of an early text by Hitler: "There lives amongst us a non-German, alien race which neither wishes nor is able to sacrifice its racial character or to deny its feeling, thinking, and striving. Nevertheless, it possesses all the political rights we do [. . .] In his effects and consequences [the Jew] is like a racial tuberculosis of the nations."[5] The terms Hitler employs to describe the conduct of this "race" ("feeling, thinking, and striving") have more to do with the characteristics of a people than with racial traits. We have here a paradoxical sign that Nazism is unconsciously at one with modernity and consciously intent on destroying it. Indeed, the notion of individual emancipation was so strongly ingrained in modern consciousness that it was "congenitally" intolerable to conceive of a Jewish collective in terms of a "people." The category of "race" served as an indirect means of designating this collective in terms no longer sociohistorical but biological and infra political (and here the paradox continues, because the racial designation denies as much the civic condition of Jews as their condition as a historical people).

Recourse to a racial category to define the Jew was therefore highly problematical in Nazi discourse and practice. The definition, notes Raul Hilberg, was "in no sense based on racial criteria, such as blood type, curvature of the nose, or other physical characteristics. Nazis commentators, for propagandistic reasons, called the decrees 'racial laws,' and non-German writers, adopting this language, have also referred to these definitions as 'racial.' But [. . .] the sole criterion for categorization [. . .] was religion [. . .] After all, the Nazis were not interested in the 'Jewish nose.' They were concerned with the 'Jewish influence'."[6] Père Jean Dujardin also points to the religious basis of the supposedly racial criteria: "According to the Nuremberg laws, a 'full Jew' was a person with at least three 'racially Jewish' grandparents. But prescriptions for the application of these laws specified that a grandfather is considered Jewish if he belongs to the Jewish religious community. This religious criterion is even more explicit in the second anti-Jewish laws [*Statut des Juifs*] adopted by the French Vichy government, which oddly confused religion and race. One was Jewish because one was a member of the Jewish people."[7] The internal contradiction that characterized Nazism is also evident in the attempt to exclude Jews from the human species. Avishai Margalit and Gabriel Motzkin have rightly observed that by humiliating and degrading the Jews before eliminating them, the Nazis aimed at excluding them not only from the German people but from the human species, just as they denied this universal category of humanity precisely by excluding the Jews from it and asserting the superiority of the Aryan race over inferior races.[8]

The debate about the "Jewish race" does not, in fact, date to the Nazi period. It haunted the nineteenth century in the form of anti-Semitism, generally defined as a category of racism. To the Jews this anti-Semitism, which constituted the first crisis in Jewish citizenship, was an inexplicable phenomenon. What exactly was being attacked in them since they had become citizens and were not a different race? There was nothing in democratic consciousness that could serve as a basis for such hatred.

Contrary to the theological anti-Judaism of the church, there seemed to be no origin for anti-Semitism in the clear consciousness of democracy. For this reason, it was ascribed to irrational, uncontrolled impulses and to atavism. Yet its basic myth, the "Jewish plot," is very explicit about what is at issue. Here again we are dealing with a Jewish group, perforce clandestine and anonymous, and outside citizenship, since it does not fit into the framework of modern politics.

The racial dimension applied to the "Jewish question" is therefore highly problematical, and we must not let ourselves be sidetracked by it. What is being designated in the "race" is a Jewish group, a "Jewish people" of sorts. It appears in a disguised form (as a "race"), since it immediately disappears as a "people," physically through extermination and symbolically through racialization (a people is not a race). This appearance/disappearance syndrome may very well be the hidden form of the singularization of the Jews; its clarification is problematic, yet it is of decisive importance. It can be seen at work in the current difficulty in naming—and therefore in defining—the extermination of the Jews. Is genocide (with its reference to race but also origin, family, and descent) an accurate term, being that Jews do not constitute a race? And what are we to make of the confusion and (heated) discussions around the concept, and whether it should be reserved to what happened to the Jews, as partisans of the singularity *of* the Shoah maintain, or applied to the many different mass killings perpetrated since the conquest of the Americas?[9] When jurist Raphaël Lemkin coined the term in 1944, he insisted on the exterminated "collectivity": "By 'genocide' we mean the destruction of a nation or of an ethnic group."[10] Robert Antelme, a survivor, has made it clear that in spite of the generic massification of individuals that took place in the camps, they were by no means places of nondifferentiation; they were, to the contrary, productive of differences, of people trying to survive in the face of their programmed destruction.[11] By the "concentration" that they produced, the camps morphologically assumed the existence of a Jewish "group," that had already become the logical target of deportation and destruction after having been erased from consciousness and from political terminology by being designated a "race." The extermination of the Jewish "race" took place outside the framework of citizenship, which could thereby dispense with retaining its memory.

In a way, we are still suffering today from the effects of the Nazi perversion of language. The Nazis devised a coded idiom, the *amtssprache*, to deal with the extermination of the Jews by camouflaging it, using words such as "final solution" or "special treatment" (*sonderbehandlung* also indicated preferential treatment to guests in luxury hotels, for instance). Their language makes it hard for us to identify and comprehend the object of their aggression in the "genocide." In practice the Nazis identified the Jews as a people within democratic citizenship and then immediately proceeded to negate this Jewish people first in language, by designating them as a race, and then in acts, by physical eliminating them.

The "People" after Auschwitz

The main question, then, is to know if the Nazi identification was a pure delusion, a fantasy of their own making, or if it rested on a dimension of reality repressed by modern political ideology and thus if, at the basis of all these developments, a Jewish people really exists beneath the cloak of a race or the false front of a "plot." The three hypotheses are plausible, and my analysis in this first part is aimed precisely at unraveling their intricately tangled skein.

I will start with an empirical observation: after the Shoah, a change took place in the singular status of the Jews. As the Jews reentered citizenship, their identification as Jews began taking hold in the consciousness of society and of the Jews themselves. Yet this identification was neither considered nor clarified by either. Democracy's "unconscious" no doubt continued to throw all its weight into the balance, and life went on as if citizenship had come out of the catastrophe unshaken. The citizen as such had survived intact. Only the Jew had been affected. This state of affairs was reflected in the legal treatment of Jewish survivors after the war. The status of the Jews as a "group" had already been admitted indirectly at the Nuremberg trials with the introduction of the category of "genocide" to designate their destruction. The French and Belgian administrations drew a distinction between two categories of concentration camp survivors: the "racial deportees," victims of a "crime against humanity," who were to receive material compensation, and the political deportees, who had been interned because of their patriotic acts and who were, for their part, to receive honors. But even this objective reality was not recognized; as one survivor recalls, racial deportees were met in Europe and Israel by "opprobrium" and "accused of letting themselves be led like sheep to the slaughter."[12] The statutory discrimination after the war only ratified a distinction that already existed in the camps where members of the Resistance, as Simone Veil remarked, "insisted, for good reason, on marking themselves off as voluntary fighters, not victims, whose passivity remained a subject of reproach for a long time."[13] It is now widely recognized that upon their return from the camps, nobody wanted to hear the testimony of Jewish survivors,[14] and that they themselves tended to stifle the expression of the plight that was theirs specifically as Jews.[15] Even at the Nuremberg trials, the Jews were not allowed to speak in the name of Jewish victims! The way in which the Jews were treated at their return drew the following comments from Jean-Paul Sartre in 1947: "Do we say anything about the Jews? Do we give a thought to those who died in the gas chambers at Lublin? Not a word. Not a line in the newspapers. That is because we must not irritate the anti-Semites; more than ever we need unity."[16]

In sum, the Jews who had been persecuted and murdered as Jews, as everyone was well aware, were held to have died as human beings, and Jewish survivors were expected to come home and join the ranks of citizens as if nothing had happened. The pretexts or explanations given, at a time when Europe was just recovering from the mass graves of the Shoah (the need for national unity after the liberation or to avoid fueling anti-Semitism again, the post-trauma aphasia on the part of deportees or even their feeling of shame, etc.), are simply stupefying in hindsight. Anyone who has retained a capacity for wonderment will recognize in the odd reception given to the Jews at their return from the camps the sign of a powerful repression, a repression bordering on a denial of reality. We are touching here upon a fundamental dimension of modernity's relationship to itself through its relationship to Jewish existence. It is this dimension, which is at the heart of the contemporary democratic debate, that I propose to elucidate in my analysis.

The Jews, for their part, accepted this situation. "Does anyone think that the Jews don't know what is happening, that they don't understand the reasons for this silence?," Sartre asks, before describing the reasons for their "resigned wisdom." "They have made a clandestine return, and their joy at being liberated is not part of the nation's joy. The following little anecdote will serve to show what they have suffered on this account. In my *Lettres Françaises*, without thinking about it particularly, and simply for the sake of completeness, I wrote something or other about the sufferings of the prisoners of war, the deportees, the political prisoners, and the Jews. Several Jews thanked me in a most touching manner. How completely must they have felt themselves abandoned, to think of thanking an author for merely having written the word 'Jew' in an article!"[17] No doubt the Jews had no choice, but also and more especially they had learned a pragmatic lesson from what had happened to them. They returned to their citizenship as if nothing had happened, but they knew from experience the fragility of it, in particular insofar as their collective condition was concerned. The catastrophe they had been through proved to them that it could be criminal for individual Jews to hold themselves aloof from their collective destiny, that they needed, on the contrary, to reinforce their collective solidarity to counter the schemes and hatred that regularly targeted them (since nineteenth-century anti-Semitism), from which citizenship and modern consciousness could not protect them. This explains the revival in the

1950s of a movement of identification with Jewish history and collective life. After the war, the *collective* destiny of Jews in the polity was an obvious fact to everyone, even though it continued to be deeply repressed on the symbolical and political levels. This collective destiny was manifested in two developments: the birth of Jewish "communities" in the Diaspora and the momentous event that represented the creation of the state of Israel. These are the two sociopolitical faces of post-Shoah Jewish singularity.

Historian Henry Rousso is not wrong in asserting that the Jews, banished by Vichy, did their best to avoid maintaining "the exclusion from the national community that they wanted to wipe out of their memory at all costs."[18] However, he seems to ignore a patent development that was happening on another level after the war: the establishment of the first Jewish "community" in France since the Emancipation. The initial sign of its birth had manifested itself in the French Resistance with the creation of the *Conseil représentatif des israélites de France*, or the CRIF,[19] a political body to represent all Jewish members of the Resistance, including the Communists, vis-à-vis the National Council of Resistance (the CNR, or *Conseil national de la Résistance*), the legitimate political authority at the time. The CRIF supplanted the representativeness of the Central Consistory, formerly established by the French state, without statutorily contesting it, since the head of the CRIF was also the president of the Consistory. On the other hand, it clearly contested the representativeness of the Union générale des israélites de France (UGIF), Vichy's interlocutor. It is interesting to note, following Annie Kriegel,[20] that whereas the CRIF subsisted, the CNR was absorbed into the newly restored Republic. The newly emerging Jewish "community" in the early postwar period was no longer an exclusively religious entity, since the CRIF brought together the entire spectrum of Jewish institutions and defended interests that were not limited to the religious sphere. Even so, with a single president at the head of both bodies, consistorial Judaism continued to play a central role in unifying the Jews of France and facilitating their return to the Republic's constitutional legality. The birth of this "community" in France was doubly revolutionary, first in terms of French political culture and its congenital Jacobin centralism and more generally in terms of the democratic system as a whole, since no such phenomenon had been seen in countries where Jews enjoyed the rights of citizenship. Community institutional structures with force of law over the Jews in each given community had subsisted in despotic states (in Eastern Europe, Russia, and the Orient) where the Jews were confined to ghettos and held collectively accountable to the state. But here were Jews who had regained their individual civic status and yet were voluntarily forming communities—symbolic communities with weak institutions, to be sure, but communities all the same; through them, Jews could express their sense of belonging to and identifying with world Jewry in general and the Jews of Israel in particular.[21] What we were witnessing was the emergence, with growing intensity, of an affirmation of the singularity of the Jews as a collective in what was theoretically an abstract and individual democratic citizenship. We have here the setting for the postwar Jewish revival.

But it was not until the creation of the Jewish state that the development of collective Jewish singularization became a massive and manifest phenomenon. The Jews redefined themselves as a singular entity, on the international plane this time, and according to the criterion of normality in force since the nineteenth century—meaning, as a nation-state. The singularity could not have been assumed and framed in terms more in keeping with the language of modernity. This development acted as a decisive relay in the continuity of Jewish existence. Symbolically leaning against the state of Israel reinforced the communities of the Diaspora and gave them the strength to continue in the wake of the collapse of their modern status. Far from the tragic negativity of their collective destiny during the war, the channeling of so much creative energy into the Jewish state restored the collective destiny of the Jews in the positive context of a freely chosen, voluntary, and constructive affirmation. The Jews came together in and around Israel as part of modernity, and they came together for life and dignity this time, not for death and destruction. This explains the central role of the state of Israel in contemporary modes of Jewish identification, even for the majority of Jews living outside Israel in a paradoxically Zionist Diaspora.

There was a third path in the postwar revival of Jewish identity, one that might seem on the surface to be far removed from a reaffirmation of Jewish singularity—to wit, the political engagement of Jews in Communism. Heir to a long socialist and libertarian tradition with which the Jews were strongly associated throughout the nineteenth and the first half of the twentieth centuries, postwar Jewish Communism identified with the USSR in its triumph over Nazism. Rejected with the emergence of the cold war as not conforming to the democratic norm, European Communism represented more than an ideological choice to the Jews. It afforded them a model of identification that reflected the marginalization and rejection by the modern system to which they had been subjected when they were stripped of their citizenship. They found in Communism a rationalization for their feelings and experiences, without ever recognizing them for what they were. Predictably, these Communist Jews were violently anti-Zionist, since Zionism directly owned up to the specificity that they themselves denied totally yet admitted indirectly. It was in the name of humanity that a sizeable proportion of Jews joined the ranks of a pariah party in the political system. Their adhesion to the Communist Party can be seen as a way of prolonging (in crisis form) their radical loss of citizenship.

My analysis, in this respect, draws on Durkheim's use of "social morphology" to try to grasp society on the basis of the social and symbolic forms of its constituent components—in this case, the conjunction of a strong Jewish presence and a segregated party. The method also could be applied to prewar socialism, which already included a sizeable, or at least a very visible, proportion of Jewish activists. They were not, of course, active in their capacity as Jews, since their engagement offered them a surrogate identity, a way out of an identity impasse. But by their proportionally considerable presence in Communist ranks, they attested with "their bodies" to the indirect Jewishness of their engagement, even as "their heads" denied it. The preponderance of Central and Eastern European Jews in this movement becomes understandable as a result. The Jews living in despotic states had modernized without benefiting from the rights of citizenship that went with modernity. Socialism and internationalism played the part of a universal citizenship for them, a global homeland without borders, an arena in which they could participate in the normal political life from which they had been excluded as Jews and for which they ideologically compensated by strongly identifying with a collectivism banished from the individualistic civic models of Western Europe's liberal states with which emancipated Jews identified. Perhaps, from a morphological standpoint again, modern Jews found in socialism the impossible Jewish collective lacking in political modernity. But then their experience concurred with that of all the democratic people of Europe who sought in socialism the social bond that liberal democracy could not give them. The extreme, peculiar activism of the Jews expressed, if nothing else, the common lot of all Europeans. This is why the collapse of the USSR in 1989 was nearly as dramatic a turning point as the Shoah for those who had sought to overcome their war experience through postwar activism. It was not until the 1990s that the Jews really left the camps behind and realized in their thoroughly censored, innermost hearts the extent of the world's desolation and the crisis of democratic citizenship.

Diasporic communitarianism (as distinguished from "communautarisme"[22]), Zionism, and Communism were, then, the three paths of Jewish renewal after the war. In what constituted a major shift away from the prewar spirit of cosmopolitanism, internationalism, and universalism, on the one hand, and religious sectarianism, on the other, the post-Shoah period has been marked by the affirmation by Jews of their singularity at the core of citizenship. This has set the tone for the last fifty years. As we will see later, the shift came about smoothly and surreptitiously, because it corresponded to a general trend in Western democracies, which witnessed a rise in "differences," group identities, nationalism, and religions and a decline in universalism. It was as if people had decided that they wanted to inhabit citizenship in their own specific names and not as anonymous, abstract human beings anymore.

The development that saw the triumph of singularity and the eclipse of the universal criterion of citizenship resulted from the impact of the Shoah on democracy, which had revealed the frailty of the social bond and the extreme vulnerability of the singular within the universality of the Rights of Man and the Citizen. The Shoah had constituted a journey into the jungle, concealed by modernity's artificial paradise, where the most civilized peoples still live. But because modern consciousness has not kept pace with historical events, this development has not yet become clear. We are still trying, unsuccessfully, with the help of outdated "modern" categories, to understand an experience that is already past modernity. The controversy around the Shoah and the extreme sensitivity of Western opinion in this regard bear witness to this fact, and dramatic errors in judgment are in the process of being committed.

CHAPTER 2

The Unthinkable Singularity

The singularity of the Jews having been recognized finally by Jews and non-Jews alike, its meaning and significance have remained unelucidated. Jewish experience over the last fifty years and the state of collective consciousness, as seen in the current controversy over the singularity of the Shoah, demonstrate as much. Democratic thought has not yet learned a political lesson from the Shoah, as if it refused to see what has become nearly obscenely obvious. The shifting terminology used to designate the "destruction of the Jews" demonstrates the growing importance of the concept of "peoplehood" and at the same time its unthinkability. At the heart of the debate on the extermination of the Jewish *people*, it is the category of "people" in general in the conception and practice of the Rights of Man and the Citizen that is at issue.

After the initial embarrassed silence that followed the return from the camps, the first term used to describe the destruction of the Jews was "holocaust"—an odd term in this event, considering it designates an animal sacrifice wholly consumed by fire, which worshippers offer to their deity. Some say the term was suggested to Elie Wiesel by François Mauriac, his literary mentor when the young concentration camp survivor was working on what would become his major trilogy (*Night, Dawn* and *Day*),[1] and that it gained widespread currency in English-speaking countries due to Wiesel's renown as an author in America. If this were true, then it would underscore the religious inspiration of the concept of holocaust. Set in the Christian perspective of the Passion, the notion is "understandable" as a death offered to God to absolve man's sins. But applied to the destruction of the Jews, it is nothing less than outrageous. In what sense can the destruction of the Jews be compared to a religious ritual? What sort of priest would offer such a slaughter, to what vile god, by virtue of what debt? Are we to understand that Hitler was the high priest of this satanic ritual? In any event, the term opened the door to the sanctification, both religious and secular, of the Shoah that was to have quite a future ahead of it.

27

In the postwar period, collective consciousness (including Jewish consciousness) was not ready to formally recognize the singularization of Jews that had taken place in the Shoah. With the focus in the United States and in Europe exclusively on the "universal" dimension of the event,[2] the more neutral-sounding, secular, and sociological term *genocide* came into use. The term shifted the Shoah from the ground of a votive offering to a deity to that of the extermination of a *genos*, or "race." "Genocide" was applicable to the premeditated and programmed murder of any collectivity. The term benefited from the universality that was lacking in the specious and specific religiosity of the term *holocaust*. It had therefore a more political significance and could be used to cover other cases in history. In this way, the singularity of the Jews was brought back to a universal norm and drowned in the biological anonymity of "race." The Jews themselves were reassured to know that they were not the only ones to have been hit by such a horrible destiny. Admittedly, the term *genocide* suited a period that was rife in crimes against humanity. But the concept of "race" applied to Jews remained problematical. In addition, against the backdrop of rampant third worldism, the term was politically manipulated in a way that stripped it of any acceptable meaning. In the 1960s and 1970s, there was even talk of "cultural genocides." As Auschwitz's specificity disappeared, so did the Jewish *people*. Suddenly the Jews realized that their silence, kept out of austerity or anxiety, could become a weakness and could leave the field wide open to revisionists who were beginning to deny in public the genocide.

A torrent of speeches, publications, and gatherings followed in the 1980s, all emphasizing the Jewishness of the "genocide" and its uniqueness. This phenomenon resembled what psychoanalysts call a "return of the repressed." "Genocide" came to be supplanted by "Shoah," a Hebrew term of biblical origin[3] that had long been in use in Israel to designate the destruction of the Jews during the Second World War.[4] Claude Lanzmann's masterwork gave the term worldwide currency. Outside Israel, where Hebrew speakers understand its meaning, it functions as an absolute designation of the uniqueness of Auschwitz and its Jewish particularity, but because it is a word from a foreign language, it also says that the event belongs to the realm of the impenetrable and the incomprehensible. To talk of the "Shoah" in French or in English is to implicitly remove the "destruction of the Jews" from the rational sphere, to deny the ability of these languages as conveyers of thought to grapple with the event, and to condemn them to aphasia and mystery, without clarifying this "destruction" in any way. A return to the myth? A concept that has become a closed book?

Today, as the controversy over the singularity or universality of the Shoah intensifies, a new term is gaining currency: *Judeocide*.[5] It is meant to express the absolute singularity of the Shoah, this time in Western languages, but the Jews who have recourse to it are merely translating the mystery of the Hebrew term *Shoah* into their own languages, because "Judeocide" still says nothing about what the Nazis killed in the Jews. By substituting "Jew" for *genos* as the object of destruction, "Judeocide" constitutes a superlative statement of the singularity of the Shoah, but it does not help us understand who this "Jew" was who was the target of murder. It is, moreover, a morally problematical notion because it implies that Jews were so far removed from human society that there is no term pertaining to the domain of mankind to name the destruction that befell them. The "destruction" is thereby hermetically isolated from anything human and therefore from anything that could carry meaning. It becomes a mystery, not in reference to the divine (as with "holocaust") but by virtue of a tautology that can do no more than refer back to a deaf and dumb ethnicity. The degree zero of intelligibility has been reached.

A Non-Elucidated Diasporic Identity

Auschwitz had conclusively demonstrated that no matter how individual Jews felt about their identity, the fate of the Jewish collective in modernity sealed their own fate as individuals who were gathered en masse and exterminated in the camps. But having acknowledged this fact, they had a hard time giving a creative, forward-looking content to this singularity. This difficulty needs to be placed in the overall context of the postwar period in Western democracies. What was happening to the Jews was in fact happening to everyone. The public space of universal citizenship was losing its positive signification and turning into a huge arena for economic transactions. By and large, the question of meaning was lost from sight. Postwar politics kept to the symbolic framework of the Second World War, informed by the struggle against fascism, even though societies had objectively left behind that context. The difficulty in keeping pace with reality was widespread.

There was, nonetheless, a major, outstanding Jewish intellectual experience in France in the early 1950s that endeavored to give meaning to a singularity that Jews had recognized as inevitable and assumed. The very nucleus of the Jewish community that was being constructed at the time was constituted by a partly secular, partly religious intellectual movement that attempted to come to grips with the singularity of Jewish identity in philosophical terms, and to do so in a way that opened onto alterity and onto a humanity devastated by the war. It was the start of the École de pensée juive de Paris,[6] or the Paris School of Jewish Thought, and an immense literary output through which Judaism recovered its capacity to speak to the nations of the world and found the strength it needed to renew its spiritual ambition after Auschwitz. We are still being transported by its momentum in France, even though, for a variety of reasons,[7] it largely gave way in the 1980s to a conception of Jewish identity driven by infrarational or irrational tendencies which lost interest in universality and intelligibility. At any rate, the movement never sought to take up the historical and political dimension of the Jewish phenomenon, and, with the exception of certain intellectuals, such as Robert Misrahi, Albert Memmi, or Wladimir Rabi, it kept within the respectable framework of metaphysical idealism. Very significantly, it was the Six Day War, and the consequent shift in ideological stances, that brought the experience to an end. Today, instead of tackling the Shoah as a challenge to the universal requiring the invention of a new avenue to it—one that modernity has failed to provide—it is taken as a brute fact governing an identity or rather an identity-based separateness that objectively accepts the singularization without understanding it intellectually. Through the increasing identity-based turn that Jewish discourse on the Shoah has taken, the Jews are indirectly and awkwardly expressing a collective identity that remains a mystery to most of them. The discourse on the absolute "uniqueness" of the Shoah evinces the unconscious need of its advocates to legitimate Jewish singularity, by which I mean Jewish *collective* identity. The issue here is to try to understand what it is in practice that "compels" the Jews (in the psychoanalytical sense of the term) to unwittingly turn this identity into something sacred and absolute to feel that they have the legitimate right to assert it.

The controversy over the Carmelite convent at Auschwitz helps us understand the inner workings of this process. The opening of a convent on the very grounds of the concentration camp was bound to be experienced by the Jews as a challenge to historical truth and an attempt to "hijack" the Shoah. By its territorial dimension (the occupation of the space, even if we are mainly dealing with a symbolic space), the affair revived the archaic Judeo-Christian conflict, with Christian identity overlaying Jewish identity and thereby occulting it. The Carmelite nuns had taken possession of the grounds and erected a very conspicuous cross that seemed to expel the memory of Jewish victims to make room for Christian symbols of the Passion, and this despite the fact that the Church's anti-Judaism may well have had its part of responsibility in the birth of anti-Semitism and that the papacy had remained silent throughout the extermination of the Jews. In addition, there was a more specifically Judeo-Polish dimension to the affair: the Communist government had systematically eliminated every trace of the Jews in its commemoration of Nazi victims. The Polonization of Jewish victims, against the backdrop of the long-standing anti-Semitism in Poland, appeared here too as an attempt to annihilate the Jewish identity of the victims. As this controversy grew, the idea began to emerge that the grounds of the concentration camp at Auschwitz should remain empty, devoid of any specific sign, and given over to "silence." This taboo on a territory (which is not necessarily condemnable considering the context of Christian activism) translated in concrete terms the idea of the "mystery" of Auschwitz by turning it into a sacred place. The grounds of Auschwitz were to remain off limits to symbolic marks. A territory (and hence an identity, a support for identification), to be sure, but condemned to emptiness and prohibition. Unthought and unthinkable but asserted nonetheless.

The fact that the affair was brought to the public eye by the very active Secular Jewish Community Center in Brussels,[8] through its review *Regards* and a sustained public campaign, shows that the concern was rooted in a secular Jewish identity, not a religious one. Curiously enough, the religious movements remained passive throughout the controversy—with the exception of the French Jewish Liberal Movement (France's Jewish reform movement). Only Réné Shmuel Sirat, chief rabbi of France, joined the Jewish delegation, initiated and directed by secular Jews (Ady Steg, Théo Klein, etc.), that went to meet in Geneva with dignitaries of the Catholic Church to find a solution to the conflict. We can see the basic ingredients of this secular Jewish identity in the patent anti-clericalism of their opposition to the Christian religious appropriation of the symbol of Auschwitz and in the centrality of *peoplehood*, as evinced by their concern for the place where Jews had been assembled en masse, as a people, before being destroyed, and this in a country where the Bundists had called for the status of a national minority for the Jews. It is, in fact, in secular Jewry, far from religious vehicles of identification, that the collective identity of Jews as it was forged in adversity over the course of history appears most forcefully. But in the Carmelite convent affair, this identity was destined to remain silent and empty, unresolved and unconscious, protected by sacredness, at once posited and prohibited. It was during this period that the term *Judeocide* began to emerge, which marks, as I have said, the degree zero of the Shoah's intelligibility because it abandons the possibility of comparing the Jewish referent to anything else (*genos, demos, ethnos*) without furthering our understanding in any way. It is a sociological fact that the Jews on the verge of assimilation are the ones whose identity is most often affected by the horrors of the Shoah, the memory of which keeps them from slipping into modern anonymity. This memory therefore is the crux of their identity, but theirs is an identity on borrowed time, because bereavement is devastating if it does not lead back into life. As a rule, the basis for such an identity is "ethnic" or "genic" in the sense that it has no *sui generis* interiority, and the condition of "ethnicity" is generally held to rank lower than that of a "people" (an ideological classification to which I will return). Even when the focus is on peoplehood, the collective condition remains unaccepted and opaque. And when, as sometimes happens, this ethnicity is offered a universal horizon in the form of a "great cause," it is merely an artificial appendage (as in some pious ideological wish or a humanitarian declaration of faith) to a purely existential condition, intrinsically lacking in content and rationality.

We are touching here on the failure of political modernity to rethink the post-Shoah situation and on the weight of the prevailing interdiction upon "peoplehood," in this case the Jewish collective condition. This is why the Jews who are most integrated in the polity and in democracy can only identify as Jews indirectly. By linking their identity to the Shoah, they are trying pathetically to legitimate this identity through the suffering and misfortune experienced in an event that designated them as Jews rather than as citizens, as if they had to find an excuse for something that conventional thinking in the society around them finds unacceptable and even shameful. It is as if they were telling the nations of Europe, "Okay, we accept this collective identity, but only reluctantly. It's your fault. Just look at the suffering it cost us." The Jews are often accused of wallowing in their status as victims, and when such is the case I am the first to deplore it. The time may be ripe to get past the psychological dimension of the syndrome (related to the fact that after the war the Jews were not allowed to give vent to their specific pain as Jews) and instead of condemning this roundabout means of founding an identity upon suffering try to understand the reason for this debilitating reaction. Maybe something in the very nature of modernity prevents the expression of the notion of "peoplehood" when it comes to Jews, even though it was as a people that they were condemned to destruction.

The Mortgage of the Shoah in Israeli Identity

Israel's existence and legitimacy are seen in universal consciousness as being mortgaged by the Shoah. Thus conventional wisdom has it that the state of Israel was created ex nihilo to compensate for the Shoah, which means the grounds on which it is based and its purpose would be humanitarian, not historical. This judgment is in no way swayed by the fact that political Zionism had been pursuing its enterprise since the late nineteenth century, and that well before the war there existed a semiautonomous Jewish administration in Palestine that had all the prerequisites of a state: the *Yishuv*, known in Hebrew historiography as "pre-state Israel." For those who believe that the moral legitimacy of Israel derives from the Shoah, Israel is an "artificial" creation established in reaction to and in compensation for the hatred of the Jews and is not the product of a genuine history. This is the prevailing view of the public at large and, at bottom, of Jews as well. It still weighs very concretely on Israel's moral image. Public opinion, governed by the media, tends to demand that the state of Israel be absolutely moral for it to have the *right* to exist. No doubt, there is no other state in the world in this situation. Even many of Israel's partisans find strength to defend it only because it is absolutely moral, when it should be a matter of common sense that its actions are informed more often by reasons of state than by moral codes, as is strictly the case of every state in the world.

This situation was bound to weigh on Israeli consciousness. Over the years, the Shoah progressively played a greater role in the reinforcement of Israeli national identity. As we have seen, in Jewish consciousness the existence of Israel redeemed the tragic Jewish collective gathered in the camps by transforming this negative collective into a positive people capable of life. The symbolic and institutional apparatus that the state of Israel set up around the Shoah are only natural from a sociological standpoint. All collectivities, especially national, forge and consolidate identity around collective experiences of happiness and strife, and collective memory always underpins national identity.

Are people sufficiently aware of the concrete morphological presence of the Shoah in Jewish existence? There are between 13 and 14 million Jews in the world today (as of the writing of this text), barely two times the number of Jews exterminated. This implacable fact has lent itself, admittedly, to wrong or improper use. There have been borderline cases of instrumental politics, as when one political leader or another cites the lesson of the Shoah to justify activist policies in the international arena. On the eve of the Six Day War, it was perfectly legitimate to invoke the Shoah to justify Israel's preemptive strike when surrounded by enemies. It was less so in 1982 for the Lebanon War. The reawakening of the memory of the Shoah that characterizes our era dates to 1967, as if the intended destruction of Israel had revived the memory of the destruction of the Jews in Western public opinion. But in 1967, as in 1982, this specter objectively haunted Israeli consciousness.

It is thus in terms of the historical foundation of its legitimacy that the postwar resurgence of Jewish singularity in its statehood form is being played out. Do the Israeli people reinstate a Jewish people with a full-fledged history of their own, or is it the a posteriori product of Hitler's persecution? If the latter is the case, then the Jews have assuredly found a courageous way to defy the challenge of Nazism, but their singularity remains under the shadow of the Shoah. To put it more brutally, does Jewish singularity precede Nazism, or is it the consequence thereof (since it manifested itself overtly after the Shoah)? This dilemma pits a humanitarian view of a singular Jewish existence against a historicist view. The choice of an answer engages a whole conception of the world. It is upon an examination of the modalities of the singular identity of Israelis that an answer is to be found. But the situation remains as unclear in Israel as in the Diaspora. If we analyze the structural components of the Israeli nation, then the singularity seems convincing enough. One could say that "it works" as well as a nation of immigrants from more than 120 countries could possibly work. A true cultural miracle of far-reaching consequences took place with the revival of a language that had not really been spoken for twenty centuries and that proved to be capable of carrying the modern world in its words and rhythms. It is in terms of the ultimate aims of the national project that the question arises. To be sure, nations seldom ask themselves why they exist. Their existence is sufficient onto itself. But such questioning is inevitable in the case of Israel because of the Jewish heritage and the fact that the state was born from a political-ideological project.

And the fact is that the aim of political Zionists (from the Right to the Left) was not to reinstate the Jewish people but to create a new people—the *Israeli* people. This is why they irremediably left Jews and Judaism in exile, bearing the victim's mark of infamy. A new man was to arise embedded in the normality common to all nations. This explains the insensitivity in some sectors of Israeli public opinion to the victims of the Shoah (accused of letting themselves be "led like sheep to the slaughter"), which the "new historians" often denounced. In historical terms, political Zionists were aware of breaking an immemorial continuity, replacing the "sickly" and "unhealthy" Diaspora Jew by the normalized, "reracinated" Israeli living in harmony with the land. This project was developed right from the outset of the twentieth century. By the Six Day War it had produced a typically Israeli culture that endowed this new singularity with real content but that broke with the culture of Judaism and the Jewish people as it had been forged in exile. In fact, it Hebraized themes from Eastern and Central Europe, peppered with the ideological conceptions of the "new man" that flourished at the time, with the birth of the great political ideologies.

From a political perspective, this project maintained the cohesion of Israeli society up until the Six Day War. What became of it in the years that followed was another story. Jewish atavism seemed to have caught up with political Zionism. The critical moment came in 1967. The danger to Israel's survival revived the memory of the destruction of the Jews in Western public opinion. This is when the Shoah resurfaced in world consciousness and more especially in the Jewish world. It was a turning point for the moral and political project of Zionism. Now that the historical lands of ancient Israel were under Israeli control, a conflict erupted between the two doctrines of Israeli singularity: the humanitarian (Left leaning) and the historical (Right leaning). Religious Zionism—which had lagged behind political Zionism until then—returned with a vengeance to become the leader of the Zionist movement, while the values and culture of Israeli identity lost ground. Judaism, the Diaspora, and the Shoah burst back onto the Israeli scene where they had been hidden for decades under the ideological-bureaucratic gloss that characterizes ideological societies. Henceforth the Shoah would be invoked as an exhortation to vigilance both by the Right (by Menachem Begin when he launched the Lebanon War in 1982 but also by right-wing religious settlers) and by the Left (to warn against Israel's loss of morality in its treatment of the Palestinians). In this respect, it is interesting to note that as the Zionist culture lost ground, the vacuum was filled by a growing investment in the Shoah as a criterion of identification for a considerable portion of Israeli society—the "humanitarians" who describe themselves as "humanists." Findings from a 1996 opinion poll on Jewish identity conducted among future Israeli teachers indicated the primacy of the Shoah as the sovereign identity-generating event in Jewish history, well ahead of the establishment of the state of Israel or religious historical events.[9] This was the case even among the anti-Zionist ultra-Orthodox—which is easily understandable, since they do not recognize the legitimacy of the state of Israel. These teachers saw the Shoah as a decisive event in their *personal* destiny, and this even though they belonged to the second or third generation after the war. More than twice as many of those polled in the nonreligious sector said that they felt concerned by the Shoah than those in the national religious and ultra-Orthodox sectors. It is interesting to compare these findings with attitudes toward Diaspora Judaism. Here the proportions are reversed: the sense of affinity to the Shoah dwindles as we go from the ultra-Orthodox to the nonreligious sector. The fact that nonreligious Israelis, the largest segment of the population, are most responsive to the memory of the Shoah but least to ties with Jewish communities in the Diaspora, means that the memory of the Shoah as the uppermost factor of Jewish identity does not necessarily imply an identification with a Jewish people, despite the fact that the latter is implicit in the identification role played by the Shoah in this case. The Shoah has become an abstract symbol, which is why it is the foremost vehicle of identification for partisans of an ahistorical, humanitarian version of Israeli singularity, unrelated to the continuity of a *Jewish* people. The Israeli thinkers who have accused their government of instrumentalizing the Shoah for purposes of national cohesion and integration are objectively right, on the one hand, yet mistaken, on the other, since the Shoah is not in fact a strong vehicle of identity. Their accusation expresses a "hyper-moral" demand upon Israel and its identification with an absolute "universal" criterion, which actually manifests their unavowed desire that Israel not exist in its *singular* embodiment.

To summarize, a look today at the substance of Jewish singularity reinstated by Israel leads to perplexity. In the days when the Zionist political culture prevailed, the singularity existed but as a substitute for Jewish singularity, so the question that concerns us here was impossible to address. With the decline of this culture, two versions of Jewish singularity emerged, pitted against one another with violence and resolution at a time when the "American way of life" was triumphing as the cultural standard around the world: the first is centered around the Shoah as the foremost factor of collective identity, while the second is carried by the rising tide of a religiousness that spells a revival not so much of culture as of archaic ghettoized modes of identity. Like Diasporic identity, the Jewish singularity reinstated in Israel remains unthinkable, vigorously reasserted, but uncertain. No doubt this is because the mechanism of repression that makes it impossible to understand this singularity is still at work. Israelis are still within the framework of political modernity, even though they stepped out of it through force of circumstance. This is the paradoxical sign that the taboo on the Jewish people inherent to modernity still weighs heavily in Israel, in the very place where an Israeli "nation" was formed in reaction to this taboo. The Jewish singularity reasserted after the war is thus more a symptom of an unresolved problem than its definitive solution. It represents an intermediary stage in an unfinished process.

The Religions of the Shoah

That there is something unthinkable about the singularization of the Jews in the Shoah is thus paradoxically embedded in the very forms of identity that Jewish singularity assumes as much in the Diaspora as in Israel, making the Jewish condition an experience that ultimately seems to have more to do with fate and atavism than with a conscious choice. It is as if illusion and authenticity were inextricably entangled in these forms of identity. Otherwise put, the Jews do not have a clear awareness of what they are living, which is what could be called a situation of alienation, to use outdated terminology. We have here all the necessary conditions for turning an experience that is not understood into a mystery as substantial as reality. Thus the singularization of the Jews, a process that concerns the whole of society, is grasped in terms of the singularity of a state inherent to the Jewish condition. It is reduced to an objective event (the Shoah) whose significance is repressed. Because it is unique, happening only once, reduced to itself and nothing but itself, the singularity is an exceptional condition, set apart from the rest of humankind and of everyday life.

This is exactly how sociologist Émile Durkheim describes the "sacred"—that is, as a break with the homogeneous fabric of the world, materialized in an object that is set apart from the rest of its environment and maintained at a distance from it. The sacral power of the Shoah has given rise to a whole set of social, psychological, ideological, and institutional mechanisms in whose synergy we can identify a "civil religion," along the lines of the secular religions that cemented secularized collectivities. (The cult of the French Republic, with all its pomp and ceremony, was the "civil religion" of contemporary France.) The former chief rabbi of England, Lord Emmanuel Jacobowitz, provocatively defined it as the "religion of the Shoah." It is not the commemorative activity with its rites and ceremonies that is being questioned here: all societies, as Durkheim again observes, survive through the periodic commemoration of their past, which acts to reinforce the bonds between its members. What is at issue is the monofunctional character of this commemoration, the way in which it has been turned into the single most powerful vehicle of Jewish social structure, the nearly exclusive point of convergence, with martyrdom becoming the foremost founding event in Jewish life. As Durkheim noted, the sacred is ambivalent. It attracts and repels at once, and society is built on this constituent tension. In the society that it unites, the singularity, thereby sacralized, paradoxically keeps those that it expressly unites at a distance from the seat of union. This is a way of approaching the "Jewish people" while keeping it at bay. We have here again the idea of the unthinkable singularity.

This sacredness may very well have more traditionally religious characteristics than those of a secular "civil religion." The notion of the Shoah's unthinkability surreptitiously leads to a line of reasoning that resembles early Christian Gnosticism and its conception of a world governed by two gods, the god of good and the god of evil, with the latter generally triumphing in this world. I have already noted the obvious fact that positing the principle of unthinkability already involves formulating a thought. And what a thought! If the Shoah is an impenetrable mystery, outside history and space, and if it is at the same time the very embodiment of radical evil, then this evil that was responsible for the destruction of the Jews remains definitively unthinkable and mysterious. There would then be a power of total, absolute, and irreducible evil at work in this world, about which we can do nothing but despair, since it is strategically and historically incomprehensible, and no supreme good, be it divine or ethical, can counteract it. One cannot fight against something that cannot be defined or located. And evil can only be defined on the basis of the intelligibility of good. If this radical evil remains a mystery, then that means that good cannot prevail against it, that good remains powerless in the face of evil's triumph in history. If this is the case, and if we are alive, then we are necessarily "guilty," guilty for living, eternally indebted to an unintelligible, taboo past. If evil is absolute, then living implies an arrangement with it. No line of reasoning disarms freedom more than Gnostic thinking. This profoundly regressive religiosity, in comparison to monotheism, is lurking paradoxically in the secular sacralization of the Shoah's singularity.

The monotheist religions also have contributed their share to this sacralization. Admittedly, the Shoah challenges one of the cardinal ideas of monotheism: the sovereign rule of a righteous God over the world. The number of victims, the repetition of the murder over the course of several years, the duration of the crime, and the very temporality of Auschwitz seem implicitly to underscore the absence of God in a world abandoned to the forces of evil. Judaism's conception of God interceding in history to save his people, as in the story of the exodus from Egypt, is profoundly shaken. Christianity, for its part, has to face its responsibility as the dominant religion in Europe, burdened by twenty centuries of deep-seated anti-Judaism. Its conception of salvation through suffering, as embodied in the Calvary of Christ, is shaken by the confrontation with a more massive "passion," suffered millions of times by the Jewish "outcasts," with the Christians playing the part of Ponce Pilate, at best, if not of the Romans who put Jesus to death. The Shoah weakens the Christian theology of the Passion not only because the Jewish martyrdom "replays" the gesture but also because it casts an ugly light on the very notion of suffering as the road to salvation. From this escalation in magnitude, this uncontrolled inflation in a spirituality of victimhood, the supposed good of the Passion emerges profoundly devalued. Christianity, in founding an identity apart from Israel, "God's people," transferred to Christ—the singular set apart from humankind, yet human nonetheless—the theologal characteristics that the Bible attributed to the people of Israel as a singular body. In the post-Shoah context, there was a massive reintegration of these characteristics into the Jewish (collective) singularity suffering a new "passion": the "passion" of the Jewish people superposed onto the Passion of Christ. On many occasions prominent Christians have interpreted this superposition in an obviously reversed manner. New York Archbishop Cardinal O'Connor described the Holocaust as "Judaism's gift to the world."[10] Pope John Paul II himself declared at the foot of the cross in the Carmelite convent at Auschwitz on June 7, 1989, "I kneel at this Golgotha of the modern world." And French Cardinal Lustiger spoke of the textual foundations of the Christian theology of the passion in the following terms: "I cannot help but recall here the words from Isaiah 52–53 whose attribution to Israel is still so painful, unbearably so. For me, I hear them without the slightest reserve but with just as much astonishment as when they are said of Jesus the Messiah whose disciple I am. Why must the Messiah endure so much suffering to enter his glory? This remains an unfathomable mystery [. . .]. The son freely walked to his annihilation saying to God his father: 'Holocausts and sin-offerings you do not require; so I said, Here I am' (Psalms 40:7-8) [. . .] I cannot bear the darkness in which Israel is plunged unless it is united to the darkness into which the Messiah penetrated to show us all the way to life, to make the light of life, the light of Resurrection that is brighter than all suns, blaze forth."[11] Such a mystical vision—apparently irresistible in some Christian circles—does a wonderful job of transposing the singularity of the Shoah into theologal categories that are regenerated by hiding the very object of the event and hence the cause of their enfeeblement. It should be noted, however, that elsewhere, in an unofficial context, Cardinal Lustiger opened a new chapter in the Christian theology of the Shoah, formulating his thoughts on the subject without recourse to the usual substitutive interpretations. "The Shoah is the radical negation of Sinai. The same elements are found in the two contrary, contradictory, and symmetrically opposed events. The giving of the Law is unique and irreversible. The Shoah, the negation or rather the refusal thereof, is equally singular and unforgettable," he writes in an essay on the singularity of the Shoah, in which he explains that by attacking the singularity of the "Jewish people, bearers of the divine word, the Law, and the Commandments," the Nazis were in fact attacking "the fundaments of Jewish and Christian cultures," that they needed to kill the Jews "to do away with the God's Commandments." "The Shoah challenged the Unique God who revealed through the election of Israel for the salva-tion of all nations the relationship between the singular and the universal that constitutes history," Cardinal Lustiger concludes. "The revelation of the One and Only circumscribes the singular space where the rejection of moral law and the extermination of the chosen people coincide."[12]

Insofar as Judaism is concerned, the main challenge of the Shoah to its doctrinal system concerns the concept of the "covenant," its central pillar. Is the Shoah a break of the divine covenant due to the unfaithful-ness of his people? This is the argument posited by the ultra-Orthodox who advocate in this way the total "thinkability" of the Shoah. To save Judaism's theological integrity, they reassert the most commonplace doctrine of divine Providence—namely, that all suffering endured by man comes in punishment for sins. Yet this is precisely the doctrine that the Shoah called into question, for who today can accept the idea that the million children who were exterminated were in any way guilty of a breach of faith? From the ultra-Orthodox perspective, the singularity of the Shoah is unthinkable not because it is mysterious but because it does not pose a problem. Since the Shoah transcends history, it can only be elucidated on the timeless plane of the relationship between God and his people. In this way, the whole thrust of the modern Jewish experience of singularization is written off. Ultra-Orthodoxy does not "know" what modernity is—even though it was born in its bosom in nineteenth-century Central Europe—and so it cannot contend with it. It has opted for withdrawal and thrown the question of Jewish singularity back to modern Judaism. In the eyes of the ultra-Orthodox, Zionism, not modernity or the Shoah, is at the origin of this singularity. Their virulent anti-Zionism takes on its full meaning here. Because political Zionism rebelled against the Jewish condition in exile, it is held morally responsible for the Shoah. This rebellion characterizes the (accursed) singularization of the Jews that is blamed on the Zionists. By taking the place of the Messiah and gathering the Jews to Zion before the coming of the messianic era, which is in God's hands only, the Zionists challenged the nations of the world and brought down God's wrath upon the Jewish people. In ultra-Orthodox thought, the singularity is not the product of modernity but rather the result of Jewish infidelity, and the symptom of a break in the covenant.[13] The huge theological output on the subject in the American Reform, Conservative, and Orthodox movements is divided between the thesis of the "mystery of Auschwitz" (the mystery of God, of the life of God to begin with,[14] or the mystery of Israel's election) and that of the divine, or purely human, miracle of Israel's marvelous resurrection after a tragedy that could have dealt the death blow to the Jewish people.

None of these theological views tackles the singularization of the Jews *in* the Shoah. The focus of questioning is on God or on the aftermath of the Shoah, but the Shoah itself remains unthinkable in this context of rationalization. These theological perspectives quite simply disregard modernity to concentrate on a metaphysical universe outside history and on the confrontation between God and his people; consequently, they are totally insensitive to the central phenomenon of the Shoah that concerns us here. The need of religious Jews to find a coherent meaning in the aftermath of such a break in Jewish history is perfectly understandable (all the more so for the prevailing form of Jewish atheism that bases its proof that God does not exist on the fact that he did not prevent Auschwitz). The fact is that approaching the question from a religious point of view seems to provide an occasion to get rid of the burden of a confrontation with historicity. Worse still, theologizing the Shoah leads almost ineluctably to its mystification. Why bring up God with respect to a modernity that rejected or forgot him? God appears, in fact, as an ideological *deus ex machina*, while the materiality of the Shoah, and its insistent social and political presence in the century, is repressed. Would it not be more appropriate to think in terms of "anthropodicy" than theodicy? After all, the Shoah is first a matter of human beings, of modernity, and of Europe! The unconscious purpose of the mystery of singularity formulated by theologians is to protect these from a critical examination. It is interesting to note in passing the theological crisis reflected in the reaction of the monotheistic faiths. By detaching the Shoah from the course of history, religion manages to patch up the breach in its coherence. Philosopher Hans Jonas gave an illustration of this mechanism when he received the Léopold Lucas award at the University of Tubingen in 1984. Speaking to a German audience, Jonas confined himself to evoking the impotence of God; he formulated a myth that was as warped as it was tedious to explain God's withdrawal from the world. I am not saying that this idea is not serious. It is the circumstance that makes it mystifying. Would it not have been more appropriate to speak to his German audience about man's lust for "power," which has triggered nearly all the wars in Europe for the past century? Invoking God's mystery in this context is a way of absolving human beings of their responsibility, rising above the historical plane—where the question of the singularization of the Jews is posed—to attain what is a world of pipe dreams, because its elevation has not assumed the burden of reality. Only after assuming the burden of political history and wrestling with it through prophetic criticism can religious meditation be genuine. But this requires monotheism to recover its prophetic spirit!

The Circumlocutions of the Jew-as-Model

Finally, there is one last arena where the unthinkable singularity is at work and which is generally overlooked: that of contemporary Western democratic society. Here, in many cases, the Shoah is the single medium of communication with the Jews. Recognizing the Jews involves recognizing the Shoah. Taking an interest in them involves evoking the Shoah. Doing something for them involves building a monument or a museum devoted to the memory of the Shoah—as if all of Jewish existence boiled down to the Shoah. The outburst of public controversy over the Shoah in the mid-1980s actually tells us a great deal about Western societies, which after forty years of repression were finally giving vent to the traumatic experiences of the war. But the turn that the debate took had something perverted about it, for it focused on Jewish singularity instead of on the crux of the question, which is Jewish singularization in democratic citizenship. The Shoah raises a crucial problem that concerns the Western democracies first of all because they were the theater of the extermination of the Jews. It is a moral necessity for Europe to face its conscience and make the effort to understand what happened. Focusing the debate on the Jews (who lend themselves to it for the reasons we have seen) is tantamount to exonerating democratic conscience from the need to take a look at itself and examine its responsibilities. To take the

French example, it would be like examining Vichy France and seeing only the fate of Jews. I am not suggesting, of course, that their fate was secondary, but reducing Vichy to the Jewish question means indirectly accepting the "rest" of its policies as if they were a tolerable part of historical normality. Recourse to the Shoah as the symbolic vehicle of communication with the Jews thus hides the fact that the Jews are being turned into symbolic mediators in the relationship of society to itself. This process could have an unexpected consequence, because it contains a grave misunderstanding. It could lead to imputing to the Jews alone responsibility for the malaise of society. The collective unconscious seems, by force of inertia, to be blaming the Jews for a situation in which they are being manipulated more than manipulating, although I too find "unbearable" what Pierre Vidal-Naquet describes as "the pose of certain individuals who, draped in the grand sash of a major extermination, believe they can elude the banal pettiness and cowardice that are part of the human lot."[15] If the debate on Vichy is confined to the Jewish policy of the "French State" instead of incorporating the Jews into an integral whole, then it paradoxically isolates today's Jews in French society. This isolation would suggest that the Jewish communal identity involves a divorce from French society, when in fact the "community" was the vehicle of the reintegration of the Jews into society after the war. One of the signs of this misunderstanding is the fact that the term *communautarisme* is commonly used to designate an "ethnic" identification of French Jews through the agency of the Shoah.

A morphological conflation is taking place in a country like France, as much on a symbolic as on a practical level, between the debate on the past with the Jews at its center and the debate on their present status. Since the Shoah has become the medium of communication between the Jewish world and the surrounding society, focusing the debate on the centrality of the Jewish singularity in the Shoah amounts ipso facto to concentrating on the singular identity of Jews in contemporary French society. We are speaking of the past when we speak about Vichy, but since we are speaking today we are also speaking about ourselves. The singularization of Jews in the Shoah, construed as the "singularity of the Shoah," thereby finds itself invested with an unexpected surplus of meaning. It is a coded language that enables its users to recognize and indirectly stigmatize the separate identification of the Jewish community in a French society whose founding political culture cannot *consciously* accept this separateness, even though it quite naturally accommodated it in practice after the war. From this standpoint, the fight for memory is necessarily seen as part of an attempt by Jews to legitimate their identity in the wake of the Shoah. They would do this using the sole legitimate language of the period (the victimhood referent of the Shoah) in whose terms they unwittingly couch what they are demanding and which cannot be expressed directly due to the weight of the collective unconscious and the deep-seated repression to which this identity is subjected. Thus the Shoah acts as an abstraction of the Jewish condition today, a language of derealization and disembodiment, which satisfies the requirements of the prevailing consensus (that is to say, the taboos of the unconscious) and adapts itself to the movement of collective repression. The necessarily sacralized singularity of the Shoah plays a role in holding at a distance the torment of postwar democracy. But the greatest paradox is that the singularization of Jews, the only real issue, disappears behind it.

The language of the Shoah has become an abstract language, a shifter that can be used for the purposes of the most diverse ideologies. Tzvetan Todorov's hope that the Shoah will become an *exemplum*, and that we will draw a "universal" ethical model from it,[16] has already come true, albeit not in the way he thought. The Shoah and the mysterious Jewish singularity have become ideological categories that are not necessarily attached to the Jews. To take the French example again, Jews are often brought up as models on different occasions in politics and civil society. Attacks against Jewish targets—from the bombing of the synagogue on Rue Copernic to the profanation of the Carpentras cemetery—have a rallying effect on French society; they have been the occasion of gatherings that have assembled the entire political spectrum, as if the "Jewish sign" was apt to bring together sibling rivals around a powerful consensus in which France contemplates itself face-to-face. No doubt the memory of the Shoah, the guilt about Vichy's role in it, and the consequent repulsion toward all forms of racism and anti-Semitism have played a role in this novel and exceptional configuration. But it cannot be understood merely in relation to the Shoah; two other factors in the current political situation must be taken into consideration—the rise of the National Front, and the problem of immigration, which for more than two decades has been shaking the established equilibrium of French society and radically changing its image of itself. This immigration can be likened to a return of the repressed for the colonial empire that had taken the French far from their homes. Now that they have retreated to their own territory, the ex-colonized peoples who were pushed to the sidelines are reemerging at the center of the French scene, which triggers a nearly automatic reaction of rejection in some sectors of the population. Commemorating the Shoah is seen as a natural prophylactic means of fighting against xenophobia. Reminders of the extermination of the Jews serve as a warning against violent reactions against immigrants.

But it is not only the "Jew as victim" that crops up regularly in public affairs, it is also the "Jew as model." The citizenship of French Jews has been regularly held up, especially since the 1980s, as an integration example for immigrants to follow in both civic and religious terms. The slogan

"Jews = immigrants," launched in the 1980s by the antiracist organization SOS Racisme, already equated immigrants to the victims of Vichy. In the 1990s, the "Debré-Pasqua" laws to limit illegal immigration were compared to the "*Statut des Juifs*" adopted by the French government in Vichy, and demonstrators at rallies in defense of the "*sans papiers*"[17] wore the yellow stars of deportees. The analogy was present in the discourse of government officials too. Alain Joxe, then minister of the interior, spoke in favor of the creation of a Moslem umbrella organization,[18] modeled on the CRIF. On the occasion of the 190th anniversary of the Sanhedrin, which was celebrated in 1997 with great pomp for the same reason, President Jacques Chirac again held up the Jews as an example of successful integration for immigrants.

Jews who see this surprising turn of events (the exact antithesis of the demonizaton of the Jews in the 1930s) as a source of pride and enthusiasm, because they think it elevates them to the status of sacred guardians of the Republic, would be well advised to look twice. Such is the ambivalence of the sacred; what is sacred today, set apart from the quotidian and hence from the norm, can become the sudden target of unconscious reprobation tomorrow. France is merely searching for itself through these fantasized representations of Jews. The Jewish-sign-of-France does not necessarily correspond to real Jews. We are dealing here with a symbolic process, but for this process to develop and be credible, it needs Jews to exist in reality. The real Jews will, at any rate, be held responsible for it if one day the wind turns. One must not forget that the sacred figure, the source of authority and legitimacy, is generally a pariah whose terrifying sacredness simultaneously attracts and repels. Despite its centrality in France's contemporary sacred landscape, the Jewish-sign-of-France is still a borderline sign, the sign of foreignness around which (or rather the vacuum out of which) the collective identity is forged. The Jewish-sign-of-the-Republic, because it is volatile and abstract, can readily be manipulated to serve very trivial, partisan political interests. Jean-Marie Le Pen has proven to be an expert in this domain, for he probably understood better than anyone else the strategic implications of a symbolic system that concentrates so much power in so very few elements. He used it as an anonymous strategic given that he drummed away on as if he were playing on an electronic keyboard. Le Pen need not even have been as viscerally anti-Semitic as he was to take advantage of what turned out to be a gold mine for the National Front, which spared it the task of formulating a political agenda. Le Pen simply pressed on the spot where the conscious mind is most fragile because of the pressure of the unconscious. Yet the National Front would not have made as much headway if it had not been for François Mitterrand, who was the first to make use of the Jewish sign. Most analysts agree that Mitterrand sought a confrontation with Le Pen to bolster the Socialist Party

(PS). At a time when Le Pen was relatively unimportant on the political scene, Mitterrand brought him into the limelight so that his party could play the role of the sole bulwark against the neo-Fascism of this diabolical figure. Faced with the decline of socialism, weakened by his own disappointing record during his first term in office and the rapid dissolution of the Communist states, the good old strategy of the "anti-Fascist front" (the inexistence of Fascism being besides the point) served as an ideological relay. To give credence to the need for this struggle, Mitterrand rallied the Jewish sign against the National Front's anti-Semitism. The survivors of the Shoah and their descendants supplied the moral authentication of the danger that needed to be fought; they conferred the ethical guarantee upon the Socialist-led anti-Fascist struggle. Likewise, the celebration of the anniversary of the Sanhedrin by the Right-leaning French government under Jacques Chirac was a way of obtaining a "moral stamp of approval" from the Jewish community at a time when the government's illegal immigration laws (aberrantly compared, as we have seen, to Vichy's *Statut des Juifs*) were coming under heavy fire, and the Socialists were taking a public stand against the National Front.

The abstract flexibility of the Jewish sign and its application in the political arena demonstrate, if need be, the potential dangers inherent in the use of this coded language for designating something else entirely. The constant mention of the Jews and the hazy, symbolic aura that surrounds them could arouse a sense of exasperation and lead public opinion to look for someone to blame (who will doubtless be easy enough to find). The figures evoked (the martyrdom or the Republican identity) lose credibility as a result. Moreover, the very existence of the Jewish sign leads to an altogether problematical massification that once inspired the myth of a "Jewish plot," and the identification of immigrants to Jews lends credence to the idea that the Jewish community is (or was) foreign to the Republic. When François Mitterrand congratulated in the same breath the Jewish *community* and the Moslem *community* (to a large extent of foreign nationality) for their restraint during the Gulf War, was he not implying the heterogeneous character of the Jews in the French nation? One cannot say that there is manifest anti-Semitism in France today, but who knows to what use this disturbing symbolic concentration could be put in case of crisis. Does the singularization that Jews came to terms with after the war pose a problem today to national consciousness? Or can it become the symbolic scapegoat for French problems as the country steps into a new era, and why?

CHAPTER 3

The All-Too-Thinkable Shoah

The singularity of the Shoah is not a mystery for everyone. In some ideological circles, it is all too thinkable. In fact, some see it as a key element in the global strategy of the powerful. The exegetes of the Shoah's "thinkability" start with an acknowledgment of its singularity, which they register as such, in all its opacity and silence. They neither deny it nor ignore it. But instead of using reason and intelligence to delve into it, they see it as a smoke screen designed to hide shameful power interests. They too sacralize the Shoah's singularity in a way but as a negative embodiment of the sacred, that is, as diabolical sacredness.[1] They turn it into the pivot of their explanation of the world, from the development of democracy to that of capitalism. They are not necessarily wrong, as we will see, but not in the way they think. This ideological view is mainly expressed by revisionists, but also by a current of thought that cannot be called revisionist, since it recognizes the existence of the gas chambers and the importance of the event, but that is close to revisionism in its view of contemporary events and the Jews' harmful role in them. We could qualify it in this respect as a form of "democratic revisionism," a description that is aberrant from a rational standpoint but that clearly evinces the inherent contradiction to which we will return later. Robert Redeker argues that it is a form of "revisionism" to be distinguished from "negationism," a term that he reserves for those who deny the existence of the Shoah.[2] I will not adopt his terminology, because I do not agree that "negationism" is necessarily the culmination of "revisionism." I see in this current of thought, to the contrary, the prodromes of a "new Left"—or a (somewhat moderate) neoleftism—insofar as it posits a *democratic* ("human-rightist") critique of democracy. In so doing, it implies that the contemporary Left, won over to economic liberalism, is not leftist anymore. The question of the Jews as a people and an identity after the war is central to the thinking of both currents of this ideology.

47

Revisionism

The most well known of these currents is revisionism. Revisionist circles
include extreme right-wing neo-Nazi groups and leftist groups hostile to
capitalism, communism, and the United States and looking for an alternative.[3] The discordant mix of Fascist and anticolonialist themes that unites
these disparate groups (and that is best exemplified by the third-worldist,
anticolonialist and differentialist stance of the New Right) resembles the
mechanism that made anti-Semitism a common ground for the extreme
Right and extreme Left in the nineteenth century. I will confine my discussion of revisionism here to some of the most significant aspects of this
pathological denial of historical reality that have a direct bearing on our
subject. The revisionist program, as Nadine Fresco observes, aims "to
prove that something did not take place [. . .] to demonstrate that instead
of the host of dead that the Jews are making so much noise about, there
is in fact but the void of a colossal lie."[4] In Louis Janover's words, "All the
revisionists have to do is see something to doubt that it exists."[5] The lie is
not the singularity of the Shoah but the Shoah itself, which they pretend
is a myth invented by the Jews to achieve their political and financial ends.
It is, on the other hand, the Shoah that is hidden behind the Jewish singularity for the broader current of neoleftists, those who suspect the Jews
of monopolizing the "patrimony"[6] of the Shoah in an attempt to conquer
positions of power or (at best) because they have remained prisoners of the
place (the camps) to which Hitler assigned them. Their aim is to demystify
it and show that it is a Jewish invention, a hoax, whence their interest in
"details," in such objective realities as the gas chambers, and their efforts
to disprove their existence. Not only is the Shoah a pure fabrication, but
the very existence of the Jews is artificial. The revisionists reformulate the
old theme of a "Jewish plot" peppered with outdated Marxist theories about
bourgeois plots to dominate the world. "It is not a race that they represent
today, but a way of living and aspirations," declares Paul Rassinier, one of
the leading revisionist writers. "And, it is not a racial problem that they
pose, as the State of Israel proves so well, but an economic and social
problem insofar as they aim, under the cover of a religious tradition, to
set up a mercantile feudal system, which, as we have said, is out to control
the whole world."[7] Throughout the development of their arguments, the
revisionists excoriate the Jewish collective, which they implicitly define as
a polity. Thus to explain the death of Jews during the war, they assert that
Hitler was merely acting in response to international Jewry's "declaration of
war" against Germany, and that the "final solution" was simply a territorial
concentration of Jews (as a people again) in Eastern Europe, Madagascar,
or somewhere else.[8]

The role of the mastermind behind the international plot is given to the state of Israel as the figure of the Jews as a nation. According to Rassinier, the Holocaust is a myth created by the "Zionist establishment" to obtain world support and moral legitimacy. And the expression "Zionist lie" crops up continually in his writings. Maurice Bardèche also sees the "Auschwitz Lie"[9] as a Zionist invention to gain financial support for the state of Israel and international Zionism. The revisionists manage to renew their leftist, revolutionary, or anticolonialist ties through this demonization of Israel as the cause of Palestinian suffering, which they compare to that of the Jews in the Second World War (and this in an altogether irrational way, even from the standpoint of their own doctrine, since they deny that the Jews were massacred during the Shoah). Louis Janover, who defends an ultra-leftist stance hostile to revisionism, aptly describes the typical revisionist as a "petty Faurissonian gofer who has left the service of a mythical proletariat to announce the revisionist Good News, that the Jews are a badly chosen people."[10] Rassinier does not hesitate to pick up old anti-Semitic themes in *Le Drame des Juifs européens.* He accuses the Jews of trying to get their hands on "the gold of Fort Knox," warns that they will "earn their bread and that of their children by the sweat of other people's brows," in which case, he concludes, "the least that we could say is that the title of 'Chosen People' that the Jews claim for themselves will take on its full meaning."[11] Considering the intellectual poverty of the revisionist argument, the fact that it became such a hotly contested question, in particular in France, may seem surprising at first, but it is less so when put back into the overall political context. There is no secret about what the extreme Right, compromised with Nazism, stood to gain from revisionism, but the needs of the extreme Left are more complex. Ultra-leftists had long defined themselves in terms of their opposition to both Fascism and Stalinism but also to democracy, which they saw as harboring the potential of Nazism. They were particularly affected by the failure of the "May 1968 revolution" and the leftist struggles in the 1970s to force democracy, as their theories predicted, to turn "into a fascist monster to overcome the trials that were supposed to overwhelm it" and thus bring about a radically new society.[12] Convinced since the 1960s of Nazism's collusion with the capitalist democracy, as expounded by Amadeo Bordiga, founder of the Italian Communist Party, in *Auschwitz or the Great Alibi,*[13] the failure of May 1968 could only be imputed to "an invisible hand pulling the strings of history."[14] It was in the genocide that they were to find an explanation for their malaise. The genocide, as the crystallization of industrial rationalist technology, was the outgrowth of capitalism and its democratic "facade." According to Janover, "To the backward generation of *soixante-huitards* (or 68-ters), the genocide and its consequences came to represent the summit of mystification, which by its very magnitude proved their own historical importance."[15] The idea of the singularity of the Shoah, to which the Jews and the public at large held so dearly, was a hoax designed to conceal the shameful nature of capitalism and its pretense of democracy. The imperialist West appropriated the victim status from its own victims in the third world and reduced them to silence by morally obliging them to feel sorry for their persecutors. In this way, the Jews were identified with the manipulators of this international lie, the great architects of bourgeois colonial domination. It would be interesting to reconsider the strange rallying cry of 1968, "We are all German Jews," in light of these developments.

That the debate around revisionism grew so heated was also due in part to the internal dynamics of the Left and the ultra-Left. The denunciation of revisionism enabled both parliamentary Socialists and ultra-leftists to adapt to the changing situation that resulted from the collapse of Communism and the decline of socialism. The ultra-Left defined itself by its twofold critique of democracy and Stalinism. Its opposition to democracy—problematical in the West, where paradoxically it could be expressed—had acquired moral legitimacy from its opposition to Stalinism and totalitarianism, which served as proof that its critique of democracy was libertarian and not Fascist. But the collapse of Communism took away the Stalinist enemy and its avatars and deprived it of the nontotalitarian certification that vouchsafed its immunity in the democratic state. Some of its members took to attacking revisionism. This was the perfect way to demonstrate that the ultra-Left was democratic at bottom, despite its criticism of democracy. In a system where Communism no longer played an active role, the critique of revisionism was the only way of keeping the ultra-leftist ideology alive. Stripped of its undesirable anti-democratic and anti-Semitic elements, the ultra-Left could keep up its condemnation of capitalism and democracy (along with globalization, Zionism, nationalism, etc.). The denunciation of revisionism acted as a purifying mechanism, the occasion for the ultra-Left to prove its democratic respectability.[16]

Distinctions of this sort between good and bad ultra-leftists did not interest parliamentary Socialists. Revisionism, as we have seen, provided them with an opportunity to reactivate their "anti-Fascist" positions. The revival of this old strategy by the declining Socialist Party, irresistibly drawn to economic liberalism, was reformulated in terms of a struggle for "human rights" against Fascism and the extreme Right. This combat posture allowed the traditional Left to gloss over its own ties with Communism and give itself a liberal democratic virginity to be defended against the assaults of an ultra-Right that was pulled out of the hat for the occasion. In addition, it forced the ultra-Left to choose between democracy (i.e., the parliamentary Left) and Fascism while obliging the Right to move closer to its own positions. We can see the extent to which the question of the Shoah and its uniqueness has benefited from a convoluted centrality in the new democratic political configuration since 1989.

The "New Left"

Otherwise more intellectually powerful and politically dangerous is the discourse that is emerging in other circles of ultra leftists and their heirs where the brunt of criticism of democracy has shifted from capitalism to globalism. The critique of the Shoah's singularity has become one of the central themes at a time when the cold war and bloc politics is a thing of the past, third worldism is losing ground, and the political and economic organization of the world is undergoing a major upheaval due to the constitution of a global market.

Tzvetan Todorov's essay "The Abuses of Memory" and Alain Brossat's book *L'Épreuve du désastre* provide a good introduction to this discourse. The texts differ in nature and in purpose, but they nonetheless present a similar argument. Neither questions the objective reality of the Shoah—which they place to the contrary at the core of the hecatombs of the twentieth century. What they do question is its meaning and the definition of the Jewish entity that it carries with it. Alain Brossat put the issue in the following terms: "To the question of knowing *who* was it exactly who entered the gas chambers with the Jews [. . .] it is clearly in the interests of anyone who has reason to side with the Zionist power to say: the Jewish people, of course, who have always been persecuted! [. . .] But one could more convincingly plead in favor of the answer given by Lessing's wise man to the question, Who are you, Jew? A man, he replied, the Enlightenment man."[17] The Jewishness of the victims, their singularity, is too burdensome. What Todorov and Brossat criticize in the singularization of the Jews is Jewish singularity itself and what they see as its manipulation by Jewish power circles.

Unlike Brossat, Todorov remains elliptic. His essay, an early version of which was delivered at a congress organized by the Auschwitz Foundation in Brussels, denounces the excessive invocation of memory in contemporary politics. The Jews are seldom, if ever, designated as such, but the examples he brings up unequivocally refer to them. His uneasy restraint in language points to the fact that they are at the heart of his critique. Citing Shelby Steele, Todorov deplores the temptation of oppressed peoples, in this case of African Americans, "to exploit this past of suffering as a source of power and privilege."[18] He speaks ironically of the competition between the ex-victims of the earth to obtain the status of "the group most in disfavor."[19] Todorov goes on to draw a distinction between literal memory, which he defines as an "intransitive fact, leading nowhere beyond itself,"[20] and exemplary memory. The latter goes beyond the singularity of the event, which it uses "as one instance among others of a more general category [. . .] a model to understand new situations." With exemplary memory, "I no longer want to bolster my own identity so much as to justify my analogies."[21] Using this binary model, he places the "literal" pole on the negative, regressive, and uncommunicative side, because literal memory subjects the present to the past and leads "to endless distress, if not madness."[22]

Exemplary memory, on the other hand, is synonymous with justice: "Justice is born in effect from the generalization of the particular offense [. . .] It is 'dis-individuation,' if you like, that allows the accession of law."[23] Todorov explicitly states that the argument in favor of singularity "is particularly frequent in the debate about the murder of Jews perpetrated by the Nazis during World War II—called, to underline its singularity, the Holocaust or the Shoah."[24] According to the author, the individual who feels that the nature of his or her experience is singular "is obviously to be pitied and helped," but "the group that does not manage to detach itself from persistent commemoration of the past [. . .], or rather those who at the center of that group incite others to live thus, are less deserving of sympathy: in this case, the past serves to repress the present and this repression is not less dangerous than the reverse."[25] What exactly is this present that is being repressed, if not another persecution, and the context implies that the victims of this persecution are the Palestinians. "Commemorating victims of the past is gratifying, doing something about those of today is troubling."[26] Todorov thus sees the relationship of the Jewish "group" to the Shoah as a matter of literalism and the mysticism of the letter. Predictably, he deems the term *Judeocide* (which posits the Jew without knowing what the Jew is: a people, a race, an ethnic group?) the most appropriate, which comes down to saying that the Shoah, in itself, lies outside the realm of intelligibility (since we no longer know at bottom who in the "Jew" was killed), and so naming the people in the murder of the Jew can be avoided. Like the letter, "the Jew" has no meaning and no intrinsic reality; the Jewish group must "dis-individuate" and dis-identify: the Judeocide must get past its Judeo-what-have-you to attain justice and truth. There is good reason, in passing, to dispute Todorov's truncated concept of justice. The exercise of justice always addresses a singular experience, a specific case, or a detail that the general law did not necessarily anticipate and that requires an act of judgment to bring the general to bear on the singular. In a judgment, the case in particular is at the center, and the universal comes down to it. There is no presence in reality that is not singular. Presence in general does not exist. That is why there can only be justice for particular individuals, identifiable by name, summoned to appear before the court to answer for their specific responsibility as individuals.

There would be, then, no intelligibility in the "Judeocide" and no morality to be drawn from it as long as the crime against humanity remains attached to the "Judeo" that is in it, and that refers to the group, its distinctive identity, its narcissism, and its lack of openness to others, all of which is borne out by the nagging obsession of the Jewish group with commemorations. Judeocide thus surreptitiously comes to designate a biological and an infrarational level and the Jewish "group" an infrapeople in the grips of a nearly racial "tribalism." One can sense that it is basically being asked to eliminate itself in order to make the Judeocide meaningful and endow it with universal import. But whatever it does, though faced with the extermination of which it was a victim, it could never gain access to Todorovian justice. Why, then, does Todorov choose the term *Judeocide*, which creates confusion by giving the impression that the Jews are at the center of all? Perhaps "Jew" is being used here in an allegorical sense to designate not a people but a universal abstraction: what we can draw from the Jews on a universal plane once we have dispensed with their historical Jewishness (described here as tribal). We will see later the Pauline origin of this rhetorical figure. Jews, who identify with the Judeocide through the idea of the uniqueness of the Shoah, are cutting themselves off from the universal and dismembering it. From this standpoint, the "Jewish group" in the postwar period—with its sense of collective belonging (the Jewish "community," the "Jewish State")—seems petrified by the past and incapable of opening itself up to "justice." Worse still, it is a factor of injustice! When it comes to the survival of postwar Jewish life and the need of the Jews to draw a practical lesson from their singularization in the Shoah, it would be hard to have missed the point more completely. "What is singular teaches us nothing applicable for the future," Todorov writes.[27] And so the Shoah, insofar as it struck the Jews, teaches us nothing for the future. On the other hand, it has a meaning for the universal.

This negative judgment is corroborated by another more disturbing classification that Todorov establishes, based significantly on the willingness of people to accept the comparison between Hitlerism and Stalinism. The hangmen and victims in these two historical tragedies are paired in this system of classification, as if they could possibly share the same point of view. Indeed, Hitler's and Stalin's hangmen find themselves cross-linked with their victims in favoring or opposing the comparison between Communism and Nazism. Hitler's victims (Jews, one would suppose) are on the same side as Stalin's hangmen.[28] The latter perceive the comparison to the Nazis as an accusation, while the former see it as a way of minimizing the Shoah and therefore Nazi guilt. This monstrous category unites victims and hangmen around common corporatist "interests," as if the "victims" had an "interest" and that it was in some way akin to the interest that criminals might have in hiding their crime! In Todorov's scheme, Stalin's hangmen and Hitler's victims are equally attached to literal memory and singularity.

According to Todorov, "Exemplary memory generalizes, but in a limited fashion; it does not make the identity of each fact disappear, but simply places them in relation with each other, establishing comparisons."[29] Indeed, there is nothing unacceptable about comparisons as such. The problem is precisely that the Shoah is taken for a brute, inert fact, with neither depth nor interiority, a numb, impenetrable obstacle, a hurdle to "leap over" in order to overcome it and open it to a meaning that lies elsewhere. Why would the opposite not be the case for Europe, which spawned such a phenomenon as totalitarianism? Why would "meaning" not be built upon the experience of the singularization of the Jews? This rationally unjustified principle of interpretation—which ignores Jewish destiny and sees only its alleged autistic insularity, its nonexistence in the realm of meaning (at best, it may be the springboard for a "humanitarian cause")—ultimately leads Todorov to a Machiavellian explanation of a power-motivated strategy, with variations on the "frantic competition"[30] to gain the "permanent privileges" that go with the status of victim! But if such a power strategy exists, then it cannot be implemented in a vacuum; in other words, the Jews cannot be the sole protagonists in this affair. As Marcel Mauss remarked, "Society always pays itself with the counterfeit money of its dreams." Why is the other party in this altogether specious relationship omitted or occulted? Who are the partners of the "Jews" in this relationship? The fact that the actors in this relationship are not clearly established, that the Jews in this regard are indirectly designated by references to Afro-Americans, Serbs, and other groups, can only lead to a mystification of the "Jewish group" laden with old demons despite Todorov's apparent formal restraint. When he writes, "Such-and-such a group has been a victim of injustice in the past, this opens to it in the present an inexhaustible *line of credit*,"[31] the classic banking metaphor is, alas, all too clear.

But it is Alain Brossat who deploys the argument of this current of thought most extensively in 500 pages driven by a strange resentment against Judaism.[32] In the framework of a hyper-"moral" project whose aim is to reveal the genocides in the world masked by the genocide of the Jews, he undertakes a radical critique of the singularity of the Shoah that turns into a violent diatribe against modes of Jewish community life after the Shoah (as much the Diaspora's *communautarism* as Israel), accompanied by an elaborate third-worldist mythology and a rewriting of history that promotes the Palestinians to the rank of a surrogate chosen people and conflates the Jews with the Nazis.[33] Brossat basically argues that the Jews as a "people" or a "group" were not exterminated (how could they have been since they are not a people?). What happened was not a genocide but a "democide" (he nonetheless make abundant use of the term *Judeocide* without questioning its meaning, and at one point he even entertains the idea of applying the term *ethnocide*[34]). "The real singularity of Auschwitz," he maintains, "is that the genocide hides a democide, that is to say that it was the regressive transformation of a *demos* into a *genos* that made it possible."[35] Thus in the victims of Auschwitz, it was the citizens who died, not the "Jews," at least not as a people.

I would not necessarily disagree with such a definition (the death of citizens) if it were not for the fact that it ignores the central fact of the Shoah: the singularization of the Jews *in* the *demos*, the disintegration of the *demos* of citizenship, which exposed the solitude and vulnerability of the Jews as a *group*, because oddly enough what was destroyed by Nazism, according to Brossat, was not the Jewish *demos* (people) but the *demos* of the Weimar Republic (in which the Jews obviously "did not exist" as such).[36] That the Nazis unduly made the Jews into a *genos* is beyond the shadow of a doubt. The problem in Brossat's argument is that the German *demos*—which is hardly an abstraction floating in the sky of ideas—did more than just contribute to the isolation and persecution of the Jews. As Daniel Goldhagen's *Hitler's Willing Executioners* and other studies have demonstrated, it did not rise up en masse against something that was more than a crime against the *demos*. It was the *demos* precisely that brought Hitler to power. The real question, which Brossat raises but does not answer, is why the assassination of the *demos*, of democracy, in the "German catastrophe,"[37] had to involve the murder of Jews. Brossat's specious piece of reasoning relies on two premises that the Shoah rendered problematical: first, citizenship is universal by nature and thus the Jews do not exist and are not a people; second, it was Hitler who made them into a group. The reasoning continues as follows. The Jews do not exist in the *demos*. They were, however, exterminated as Jews. But since they do not exist, what was it in them that was exterminated? The *genos*. The Jews, though, are not a *genos*; it was Hitler's folly that saw them as a *genos*—a Nazi category. This leads Brossat to regard Nazism as the source of all the makings of Jewish survival after the Shoah, since this survival plainly revolved around Jewish identity, collectivity, and singularity. "Defining today what is specific to the Jews is a way of reactivating the terms of the final solution. The Jews are the people who the Nazis marked as Jews in order to exterminate them. As to the rest,[38] we must admit, despite all opposition, that the difference of the Jews comes down to this: its indefinable character, unassignable to a fixed characteristic. The only way to univocally pin down Jewish identity (to form

Jews as a "real group") is to act like the persecutor and decree: 'I am the one who decides who is Jewish and who is not.' "[39] In sum, the common identity among Jews, the sociohistorical reality of their existence for thousands of years, and their desire to organize their own collective life (which has to do with the makings of history and not with some humanitarian cause) all derive from the persecutor's language! "It is from the Nazis' exterminating perspective that 'the Jews' form 'a real group,' that they can be named adequately and without exception as an ethnic or racial group. The orthodox will name the Jews as a religious sectarian group, and the Zionists as a national group." The case of Israel is the height of perversion in Brossat's eyes: "The naturalization[40] of the 'Jewish question' is, of course, the ground on which the Zionist view of history stands; it underpins the establishment of the State of Israel as a *Judenstaat*, the State-of-all-the-Jews. It is not for nothing that the ongoing practices of the 'Hebrew State' involve racializing the national and nationalizing the racial."[41] It does not occur to Brossat that the Jews existed as a "people" before Hitler turned them into a *genos*, or a race, which they are not, of course. If he had considered this idea, he would have had to rethink the entire makings of modernity, which his book fails to do. By referring all forms of real Jewish collective existence back to the *genos*, he imprisons Jewish consciousness in a magic circle that adopts the Nazi definition of the Jewish condition that he so vehemently denounces: "The dual Jewish catastrophe contained in the emblematic term of 'Auschwitz' is situated first and foremost in the German Crime that reduced an element of the modern demos to a zoological condition before being pursued in the crime-contaminated response that Jewish and non-Jewish posterity alike brought to the catastrophe: the massive re-tribalization of the 'Jewish question,' a process of re-particularization at the core of which the State of Israel is installed."[42] Elsewhere he says that "State Zionism, like its Communist counterpart in the popular democracies of Eastern and Central Europe, has been irremediably contaminated by its despicable origin: Auschwitz plays the same role for the former as Stalin's murderous regime for the latter [. . .]. Israel 'comes' from Auschwitz like the East German regime or that of Novotny come from Stalin's crimes; the trap has closed in upon a victim, twice assassinated: first physically and then ethically."[43] This dialectical reversal that identifies the victim with the hangman is a common ideological device used by revisionists, which I do not consider Brossat to be. It consists in referring the victim's condition back to the hangman's position, just as Todorov did in the topological classification described earlier. The main part of Brossat's demonstration aims at undermining the discourse of the victim, under the pretext that it has been contaminated by the hangman's reasoning. And so the victim is the one who paradoxically becomes the main focus of criticism. In the same way, criticizing the discourse of the singularity of the Shoah as a smoke screen to hide reality serves to divert attention from the main subject—namely, the hangman. The explanation that Brossat gives for this rhetorical figure is interesting for the ideological construction upon which it is based. "What characterizes the Jews in modernity is precisely their non-coincidence with any definition of them as a group. Whether you define them as a religious, national or ethnic group, you always find a surplus or a remainder: one can 'be' Jewish and agnostic or Catholic [. . .] Jewish and a patriotic Frenchman or German, etc."[44] Further, "For readily comprehensible reasons, Zionist ideology has worked to obscure the fundamental dimension of 'modernization' of the Jews—what can be termed their *'demos*-ization,' a process of detribalization that amounts to something different and much greater than assimilation or integration. The political constitution of the Jews as adult subjects in modernity is the process by which they become not only citizens of a State and members of a nation, but also *men*, the bearers of universality, of the humanitarian construction of modern civilization."[45] We will return later to this philosophy of modernity's history, which demonstrates the author's sudden, unexpected endorsement of modernity when all through the book he lambastes democratic modernity and its "conservative laissez-faire ideology"[46] (to the point of blaming globalization of the democratic paradigm after the collapse of the USSR for recent "rural genocides" and "urbicides"). It seems from this apparent contradiction that Brossat holds the Jew to be the sole witness and guarantor of democracy; democracy has become corrupted through and through, but the Jew and the Jew alone is expected to continue to attest to and embody it by staying within a *demos* that has disappeared. By murdering the Jews, the Nazis "assassinated the new political citizen promised by modern constructions [. . .], the philosophy of democratic political individualism. Murdering Jews was a way of endlessly prolonging the assassination of the Weimar republic."[47] This reasoning allows Brossat to avoid dealing with the central question raised by the Shoah: the collapse of political modernity, the failure of citizenship to safeguard the singular. He is willing to examine East Timor, Rwanda, Cambodia, or the aborigines in Australia from this perspective but not the Jews who, for their part, must embody modernity.

Thus it is not so much the principle of the Shoah's comparability to other genocides in the twentieth century that is problematical as it is the myth that those who make the comparisons attach to it. In Brossat's words, "As a constituent component of the self-centered narrative of European history as universal history revived after the collapse of the totalitarian regimes, the discourse of the Shoah's singularity has a place in the new democratic theodicy, in radical contrast to all the bloodbaths that were part of French colonial history until the very end."[48] Such arguments lead to turning around the consequences of the idea of the Shoah's singularity (and its exclusivism): instead of the "ethnocentric" Shoah blinding us to other genocides, it is the latter that, in the name of universal "justice," will end up blinding us to the Shoah.

The Comparison with the Communist Crime

Both Todorov's and Brossat's critique of the singularity of the Shoah culminate in a comparison between the Nazi crime and the Communist crime. As we have already seen, the new emerging Left had to walk a fine line when formulating its criticism of democracy to avoid being accused of Stalinism on one side or revisionism on the other. Denouncing the "crimes of Communism"[49] became therefore a prerequisite for its declaration of faith. But who would think of disputing the criminal nature of Communism? Certainly not the Soviet Jews, who suffered so much from it, or worldwide Jewry, whose efforts to counter Soviet oppression contributed to the process that led to the collapse of Communism. What, then, makes Stéphane Courtois think that the "unique nature of the Shoah" would lead people to deny the fact that "the deliberate starvation of a child of a Ukrainian kulak as a result of the famine caused by Stalin's regime 'is equal to' the starvation of a Jewish child in the Warsaw ghetto as a result of the famine caused by the Nazi regime."[50] This same line of reasoning is employed by Tzvetan Todorov, whose comparative analysis is quoted extensively in *The Black Book of Communism*: "As has often been pointed out, Jews are persecuted not for what they have done but for what they are, and Communism is no different. It demands the repression [. . .] of the bourgeoisie as a class."[51]

Stéphane Courtois insists that he is not trying "to devise some kind of macabre comparative system for crunching numbers,"[52] but by focusing on the suffering and the number of victims, he skirts around the real issue involved in the singularity controversy. Obviously the suffering of a human being is the same everywhere, whether this human being is a kulak or a Jew. And it is beyond dispute that Communism was a murderous ideology. But if we stick to this aspect of the question, then we will never understand why the Jews were specifically exterminated as a people in the heart of citizenship. Because the crux of the matter is precisely the political (and not the human) criterion that was the "cause" of the suffering inflicted programmatically on this occasion. The Jews were not exterminated because they belonged to a "class," like the kulaks. If this had been the case, then why does an analysis of established facts with their own intrinsic basis in reality (i.e., the extermination of the kulaks) seem to necessitate a "comparison" to the Shoah? Why use the Shoah as a yardstick for this assessment? "The crimes of Communism have yet to receive a fair and just assessment from both historical and moral viewpoints," Courtois complains. The reader may fear that I am about to launch into a specious argument, in the manner of Bourdieu, explaining that this assessment is a way of appropriating the "symbolic capital" of the Shoah, by divesting the latter of its singularity and investing it in the Communist crime. The implications of this debate are, in fact, otherwise subtler, and they touch on the crux of the question of peoplehood with which we are concerned.

The comparison of Nazi and Communist crimes comes up against an obstacle, for although it is true that Stalin deported the peoples of the Soviet empire, he also attacked socioeconomic classes that were not historical peoples. And the comparison between the kulak and the Jewish child feeds the confusion between the two. The difference between a social class and a people is blurred when the massacre of the kulaks is identified with the extermination of the Jews (via the rhetorical figure of the child). The implied conclusion to which this confusion leads is that it was not a people that was the object of destruction in the Shoah. If this is the case, then the "unique nature of Auschwitz" makes no sense. The only thing that would make it stand out were the methods: "the mobilization of leading-edge technological resources and their use in an 'industrial process' involving the construction of an 'extermination factory,' the use of gas, and cremation."[53] And so Courtois concludes that "the genocide of a 'class' is tantamount to the genocide of a 'race,' "[54] and "class totalitarianism" stands side by side with "race totalitarianism." This terminology brings us to the degree zero of the notion of genocide.

To make possible the confused alignment of these two historical forms of totalitarianism, the singularization of the Jews as a people in the Shoah had to be minimized. The Jews are thus seen as "the third group of victims," targeted by the Nazis, after "left-wing militants" and the "mentally or physically defective"[55] in Courtois's strange classification of victims. By divesting the Shoah of its singularity, the notion of genocide becomes so disembodied that the author can maintain that the enemy in totalitarianism is "a totally elastic category," which I understand as meaning that it can be either a social category or a people. This indifferentiation is tantamount to an insidious depoliticization of the phenomenon. "The purpose of terror was to exterminate a group that had been designated as the enemy. Even though it might be only a small fraction of society, it had to be stamped out to satisfy this genocidal impulse."[56] By designating the Jews, the Nazis were designating an abstract enemy with no substance in reality. "This process of abstraction, closely linked to ideology, is another key factor in the birth of the terror," Courtois asserts. "It was not human beings who were being killed, but 'the bourgeoisie,' 'capitalists,' "[57] "Jews" then.

But what does Courtois make of the real Jews who defend the idea of the singularity of the Shoah? He basically takes up the same line of argument as the New Left, but his judgment on present-day Jewish singularity is framed in practical, not theoretical, terms. After having suggested that the Jews were exterminated as victims among other victims, the idea of an "international Jewish community" crops up all of a sudden to explain the "blackout"[58] on Communist atrocities. "In contrast to the Jewish Holocaust, which the international Jewish community has actively commemorated, it has been impossible for victims of Communism and their legal advocates to keep the memory of the tragedy alive, and any requests for commemoration or demands for reparation are brushed aside."[59] Here the expression "demands for reparation" only hints at the sordid financial interests behind the "blackout." In an article published elsewhere, the author explicitly denounces the lack of sensitivity of Jews to the suffering caused by Communism: "Those who should be particularly sensitive to the atrocity of these crimes precisely because of their proximity to the Jewish genocide seem indifferent to the twenty-five million victims discussed in *The Black Book*. Is the starvation of a Ukrainian child during the deliberate famine provoked in 1932 equal to the starvation of a Jewish child in the Warsaw ghetto in 1942 or isn't it? Alas, there are people in the Jewish community who pretend to have a monopoly on crimes against humanity. It's a terrible shame. And, in the name of history, it's unacceptable."[60] But the main explanation for the blackout lies elsewhere. It was the Allies, "the victors of 1945 [who] legitimately made Nazi crimes—and especially the genocide of the Jews—the central focus of their condemnation of Nazism."[61] This is the classic leftist anti-American refrain that accuses the victors of rewriting history for their own purposes. And among the victors, there was Stalin of course! "After 1945 the Jewish genocide became a byword for modern barbarism, the epitome of twentieth-century mass terror. After initially disputing the unique nature of the persecution of the Jews by the Nazis, the Communists soon grasped the benefits involved in immortalizing the Holocaust as a way of rekindling antifascism on a more systematic basis."[62] In this way the "international Jewish community" finds itself identified with those who seek to gloss over the Communist crime in particular and more generally all of the twentieth-century genocides for their own political interests. If, as Courtois admits, the "extraordinary attention paid to Hitler's crimes is entirely justified," then this is only because "it respects the wishes of the surviving witnesses, it satisfies the needs of researchers trying to understand these events, and it reflects the desire of moral and political authorities to strengthen democratic values,"[63] not because of a need for factual truth. Justified as the attention may be, Courtois nonetheless maintains that "a single-minded focus on the Jewish genocide in an attempt to characterize the Holocaust as a unique atrocity has also prevented an assessment of other episodes of comparable magnitude in the Communist world."[64]

Beyond all these explanations, which are based on the usual presuppositions of strategic analysis, the pioneering theorists of the New Left are driven to deny the singularization of the Jews in the Shoah by more than just a new reading in support of an ideological reformulation. Their stance in this respect not only raises the fundamental question that concerns us here (of "peoplehood," singularity, and the singularization in the universality of citizenship?), but it also points to the intellectual foundations that underpin their theoretical enterprise. In light of this question, we can see the extent to which Marxism is still a major source of inspiration. With the question of peoplehood, the New Left is faced once again with the key problem in Marxist theory, that is, its incapacity to deal with the concept of the nation. And Marxist theory is exemplary in this respect of the failure of political modernity in general to conceive of "peoplehood."

Marxism undertakes its social analysis from the perspective of Man and the individual. It regards the national historical bond that unites individuals as a lie, which only serves the domination of the class (the bourgeoisie) that controls the (class generating) division of labor that in turn reduces people to a distinctive condition within the economic system. This is why Marx and Engels tend to conflate the state (instrument of this domination) and the nation. They imagine the historical process that drives capitalism toward globalization, leading to a global market where the different nationalities will disappear and the proletariat will become a universal class. The leap into the classless paradise of Communist society will become possible when the proletarians regard themselves as abstract individuals without ties, "naked" men in a way. This stateless, universalized proletariat emerging in the wake of the collapse of bourgeois society along with its classes and nationalities will then become a universal nation of sorts. Marxism aspires to rebuild humanity on a rational and universal foundation over the rubble of old nations and distinctive identities, which it sees as nothing but interchangeable prisms of the same alienation. These principles inspired, of course, the strategy of the global Communist movement, which came up, however, against the obstacle of nations and European nationalisms during the world wars and was forced to tone them down in practice.[65]

The Marxist inability to grapple with the national phenomenon was not limited to the practical side of things. Marxist rationality was unable to deal with it either. The same two-sided picture of the conscious and the unconscious that we saw at work in political modernity can be found in Marxist theory. Here again the "people" (that the Marxists understood as the "national") resurfaced in the very theory that denied its existence. The class concept, upon which Marxist doctrine stands, can in fact be seen as a spectral resurgence of the people that had become invisible. Marxist analysis breaks down society into classes that are so many "peoples" in a central framing unit whose sole coherence is ideological (in the Marxist sense of the term), with social ties woven on the level of a class rather than a historical people. Yet even in conscious terms, Marxism does not relinquish the idea of a global unit, like that of a people. The "proletariat," the class that encompasses all classes, the "universal" class to come, is a fantasized, twisted representation of a surrogate people. It becomes the absolute people promised as the apotheosis of class war. When Marxism thinks of "people," it thinks in terms of the "proletariat."

The singularity (especially national) of the Jews has always presented a problem to Marxism, both theoretically—Marx's *On the Jewish Question* already bears this out—and in practice—witness the history of relations between the Communist and Zionist movements. It also presented a problem to the individual Jewish Communist militants who were always forced to choose.[66] The New Left's critique of the unique Jewish nature of the Shoah is the latest expression of what is now a timeworn discourse. The aim is to eliminate the category of people from an event of such strong symbolic import as the Shoah and replace it with that of class, and, in so doing, to stigmatize the Jews, accused of standing in the way of a universal reality by their senseless particularity. The occultation is twofold: that of the people (of peoples) and of the Shoah. The New Left has thus retained one of the characteristic features of Marxist thought, which it tries to revive in secret (unaware?), in a utopian fashion. This was precisely the root of totalitarianism—the political enterprise of totally and rationally controlling the social bond that modernity had lost. It was peoplehood as a category of social cohesion that was fundamentally challenged in Communism. The latter radically criticized and denied it while trying to recreate it ideologically in a controllable way. In the end, Communism came up against the rock of peoples and was perverted by it. Behind the "motherland of Socialism" stood the age-old Russian imperialism from whose grips the dominated historical peoples had to break free after the collapse of the Soviet Union. By reiterating this occultation of the people, the least we can say is that the New Left is making any comprehension of totalitarianism impossible, when this is precisely the key to an understanding of the Communist crime, the legitimate subject of analysis of *The Black Book of Communism*.

The New Israeli Historians

In its wildest dreams, the New Left would never have imagined that it had soulmates in the despised state of Israel, people whose writings and stances coincided so amazingly with their own! It is interesting to observe in this regard the overall political shift that was taking place at the time in a number of democratic countries. The 1990s witnessed the emergence in Israel of circles of thinkers who came to be known alternatively as "new historians," "post-Zionists," or "critical sociologists," and who undertook a "revisionist" retelling of the history of their country. And their enterprise was by no means revisionist in the neutral sense (of revising the past in light of present-day knowledge), for it contained a critique of Zionism, Israeli society, and the relationship to the Shoah that was devastating to the point of pulverizing not only the singularity of the Shoah but Jewish singularity period. It cast the Palestinian national movement in the role of hero in a new historical narrative and gave pride of place to the Palestinian view of Israel (which appeared in leftist and revisionist theories in Europe only as a counterpoint). Such a reversal in perspective obviously led to drastic historical revisions. The main problem for us is to understand the overall rationality informing this current of thought. How can we rationally account for this overturning of the most evident ideas? It is clear that, even before the establishment of the state, Israeli society was an ideological society, with all of the bureaucratic consequences that go with this situation. It could hardly have been otherwise: after all, it was the product of a willful, activist political project and the instrument of an attempt to create a "new man." Until the Six Day War, the labor union, the Histadrut, embodied to perfection this bureaucratic and ideological power, which was highly elitist (and in practice its *nomenklatura* is still in a dominant position at the time of this writing). The "new historian" phenomenon constituted a challenge to this state of affairs, a positive sign of a loosening of the bureaucratic hold, but not unfortunately of the ideological hold, because to justify their paper revolution, the "new historians" and "critical sociologists" ended up paraphrasing the thesis of "Zionist plot," one of the last fossils of Communism. This thesis is implicitly formulated in their attacks on the Zionist elite and the Socialist politicians who presided over Israel's destiny in the early years and who are accused of hiding their real intentions and their reprehensible acts behind the "values" of political Zionism. The history of the 1948 War of Independence is rewritten so that Israel is found congenitally "guilty" for the Palestinian tragedy. But it is the Shoah that is their favorite object of investigation. They accuse the Socialist elite of having acted cynically and heartlessly toward European Jews, having first refused to help them before shamelessly turning around and manipulating the memory of the Shoah for its own internal and international political purposes.[67]

According to professor Yosef Grodzinski of Tel Aviv University, "The way in which historians forge the collective memory of the Shoah is decisive for the continuation of Zionist ideology in its present form. We are embarking upon a new era: it is finally admissible to criticize Zionist historiography and propose new explanations for what happened."[68] Putting an end to the ethnocentric explanation of the Shoah ("the whole world is against us") is, in Grodzinski's opinion, an important step in changing the collective identity of the state of Israel and moving it away from the Zionist ethos.[69] "The Israeli treatment of the Shoah is a danger for the people," chimes in adman Boaz Evron.[70] Tom Segev's *The Seventh Million* is obviously at the heart of the debate, but the Shoah in itself is not really what interests these "new historians"; they merely use it as a means to advance their cause—an end to the Zionist entity, a separation between Judaism (and not simply the Synagogue) and the state, between the Israeli nation and the Jewish people, and between the Israeli nation and the state of Israel (which would make it a state with no specific national identity). One of the recurrent demands of the "new historians" is the abolition of the Law of Return. According to Uri Ram and Baruch Kimmerling, the political credo of post-Zionism can be defined as a politico-cultural project based on an ideologico-political combat to change the Israeli collective identity. It involves a number of changes in the current situation: granting sovereignty to the Palestinians in the occupied territories, granting national minority rights to Palestinian Israeli citizens, and the progressive separation between nationality and the state of Israel, that is, the creation of a universal democratic legal framework in which no national tradition or ethnic group would have a special status.[71] The main thrust of this new historical doctrine is plainly the negation of the state of Israel's Jewish singularity (and even its Jewish identity). Here too the "denationalization" of the Shoah—or, to use their own terms, its "de-Zionization"—serves to denationalize the state of Israel, to eliminate the nation in the state. Jewish singularity, both religious and secular, is the focal point of their criticism.

The "universalization" of the Shoah, like the idea of a state with no national identity—an unprecedented occurrence in international life—amounts to a pure and simple negation of the Jewish experience of modernity, as much the Jewish experience of emancipation (marked by the anti-Semitic phenomenon) as that of auto-emancipation (Zionism). As the single most catastrophic "accident" of (Jewish) modernity, the Shoah has to be eliminated symbolically to restore vitality to the definitively faded ideal of a modern utopia. This is possible only by turning a blind eye, in an obscenely visible manner, to the fact that the Jewish state (which made the "new historians" what they are) was established precisely because political modernity failed to integrate the Jews as a people. The "new sociologists" end up reviving in all its utopian splendor the eighteenth-century Enlightenment model, the very model that was never actually realized in Europe because the nations, as of the 1789 revolution, weighed so heavily (and unconsciously) on the universality of democratic citizenship[72] that the democratic state of citizens was irremediably tied to the very specifically singular identity of the nation. Considering the way in which these ideological tenets gloss over the Jewish historical experience and reproduce modern ignorance of the Jews, it is not surprising that the defense of abstract citizenship in the state of Israel goes hand in hand with a denial of the Jewish collective identity, seen as neither modern nor meaningful in Israel. In the words of Amnon Raz-Krakotzkin, "Choosing to be Jewish means choosing exile and nothing more."[73] Back to square one of the Diaspora, which culminated in the catastrophe of the Shoah.

We are touching here on a very sensitive knot of contradictions. The "new historians" prefer to blame the idea of the singularity of the Shoah rather than face the crisis of political modernity, as this would force them to recognize the validity of political Zionism, which was a product thereof. In this way they safeguard the integrity of the modern model (the universal citizen) despite the crisis. Yet they are led in spite of themselves to an internal contradiction. When they denounce Zionist colonialism, it is not so much to promote a third-world model (in this case, one based on Arabism, since they are in the Middle East) as it is to adopt a model more "Western" than the West. But the "new historians" are hardly in a position to reproduce the posturing of European or American third worldists, who can criticize the past and present colonialism of their own states while remaining comfortably installed in a West that is stable and sure of itself. As Westerners in an Eastern land, and therefore objectively on the side of the colonialism they condemn, the "new historians" inevitably find themselves advocating Western modernity, their anti-colonialist declarations of faith notwithstanding. This trait is of decisive importance to an understanding of their attitude. Their animosity toward Judaism as a historical culture and affiliation, and not only as a religion, is in fact so strong that they cannot imagine that the Jewish people would have the necessary resources to develop a secularism separate from the Synagogue but still part of Jewish culture, just as France and the Third Republic remained immersed in the Christian culture of French history. And so their only choice is to settle for the very modernity that, as third worldists, they feel obliged to verbally attack. The refusal of an Israeli state in the Orient is a predictable outgrowth of their refusal to face the crisis of Western political modernity that made them what they are—to wit, Israelis. But being that they are Israelis, their hostility toward the state of Israel and what it represents can be seen as a retrojection of the crime (whose mark is worn by the victims of Nazism) onto the victims themselves. Instead of criticizing the failures of political modernity, they criticize the Jewish victims, by shifting the burden of responsibility onto them and onto the singularization that isolated and distinguished them. It is through accusation against the Jews that Nazism is condemned. "It's the old Jewish tactic of self-accusation," observes Dina Porat. "It spares them the embarrassment of confronting their own impotence and the realization that nearly all of Western world, whose values Zionism adopted, was ready to renounce the very existence of the Jewish people."[74]

With the new historians, confused thought reaches its highest pitch. It is Zionism that is put on the hot seat, not Nazism. To reactivate the modern paradigm, Jewish singularity is denied. Thus there would be no justification for Jewish claims of identity if not the persecution of the Palestinians via the outrageous, narcissistic continuity of this identity in the Zionist state. We may not know why the Jews as such were attacked, but we do know that they are attacking others. Modernity has been saved. And so the new historians rebuild the myth of a "civil society," with Israelis, Palestinians, and others as equal citizens in a state with no national identity. We have here the spectacular resurgence of the ex-PLO's old idea of a "secular, democratic Palestine."

These developments evidence a repositioning of the Israeli ultra-Left, by this time well established in mainstream university, press, and publishing circles, when in the 1970s its ideas were confined to a few bohemian haunts. This repositioning can be explained by the same reasons as the emergence of the New Left in Europe. One could even say that the collapse of Communism had a more violent impact on Israeli political circles because of the ties between Socialist Zionism, born in Eastern Europe, and Communist circles, especially in East European countries. Until 1967, Israel very much resembled a Socialist democracy, with the predominance of the Socialist Party, its permanent management of power, its official ideology, and its policy of integration of immigrants into the national society. That its elite was nearly exclusively of East European origin underlines moreover the cultural dimension of these political-cultural syndromes. The Right's rise to power in the 1980s represented a cataclysm to the Left. The ultra-Left could no longer be held at bay by the Left-leaning government. Israel's shift to the Right, demonized by the vanquished Left, could only fuel the ultra-Left's radicalism, its condemnation of Israeli society and its fundamental values. The Oslo process brought to a head the idea that the enemy was within. By basing its denunciation of Zionism and its nationalism on a defense of the Enlightenment utopia, the Israeli New Left, like its European counterparts, was killing two birds with one stone. It gave itself a democratic virginity, even as it rather undemocratically denied the legitimacy of Israeli society and the Israeli people, accused of harboring the darkest designs. At the same time, it rejoined the West despite its anti-colonialist stance, and this at a time when third worldism was losing credibility, as third world states seemed set on proving that the freer they were, the less democratic and the more prone they could be to violence, terror, and injustice.

What part do the "people" and its singularity play in the overall economy of such a phenomenon? The "people" is the preeminent target of criticism of the "new historians." Boaz Evron, for instance, claims that there has never been such a thing as a Jewish people, and that the religious ties that united Jewish communities do not suffice to found a national identity.[75] In their endeavor to rid themselves of the people, the "new historians" have to rid themselves of the weight of the Shoah, because it was the Jews as a people that the Shoah targeted; it was the mechanism of singularization at work in the modern universal that it so scandalously revealed. As a rule, they reject any "meta-narrative" likely to account for the unity and coherence of a collective history of the Jews, because it allegedly works to mask minority "narratives." The "myth" of the Jewish people is destroyed, and discredit is cast on all forms of Jewish identity in several ways. First, the "Zionist entity" is blamed for the expulsion of the Palestinian people and the abandonment of the Jews in the Diaspora. Such a judgment involves a retroprojection. It supposes that the *Yishuv*, which counted 600,000 people, could have saved 6 million European Jews. What the state could have done in the past (when it did not exist) is judged by the yardstick of what it can do today. The leader of the "new historians," Ilan Pappe, justifies such a procedure, which runs counter to historical methodology when he says that, "The past is the product of an ideological relationship with the present."[76] The blaming of Israel (which German revisionist historian Ernest Nolte would have heartily approved) goes hand in hand with a "normalization" of the Shoah, seen as just one more genocide in a long litany of such events. Predictably, the "new historians" develop a humanitarianist theory of Jewish identity. They deny that Jewish identity has any basis in reality, or that the Jews have any original historical nature, and they are only willing to recognize that Israel may have a humanitarian significance, whence their hypermoralism—if Israel acts for reasons of state it oversteps the bounds of its legitimacy as a shelter for the persecuted, knowing that the latter have no historical ties, either with one another or with the place where they are gathered. From this prism, the state of Israel cannot fail to appear murderous. It is interesting to note that the "new historians" do not take their historical investigations back any earlier than the nineteenth century, as if the Jews did not exist before the rise of modern anti-Semitism. Theirs is a wholehearted confirmation of the Enlightenment's conception of the Jewish people.

An often naïve, typically well-intentioned form of self-righteous hypermoralism goes with this outlook. Benny Morris, for instance, expressed astonishment over the fact that the War of 1948 (provoked by the Arabs) led to the expulsion of Arabs, as if he were unaware that expulsions are part and parcel of all wars, past and present. The Jews themselves were

driven out of the West Bank by Transjordan's Arab legion. Similarly, the
great majority of Sephardim were unable to continue living in Arab countries after the nation-states were created. But how can one even see this
expulsion of a Jewish people that does not exist? There is a homeostatic
relationship in this respect between the New Left and the opposite pole
of the ideological-political spectrum, namely, the religious Right, which
occupies in positive terms, as if by defiance, the place of the singularity
denied, and at the same time designated as such, by the New Left. Thus
the hypermoralism of the New Left counterbalances the hyperrealism of
Jewish singularity, denigrated by the New Left as a form of tribalism, which
all national identities are in its eyes.

The "new historian" movement is not numerically important, but it
has a great impact on the public (which only confirms the fact that far from
being persecuted, it too is part of the "establishment" it denounces). The
movement testifies to a profound crisis in Israel's *intelligentsia*, developing
as it does to the point of caricature ideas that have always had a strange
appeal on the later.[77] It can be seen as part of the process of globalization
and the emergence of a "high-tech" elite that has broken away from nations
and national identities and pitted its imperial universalism against the
pseudo-"tribalization" of their peoples in an effort to found the legitimacy
of the power to which it aspires. Significantly, there are few professional
historians in the "new historian" movement, which is mainly composed
of sociologists, political scientists, psychologists, or linguists. In a similar
vein, many of the intellectuals in New Left circles in France are adepts of
a postmodernist hermeneutics that sees reality as a "narrative," and each
group as producing its own story, world, and identity. In the words of Ilan
Pappe again, "Historians are free to add pieces of reality as required by the
historical narrative that they are telling, even if they have no documentary
basis." Comparing history to archaeology, he recognizes that "there are
things we add because we do not have all the evidence. You add what's
missing from a present-day standpoint."[78] History, from this standpoint, is
no longer tied to what actually happened, since even facts are an illusion.
"Thus a description of what did not happen carries equal weight," notes
historian Anita Shapira, "Why did Israel fail to establish a peace treaty with
its neighbors in the early nineteen fifties? Why didn't it avoid the War of
Independence? Why didn't the Zionists leaders save the Jews of Europe?
The question, What would have happened if . . . ? is not a valid intellectual
method and cannot replace a description of what really did take place." The
aim of this "new history" is not to analyze historical reality but, as Anita
Shapira pithily states, "to prove that something that could have happened
did not." Nadine Fresco, as we saw earlier, describes in similar terms the
revisionist endeavor "to prove that something *did not* take place."[79] The

sum and substance of the difference between the revisionists and the "new historians" may well boil down to this "could have happened."

All of the variations on the Shoah's "hyper-thinkability" discussed earlier participate in the resurgence of the New Left in Western democracies. They all agree, so to speak, to deny the singularity of the Shoah, which they see as the sign of a regression in the values of modernity, connected either to Nazism (as the effect thereof) or to strategies of domination (in the form of the classic international "Jewish plot" or of an Israeli state identified with oppression). This singularity universally delegitimates "peoplehood" in the Jewish condition, which is generally expected to be exemplary of the condition of modern man—the Jew as the absolute referent for Mankind! The recurrent glorification of the Jewish figure is among the most surprising aspects of these texts. It may be tempting to see in this a rhetorical device designed to hide a crypto-anti-Semitism. But this is not the case. (And if it were, it could only be a "postmodern" form of aesthetic, literary, and post-theological anti-Judaism.) On the contrary, we must take seriously this glorification of the Jewish figure and realize that we are dealing with an allegorical Jew, lifted onto a pedestal—precisely because he or she does not exist—while the real Jew is trampled in the dust.

What, then, could possibly account for such an ideological fixation on the figure of the Jew in the Shoah? Is it because the Shoah is a capital event in the West, or because the Jews abusively put it at the center of public debate? Why must the constitution of a new political discourse develop a theory about Jews? We could posit the Christian origin of the symbolic figure of the Jews, which, as we will see, tells us many things about the "narrative" that is being constructed around the Jew in the Shoah, but if we content ourselves with such an explanation, we will never leave the realm of mystery and mystification. We also could posit a new and much more abstruse cause and see in the "singularity" of the Jews the sign of a structural problem in political modernity, in its relationship to Jews, as well as in its relationship to itself and to its humanity. This is the direction in which I will be taking my analysis. But before embarking upon it, it is time to look at this singularity and its problematical history in greater detail and examine the conditions of the (Western) narrative constructed around it.

CHAPTER 4

The Unthought Singularity

Unlike the theologies of the Shoah that sacralize Jewish singularity and make it a taboo subject, New Left discourse undertakes to reason it to excess, in an ideological mystification, as if everything followed from a single cause. From both standpoints, Jewish singularity, indeed, singularity in general, be it glorified or demonized, remains unthought. Yet it is the New Left's narrative that takes us in the right direction, because it is framed in the political-historical terms that must be given priority in the examination of the singularity of the Shoah. This is because the Shoah implicated the Jews as a people;[1] it was the people in them that the Nazis targeted. And peoples exist only in political and historical fact. The "Jewish people" has remained one of the most obscure enigmas in history, even in modernity, despite its break with religion. The reason for this strange fact is one of the aspects of the subject to be defined.

The Historicity of Jewishness

The term *Jew* is not a hollow rhetorical category. It refers to a cultural, anthropological, sociological, and historical reality of generally unsuspected reach. All one has to do is step out of the clouds of rhetoric and ideology and examine the subject in sociological, historical, political, and textual terms to see that this is the case.[2]

Like any other people, the Jewish collective traces its existence back to a founding act, recorded in the first two books of the Bible. Unlike most origin myths, theirs is not a myth of foundation and autochthony, of roots in the land, but of exile and mobility. To bear the project of a humanity restoring justice and forgiveness, Abraham, the eponym ancestor, leaves the civilization into which he was born. The theme of departure reappears on the scale of the people when, freed from the bonds of slavery, the Jewish people leave Egypt to find unity in the wilderness. "A nation from amidst a nation" (Deuteronomy 4:34)—the identity of the Jewish people is thus ambivalent in their own eyes, and so Abraham the Hebrew does not forget that he was once Abram the Aramaean. This identity, nomadizing between the borders of the identities of other peoples, is borne, nonetheless, by the promise of the Land and hence of a way out of the desert. This departure from sociality does not lead, as Hegel thought, to a transgression of common norms of morality[3] but rather to the Sinaitic law, recognized as the guarantee of a covenant, the foundation of humanity's future moral redemption. The concept of a covenant is what makes the "Jewish people" a sociality bound together not by ethnic ties but by formal and rational contractual terms. As ninth-century philosopher Saadia Gaon stated, the Jewish people is a people only by virtue of its laws. As far as political culture is concerned, even novice historians of Judaism know that medieval Jewish communities, for instance, were governed by charters of rights and obligations that tied their members to one another but also by what was as pernickety a practice of separation between religious and lay authorities as was possible at the time. Eight centuries before Greece, this so-called "tribalism" forged a social organization based on consent and responsibility, freedom, and respect for a moral code,[4] which gave rise to the "Mosaic commonwealth" upon which sixteenth- and seventeenth-century Protestant theologians modeled the republican idea in opposition to royal absolutism. The Hebraic idea of the covenant was thus one of the key sources of modern democracy. It was also from this "tribalism" that early seventeenth-century theorists of international law drew the idea of humanity upon which universal law was founded. This is why the Jews can be counted (on the basis of the experience of Jewish medieval philosophy) alongside the Protestants of the Reformation, as pioneers who paved the way to political modernity,[5] without forgetting their direct contribution to shaping it during the course of its development. Freedom from bondage, moral obligations, and austerity, in the hopes of the fulfillment of the promise to come, have all counted among the most powerful constructs in the Jewish collective imagination.

Specific morphological structures correspond to these constructs. Their strongest characteristic is governed by the symbolism of exile and the hope of return. The lack of a territory did not put an end to Jewish continuity, which survived it, living in hopes of return. Thus despite the great divisions in the Jewish collectivity (two states in antiquity, the Ashkenazic and Sephardic cultural worlds, the Diaspora and Israel), the collective framework has never ceased to exist, from the point of view of the Jews or the world at large. This tension and constant mobility have been sustained by the messianic faith that produces a suspended temporality in which the ideal of unity is kept alive despite an extremely fragmented and divided reality.[6] The Diaspora constituted, in this respect, an original model of social morphology: the symbolic-geographic center (the Land of Israel), the book (the Torah), and the international solidarity that united Jewish communities in the defense of persecuted Jews since Antiquity worked together to sustain what was an inevitably problematical continuity for twenty-five centuries. In the countries of their dispersion, the Jews were totally part of the body politic (when it was willing to accept them), but they harbored something over and above it, a surplus of being and identity that transcended the confines of nations and empires, namely, their Jewishness, their belonging to a Jewish people. This extra measure of identity testified to the prospect of a humanity beyond the compartmentalization of peoples. It so happens that this surplus of identity was carried by Jewish *singularity*, by the singularization of Jews in the nations, which bore witness to a dimension beyond each nation. In humanity, the Jewish people remained a sort of "people within." Contemporary Israeli society, bringing together Jews from more than 120 nations (from Ukrainians to Moroccans and Falashas), illustrates that, above and beyond a diversity that is as great as that of humanity, the Jews form a people, notwithstanding the difficulties involved.

What nobody has considered, what seems to be so inadmissible to modern consciousness that everyone has repressed it, is what can be defined as the historicity of Jewishness. The state of being Jewish is not the result of a decree by the "persecutor," as Alain Brossat pretends, one that constitutes the Jews as "a real group" by deciding "who is Jewish and who is not."[7] Jewishness is an empirical fact of history. Historicity can be defined as the quality of the historic experience of a people. There is no history where there are only individuals.

The Pariah People

The Jewish problem in modernity stems from the fact that the "Jewish people" did not find a place for itself in Europe, when the nation-states were first established (the major expulsions of Jews in Western Europe in the Middle Ages can even be regarded as benchmarks to date the birth of the European nation-states), and then, in a more radical way, after the French Revolution, when the peoples of Europe were divided into territories and nations. The declarations by Comte de Clermont-Tonnerre and Abbé Grégoire,[8] cited earlier, are significant in this respect; the entry of the Jews into the French nation had a price—the dissolution of the "Jewish people." Equally significant was the resolution adopted by Napoleon's Grand Sanhedrin, relinquishing the "political laws" of the "Jewish nation" and maintaining only the "religious laws" (which continued, morphologically, to bear the trace of their former relationship to the "political laws";

thus the problem of "peoplehood" would be based on a misunderstanding and framed first in religious and later, with anti-Semitism, in racial terms). The Enlightenment-era ideology was thus driven, for the best reasons in the world, to ignore the historicity and singularity of the Jewish people, who could not benefit at the time from the constitution of a political state in Europe because they had no territorial basis and therefore, to all intents and purposes, no formal existence. This was the lot of many peoples at the time. The French revolutionaries were also intent on eliminating *patois*, or regional languages, which Abbé Grégoire described as "foreign" idioms and which was a way of designating the peoples and cultures that spoke them. But the Jews never had a recognized geographical area where they could enjoy concrete if not formal continuity, and they were among the first to be hit by the process of modern urbanization. Thus modernity necessarily "ahistoricized" the Jewish people and spoke, from then on, about a "Jewish condition" (as one might speak of the "condition" of women or of Afro-Americans), a state that comes under the heading of biological atavism (the subject of romantic mysteries, at best, when it was not of darker fictions). The current terminological difficulty in designating the destruction of the Jews derives from this overall difficulty in qualifying Jewish existence. The scores of books written on the unfathomable mysteries of "Jewish identity" apparently have not succeeded in penetrating its secret.

Political modernity emancipated individual Jews but had no place in its midst for the Jewish people. This is an obvious fact. Yet the Jewish people did not in actual fact disappear as a result. The anti-Semitism that political modernity produced from its outset objectively demonstrates, by its unconscious dimension, that from its own perspective the Jewish people continued to exist, albeit unrecognized and therefore doomed by iron necessity to be swept into the erring impulses of history. But even before anti-Semitism emerged as it did chaotically in the democratic world, the Napoleonic model with the Grand Sanhedrin, briefly discussed earlier, had formalized and institutionalized the ambiguity of the Jews in citizenry in a very perverse manner. By organizing the Jews of France into a consistory, that is, a religious confession and hence a "community" in a way, Napoleon reinstated a collective form of Jewish life that the revolution had not foreseen and that once again designated the Jews as a group and a singularity (this time authorized, legitimate, and legal). Napoleon's later policies make his purposes clear: to single out the Jews from French citizenry in an infamous way (the "infamous decree" of March 17, 1808, excluded the Jews for a period of ten years from economic laws applicable to all citizens). It was, then, institutionally and not just in civil society (through anti-Semitism) that even after the revolution the Jews were regarded, consciously and unconsciously, as a "Jewish people." But this people was ideologically impossible to see or to conceive, fundamentally banished to the point of becoming a mystery and a fatality for the Jews themselves. When anti-Semites attacked Jews, they were always attacking a species outside of history and outside of humankind (and hence as a "race"). This is what Alain Brossat calls the "zoologization" of the Jews, their reduction to the status of a "natural group,"[9] but he does not realize that his own approach to the Jewish condition before the Emancipation obeys a similar mechanism to the one he denounces in his analysis of Nazism. Indeed, he cannot imagine the possibility of a Jewish existence before the Emancipation or in the wake of its failure: the only Jews that exist in his eyes are the Jews of modernity, the ones who have disappeared behind the citizen. In the saga of modernity, democratic Emancipation is what allowed the Jews to gain access to the human condition. Outside modernity, either they are *nothing* but men (and so they do not exist), or they are *nothing* but Jews,[10] whence the impossibility to conceive of them other than in infra-rational terms (race, pathos, visceral drive, tribal affiliation, fate, condition, identical identity, brute singularity, etc.). Anti-Semitism is a paradoxical, still inexplicable phenomenon that emerged with the Emancipation. We have not yet understood why modern human beings, citizens of the *demos*, attacked other citizens on the pretext that they were Jews when "Jewish" had supposedly ceased to exist in the citizenship and rationality of the Enlightenment. These citizens found themselves attacked not because they were different from others (this is supposedly the case for the Jews who are accused today of *communautarism*, that is, of living in a Jewish community apart from mainstream society[11]) but precisely because they were like them, the same and therefore unidentifiable (which is why they had to be marked with a yellow star). What can explain such an aggression that singled out the Jew in the citizen? The collective imagination? The need for a scapegoat? Some sort of "diabolical causality," to borrow Léon Poliakov's term?[12] The great historian of anti-Semitism wrote a sweeping history of the world from the prism of anti-Semitism, but the reader comes out without understanding why it happened to the Jews. Setting aside the theological explanation, we are no doubt dealing with a very powerful knot in the unconscious of modernity that deprives it of words and thwarts any clear expression. The anti-Semitic phenomenon is surely one of the most important phenomena of modernity that has remained as mysterious (in modern terms) as Fascism and totalitarianism. It is the blind spot of what anthropologist Louis Dumont calls "modern ideology," the ideology of the Enlightenment that structures our worldview and in whose terms "peoplehood" becomes unthinkable. It runs through modernity with a depth that was forcefully thrown into relief on the occasion of the Dreyfus affair, or with Nazism, nationalism, or Communism. As long as we have not understood the underlying mechanisms of the symbolic system that sustains it, we will fail to understand modernity and hence to free ourselves from Enlightenment's magic circle (that is, from the darkness it needs to shine), to get out of the fatality of chronic catastrophe that haunts it and that we can only explain in terms of the irrational. When I speak of the unconscious of modernity, I am referring to its latent *structures*, not to a purely psychological mechanism. From the morphological perspective of my analysis here, the conscious and the unconscious, while being very precisely separated and delimited, as I have already said, appear together at the same time as part of the same coherence and the same systematic, yet dialectical, unity. To illustrate this, let us say that the emancipation of the Jews, their admission to citizenship, appeared at the same time as anti-Semitism, and that Enlightenment man, citizenship, and universality appeared at the same time as imperialism, colonialism, and racism. In the aftermath of the Shoah, it is impossible to ignore this.

The perseverance in the obliteration of the Jews as a people, as much institutionally as through violence, in flagrant contradiction to the conscious ideals of human rights that presided over the Emancipation, is nonetheless a "functional" product of modernity, structurally embedded in its spirit and not the result of erratic acts or intentions by individuals or groups who would be enemies of the Jews. Both the emancipation of the Jews and the concept of democratic citizenship in general were flawed from this perspective, and this is the subject of my investigation. The fact that the Nazis consciously decided not to call the mass murder of the Jews by its name, but to use *amtssprache*, a coded bureaucratic language instead, was a sign of the "modernity" of their crime. Even in destruction, they could not name the Jews as a people. And what reason would they have had to name them, since they did not consider that the Jews came under the heading of humankind? The race (that is assassinated) is below the threshold of what language can express. Modernity had opened its doors to individual Jews as citizens (which was, of course, a great step forward toward freedom from oppression), but it lacked the basis upon which to found in its midst the legitimacy and recognition of the Jewish collective that is a fact inherent to the order of the world (even though it is a factor of disorder in the classification of human beings—the very core of modern politics and power).

We have here all of the ingredients of the "Jewish question." The Jewish people could not fit into the European nation-state framework. Having become citizens, however, the Jews (in the very eyes of the moderns, of the civic *demos*) continued—against their will—to belong to a people that had become a specter, a subrational group, implacably *alien* to the political normality of states, testifying to another view of world history, an archaic figure out of the past or a harbinger of the future, in any case, a spoke in the wheel of the nation-states. The concept of the "pariah condition," as forged by Hannah Arendt (after Max Weber) to define the condition of the Jews, brings home what such an experience involved (and still does in a way). The "Jew" is the system's outsider and, as such, one of its key components, embodying at once the failure of the modern system and its opportunity to come to terms with itself and shake off the yoke of fatality. The "Jewish people" is the unthought, incomplete, and unfinished facet of the emancipation of the Jews, so much so that it cannot even be named. It is this omission—conveyed by the singularity and the singularization of the Jews—that is of universal import for all of political modernity and that must be tackled urgently in the wake of the Shoah.

Zionism's Avenue to Humanity

It is on this level that we can take up the question of Zionism at the core of the question of Jewish singularity. Based on the presuppositions of modernity and the Emancipation, Zionism is unimaginable and unthinkable. Yet it is, in fact, a product of the unconscious of the modernization of Jews, part and parcel of it (and even a choice piece).

Political Zionism is the second avenue of Jewish modernity, that of the national auto-emancipation through statehood, after the civic emancipation that regarded individuals only. To a certain extent, political Zionism resulted from the failure of (emancipated) citizenship; its existence is a living (albeit an implicit) challenge to the normative validity of individual emancipation and its resignation to the demise of peoplehood. The conditions of its birth are telling in this respect. With the explosion of anti-Semitism during the Dreyfus affair, it became clear to non-French Jews in particular that the hostility of the anti-Dreyfusards targeted the "people" (the Jewish "plot") in the Jewish citizens and, drawing the necessary conclusions, they set out to emancipate the Jewish *people* and not only individuals. Political Zionism is thus modern in the sense that it was created in and by modernity and at the same time anti-modern, because it was created in reaction to the partial failure of the Jewish Emancipation (partial because it did not so much contest emancipation as add "auto" to it by integrating the Jews into the family of nations). Zionism, at the time of its birth, betrayed the two facets, conscious and unconscious, of modernity. Thereafter it took its place within the conscious framework of modernity and was formulated in its terms, aspiring as it did to establish a Jewish nation-state and nationality based on the model of political modernity. What could be more "modern" than the nation-state? But because Zionism remained a modality of modern emancipation, it also remained prey to a contradictory tension between the logic of the nation (a *Jewish* state, if such a thing is possible[13]) and that of citizenship (a state of Jews, but not necessarily Jewish), although this tension would not manifest itself until the end of the twentieth century. In the aftermath of the Second World War, when everyone saw that anti-Semitism had led to the Shoah, the accuracy of the Zionist analysis became shockingly obvious. In the Jewish people, bled white by the Shoah, it aroused an incredible outpouring of energy, and the state of Israel became the rallying point as much for the Jews of the *Yishuv* as for the Jews of the Diaspora.

The new state was clearly lodged within the tradition of political modernity and embedded in the symbolic universe of Europe. Thus Theodor Herzl's analysis in *The Jewish State* was based on the conviction that the creation of this state would compensate for the failings of democracy that he had seen at work "in every country, "even in those highly civilized—for instance, France."[14] Herzl imagined a fair exchange of sorts: the future Jewish State would welcome the Jews who did not benefit from the Emancipation, the miserable masses from the despotic states of Eastern Europe and the Jews who have difficulty assimilating (liable to endanger the status of emancipated Jews by exacerbating anti-Semitism), and, in return, the future state of Israel would be admitted into the family of European nations.[15] The fact that it did not much matter to Herzl whether this state was in Africa or Asia is typically "modern" (by its unrealistic abstraction and faith in acts of will), and here again historicity was to return with a vengeance. There is only one place where the Jewish people, by the weight of its own history, could choose to set up an institution of power and that is in the land of Israel,[16] which is not only the "promised land" in the Jewish people's representation of its origins but also the actual and symbolic node in the articulation of nearly all of its dispersions throughout its history. In fact, if Herzl was willing to accept Uganda, it was only because there was a pressing need to save Russian Jews from the pogroms. But when the question of Uganda came up at the World Zionist Congress, the Russian representatives themselves took a stand against this temporary solution. The Jews who needed a solution most urgently knew that the humanitarian emergency could not prevail over historicity.

Those who maintain that the specificity of Israel is an artificial product of the manipulation of the Shoah act as if the country was peopled exclusively by European survivors of the Shoah. This picture exists in the Western collective imagination but not in reality. A great majority of the population comes from Arab countries, and the Jews did not leave them because of the Shoah. They left when the Arab nation-states were founded in the postwar period and the colonial countries could no longer protect them, because there too there was no place for the Jews, and so they emigrated en masse to Israel, among other destinations. Yet the memory of these Jews, as if by common consent, is treated as if it could be tallied in the profits and losses of decolonialization, in total disregard of the fact that well before the Arab invasion these Jews had lived in the countries they were forced to leave. If they opted for the West during the colonial era, it was because they were second-class citizens under Moslem rule, assigned to the infamous status of *dhimmi*, and they saw the arrival of the Europeans as a liberation. Thus at the time of the establishment of the state of Israel, there was an exchange of populations, which was the case in many other places in the world. The oppression that Sephardic Jews had long suffered in Moslem societies intensified with the birth of the Arab nation-states and their objectively xenophobic policies (as if the Jews were "foreigners" in these countries). Their accession to Israeli citizenship was thus lodged within the process of national auto-emancipation. Behind the real drama of the Palestinians lies this drama that implicates the responsibility of the Arab world this time.

The intention of the early political Zionists was to establish a Jewish state outside of Europe because Europe had failed in its emancipation of the Jews. Theirs was not a desire to leave Europe as much as to find a way to reintegrate it on a basis more suited to its norm, one that rested on Jewish singularity, since this was what posed a problem in civic emancipation. This intense paradox that sees the telescoping of the singular (the national) and the universal (emancipating modernity), of the Jew and the citizen, in the appearance of the Jews as an autonomous, collective actor on the modern stage is, in fact, intrinsic to political modernity, which saw the rise of the national(ist) phenomenon in citizenship and the democratic state.

The Zionists leaned on the concept of man-of-the-citizen (from the standpoint of the dual notion of the "Rights of Man and the Citizen") as a foundation for the entry of the Jews into modernity, where they had no place as a people. The problem is that Zionism obviously identified the man-of-the-citizen with the Jew, while for modernity (on a conscious level) the Jew became a citizen because he was a man, not because he was a Jew (a point to which I will return later). In Zionism, the facts are reversed (but they are still the same facts). It is because the Jew is a Jew that he becomes a man, that is, an Israeli, a new substitute category for the Jew in exile. This reading is what embeds Zionism in the same logic as "the Rights of Man and the Citizen." The Zionist restoration of Jewishness via the invention of an Israeli citizenship is a way of restoring the humanity persecuted in the citizenship of the emancipated Jew, attacked by the anti-Semite as a "Jew," and regarded by the Zionists as a "human being." In their eyes, it is the man in the citizen who was attacked (which is why the Zionists were intent on "normalizing" what they saw as the "pathological" and "unhealthy" Jewish condition). And it is the real question, which explains (as few people have realized) why Herzl considered the Jewish State "necessary to the world."[17]

What is happening in this transposition ought to concern (or have concerned) democracy as a whole, calling upon it to rethink the status of the man in the citizen. Indeed, this is the wider aim of my analysis. However, Zionism runs the risk of a misunderstanding: by taking the Jew out of the emancipated citizen, even if it is to establish a new citizenship and restore the Jew in the abstraction of man, Zionism can give the false impression of breaking with the professed universality of modernity and disputing its validity. This is, of course, but an optical illusion.

In Zionism, it is the avenue to humanity (and not to citizenship) that becomes the central issue (because this humanity is what the anti-Semite denies at bottom to the Jew, by dissociating it from citizenship without recognizing it in his or her Jewishness which is his or her form of humanity). The establishment of a Jewish citizenship, condition of the normalization of the Jews and of their successful entry into the family of democratic humanity, on the same basis as the citizen nations of the European states, was only a means of gaining access to this humanity and not an end in itself. The Israeli experience allowed Jews after the Shoah to return to humanity on the basis of singularity (of the nation and the state), just as the Diasporic Jews returned to the citizenship of which they had been divested through a reaffirmation of community values and an identification with the state of Israel. Consequently, the singularization of the Jews in the Shoah led overwhelmingly to a reversal in the emancipatory logic without destroying it. It rests henceforth more on the singular than on the universal. Otherwise put, citizenship in the way that Jews would invest it as Jews and not only as "citizens" or as "men-of-citizens" became for them the foundation of humanity and not the opposite. One must be Jewish to be a man, to be present in the polity, to be a citizen, and not "human" (and repress one's Jewishness like modernity repressed it) to be a citizen. This is the lesson Jews learned from the Shoah. But (and this is the dilemma to which we will return later) it is the Jew-of-the-citizen, the Jew repressed in and by the citizen, that underpins the invocation of man. This Jewish being that political Zionism set out to reinstate remained a particular and singular modality of a humanity still conceived in terms of abstraction and anonymity, in terms of the universality in the name of which the Emancipation had removed Jewishness from an equally abstract and anonymous citizenship.

The Bright Spell after the War

By reaffirming Jewish singularity after the war, the Jews were not staying in the place that Hitler had assigned to them; if this had been the case, then Hitler would have won a posthumous victory, and the Jews would have been doomed to perverse Nazification. Should the Jews have picked up their prewar mode of existence and blended back into the civic *demos*, as critics of Jewish singularity maintain? This is not, at any rate, what happened. The Shoah had brought home to them the fact that they would always be exposed to a mortal danger if they continued to relinquish their condition as a people in the civic condition. The fact that they had repressed, dismissed, and neglected their peoplehood to join in with the modern chorus had led them to this terrible situation of solitude and abandonment, with no help from anywhere, rejected by all states, because the Jewish *people*, deprived of existence in the jungle of nation-states and no longer falling within any category of modernity, had become a pariah people. In the concrete brutality of history, far from the wonderful legal categories that were useless when it came to saving them, they had been hit where they least expected it, in the part of themselves that they had left behind and repressed, that is, in their communal existence, in the dimension of peoplehood that many of them had decided was senseless in light of modern progress. After what hit them, this dimension came back to the fore and with it the extent to which it had been neglected. By reaffirming their collective identity, the Jews were not letting themselves be "zoologized" or racialized, as if they were accepting the Hitlerian norm. On the contrary, it was the Hitlerian norm that had seized them by what they had repressed, by what modernity had repressed, designating them exactly where political modernity had abandoned them and failed. After such a tragedy, the repressed could no longer be dismissed. The unconscious was brought back to the surface of consciousness. In Emmanuel Lévinas's words, "Hitlerian anti-Semitism's recourse to the racial myth reminded the Jews of the irremissibility of their being [. . .] to renounce Judaism or to make light of it, is to accept the supreme disgrace, and there is nothing more terrible than accepting this."[18]

Behind Hitler's category of singularization ("zoologization") stood a Jewish people and a Jewish historicity ignored by modern consciousness. The fact that it was so easy for Hitler (and the anti-Semites before him) to swoop down on it like a vulture evidenced that this repression of the condition of peoplehood in the condition of the Jews was criminogenic, that it was the source of the catastrophes that struck the Jews for two centuries. But to undertake such a reversal in perspective and to unravel this tangled skein would necessitate recognizing that the Jews exist, that they are men by nature and not by decree, that they have constituted a people for thousands of years, hence well before modernity. This historicity was repressed by modernity (albeit ambiguously, since it was recognized by Zionism, a product of modernity), but it did not totally disappear. It resurfaced in the Shoah. And its reconstitution after the Shoah is a sign of great import for the symbolic of modernity, a major sign (and not the cause) of its end or, at any rate, of an upheaval in democratic citizenship. In reaffirming Jewish singularity and identifying with Zionism, the Jews very logically acted upon their desire to start over again, to renew their ties with others, and to return with more security to a modernity that had had tragic consequences for them. Jews began realizing that it was impossible to encounter alterity when their own existence was uncertain, and that they had neglected the vital needs of their communal existence for more than a century. Zionism and the state of Israel—which had engendered the only *democracy* in the Middle East[19]—gave the Jews a way to return to democracy, after having been abandoned by it, and it gave democracy a chance to continue and find a remedy for its own failings: the creation of a (democratic) state of Israel was a sign, even proof, that the democratic ideal had not lost all credibility. It would be a mistake to underestimate the widespread support for the state of Israel that existed until the 1970s and still does in a way in Western democracies. This support represented a vital moral and spiritual need for Western democracies and was not merely the expression of compassion and pity. The state of Israel is therefore an important symbol in the system of contemporary democratic values. Seen in this light, it is clear that the infamous resolution adopted by the United Nations in 1975 equating Zionism and racism evinced a moral crisis in the global system of values. Just as democratic anti-Semitism is negative proof of the continuity of the Jewish people in modernity, this accusation of racism is negative proof of the origins of Zionism as I have defined it—reinstating the *humanity* of the Jew after the destruction of the Jews, by positing it more in relation to Man than in relation to the emancipated citizen. The accusation that Zionism is a form of racism implies that it is infrarational, antimodern, Nazi of course, and adverse to Man, that it is "zoological," just as anti-Semitism made a race of the Jews. The practice of reversing responsibility is already at work in this accusation. Israel is accused of racism in the name of morality, of course, but the accusers are suggesting something more than the exercise by Israel of racism (against Arabs)—they are pointing an accusing finger at a racial condition, an infrarational, inframodern identity that would set Israel apart from universal humanity.

The birth in France of a "Jewish community" after the war is to be understood similarly against this backdrop of a Jewish historicity that had slipped out of modernity's conscious (but not unconscious) mind. It was a new invention that allowed Jews to rehabilitate the citizenship from which they had been excluded en bloc under Vichy, when they had been left in a state of total abandonment and fragility. It did so by compensating for the failings of a system that had set the banquet table for citizenship without providing a roof to protect the guests in case of bad weather. This change took place in complete symbiosis with changes in French society, whose

search for a new social bond, starting at the end of the 1960s, produced
the considerable development in the grassroots movement that we can still
see today and which evidences the absence of sociality in the centralized
French system characterized by a deep gulf separating individuals from the
government. It was in civil society that the Jews abandoned by their state
had found help, and it was in civil society that the reconstruction of Judaism
took place. France made this enterprise possible, because it had not been
totally compromised by Nazism. Thanks to the French people, 80 percent
of the French Jews, whom the state (admittedly misgoverned by Vichy) was
ready to hand over to the Nazis, were saved. These events also marked a
turning point in the French political mentality. After having witnessed the
confrontation between two figures of state, De Gaulle and Pétain, civil
society could only assert its predominance over the state, something that
had never occurred in the Jacobin nation before.

Thus the Jewish community, born from the heart and hollow of citizenship, is not to be understood as a "less," a penurious element for the
republic, a reservedness separated from the surrounding life, but rather as
an increase, a gratuitous beyond, a "more," an affirmation of republican
citizenship. It is this increase that may be at work in the centrality of the
Jewish sign in the French debate discussed earlier (in an affluent and no
longer penurious reading thereof). French Jewish identity is the particular
in addition to (and not in subtraction from) the universal. So close to the
apocalyptic landscape of the war, the École de pensée juive de Paris, the
school of Jewish thought, boldly theorizes that the Shoah obliged Jewish
consciousness to take on a responsibility toward man by virtue of a renewed
fidelity to Judaism.[20] The genocide mainly affected one people, but by its
systematic character it engaged modern man and therefore enjoined Jewish
consciousness to search in the depths of its Hebraic (and notably biblical)
past for a response to the failure of modernity and a way of redeeming
it. By maintaining their singularity, the Jews were thus bearing witness to
the human. This is what was involved in the return that took place at the
time to the traditional texts and to Judaism. It was not a matter of dissolving the specificity of the Jewish martyr in an abstract universal, as certain
historians who ignore Judeo-French history believe, but of considering it at
the center of universal human destiny, which meant affirming its singularity.
Jewish destiny, by its very singularity, bore witness to the universal destiny
of humankind. "In speaking of our universalism," explained Lévinas in a
speech given in 1963, "as strange as it might seem, because it is almost a
contradiction in terms, we wanted it to be a 'particularist universalism.'
The Jews are not willing to be evaporated, sublimated, or volatilized to
become universalist; on the contrary, they want to be universal in full consciousness of their own particularity. This is precisely the mystery of the

moral phenomenon: to accomplish the moral act, to undertake the sacrifice that is morality itself, I must be as deeply myself as can be. The idea of a universal humanity, of a great human family is fine, but a great human family founded on the unique consciousness of my irreplaceable duty which institutes as strongly as possible my existence as a person."[21] This was the starting point of a specifically Judeo-French school of thought that sought to express the spiritual and philosophical message of Judaism in the very terms of contemporary thought. It needed therefore to defend and illustrate the "presence" of the Jews in the world at the end of this twentieth century during which they had nearly disappeared and which had seen Judaism as well as modernity shaken to their very core. Thus was born the "community" that attested to the presence and openness of a genuine Judaism that set out to be faithful to itself and at the same time part of the polity, at the core of modernity and speaking in its language. The "Community" and the restoration of Jewish identity were the means through which the Jews returned to citizenship after the war, a citizenship reread and rectified in light of experience. The same reasons that accounted for the reconstitution of Jewish singularity and grounded its legitimacy argued in favor of its openness to the universal. France, in its singular identity, and for reasons evoked earlier, inherited the European philosophic vocation that had been assumed until then by Germany but that had deserted it with the Shoah. It was in this one place, in France, where the memory of and the search for the universal had been kept alive, that European Judaism was so swiftly reborn after the night and fog.

CHAPTER 5

The "Universal" Narrative
of Singularity

The discourse of singularity does not pertain to Jews and to Jewish history only. It is also the product of the Western imaginary in which it is professed and upon which it implicitly relies. It is always articulated in a tacit relationship to a "universal." It would be an ethical and a historical mistake to neglect this dimension in trying to understand the issue with which we are concerned here, because it was the Western imaginary that implemented the mechanisms of the singularization of the Jews. And they are fundamental to our understanding of Jewish singularity, which is the product of Jewish history but also of the history of the West, insofar as it is framed in the terms of Western discourse. Is not the Shoah also and first of all the problem of modern Europe, the outcome, as Arno Meyer argued, of a European crisis that began with the First World War? The Jew of history was effectively destroyed in it, but so was the Jew of Europe, the Jew as he or she appeared to Europe. In the course of its history, Europe forged "its" own Jew, one that does not necessarily correspond to the real Jew but that requires his or her existence as a prop. For this reason we cannot turn only to the Jews for an understanding of the "mystery" of the Shoah's singularity or the European singularization of the Jews in the Shoah. If the "trees" are the Jews, then the "forest" that needs to be seen is Europe! There is a "Jewish sign of Europe" that tells us a great deal more about Europe than about the Jews. The Shoah's incomprehensibility stands at the crossroads of these two histories. To understand why the Jewish singularity of the Shoah is so hard for Europe to see, we must grasp the impact of the Shoah on the symbolic economy of this "sign" and what makes for the fact that modern European consciousness, structured as it is by the history of its relationship to the Jewish sign, is naturally blind to the singularization of the Jews in the Shoah.

This situation is the culmination of a long process that developed over the course of twenty centuries. It is rooted in the Christian foundation of a European identity that took shape in a dialectic between the singular and the universal in which the Jewish sign was forged. Indeed, it was because nascent Europe (and there is no Europe outside of Christendom) said something about the Jew (as a signifier for it) that it was constituted as an identity (identical to itself). Thus the Jew was "spoken" by Europe even before speaking to it. This phenomenon is what I am defining as "Europe's Jewish sign." From the outset, Europe defined itself in Judeo-centric terms, since Christianity saw itself as the "new Israel." The case of Europe is unique in the history of civilizations: according to philosopher Rémy Brague, Europe is an identity that conceives of itself as second, as a substitute identity. Before Christianity, pagan Rome found the source of its identity in Athens. With Christianity, Israel became the new horizon. But Europe's need of the Other to conceive of itself, its need of alterity, is not necessarily altruistic. The relationship to the Other is experienced as a relationship to the self as sameness. Brague maintains that "Europe stands apart from other cultural worlds by its particular mode of relationship to what is proper to it: namely, the appropriation of what is perceived to be foreign."[1] Which is also a way of negating what is foreign. To pagan and then Christian Rome, Athens and Jerusalem appeared as models in all their glowing splendor, only to vanish from history once and for all, at least from the vantage point of Rome. This observation is particularly true when applied to Europe's Jewish sign. We have in our possession a text that in a few sentences puts the economy of the Jewish sign into place for twenty centuries: *The Letter of Paul to the Romans*. This assertion is no doubt excessive, but it is valid for the symbolic sphere and pertinent on the level of symbolic morphology. All civilizations could be seen as having a kind of fundamental symbolic map on which their successive configurations throughout history can be plotted. Forms of thought, as formulated in writing, would express something of the group's founding identity. The Pauline text could thus be regarded as the very matrix of the European narrative of singularity, the traces and remote consequences of which could be seen in contemporary narratives concerning the singularity of the Shoah. What would be at issue in it is not only history but also the literary structure of Western discourse.

The Symbolic Economy of Europe's Jewish Sign

It is a matter of widespread agreement that the founding paradigm of Christianity is the Pauline model, where the relations between Jews and Christians are systematically defined. These relations are of decisive importance because Christianity derives from Judaism, and the early Christians in Paul's days were still Jews of the Synagogue. Paul's description of the Jews is based on a dialectic (emphasized at about the same time by Philo of Alexandria) between the "letter," or the "flesh," and the "spirit."[2] In Paul's words, "a Jew is someone who is [. . .] so [. . .] in Spirit and not by the Book" (Romans 2:29), and further "they were not the children of the flesh that became the Children of God" (Romans 9:8). The nascent Church (on its way to becoming the Church of Imperial Rome) would gradually end up interpreting this text as meaning that the Christian had replaced and superseded the Jew by attaining a superior rank of being.[3] Europe is thus inaugurated as the "new Israel," the "Verus Israel" (the true Israel), whose truth derives from the fallen state of "old Israel." Henceforth, "Israel after the flesh" and physical circumcision will be pitted against "Israel of the spirit," Christian Israel, and the "circumcision of the heart," to borrow an expression from the language of the prophets that flourished in Christian thought. The letter is Hebraic, the meaning is Christian. The letter is thus seized in an economy of meaning that it did not carry before, overwhelmed by a signification that sweeps it in its flow. The same Israel is at once recognized and denied. It is split in two, and henceforth Jews and Christians flock to the same being "of Israel." This movement (in the way of an implosion?) released a considerable amount of symbolic energy in the Hellenistic and Roman world. It enabled Christianity, once it was theologized, to pass itself off as universality, generality, and totality (on an equal standing with the worldwide empire of Rome) at the cost of reducing the Jewish sign to particularity and materiality, to an inert body doomed to death and caducity. It is by establishing the Jewish sign as restrictive, by confining the Jew to a carnal, ethnic, and spiritual singularity, that the Christians established themselves in the universal. The Pauline coup de force opened the Roman Empire to the Christians by providing them with a structure that allowed them to pit themselves against it.

The Roman Empire, turned Christian, gave way to a medieval "Catholicity" (etymologically, "universality"), which affords a perfect illustration of a dialectical model that did not remain a mere theological figure of style but was translated into a sociohistorical fact. In Catholic Europe, under the leadership of the pope and the emperor of the Holy Roman Empire of the German Nation (in a political echo of the division between the spirit and the flesh), the Jews, restricted within the bounds of their ghettos, were seen as personifying the only singular "people" in all imperial, "universal" Europe. All the theories about Jews as witnesses to the truth of Christianity are lodged in this framework. With modernity, Europe is the only civilization in history to go through such an extensive revolution (that overturned the world order) and yet perpetuate itself within the same civilization. It was as if, to borrow Marx's metaphor, the European civilization had been "standing on its head," and modernity had "set it back on its feet." Henceforth, the world will be explained not by ideas (the "head") but by materiality (the "feet"), not by metaphysics but by economy, history, society, and politics. Yet the end to the preponderance of the Church did not put an end to the referential Pauline dialectic. It was as if the Pauline model continued to be active in modernity, even though Christianity had lost its power. To pick up the terms of Pauline discourse again, what was on the "spirit" side was reverted to the "letter" side. In concrete terms, it was the end of Catholicity. This was materialized in the Protestant schism by a return to the Hebraic letter, to the "Old Testament" of "carnal" Israel, which was given a new translation directly from the Hebrew. With its focus on philology rather than exegesis and on scientific study of texts rather than metaphysics, Protestant-ism re-Judaized Christianity (but we are dealing here with a "Judaism" as it grew out of the Pauline dialectic). It was as if Israel "after the flesh" had stepped back on the stage of Catholic Israel. On a symbolic level, Europe Judaized by identifying with the Jewish sign (the "letter") that it itself had produced, and at the same time it distanced itself from Catholicity. This crucial turning point also found expression in sociological forms. It was the end of the empire and the beginning of the era of nations and states, in an apotheosis of individualist and collective particularisms. "Catholicity" living according to the "spirit" was over.

And what about the Jews? What was the sociological effect of this major upheaval in civilization on the Jews? One would have imagined that as Europe "Judaized" it would rediscover the Jews exactly where they had been relegated (to the material, the flesh, this world, singularity). And yet it was exactly the opposite that happened. The Jewish sign still remained (dialectically) doomed to absence! At a time when Europe was breaking down into particular (and particularist) peoples—first in nation-states and then in nationalism—the Jews found themselves identified with the "spirit" and the universal (and this after having personified absolute singularity in medieval Catholicity). Sociologically speaking (as we have seen), when the Jews were admitted to citizenship in the nation-states, they were expected to become citizens like all others. Judaism was supposed to disappear as a singularity, an identity, and a historical "people" to become, in psychological and legal terms, a religious confession. The Jews who were unwilling to accept this excluded themselves from geographical Europe (but not from symbolic Europe) by creating Zionism, which took them to the Middle East (and turned them into a people and a nation "like all others"). By doing so they extricated themselves from their predetermined (confessional and abstract) destiny and fell in line with the norm of singularity. In the meantime, in concrete terms, the Diasporic universalization of the Jewish sign spelled the end of local communities (the medieval *kahal*) and the appearance of major worldwide Jewish institutions. And, for the Europeans, it marked the development of the fantasy of cosmopolitism and of an international Jewish plot (plutocratic capitalism and international communism). The Jew was no longer seen as the negative embodiment of the singular but rather as the sign of the universal threatening European national identities. Today, on the other hand, leaving aside the archaic exception of the National Front, the Jew is identified as the singular (Zionism, ethnicism, or tribalism) threatening the universal.

As we can see, the Pauline economy of the Jewish sign can be regarded as symbolically structuring the history of Europe. It was as if the "narrative identity" of Europe, to pick up Paul Ricœur's notion,[4] was condensed into the Pauline tale of Christian origins, the main line of which is the Jewish sign. By following its successive configurations, we follow its development over the course of history. Thus Europe rediscovers the Jewish sign at every crucial turning point in its history, as if it drew a permanent force of renewal from this sign, a symbolic energy that allowed it to make its way through its own universe and to occupy at times the top, at other times the bottom. For the founding moment that Christianity constituted, the thing is evident. For the modern turning point, Protestantism attests to it. Neither should we overlook the moment of revolutionary emancipation, when the admission of Jews to citizenship was regarded as such a significant test that it generated a whole corpus of philosophical and political texts (pamphlets, "apology" of the Jews, literary competitions, etc.) Finally, in democratic modernity, anti-Semitism demonstrates that the Jewish sign is still lodged in a mysterious way within the core of European identity. The question of Jewish singularity is inseparable from European identity.

It is in this economy of the Jewish sign that Europe regards itself as at the center and even conceives of the center, by pushing to the margins (but it is the margins that set the center) the Jew as sign, a wandering sign, always elsewhere, but always a source of renewal for Europe and of a glorious eclipse for the Jews—Europe's Jew as glorious pariah, divine beggar, and a necessity for Europe!

The "Rhetorical" Jew after the Shoah

The Pauline dialectic designates the Jewish people not only by its supposedly negative aspect and its temporary exclusion (as long as it has not become Christian) but also by its positive, glorified aspect. This positive dimension is paradoxical, because what is appreciated in "the" Jew is the Christian, not the Jew; it is the Christian who has become the "true" Jew who finds himself or herself indirectly glorified. To occupy the still glorious and honored signifier "Israel," Paul introduced some leeway into the signifier "Jew." Thus Jews need not be Jewish, and Israel need not designate the Jewish people. Behind the fallen Jew rises the chosen Jew who does not necessarily coincide with the "historical" Jew. This dissociation is Paul's invention. It did not exist before him. When the prophets criticized the Jewish people, it was in terms of what they could and should be. Paul ethnicizes, in a nearly Gnostic dualism, the relationship between the moral injunction and the enjoined, dissociating an exclusively ethnic Israel from an exclusively symbolic Israel. This hidden, chosen Jew, who is the Christian, had, of course, its own symbolic history within the West. It is, for example, this Jew who Luther identifies with the Protestant (who is born at the same time), in opposition to the "false" Jews of Roman Catholicism. The same symbolic mechanism that Paul had applied to "carnal" Jews Luther used against those who were to be Catholics and Catholics only henceforth (and no longer representing the totality of Christendom).

This dialectic shows us the extent to which "the Jew" had been turned into a concept and a rhetorical figure expressing something altogether different than the real historicopolitical "sociological" Jews (in fact, this was when the Jews found themselves reduced in the Western collective imagination to the minor category of "sociological Jews"). Thus a sophisticated discourse could concern Jews without real Jews being concretely or willingly involved even for a moment. The discourse "runs" on its own power. The Jewish signifier (Israel) has fallen into the "Jewish sign" (the word "Israel"), and as a result the latter has became detached from its signifier. As to the signified (the "chosen people"), it has nothing more to do with either the sign or the signifier. Ultimately this derealizing discourse had catastrophic consequences for the "sociological" Jews, because whereas the discourse runs on its own power, there are still real Jews to bear the consequences, testify to its reality, or be scotomized under laurel wreaths.

After the Second World War, a brand new version of the glorified-denied Jew emerged in France, a totally novel version in a number of respects. In particular, it had a secular, non-Catholic, and philo-Semitic character. What was glorified was no longer Catholic Israel but Israel of the word, Israel-as-writer; the glorification was grounded this time in a full-fledged mystique of the letter and of the Jew as letter. This marked a new era in the symbolic history of the Jewish signifier, characterized by the "spiritualization of the letter" not the spirit versus the letter (the age of tradition) or the letter versus the spirit (modernity) but the spirit in the letter (the "postmodern" age?). It was a whole *literary* current in the 1960s and 1970s that expressed this new variant on the Pauline dialectic. Many of the writers who were part of it were Jewish (another novelty), and they wrote profusely about their literary Jewishness (it is in this respect that we can qualify them as "Jewish" authors, a designation that their [residual] Paulinism would have driven them to refuse). The figure of Edmond Jabès is central from this standpoint, but it holds court in a galaxy surrounded by such imposing figures as Maurice Blanchot, Emmanuel Lévinas, Jacques Derrida, and, more remotely, Georges Perec. An identifiable literary movement, the *Collectif Change*, or the "Change Group," with its own journal, the *Cahiers du Collectif Change*, was founded by Jean-Pierre Faye. Issue 22, dated February 1975, is significantly entitled *"L'Imprononçable, l'écriture nomade"* ("The Unpronounceable: Nomad Writing"). Focused mainly on Jabès, it presents a kaleidoscope of the new myths of the Jew embodying writing, of the writer as Jew, the Jewish letter as the guardian of the secret of existence, and the Jew's eternal exile as the quintessential expression of the human condition. What is of interest to us here is not the assumptions in their own right (they may contain some truth and have their literary justification) but rather the relationship to living Jews that are stated or implied in them.

Some twenty years after the Shoah, the absent (exiled) Jew was being glorified, in a patent, deliberate break with the real situation of Jews who were struggling at the time to reconstruct their destroyed lives but who remained significantly deprived of meaning, despite the irreproachably genuine philo-Semitism of this intellectual current. The most interesting observation that we can make in this regard is to note that the conceptual machine of the signifier "Jew" runs on its own power, independently of the real existence of Jews who had just survived the fatal consequences of early twentieth-century mythical representations of the Jew (the "Jewish plot"). This "machine" depends, nonetheless, on the condition of real Jews. Its new productivity required procedures adjusted to the new post-Shoah situation: with the letter destroyed and the spirit having lost its foundation, spirit was drawn from the missing letter, from its hollow, its vacuum. This did not prevent the concrete letter (the "sociological Jews") from being, if not excluded, at least held at bay, disconnected from meaning. Behind the glorification of the (rhetorical) "Jew," the real Jew disappeared again, even as he or she found himself or herself surrounded by an enormous sympathy. It would require another book to analyze in detail the theory of the "Jew" developed in the great many texts written by this intellectual current.

Philippe Boyer announces very clearly in this issue of *Change* that the point is to "grasp the effect of Jewishness [. . .] insofar as it is a factor of *disturbance* in the very order of writing, and more generally of subversion in the established order of stabilized forms of discourse."[5] This effect can be considered only after having eliminated the real Jew, who is (classically) identified with closure (no doubt the "religious" and "national" particularism of Jews): "It remains for us to note the sign if not of a paradox at least of a double articulation, of which Jewishness would ensure a production of meaning in the exteriority of its own closure—and hence, less a production of meaning per se as a pure gesture of production, disturbing to say the least, never guaranteeing the assurance of stabilized significations."[6] This statement can be read in several ways, but it can be interpreted as meaning that "the Jew" generates an absence of closure in Western (and hence universal) discourse because of the fact that he himself is closure. The writer could hardly be more Pauline. The letter by its closure generates the spirit. Boyer goes on to quote Maurice Blanchot: "There is a Jewish thought and a Jewish truth, that is to say that there is, for each of us, an obligation to see whether we can find in this thought and this truth a certain relationship of man to man that we cannot get around without avoiding a necessary interrogation." "Jewish truth," Boyer continues, "as it is formulated in the text in terms of a questioning, can only be read outside the discourse that harbors it." Whereupon he quotes Blanchot again, "Certainly, this inquiry will not be entertained here as proceeding from a religious exigency. Let us acknowledge this beforehand. Let us also declare that it is not a question of the interest we bring to facts of culture. Finally, let us acknowledge that what the Jewish experience can tell us at this level cannot pretend to exhaust the meaning that gives it its richness." And Boyer concludes that "[r]efusing closure, be it religious or cultural, may be a way of giving ourselves the chance to grasp the effect of Jewishness in its own originality."[7] Its "own" being of course without any relationship to real Jews. Boyer very explicitly states that "the effect of Jewishness" is to be perceived "in the exteriority of its own discourse, [. . .] outside the bounds of a strictly Jewish discourse," reduced to what the "single word Jew" means.[8] Jean-Pierre Faye evokes another idea in a citation from Edmond Jabès: "I am speaking of the Jew. I say: JEW, but I am thinking mostly of the word itself, any word, the letter, the last sign which is a point—the center of Nothing, drenched with ink and blood—which holds up the book and all its weight of light and night: a minuscule star, a yellow star. [. . .] The book is Jewish. The book is made of Jews. Because the Jew has for centuries wanted to be a sign, a word, a book."[9] According to Evgen Bavcar, "This is what makes Jabès a Jewish writer, since being Jewish means being conscious of one's non-identity. This is what makes for the Hebraic wandering and for Jabès's wandering as manifested in his writing."[10]

But what happens when this nonidentity (with which I could agree[11]) has constituted a historical identity? The schema of derealization of the Jew revolves in this perspective around the figure of the "book." Faye even writes of the "migration of the narrative on the book *or* the Jewish people."[12] This book, writes Boyer, is "the uninhabitable territory. The place where no one ever resides, the place without boundaries that can only ever be reached in the shifting margins along its edges, this is the non-place of the book. 'Writing does not reside in any way'[. . .]. Separating the law of watchwords and the fictions of the non-place is a gap where the word 'Jew' may for a moment name the 'question.' "[13] And the Jewish people, according to Boyer, is "a people that has only ever lived in this non-place that is the Book, the sole territory that guaranteed the specificity of its History."[14] Faye, despite his eminent sensitivity to the ideological dimension, lets himself go to a cascade of conceptual substitutions that clearly illustrates the mechanisms of "change"—the apt designation for a movement that uses the Jewish sign, in a very Pauline way, as the vehicle of an infinite interchange that it hopes will underpin a "third critic," after Marx's critique of political economy and Nietzsche's critique of philosophy. "A people is present in history in an absent state; continually unaccepted. This people is not a people: it is a law. This law is nowhere promulgated: it is a word. This word is nowhere written: it is a language. This language is spoken at times (nearly) nowhere: it is dispersion. This dispersion is (almost) concentrated at times at a point: it is a center. This center, at regularly irregular intervals, is subjected to denunciation and destruction: it is erasure. This erasure is never (totally) erased: it is a memory. This memory is continually forgotten (by others): it is oblivion. This oblivion cannot be forgotten: it is the rest. This rest cannot be annihilated: it is fragility."[15]

The Jew of the book (with a lower-case "b") is substituted for the Jew of the Book and of religion, of "Jewishness insofar as it characterizes what is at stake in a certain relationship to writing and to the book."[16] But unlike the Book, this book says nothing: it is eternal exile. Boyer quotes Emmanuel Lévinas: "The subject in saying approaches a neighbor in expressing itself, in being expelled, in the literal sense of the term, out of any locus, no longer *dwelling*, not stomping any ground,"[17] and comments that "this Other inalienable in his alterity, who lets himself be approached only under the prohibition of residence [. . .] this mark of the Other [is] the sign of Jewishness to the extent that it cannot be dissociated from active 'de-residence.' "[18]

One could hardly overemphasize how such a rhetorically fascinating theoretical formulation falls flat and betrays the full thrust of its symbolic violence when applied to living Jews, survivors, "displaced persons," forced to reside in those place that were not places—that is, in the camps—real Jews who were struggling to leave all that behind and gain a foothold somewhere, in the Israeli experience, for example. Just as Jews find themselves glorified, they also find their very existence radically denied. Now there is no mistake about it: behind the rhetoric, it is this Jew that is the focus of the Change movement. It is upon this Jew's historical experience (and notably the Shoah) that its theory is founded.

In the 1980s (and this is very important from the standpoint of the controversy over the singularity of the Shoah), the "rhetorical Jew" surged back to the fore in a major essay by Jean-François Lyotard, *Heidegger and "the jews."* By putting "the jews" between quotation marks in the title, Lyotard announces straight-out where he stands. Indeed, it is one of the rare books to put things so clearly. The author starts with the following explanation: "I write 'the jews' this way neither out of prudence nor lack of something better. I use the lower case to indicate that I am not thinking of a nation. I make it plural to signify that it is neither a figure nor a political (Zionism), religious (Judaism), or philosophical (Jewish philosophy) subject that I put forward under this name. I use quotation marks to avoid confusing these 'jews' with real Jews. What is most real about real Jews is that Europe, in any case, does not know what to do with them. Christian Europe demands their conversion; monarchs expel them; republics assimilate them; Nazis exterminate them. 'The jews' are the object of a dismissal with which Jews, in particular, are afflicted in reality. They are that population of souls to which Kafka's writings, for example, have given shelter only to better expose them to their condition as hostages."[19] The statement is surprising, to say the least, since the first prudent proposition is contradicted by the second. The concept "the jews" has no (political, religious, or intellectual) meaning specifically related to "real" Jews, but the (necessarily objective and external) destiny of real Jews proves the relevance and the reality of the concept! Witness the acrobatic feat that involves confirming the universality of the concept on the basis of the destiny of "Jews, in particular," who, in good logic, are described as "hostages," and referred to Kafka's writings and to the Kafkaesque. Yet it becomes clear in the course of Lyotard's text that the concept "the jews" does not exist outside of existential Jews. The reference to the Shoah is explicit. "Indeed, it is not 'by chance' that 'the jews' have been made the object of the final solution."[20] "One converts the Jews in the Middle Ages, they resist by mental restriction. One expels them during the classical age, they return. One integrates them in the modern era, they persist in their difference. One exterminates them in the twentieth century."[21] The reference to Jewish thought is also formulated, which gives rise to a remarkable mistake on the part of Lyotard concerning the absence of the question of origin in Jewish thought.[22]

My point here is not to pass judgment on the great mystery that the concept, "the jews," harbors, according to Lyotard, and that Heidegger's thinking would elucidate: "What, in Europe, reminds us, ever since the beginning, that 'there is' the Forgotten."[23] Through them "the Forgotten never ceases to return to claim its due. The Forgotten is not to be remembered for what it has been and what it is, because it has not been anything and is nothing, but must be remembered as something that never ceases to be forgotten [. . .] that one is obligated before the Law, in debt, It is the 'affection' of this 'fact' that the dismissal persecutes."[24] "Paulinism" may perhaps shed light on the condition of this "forgotten," reduced to an irremediable past, which may very well be carnal Israel in the consciousness of spiritual Israel. "[T]he West is perhaps inhabited, unknowingly, by a guest, [. . .] holds something hostage that is neither 'Western' nor 'its' hostage."[25] "The West is thinkable under the order of *mimesis* only if one forgets that a 'people' survives within that is not a nation (a nature). Amorphous, indignant, clumsy, involuntary, this people tries to listen to the forgotten."[26] These "jews" play the same role as the Jew of the book in the 1970s: " 'the jews' are within the 'spirit' of the Occident that is so preoccupied with foundational thinking, what resists this spirit; within its will, the will to want, what gets in the way of this will; within its accomplishments, projects, and progress, what never ceases to reopen the wound of the unaccomplished. 'The jews' are the irremissible in the West's movement of remission and pardon. They are what cannot be domesticated in the obsession to dominate [. . .]. 'The jews,' never at home wherever they are, cannot be integrated, converted, or expelled. They are also always away from home when they are at home, in their so-called own tradition, because it includes exodus as its beginning, excision, impropriety, and respect for the forgotten."[27]

Lyotard's analysis is not completely erroneous. What is problematical about it is precisely the rhetorical play on "the jews" and the Jews. In his discussion of the exclusion of the Jews in the West, he himself excludes the Jews from his discourse, because he turns them into inert objects, intrinsically devoid of meaning, irremediably elsewhere. History has given us the example of a similar discourse on "the woman," who is glorified and denied in the same breath. Is this parallel an accident? Did not Paul himself declare: "There is no longer Jew or Greek, there is no longer slave or free, there is no longer male and female; for all of you are one in Christ Jesus" (Galatians 3:28)? In Lyotard's essay, the historicity of the Jews is totally omitted, even though it is manifestly necessary to the credibility of the thesis. His reflections ultimately lead to a vague reality in which the Jews are seen as a condition of humanity that includes others besides Jews, all of whom are defined as "survivors." Thus the singularity of the Shoah is placed at the center and at the same time clearly evaded.

"[T]he debt that is our only lot—the lot of forgetting neither that there is the Forgotten nor what horror the spirit is capable of in its headlong madness to make us forget that fact. 'Our' lot? Whose lot? It is the lot of this nonpeople of survivors, Jews and non-Jews, called here 'the jews,' whose Being-together depends not on the authenticity of any primary roots but on that singular debt of interminable anamnesis."[28] Exit "the Jews."

The Shoah: A Nonevent?

It is in this web of meaning that the Shoah "takes place," and to understand the "impact" of the latter on Europe, we have to understand what the former represents for Europe, at the very heart of its symbolic construction.

Against such a backdrop, the "appearance" of the Shoah runs a strong risk of being visible only from the prism of a disappearance! In practice, can European consciousness even *see* the Shoah through such a symbolic grid? Objectively, in its very perception, the Shoah constitutes a sort of destruction of the signifier (the letter, the body, the flesh, even the name) of the Jew. The extent of the physical dimension of its destruction can be evaluated on this occasion. For the continuity of Europe, it has a signification that is almost more important than its symbolic dimension. The "practical" foundations of the economy of Europe's Jewish sign were destroyed. In the medieval period the Jews had been—wittingly—*preserved* and fitted into imperial Catholicity as eternal negative witnesses to its truth. They were held outside of historical time and at the same time confined—albeit unwittingly—in the most concrete terms in history—imprisoned in ghettos and reduced to the barest form of historicity, a historicity stripped of meaning. In its own mind, Europe saw itself as suspended in an unchanging eternity, since it embodied the absolute truth of history as against the Jews who were caught in the "human, all too human" history, and who remained fossils of humanity, behind the end of time proper to Christian redemption. The eternity of the spirit could be cast as the negative of the letter, but only if the letter was preserved. Then, with the advent of modernity, while the European polity was moving (morphologically) into the now well-regarded symbolic field of the Jewish letter (the historicity of *this* world) and building itself up within bounds that were once assigned to the ghetto, one could say, the Jews found themselves pushed toward the horizon—"spiritualized" when everything was becoming material, "extra/de-temporalized" when everything was becoming secular. Henceforth, Europe would be lodged in the "human, all too human" history, whereas the Jews were not supposed to have any part in it as Jews. But surreptitiously democratic modernity preserved them: in fact, with anti-Semitism, it kept them in a more explosive and changeable place than that of the ghettoized letter that was the prism of their medieval "preservation." All modern men had become "jews" in a way, as long as they identified with the letter, and the Jews had become men, but there was no place in the polity for them to reside as Jews, that is, under their human name. And so they were classified by others and by themselves in the very categories that the modern nation-state had suppressed: the religious, the spiritual, and the universal. The Jews were everywhere and nowhere, while, concretely, exclusion pursued them wherever they went, since they remained

Jews under anti-Semitic fire. This exclusion was on a vaster scale. No longer confined to the ghetto, it assumed universal dimensions, became insidious and abstract, at times excessive and radical, even murderous, because it had no bounds anymore.[29] It was as if the letter (the flesh) had universalized into an explosive mix.

It just so happens that, with the Shoah, the Jews were really, massively, rationally, and, hence, significantly destroyed. This is the reality the Shoah established in Europe, a reality that cannot be overlooked and that has had far-reaching consequences on the signification system of Europe's Jewish sign. Thus the systematic attempt by the Nazis to belie the destruction of the Jews through the use of *amtssprache*, or "office talk," in implementing the "final solution" can be seen as expressing their awareness of the importance of the "literary" system involved in Europe's Jewish sign. Indeed, why would they have felt the need to "conceal" the extermination of the Jews, to eliminate every slightest trace of their hideous crime if they had not sensed that the disappearance of the "Jewish sign" (caused by the eradication of the Jewish body) undermined the (demonic) Europe that they were building? They knew unconsciously that they could not destroy the Jewish sign without destroying Europe. Paradoxically, their definition of themselves and of the West they were planning to construct was dependent on the Jews . . . those they were exterminating. The destruction of the Jews fed their identity. It was on the basis of a dialectical relationship with the Jewish sign that they identified themselves as supermen and as a superior race and designated the Jews as inferior.

The "writing operation" involved in *amtssprache* could not, however, hide the fact that the signifier of Europe's Jewish sign had been destroyed. Within the logic of modernity, it was as if Europe had destroyed itself, because the agency of the letter, of the body, modernity's elective agency, found itself symbolically destroyed in the process. By destroying the Jew reduced to the body (defined by "race," made into a depersonalized "object" by the camps, into skin for lamp shades and fat for soap), by breaking the corporealized and materialized sign of the Jew, it was modernity that destroyed itself. In this new context, the Jewish sign necessarily eludes the signification operation, because the signifier that carries it has vanished. The universal has lost its foundation, as has the particular. A gaping vacuum is all that is left at the core of Europe, an extremely dense black hole that sucks up all the light; an immense abyss has opened up, an abyss of meaning, an abyss of being, a real abyss. What is left of Europe after the Shoah? The purpose of my investigation here is precisely to elucidate the nature of this vacuum and what may eventually become of it.

In a way, the history of post-Shoah Europe could be written in the shadow of this vacuum: the successive interrogations concerning the "death of God" and the "death of man," the collapse of the universal, the dislocation of European identities, and the rise of a consumer society bent on filling this vacuum with pipe dreams. Europe has apparently managed to come together and create an economic union, but it is a soulless entity built upon massification and the elimination of the singular. The European Union is a bureaucracy, not a spirit, and its universal dimension seems to have died. The reality of this landscape of being that I outlined previously was masked by Communism, which artificially divided Europe in two. Its collapse has made the vacuum look even bigger. And it is perhaps only now, fifty years after the Shoah, that European consciousness can truly face it and realize the enormity of what happened. Yet it does so only indirectly and confusedly, as if it were confronting a mystery. A logic is at work in the structure of contemporary consciousness that makes it impossible to "see" the Shoah, because to look the Shoah in the face is to lose oneself; it is to sink into an immeasurable abyss, since it means facing the destruction of the Jewish signifier and hence the loss of one's own fabric of meaning. In this respect, the Shoah almost qualifies as a "non-event." Something that happens is not an event if there is no awareness of it, no sensitivity to it. What constitutes an "event" in one civilization may not in another. Every civilization has a certain amount of natural blindness (commensurate perhaps with the dimension of the unconscious). How can an event be perceived when it overwhelms consciousness (modern consciousness, in this case) as it is happening?

From this vantage point, focalizing on the singularity of the Shoah, referring it to the Jews alone, even sacralizing it, can serve as a means to cover up reality and avoid the abyss. By linking the Jews again to the "letter" and to the singularity of the Shoah, Europe reinvests a spiritual identity—an operation that sets the symbolic machine back into motion. The dialectic of the letter and the spirit lends itself surprisingly well to an analysis and a classification of all the theories of singularity discussed earlier. They are all informed by what can be called a "literary" theory, the main line of which is an overemphasis on the "letter" in comparison to the "spirit." In the theological approaches, the letter is sanctified and becomes an opaque screen. It conceals the universal and meaning (the "spirit"), the better to approach them, as if everything that the letter repressed was so hidden inside it that a halo of energy was released from its materiality. The revisionists, for their part, defend the letter *against* the spirit, only to destroy its meaning. The letter is understood as a deceptive mask hiding the truth (and in this way they manage to quickly fill the void that makes naming impossible). The failure of consciousness is explained as the consequence of the doctored let-ter, the result of a plot. Faurisson (who significantly enough has a literature and humanities background) explains his method of interpreting texts in the following terms: "We must look for the letter before looking for the spirit. Texts have only one meaning, or there is no meaning at all. [. . .] Literary criticism [should] accept this hard law of meaning just as physicists accept the law of gravity."[30] This method, he continues, "is an excellent means to detect all kinds of falsifications and fabrications."[31] We are dealing here, in Nadine Fresco's words, as we have already seen, with an attempt "to prove that something did not take place." For this purpose the letter is destroyed, as is the materiality of meaning; the objective reality of the event is denied, since there is no meaning to be drawn from it, and one must break with the " 'universal creed' of official history."[32] The letter is obviously Jewish. Proof thereof is that the extermination of the gypsies and of the mentally ill never gave rise to revisionism. In the same vein, the revisionists are primarily interested in the written word when they point to the lack of a written order by Hitler to exterminate the Jews or discrepancies between the testimonies of survivors and their written transcriptions. In sum, the revisionists gain access to the spirit through the destruction of the letter. But they have a vital need for the letter. Insofar as the destruction of the letter is concerned, the revisionist aim is not far from the goal of the Nazis.

The dialectic of the letter and the spirit is also at work in New Left circles. Tzvetan Todorov is most explicit in this regard. He implicitly reiterates the Pauline conception in his criticism of "*literal* memory" (as opposed to "exemplary memory"), its limited, egocentric, intransitive character, outside justice and leading, if left to its own devices, to madness. The author identifies the Jews who defend the singularity of the Shoah with this literal memory. Alain Brossat formulates the same idea in different terms, when he pits the "reterritorialization" that characterizes the Jewish condition today against what he sees as the lesson of the Shoah, "because what is peculiar to the Shoah [. . .] is to state its illimitation in its resistance to any form of specific territorialization or confinement."[33] There is not the slightest doubt that from Brossat's perspective the singularity of the Shoah stands with the Pauline letter versus the universal that is hidden in it.

All of these ideological constructions are informed by an attempt to produce a new European universal, either in opposition to the (traditionally Jewish) letter or centered upon it, as if the letter had not been destroyed in the course of the Second World War, as if it were possible even now to return to a (neo-Kantian) idealism whose failure has been demonstrated by modern experience.[34] This attempt is doubly significant for Europe. In symbolic terms, it marks a regression in relation to modernity, since the resurgence of the spirit versus the letter unwittingly harks back to the religious model of medieval Catholicity (is this not what is called a "resurgence of religion," even if it is beneath an ultrasecular veneer?). Moreover, in terms of reality, it has no substance and no future: it acts as a mask that prevents

Europe from seeing the profound crisis of modernity and the vacuum that constitutes it. In this sense, it is inclined, despite itself, to overlook the Shoah in the end.

The meaning-making machine has broken down. All of the interpretations of the Shoah are inextricably stuck in the antinomies of the universal and the particular; they inevitably lapse into fabrication, occultation, or mystification. If the Shoah and modern politics have shown us anything, it is that a universal whose construction is founded on the exclusion of the singular can lead to catastrophe, but also that the singular divorced from the universal is exposed to all sorts of perversions. The singular is drawn to the universal which channels it, captures and diverts it or represses it. It is another problematic of universality that political philosophy has to think through in order to pull democracy out of the vacuum that has been created in it, and that is nothing other than the negative of the fallen universal, the eclipse of the man in the citizen. It is this avenue of exploration that was opened by Jean-Paul Sartre and Hannah Arendt.

CHAPTER 6

Democracy's Jewish Question

Sartre and Arendt

Immediately after the war, two major philosophical essays appeared that undertook to comprehend the singularity of the Shoah and to draw a lesson from it that would reinforce democracy: Jean-Paul Sartre's *Réflexions sur la question juive* in 1947 and Hannah Arendt's *The Origins of Totalitarianism* (in particular, *Part One: Antisemitism*) in 1951. Both were brilliant essays whose profound meaning has generally been overlooked, even by the greatest experts. Very little thought has been given to the significance of Hannah Arendt's basing her study of political modernity (and hence of the democracy-totalitarianism couple) on an analysis of anti-Semitism, as if this phenomenon could cast some light into the darkest depths. Similarly, so much attention has been paid to the most anecdotal aspects of Sartre's remarkable depiction of the Jewish condition in anti-Semitism that his extraordinary perspicacity in analyzing the implications of the Jewish question for democracy has been ignored. Here again, the focus on Jewish singularity has hidden the system that produced it. Sartre continually warns against this mistake: "anti-Semitism is not a Jewish problem; it is *our* problem," he declares.[1] Similarly, when he states, "It is for the Jews *also* that we shall make the revolution" (182), this "also" is not to be understood as superfluous but as the over and above that gives us in return the sense of what is essential. Sartre, however, was not necessarily fully aware of this, because his thinking leads to an impasse,[2] and this is what probably caused many of his readers to miss the significance of his analysis.

Sartre's *Anti-Semite and Jew* marks an important milestone. Out of the two essays, it is the one that was written closest to the war. It shattered the polite silence of the period, emphatically underscoring the Jewish singularity and putting forward some striking ideas about democracy—that nobody heard. Arendt's *Antisemitism*, published four years later, was obviously stimulated

by Sartre's reflections.³ Whereas Sartre goes to the heart of the matter with
a typically French sense of abstraction and universality, Arendt steps right
into the meanders of modern Jewish history—which Sartre ignores—and
provides a detailed historical, political, and cultural description of the pariah
condition of the modern Jew. Was the importance of her analysis recognized at the time? Arendt, a Jewish refugee from Germany who emigrated
to the United States, took a direct part in the reconstruction of postwar
Jewish life and was actively involved with Zionism, but her message was
not heard in the Jewish world and in the international intellectual arena.
The controversy sparked by *Eichmann in Jerusalem: A Report on the Banality
of Evil*,⁴ first published in 1963, is telling in this respect.

Both Sartre and Arendt were reviving a genre that had won its spurs
with Marx, who was the first, at least formally, to tackle the "Jewish question," the problems posed by the emancipation of the Jews, and what they
revealed about the essence of the liberal economic democracy. Marx's 1843
On the Jewish Question can be seen in the background of Sartre's and Arendt's
essays, even though it is never directly examined or even cited. Arendt is
most offhanded about it. In discussing the anti-Semitism of the lower middle
class in France and Toussenel's *Les Juifs, Rois de l'Epoque*, she mentions
Marx's name in passing and observes in a note that "Marx's essay on the
Jewish question is sufficiently well known not to warrant quotation" (47).
Yet Arendt adopts one of Marx's main positions vis-à-vis the Jews, making
them responsible for their destiny and hence, in the final analysis, for their
own oppression. Marxist themes (class struggle, proletarians, revolution,
etc.) abound in Sartre's essay, but it contains no historical genealogy of
the Jewish question and no specific mention of Marx's study of the subject.
Nevertheless, the latter's presence can be strongly felt in Sartre's analysis of
democracy, although there is a fundamental difference: Sartre focuses more
on the "Jew" than on the "Man," even if the final goal is to achieve the
Marxist ideal: "anti-Semitism would have no existence in a society without
classes and founded on collective ownership of the instruments of labor, one
in which man, freed of his hallucinations inherited from an older world,
would at long last throw himself wholeheartedly into his enterprise—which
is to create the kingdom of man" (150).

As we can see, the ahistoricity of the Jew, even in "the Jewish question,"
has an illustrious history, which only underscores its "modern" character.
Totally ignored by Marx, or demonized as an economic figure (which Sartre
rectifies), the historicity of the Jews, that is, the singular experience of the
Jew (the self-same experience that led to raising the question of democracy),
has been widely misunderstood or belittled. Thus in a critique of Marx's
argument in *On the Jewish Question*, Claude Lefort speaks of "the Jews,
who imagine themselves to belong to *a people apart* and whose beliefs are

apparently in contradiction with their belonging to a political community,"[5] without considering for a moment what could be the basis of this "imagination" in reality, as if the "Jewish" element in the "Jewish question" was nothing but a rhetorical device a purely instrumental concept. Admittedly, Claude Lefort's judgment conforms to Marx's thinking. If Jewish singularity is the main tool that Marx uses to grapple with a fundamental problem in democratic theory, then it is nonetheless denied in his thinking and discourse, as it will be, in his wake, by the whole socialist current.

This brief reminder of Marx's influence is necessary insofar as it demonstrates that the two essays that appeared in the wake of the Shoah participate in an interrogation that is nearly as old as the theory of the rights of man and the citizen in its successive political incarnations. The question that the Shoah poses to postwar Europe also can be appreciated in light of the long-term history of Jews in modernity confronted with anti-Semitism and democracy confronted with its ambiguity. The question that Jewish singularity posed to democracy from the outset helped bring home, in the most concrete historical terms, a fundamental problem in political modernity. It is toward an understanding of this problem that my efforts are directed here.

Jean-Paul Sartre: A Critique of Democracy Seen in the Mirror of the Jewish Condition

Sartre manages to paint a striking portrait of political modernity (in its twofold democratic and totalitarian aspect) simply by portraying the difficulty of the Jewish condition in the citizenship based on the rights of man and the citizen: "Enemy of the Jews, the anti-Semite has need of them. Anti-democratic, he is a natural product of democracies and can only manifest himself within the framework of the Republic" (33). Sartre's approach is dichotomic—Jew versus the others, democrat versus (nationalist) anti-Semite, authentic versus inauthentic Jew, and so on—as if the destiny of the Jew provided a true reflection of the destiny of the body politic as a whole. When he writes that "anti-Semitism is not a Jewish problem; it is *our* problem" (152), he is making not a psychological or moral statement but a strategic one, as is borne out by his assertion that "we are all bound to the Jew, because anti-Semitism leads straight to National Socialism" (151). Sartre is not out to "bury" the problem in a generality. On the contrary, he accomplishes the equivalent of a Copernican revolution when he places the Jewish point of view, or more precisely the Jewish condition, at the center of his work. The democratic definition of Man is reexamined from the perspective of the Jewish condition in citizenship.

Confronted with anti-Semitism, the Jew finds "his situation even more incomprehensible," insofar as "he has the full enjoyment of his rights as a citizen, at least so long as the society in which he lives is in equilibrium" (79). Instead of confining himself to analyzing the figure of the anti-Semite, Sartre takes up the figure of the democrat as its counterpart: "The anti-Semite reproaches the Jew with *being* Jewish; the democrat reproaches him with willfully *considering himself* a Jew. Between his enemy and his defender, the Jew is in a difficult situation: apparently he can do no more than choose the sauce with which he will be devoured" (58). Thus Sartre does not look for the causes of anti-Semitism outside of political modernity. The democrat's position may well be preferable to the anti-Semite's, but fundamentally it is equally problematical; this is because there are processes at work in democracy that can lead to the negation or the alienation of the Jew. In this connection, one could add the adjective "bourgeois" to "democracy," since Sartre sporadically evokes the class struggle of bourgeois society, a society defined by "the *separation* of men": "anti-Semitism is a mythical, bourgeois representation of the class struggle, [that] could not exist in a classless society [. . .]: it can exist only in a society where a rather loose solidarity unites strongly structured pluralities; it is a phenomenon of social pluralism" (149). And not of totalitarianism, at least at its origins. Hence Sartre's essay set out to analyze anti-Semitism at the heart of democracy, and not only among his enemies.

The Jew as a Vehicle of Social Cohesion

Upon examination of Sartre's argument, his reference to the "bourgeois rep-resentation" of the people seems to fall more under the aegis of Durkheim's *Elementary Forms of Religious Life* than under Marx's *Capital*. He demonstrates again and again that citizens of the modern nation-state have difficulty uniting, and that democracy is faced with a lack of social cohesion. "[A]nti-Semitism is a passionate effort to realize a national union *against* the division of society into classes. It is an attempt to suppress the fragmentation of the community into groups hostile to one another by carrying common passions to such a temperature that they cause barriers to dissolve. Yet divisions continue to exist, since their economic and social causes have not been touched; an attempt is made to lump them all together into a single one—distinctions between rich and poor, between laboring and owning classes [. . .]—they are all summed up in the distinction between Jew and non-Jew" (149). This provides us with the explanation of Sartre's dichotomic perspective.

In this regard, Sartre underscores the split in the real in democracy, "Thus for the anti-Semite there is a *real* France with a government *real* but diffused and without special organs, and an abstract France, official,

Jew-ridden, against which it is proper to rebel" (31). For the Jew too, as
we have seen, democracy is split. Anti-Semitism is "incomprehensible" to
him, considering his civic status, while the democrat refuses to see in him
anything but an abstract Jew. In the same way, the democrat refuses to recognize anything but an abstract nation devoid of identity and lodged within
historical genealogy. "[T]his permanent rebellion [of the anti-Semite against
an "abstract France"] is the act of a group" (31), but this group cannot be
reduced to a political party (even if it gives rise to such a party); it identifies,
rather, with the whole nation beyond divisions, and aspires to restore the
"*social* order" (32) that has been damaged, because "the Republic is weak"
(31). In the anti-Semite's eyes, "the social order [is] a society that, by virtue
of juxtaposition, is egalitarian and primitive, one with a heightened temperature, one from which Jews are excluded" (32). In Durkheimian terms,
the anti-Semite wants to recreate the "mechanical solidarity" of traditional,
religious, and "holistic" societies in which individuals are interchangeable
and anonymous and substitute it for the typically modern "organic solidarity" founded on the differentiation and complementarity of functions of
individuals and hence on individualism.

The Jew thus provides the fragmented, individualist society of democracy with a vehicle of cohesion, otherwise impossible in the framework of
a citizenship that is necessarily abstract, since it is egalitarian and hence
anonymous. If democracy does not distinguish between its members, equal
in citizenship, then it nonetheless divides them into "classes" in civil society and economic life. (The Marxist argument, to which we will return, is
recognizable here.) Similarly, if the anti-Semite opposes democracy because
he "understands nothing about modern society" and yearns to return to a
premodern community, he is nonetheless "a natural product of democracies"
(33). In other words, he is a typically modern phenomenon. The unresolved
ambivalence of modernity, not to say its failure, could hardly be stated more
clearly: modernity produced from the start—at least in one of its strata—a
nostalgia for the premodern. Citizens in modern democracies thereby see
themselves "driven" (this irrational aspect is what needs to be rationally
analyzed) to exclude the Jews in order to form a "group" among themselves
and to unite. The anti-Semitic crisis necessarily produces massification. "The
phrase, 'I hate the Jews,' is one that is uttered in chorus; in pronouncing
it, one attaches himself to a tradition and to a community" (25) ("the tradition and community of the mediocre," Sartre adds). The anti-Semite is
"a murderer who represses and censures his tendency to murder without
being able to hold it back, yet who dares to kill only in effigy or protected
by the anonymity of the mob" (53). "[T]he society which the anti-Semites
form remains in a latent state during normal periods, with every anti-
Semite celebrating its existence. Incapable of understanding modern social

organization, he has a nostalgia for periods of crisis in which the primitive community will suddenly reappear and attain its temperature of fusion. He wants his personality to melt suddenly into the group and be carried away by the collective torrent. He has this atmosphere of the pogrom in mind when he asserts 'the union of all Frenchmen.' In this sense anti-Semitism is, in a democracy, a covert form of what is called the struggle of the citizen against authority" (30–31). The anti-Semite affirms his citizenship through his anti-Semitic act, in fact, it is the only way he gives himself of doing so: "It is vis-à-vis the Jew and the Jew alone that the anti-Semite achieves self-realization as a legal subject" (28).[6]

How can this contradiction be understood? The anti-Semite becomes a citizen (in his or her own eyes) by denying the citizenship of the Jew and therefore breaking with the very principle of democratic citizenship. The only possible explanation—which Sartre does not clearly consider—raises the question of peoplehood and collective identity in the social bond. By hating and excluding the Jews, anti-Semites undertake to constitute the people (the "nation" in their discourse) as the "legal subject" of the republic, which they feel does not embody it enough, or, worse still, has emptied it of all of its content because the civic contract binds abstract individuals only. This is why, for anti-Semites, the only way to unite in a meaningful way and step out of the abstraction of the social bond is to reject the Jews, set themselves apart and identify. With what, if not with the people that modernity abandoned (as a form of sociality) and the division that characterizes organic solidarity renders impossible? The anti-Semite wants to identify; he or she is looking for a collective identity in a place where it lacks sufficient rational foundations to become a "legal subject" (and thus remain within the republican norm). Sartre considers that the anti-Semite's observations concerning democracy contain a partial truth: "We are in agreement with the anti-Semite on one point: [. . .] we cannot conceive of society as a sum of isolated molecules; we believe that it is necessary to consider biological, psychical, and social phenomena in a spirit of synthesis" (59). It is precisely this "indivisible totality of the country" (29) that the anti-Semite is seeking by excluding the Jew, this "synthetic whole" (56) that he assumes exists in the Jew (conceived therefore as a "Jewish people"). Sartre, though, does not "follow" him on this last point: "But we take leave of the anti-Semite when it comes to applying this spirit of synthesis. We certainly do not know of any Jewish 'principle,' [. . .]. Neither do we admit that the 'true' Frenchman benefits so readily from the experience or the traditions left him by his ancestors [. . .]. We are willing to utilize ethnic concepts only in the areas where they have received experimental confirmation—in biology and pathology, for example. For us, man is defined first of all as a being 'in a situation' " (59).

Herein lies one of the impasses to which the Sartrian explanation leads. Indeed, despite Sartre's extraordinary perspicacity, he has trouble recognizing the phenomenon of collective identity and the historicity of collective realities (the empirical reality of Jewishness [*le fait juif*] in this case), which is the condition sine qua non—in his own conception—of an explanation of anti-Semitism. For this reason he is unable to understand fully that anti-Semitism, a "product of democracies," serves as one avenue by which democracy can reach (in a totally perverted way, of course, because of the repression that took place here) the peoplehood that was rendered intolerable by modernity, and the singularity and identity of all social bonds that were refused by the rationality of the rights of man. The Jew embodies the unacknowledged singularity of the collective, repressed by democratic consciousness and, hence, doomed to savagery and the irrational. The anti-Semite thus tries to get to his people through the "repressed peoplehood" in the citizenship of the Jews, a repression that remains highly identifiable because of the supposed allogeneity of the Jew, his indelible historical past, and his symbolic value in the West. The Jew appears to the anti-Semite as the quintessence of the forbidden people in modernity, as the embodiment of the "peoplehood" for which he so yearns, for himself and his family, but which is out of his reach. By excluding the Jew, he approaches and identifies with him *a contrario*; in this way, he achieves self-realization—in a group—as a people. The process of massification that enables the anti-Semite to get away from democratic individualism requires that he apply the process of massification to the Jews and take away their citizenship. This process, according to Sartre, does not take place outside the framework of democracy, even if it results from an opposition to democracy. "If the Jew did not exist, the anti-Semite would invent him" (13).

Sartre does not, however, take this explanation to its conclusion. He comments more or less clearly on the question of singularity in several passages. "[T]he principle underlying anti-Semitism is that the concrete possession of a *singular*[7] object gives as if by magic the meaning of that object" (24). "[A]nti-Semitism channels revolutionary drives toward the destruction of *certain men*, not of institutions. An anti-Semitic mob will consider it has done enough when it has massacred some Jews and burned a few synagogues. It represents, therefore, a safety valve for the owning classes, who encourage it and thus substitute for a dangerous hate against their regime a beneficent hate against *particular people*" (44). "Anti-Semitism, a bourgeois phenomenon, appears therefore as a choice made to explain collective events by the initiative of *particular people*" (37). It is the singular that is the target in the Jew, and here the singularity masks the rest of reality and protects it in this way. But by excluding the singular, the anti-Semites singularize themselves as a mass. Sartre is basically arguing here that the anti-Semite seeks to establish the universal by rejecting the singular, but given that the singular is rejected from the universal, this comes down to saying that he particularizes the universal.

Sartre shrugs off consideration of the singular Jew in this whole process because he considers that the object of the anti-Semite's desire is property and appropriation and not singularity or identity (even if property, if we are to believe Durkheim, is an extension of the person). In his argument here, Sartre sounds more like Marx in *The Eighteenth Brumaire* explaining the peasant vote in favor of the future Napoleon III by the fragmented, juxtaposed structure of their property. "The society that the anti-Semite conceives of is a society of juxtaposition [. . .] since his ideal of property is that of real and basic property" (29). Admittedly, Sartre identifies the object of appropriation with the "nation": "the anti-Semite lays claim to a concrete and irrational possession of the nation's assets" (109). But is not appropriating the nation appropriating oneself, affirming a collective identity by laying an exclusive claim to it? The nation, in fact, is the source of values that "derive in large part from the spontaneous condensations that fall [. . .] like a light dew[8]; they are strictly national and result from the normal functioning of a traditionalist and historical society" (80). The Jew, like the worker, "is a man who is refused access to these values on principle" (81). "To be a Frenchman is not merely to have been born in France, to vote and pay taxes; it is above all to have the use and the sense of these values" (80). Sartre does not really ask himself why the "nation's assets"[9] would be out of the anti-Semite's reach altogether but confines himself instead to an explanation based on alienation resulting from the class struggle, and so we do not understand why the anti-Semite singles out the Jew in particular and not any other, to use as a lever that enables him to appropriate these assets. Moreover, because Sartre does not recognize that the Jewish sign has an intrinsic, relational historical signification and believes that the Jew is determined by his "situation" (of oppression) and not by his historicity—that is, his real, intrinsic collective condition—Jewish destiny in modernity remains a senseless, utter mystery to him.

Yet anti-Semitism exists, the Shoah happened, and Jews suffer. How does Sartre account for this? It is here that Sartre provides his most far-reaching explanation, one that clarifies the modalities and processes that characterize democracy's unforeseen impasse more than its meaning (and its consequences for Jewish destiny). Several lines of reasoning overlap in his thinking. The most manifest is strongly reminiscent of the Durkheimian analysis of the origins of religion. Durkheim notes the alternation of two states in the condition of all societies.[10] There are periods of spatial dispersion and ordinary routine when individuals take care of their private affairs, and there are periods of gathering in a place (the "corrobori").

These are times of heightened effervescence when individuals accomplish out-of-the-ordinary acts. They feel invested with a superior force that they draw from the enthusiasm of the gathering and attribute to the action of a god exterior to them. It is on such occasions that the society is founded, at the same time as religion, according to Durkheim (its god is the projection of their collective identity into transcendence). All societies need periodic gatherings of this type (festive, ritual, etc.) to reinforce the original bond that loosens in everyday life. Ethnologist Victor Turner picked up this theory and gave it a more pragmatic turn. In his version, it concerns not only the origins of human society but all societies throughout their existence, even in modern times. According to Turner, their lives are punctuated by an alternation between periods of *societas*, during which ordering, hierarchy, and competition are predominant, and periods when the *societas* becomes so oppressive that individuals no longer know what they are doing together. At such times, people feel the need of the *communitas*, an ecstatic, disorderly (revolutionary) experience of communion, when all class distinctions are suspended and the social bond is revitalized.

Besides these specific periods when the *communitas* submerges social life, the *societas* keeps within it, on a permanent basis, the signs and vehicles testifying to the *communitas*. Anyone with a low status (beggars, poor men), on the margins of society, or in a situation of liminality (between two categories, ages in life, or statuses) is regarded as being representative of the *communitas* in a way that others are not; one's condition compels the others to step outside of their assigned social position and to remember their common humanity That the Jews are a vehicle of *communitas* in citizenship is something Sartre notes on several occasions, without being able to see it in terms other than psychological: "By treating the Jew as an *inferior* [emphasis added] and pernicious being, I affirm at the same time that I belong to the elite. This elite, in contrast to those of modern times which are based on merit or labor, closely resembles an aristocracy of birth [. . .]. Whatever [the anti-Semite] does, he knows that he will remain at the top of the ladder" (28). "Since anti-Semitism survives the great crises of Jew-hatred, the society which the anti-Semites form remains in a latent state during normal periods, with every anti-Semite celebrating its existence. Incapable of understanding modern social organization, he has a nostalgia for periods of crisis in which the primitive community will suddenly reappear and attain its temperature of fusion." Anti-Semitism thus makes it possible to compensate for the discrepancies in hierarchy and the lack of humanity in the triumphant *societas*. "[W]when he reaches the summits of legal society," the Jew discovers behind the rational civic order "another society—amorphous, diffuse, and omnipresent—[which] appears before him as if in brief flashes of lightning and refuses to take him in" (79–80). From our standpoint, this society is precisely the *communitas* that the anti-Semites form via the exclusion of Jews; it is the very experience of community rendered intolerable by citizenship in the nation-state. "Thus the Jew remains the stranger, the intruder, the unassimilated at the very heart of our society" (83). And this strangeness has nothing to do with a "metaphysical disquietude": "it is social" (133) and political. The other society behind the rational civic order may very well be what I have been referring to as "peoplehood," and the amorphous, diffuse character of the group's identity may very well be due to the fact that democratic rationality repressed "peoplehood" and left it lying by the wayside. It is interesting to note the implications of Durkheim's analysis in this regard: He was one of the founding fathers of the Republican ideal during the Third Republic, yet his idea of society as having an implacable "religious" dimension, embodied in the *communitas*, suggests that the democracy of the rights of man and the citizen has impassable limits, that it cannot function without the religious dimension upon which it is founded, no matter what it thinks about religion and no matter what Durkheim himself thinks, since he was an atheist. As we have seen, for Durkheim the collective identity, without which there would be no social cohesion, is embedded in the religious sphere. Yet democracy, he insists, is supposed to be founded on rational bases, on individualism and organic solidarity. The contradiction is dialectical as in Sartre's essay. The two opposed elements must be understood as being of one piece. At the heart of this ambivalence that citizenship cannot resolve and that it may even generate by its abstraction and universality stands the Jew.

Anti-Semite and Democrat: Democracy as a System

Sartre, however, does not go so far as to draw such a conclusion, even if it is there, just beneath the surface, in his parallel between the anti-Semite and the democrat, and more especially in his description of the relationship of the democrat (as, we may assume, the personification of citizenship) to the Jew. One of the originalities of his analysis is that he takes up not only the figure of the anti-Semite (which is the usual focus of attention) but also that of the "democrat," thereby implying that the latter too has a part in the exclusion of the Jew. This is why it can be said that Sartre's perspective embraces the whole of the democratic system, democracy as a general dialectical system and not only as a value. This approach has the impact of a judgment, even though Sartre does not consciously assume the theoretical consequences. By pairing the anti-Semite and the democrat, Sartre underscores the systematic character of anti-Semitism that is crystallized at both poles of democratic reason: singular-universal. Citizenship represses the singular in the name of an abstract, theoretical universality (since, in civil society, individuals are de facto unequal and singular) upon which the democratic political arena is founded. This repression concerns the individual, of course, but more especially the collective identity that cannot be reduced to a question of rationality because it pertains to the realm of the imaginary (the "mystery" of origins of the collective, its saga, its mystique). Is this not what Sartre is implying when he states that "anti-Semitism is, in a democracy, a covert form of what is called the struggle of the *citizen* [emphasis added] against authority" (31)? But what the anti-Semite seeks is not, as Sartre supposes, a strong state to replace the "weak" Republic; by opposing the power of abstraction of the state, he is trying to belong again to the people absent in the vacuum of the polity. By removing the Jew from universal citizenship and accusing the Jew of fomenting a secret, domineering Jewish people, he restores the principle of singularity and identity, for his own benefit, of course.

   Such an interpretation takes to its logical conclusion the Sartrian portrayal of the "democrat" in the posture of the universal suppressing the singular. "The Jews have one friend, however, the democrat. But he is a feeble protector" (55). Unlike the anti-Semite, he has chosen "the analytic spirit. He has no eyes for the concrete syntheses with which history confronts him" (55). This means that he disregards on principle, like the Emancipation thinkers, the Jew in the man. "He recognizes neither Jew, nor Arab, nor Negro, nor bourgeois, nor worker, but only man—man always the same in all times and all places" (55). To him, all collectivities are a sum of atoms, or individuals, and "by individual he means the incarnation in a single example of the universal traits which make up human nature" (55). Whereas the anti-Semite thinks that there is a "synthetic whole" that defines "the Jewish *person*," the "democrat, like the scientist, fails to see the particular case; to him the individual is only an ensemble of universal traits. It follows that his defense of the Jew saves the latter as man and annihilates him as Jew" (56). As a democrat, he defends the Jew not because he is a Jew but because he is a man. In spite of his generosity, he ignores the Jew in the man whom he defends and considers in him only the suffering of all men. There is no understanding here of why it is specifically the Jew who suffers. " 'There are no Jews,' [the Democrat] says, 'there is no Jewish question.' " (57) Sartre goes on to write some of the most powerful and absolutely unique pages on this subject in democratic literature. "This means that he wants to separate the Jew from his religion, from his family, from his ethnic community, in order to plunge him into the democratic crucible whence he will emerge naked and alone, an individual and solitary particle like all the other particles. This is what, in the United States, is called the policy of assimilation; immigration laws have registered the failure of this policy and, on the whole, the failure of the *democratic point of view*" (57, emphasis added). "For a Jew, conscious and proud of being Jewish, asserting his claim to be a member of the Jewish community without ignoring on that account the bonds which unite him to the national community, there may not be so much difference between the anti-Semite and the democrat.[11] The former wishes to destroy him as a man and leave nothing in him but the Jew, the pariah, the untouchable; the latter wishes to destroy him as a Jew and leave nothing in him but the man, the abstract and universal subject of the rights of man and the rights of the citizen" (57). Thus if the democrat defends the Jewish victim, then he condemns the Jew in him, and more specifically his belonging to a "people"; what he has "against the Jews is their clannishness" (58); moreover, "he fears the awakening of a 'Jewish consciousness' in the Jew," that is, of a "consciousness of the Jewish collectivity—just as he fears that a 'class consciousness' may awaken in the worker. His defense is to persuade individuals that they exist in an isolated state" (56–57). It is striking to observe the effective permanence of the situation that Sartre describes. These lines were written just after the war, but they were as valid in the eighteenth century for partisans of the Emancipation as they are today, when it is fashionable for human rights advocates to preach universalism and denounce the Jews' supposed "tribalism" and "*communautarisme*." At bottom, this ideological stance betrays a refusal to grant any sort of intelligibility to Jewishness [*au fait juif*] and its historicity.

Sartre does not mince his words when it comes to criticizing the democrat, whom he quite simply compares to the anti-Semite, when seen from the point of view of the Jew: "[T]here may be detected in the most liberal democrat a tinge of anti-Semitism; he is hostile to the Jew to the extent that the latter thinks of himself as a Jew" (57). The democrat turns the Jew into an object, "objects of commiseration, of pity, of what you will—but objects" (76–77); "[t]he liberal, when he met a Jew, was free" to make a generous gesture if he chose, "but the Jew was not free to be a Jew" (77). Because the democrat "has much to do" because he has other members of humanity to defend, "he concerns himself with the Jew when he has time" (73). In a striking tableau, Sartre suggests that the democrat acts "as if he were fascinated by all who plot his downfall" (72), because "[p]erhaps at the bottom of his heart he yearns after the violence which he has denied himself" (73) and which can paradoxically be exercised against the Jew, in all good conscience, since he is a defender of the Jew.[12] But it may very well be that what fascinates the democrat (like the anti-Semite) is the very "peoplehood" that he overtly abhors (and that is the problem of democracy as a whole). He thus reproduces the anti-Semite's rejection of the Jew, but for diametrically opposed reasons. When he considers the Jew in the victim of anti-Semitism, what he sees is an abstract Jew "tacked onto" an abstract man. "[T]he Jew has a personality like the rest of us," writes Sartre, "and on top of that he is Jewish" (79). This ("on top of that") is precisely what is at issue, because it "amounts in a sense to a doubling of the fundamental relationship with the Other" (79), and this is something that the democrat refuses to see. The failure of the democrat to consider the Jew in the citizen and in the man evidences the failure of the principle of democratic universalism, which in this respect does not conflict with the particularism of the anti-Semite. The democrat is seeking "a contractual community in which thought itself would be established under form of contract [. . .] and in which the 'social contract' would be the sole collective bond" (117), where "Jews, Chinese, Negroes" would have rights because they are "men and not because they are who they are in history and in concrete fact." I will return to this question, which is at the center of my analysis, and which will be guiding the discussion in the second part of this book.

The Ignorance of Jewish Historicity

Sartre challenges the democrat's stance. He declares that he agrees with the anti-Semite "on one point: we do not believe in 'human nature' [. . .]; we believe that it is necessary to consider biological, psychical, and social phenomena in a spirit of synthesis" (59). "[W]hatever effort we made to reach to the *person*, it was always the *Jew* whom we encountered" (77). Yet despite his altruism, Sartre does not really encounter him at all, because he fails to recognize the historicity of the Jew. Admittedly, few people understood what was going on in the Jewish world after the war as well as he did. Shocked by the "clandestine return" (72) of the Jews and the silence with which they were greeted, he praises the "free effort of the Jew to live in and master his situation" (118). This is an accurate description of what was behind the construction of the diasporic Jewish community and the Jewish state after the Shoah, which is what the anti-Semite, to the contrary, denigrates as proof of "a fixed characteristic manifesting the Jew's incapacity to become assimilated" (118)—a position that defines the attitude of critics of Jewish identity after the Shoah. "The Jew can choose to be authentic by asserting his place as Jew in the French community, with all that goes with it of rights and martyrdom; he may feel that for him the best way to be French is to declare himself a French Jew. But he may also be led by his choice of authenticity to seek the creation of a Jewish nation possessing its own soil and autonomy; he may persuade himself that Jewish authenticity demands that the Jew be sustained by a Jewish national community. It is not impossible that these opposing choices might be reconciled and made complementary as two aspects of Jewish reality" (139–40). It would be hard to find a more lucid description of the system of postwar Jewish identification and the way in which it restored their humanity: "The Jew is to another Jew the only man with whom he can say 'we' " (101)![13] Sartre takes a stand against the very principle of assimilation through "inhumane" coercive measures, that would seek, as Napoleon did, "the sacrifice of the person [the Jew] to the community [the French nation]"(144) in the name of democracy.

But Sartre's critique of political modernity (as generator of the "anti-Semite" and the "democrat") and his programmatic and declaratory recognition of the Jew's historicity are not taken to their term. He provides a unique analysis and criticism of the pariah condition of the Jew in democracy, but he does not pursue to its logical conclusion his investigation of the impasse of democracy reflected in the condition of the Jew-as-citizen. He limits his criticism of the democrat to a criticism of his relationship to the Jew without trying to understand what the democrat's failure says about democracy itself. Once again, the specificity of the Jewish condition masks the system that produces it. Sartre reaches a limit point here: from his position as a declared democrat (which I share with him), he criticizes the figure of the democrat in a way that leaves the very problem that he raises so well in the dark in the end. In fact, it is astounding to see in this essay the way in which the position of the democrat ultimately triumphs.

I believe that this is due to his failure to come to grips with the historicity of the Jew and, more generally, with the question of peoplehood (and social cohesion) in democracy. As we will see later, this may be linked to the conception that he has of the relationship (?)[14] between the Jew and the man. "We must now ask ourselves the question: Does the Jew exist? And if he exists, what is he? Is he first a Jew or first a man? Is the solution of the problem to be found in the extermination of all the Israelites or in their total assimilation?" (58), as if in light of this last dilemma, not only are the Jew (extermination) and the Man (assimilation) mutually exclusive, but each excludes the possible recognition of the Jew.

Thus recognition of the Jew alternates with an inability to see him. How, after everything Sartre has said concerning the Jew's objective condition, could he reproduce the reduction of Jewishness to a biological and pathological fact? "We certainly do not know of any Jewish 'principle,' [. . .]. We are willing to utilize ethnic concepts only in the areas where they have received experimental confirmation—in biology and pathology, for example" (59). Is the alternative between metaphysical essentialism and biological ethnicity? The third possibility is simply that of historicity, but Sartre could not conceive of this in 1947, just as he could not conceive of the intelligibility of peoplehood and the social bond. In this way, he identifies the Jewish community as "a quasi-*historical* community" and in the same breath, he states that it "is neither national nor international, neither religious, nor ethnic, nor political" (145). For an explanation for this contradiction we might look to the Sartrian notion of "in a situation": "For us, man is defined first of all as a being 'in a situation.' That means that he forms a synthetic whole with his situation—biological, economic, political, cultural, etc. [. . .]. To be in a situation, as we see it, is *to choose oneself* in a situation. [. . .]. What men have in common is not a 'nature' but a condition, that is, an ensemble of limits and restrictions [. . . and] this condition is nothing more than the basic human situation, or, if you prefer, the ensemble of abstract characteristics common to all situations. I agree therefore with the democrat that the Jew is a man like other men, but this tells me nothing in particular [. . .]. If I wish to know *who* the Jew is, I must first inquire into the situation surrounding him" (59–60). Now Sartre see the Jew's situation as governed by the hatred of the anti-Semite and the nonrecognition of the democrat. This is what makes him a Jew. "The Jew is one whom other men consider a Jew" (69): this is Sartre's famous theory, which for most people sums up his thoughts in this essay but which in fact occults them.

It is in the confrontation with this fundamental given of his situation that the Jew decides who he is. He has a choice between two alternatives: authenticity and inauthenticity. The identity of the inauthentic Jew is readily understood. He is the one who chooses "flight" but cannot get rid of "the image which haunts him" (100) and who, by denying it, only makes it more offensive. "He conquers a position in his capacity as Jew; he keeps it with the means he has at his disposal, that is with 'Jewish' means, but he considers that each new conquest is a symbol of a higher step in the process of assimilation" (99). But he is the only one to regard it as such; in everyone else's eyes the Jewish singularity is obvious, grossly so: "The inauthentic Jew wants to lose himself in the Christian world and yet he remains fixed in Jewish milieux" (121). He is characterized by "this perpetual oscillation between pride and a sense of inferiority, between the voluntary and passionate negation of the traits of his race and the mystic and carnal participation in the Jewish reality" (129–30). The identity of the authentic Jew is not quite as easily comprehensible, because this "authenticity" is not what one may have expected. Sartre conceives of authenticity not in terms of a moral and an intellectual project or an intrinsic historical reality but rather in relation to a "situation." To be authentic "is to assert that one is a Jew [. . .] authenticity is manifested in revolt." The authentic Jew stands up against persecution and asserts his Jewishness loudly and clearly, but he remains determined by this persecution. "Authenticity, it is almost needless to say, consists in having a true and lucid consciousness of the situation [. . .], in accepting it in pride or humiliation [. . .]. There is no doubt that authenticity demands much courage" (90). "[T]he authentic Jew is the one who asserts his claim in the face of the disdain shown toward him" (91), the one who "*makes himself a Jew*, in the face of all and against all. He accepts all, even martyrdom, and the anti-Semite, deprived of his weapons, must be content to yelp at the Jew as he goes by, and can no longer touch him" (137). But Sartre does not regard authenticity as a solution to the Jewish problem, individually or collectively, because the Jew will always be suspected of trying to "hide his origin" (138), and because he still depends on opinion, this authenticity leads "straight to the ghetto" (139). Since this is precisely the form of authenticity that many Jews asserted after the war (and which Sartre says is due to "the suffering that the Jews have under-gone during the past few years [which] has does much to open their eyes" [138]), a negative judgment is being implied here that stands out against the positive appreciation of postwar Jewish identity that Sartre expresses in the same pages. In fact, to Sartre, the authentic Jew takes up the gauntlet but remains lodged in a system that excludes and denies him, and this marks him congenitally. It becomes clear, then, why Sartre sees authentic-ity paradoxically leading to assimilation in the end: if the situation against which the Jew revolts in choosing authenticity disappears, then the reason for his revolt (the authenticity) disappears too, and the Jew can finally take the place he could not find before in the order of things. At bottom the authentic Jew is dreaming of one thing only, and that is to be like everyone else, to stop being Jewish as soon as the war against him stops. "Thus the authentic Jew who thinks of himself as a Jew because the anti-Semite has put him in the situation of a Jew is not opposed to assimilation any more than the class-conscious worker is opposed to the liquidation of classes [. . .]. The authentic Jew simply renounces *for himself* an assimilation that is today impossible; he awaits the radical liquidation of anti-Semitism for his sons. The Jew of today is in full war" (150). Sartre proposes "the socialist revolution" for the "suppression of the anti-Semite." "And while we wait for it?" (151); well, we'll simply have to make do with appreciating the authentic Jew—as if to compensate for the democrat's failure—and fighting the anti-Semite. This is, of course, but a transitory, provisional solution. In the last resort, the community option and Zionism, both of which Sartre fully appreciates (since they are forms of freedom and revolt on the part of persecuted Jews that leave anti-Semites without resources), are only temporary mechanisms of authenticity that contain no essential depth, even if they have existential substance: they hide, to his mind, a deep-seated desire to stop being a Jew and to join the ranks of all men. Waiting for the revolution.

This analysis is profound, and I will not say that it is altogether wrong: paradoxically it may even be true when applied to political Zionism that has oddly reincorporated in its separate identity the desire for assimilation and that has remained, as Sartre says, dependent on opinion—in fact, even more sensitive to opinion than others, because its longing is to be accepted among others, even though it is through separation from them. It also may be true for the revival of the community, which aims at reincorporating the Jews in the polity from which they were collectively excluded, but to do so this time on the mode of authenticity. But what Sartre overlooks is that both postwar phenomena gave rise to a culture, a consciousness, and a social structure, and—most importantly—they encountered (perhaps despite themselves) the historical and cultural foundation of Jewishness: the land of Israel with its historical and symbolic heritage for Zionism, and eternal Judaism for the Diasporic community—both age-old "repositories" of Jewish historicity. The posture of authenticity reactivates and revivifies Jewish historicity by reintegrating its premodern past and not by a wave of the ideological wand (we will return to this question later).

The difficulty Sartre has in conceiving of a Jewish historicity that is not wholly reactive[15] (and if historicity is always structured in a relationship, the latter does not constitute the whole of its reality) is a powerful sign of his difficulty in dealing with the question of peoplehood in democracy and of singularity in citizenship, in facing up to the problem that he raises in exceptional terms. This is why he does not succeed in coming to terms with the Shoah's challenge to democracy, even though he brilliantly perceives the implications thereof. All he can do is implicitly reiterate the order of things and leave the rest to some hypothetical revolution, which is no more than a pious hope or a militant declaration of faith. The revolution will put an end to anti-Semitism, but the latter will remain incomprehensible at bottom, even though all of its modalities and mechanisms will have been clarified. Sartre looks for his vague explanation and his "faith" in the Marxist concept of class struggle, but he does not really seem to believe in it since he neither argues in its favor nor theorizes it. All of his attention is concentrated on the Jewish condition: the entire reality of the overall system is discussed in its light, yet he does not see the way in which this light reflects back onto the same system. This is precisely what I have tried to do in analyzing his conception, but it is only possible if we accept the hypothesis of the historicity of the Jewish condition, the existence of Jews independently of anti-Semites (and of democrats).

Irrationality as a Way Out

Because the Jewish condition is senseless and lacks historicity (other than the historicity in the suffering and persecution imposed by the anti-Semite[16]), and because the fundaments of the system that produces it are not questioned, all Sartre can do is resort to the argument of irrationality to account for the strangeness of the pariah condition of the Jew, which he depicts so brilliantly because he understands its systematic nature. We have seen how he did not extend his critique of the "democrat" to the democratic system, even though he diagnosed its failure, at least insofar as Jewish destiny is concerned. Understandably, the explanation based on irrationality is not something Sartre states or theorizes overtly. However, it is present between the lines throughout the essay and can be reconstructed by a textual exegesis. Sartre picks up the Weberian term of pariah (that became famous with Hannah Arendt). The anti-Semite wants "to destroy [the Jew] as a man and leave nothing in him but the Jew, the pariah, the untouchable" (57). He often writes about the condition of the Jew as one of abandonment and continual danger,[17] and he compares it to the situation depicted by Kafka in *The Trial*: "Like the hero of that novel, the Jew [. . .] does not know his judges, scarcely even his lawyers; he does not know what he is charged with, yet he knows that he is considered guilty" (88). Sartre pens a deeply insightful description of a martyr figure that neoleftists, out of a lack of generosity, never even thought of considering in their speculations on current Jewish victimhood; "[the Jew's] effort is to constitute himself a martyr, in the proper sense of the term, that is to prove in *his person* that there are no Jews" (95). And not to consolidate his identity and get others to admire it. Thus behind the Jewish assertion of the Shoah's singularity would also lie the desire not to be Jewish anymore, to find a place among others by asking for their pity and consolation. Sartre goes so far as to maintain that "[i]t is not the man but the *Jew* whom the Jews seek to know in themselves through introspection; and they wish to know him *in order to deny him*" (97). The Jew, within himself and in the company of Jews, is a stranger to himself from whom he tries to break free. But why this is so we do not know, if we follow Sartre's reasoning—unless we are dealing with the sacrificial mechanism of the scapegoat, common in ethnological theory and in essays on anti-Semitism, and which Sartre advances too. He compares the anti-Semitic crisis with "a rite of initiation which admits [the anti-Semites] to the fireside of social warmth and energy. In this sense anti-Semitism has kept something of the nature of human sacrifice" (51). As far as the anti-Semite is concerned, he is described with the characteristics of the ambivalence of the sacred, a negative "criminal" (49) sacredness in this case, that inverts all values for the purposes of accomplishing a sacred duty. In this connection Sartre provides religious examples, such as the "sacred prostitution," in India (50). "[T]he *real* France has delegated to [the anti-Semite] the powers of her High Court of Justice," and "he looks upon himself as a sanctified evildoer" (50).[18] The classic term of scapegoat is finally pronounced: the Jews are the "scapegoat for a still pre-logical community—this species that bears witness for essential humanity better than any other because it was born of secondary reactions within the body of humanity—this quintessence of man, disgraced, uprooted, destined from the start to either inauthenticity or martyrdom. In this situation there is not one of us who is not totally guilty and even criminal; the Jewish blood that the Nazis shed falls on all our heads" (136). For our purposes here, this crucial statement (which contains an unexpected significance to which we will return later) demonstrates that Sartre basically sees anti-Semitism as an archaism, a vestige from traditional society in the heart of modernity that has nothing to do with modernity,[19] which is a typically Marxist explanation. The kernel of this Marxist problematic can be heard in the word "pre-logical." We are now in a position to understand why Sartre resorts to the "religious" argument to explain anti-Semitism, which he explicitly identifies with Christianity. "What weighed upon [the Jew] originally was that he was the assassin of Christ," a "legend created by Christian propaganda during the dispersion" (67) that made the Jew a subject of "taboo" and inspired "religious horror" (68). "Thus it is no exaggeration to say that it is the Christians who have *created* the Jew in putting an abrupt stop to his assimilation" (68), "to know what the contemporary Jew is, we must ask the Christian conscience [. . .]. The Jew is one whom other men consider a Jew [. . .]. In this sense the democrat is right as against the anti-Semite" (69). But Sartre does not tell us why this "vestige," this relic of traditional society dominated by religion, has continued to be so powerfully active in modernity, nor why instead of disappearing in democracy anti-Judaism turn into anti-Semitism. We are touching here on the crux of the impasse in the Sartrian analysis: to safeguard the integrity of modernity, he gets rid of discordant and malfunctioning phenomena (which he brilliantly analyzes elsewhere) by attributing them to traditional society, the religion of "pre-logical" days, and antimodern Christianity, when in fact they were manifested—and with what terrible force—at the very heart of modernity. Sartre does not help us understand why political modernity produced this aberrant religiosity that uses the Jew as the sacrificial animal, nor why Christianity remained so influential in a secularized world. Nearing the end of his analysis, he is reticent to "take the plunge" and changes his mind. It is the irrational and the archaism (yes, but then what is the modern?) that explain the anti-Semitism in modernity. Hence, modernity as a value survives intact. And while the question that the Shoah poses to modernity is formulated, it remains repressed, limited to the Jew, who is not credited with the possibility of hearing it clearly and responding to it, other than through the heroism of martyrdom (symbolic for Sartre, that is obvious: whatever the Jew does, be he authentic or inauthentic, the Jew remains "Jewish," that is, the product of the relationship of others to him), a martyrdom that is the (less cruel) flip side of his (bloody) sacrificial destiny.

This last analysis may very well make more sense than we have imagined until now, if it is taken not as the ultimate explanation that Sartre implicitly thought it was but as a central given, an unquestionable fact characterizing the nature of political modernity and notably of democracy. The Sartrian analysis thus proves to be extraordinarily rich, even in its impasses, which will ultimately open avenues to new horizons.

Hannah Arendt: A Critique of the Emancipation Seen in the Mirror of the Pariah People

The Jewish history that Sartre ignored, the historicity of the Jewish condition that he had so much difficulty formulating that he ended up denying its reality, is extremely well elucidated in the first part of Hannah Arendt's brilliant treatise *The Origins of Totalitarianism*. Indeed, the author's discussion of Jewish destiny in modernity shows proof of extraordinary perspicacity. Whereas Sartre focuses on the strangeness of the pariah condition of the Jew in democracy and resorts to Marxist arguments (which he does not even revise) to explain it, Arendt examines in detail the process of emancipation of the Jews in order to understand the historical genealogy of the Catastrophe but also the tragedy of modern politics that produced a phenomenon unlike any other: totalitarianism.

An Epistemological Reversal

There is neither strangeness nor communist hopes in Arendt's essay, which provides instead a description of a dark and tragic historical impasse. Her explanation draws its strength from the three hypotheses that underpin it: the historicity of Jewish identity; the definition of the Jewish condition as the condition of a "people," even and including in modern citizenship (Jewish discourse notwithstanding); and, finally, the historical rationality of events as the condition of their intelligibility. The inaugural act of her analysis constitutes a kind of "Copernican revolution," implemented, incidentally, not without a degree of immoderation. Arendt challenges the common fallacy (among Jews and non-Jews alike) that "Jewish separateness was due exclusively to Gentile hostility and lack of enlightenment" (viii). According to Arendt, the widespread notion "of an 'eternal anti-Semitism,' in which Jew hatred is a normal and natural reaction," is a doctrine that "gives the best possible alibi for all horrors" (7), because it clears anti-Semites of responsibility. It also makes a serious analysis of anti-Semitism seem superfluous, since "Jew-hatred is justified beyond the need of argument" (7) and can be filed neatly into the category of irrational passions. The scapegoat theory crystallizes these commonplace fallacies. It was "one of the principal attempts to escape the seriousness of anti-Semitism and the significance of the fact that the Jews were driven into the storm center of events" (7). It is essential, she argues, to restore the rationality and explicability of the anti-Semitic phenomenon, which she considers an "outrage to common sense" (3), for the purposes of comprehension, of course, although this comprehension "does not mean denying the outrageous, deducing the unprecedented from precedents, or explaining phenomena by such analogies and generalities that the impact of reality and the shock of experience are no longer felt. It means, rather, examining and bearing consciously the burden that events have placed upon us—neither denying their existence nor submitting meekly to their weight as though everything that in fact happened could not have happened otherwise" (x), for the purposes of freedom too and of maintaining the dignity and intrinsic liberty of the victims of the horror. From this perspective, Arendt regards the victims neither as bound to eternal victimhood nor as the intensely tragic passive object of a violence that wholly depends on the goodwill of others.

This attempt at understanding can meet with opposition from the victims who have adopted a form of "Jewish apologetics" (x) and who cannot accept the very principle of an explanation, which they feel is prejudicial to their suffering, because it necessarily refers to social patterns based on an interplay of actors and hence on the responsibility of persecutors and victims alike. "[T]his self-deceiving theory, accompanied by the belief that the Jewish people had always been the passive, suffering object of Christian persecutions, actually amounted to a prolongation and modernization of the old myth of chosenness" (viii–ix).

Arendt is as critical of the hypothesis implicit in such Jewish apologetics as she is of the scapegoat theory, since both posit irrationality to explain (or rather to avoid explaining) anti-Semitism. Her approach therefore carries a potential misunderstanding. But in setting out to break definitively with the apologetic bias, her aim is not so much to criticize the mythical cast given to Jewish suffering insofar as it masks the Jews' responsibility in their unenviable position, as to assert the principle of Jewish freedom. The Jewish people is an autonomous actor in history—even in its failings. It takes an active part in the global game, pursues its interests with no sanctimoniousness, makes mistakes, and behaves questionably, just as other actors do, even though it has suffered disproportionate setbacks unlike any others. This reaffirmation of the fundamental liberty of the Jew—which Sartre could not postulate despite his generosity and his efforts—is the condition sine qua non for the recognition of the historicity of the Jewish people as an implacable fact of history that requires objective observation to be rationally analyzed. "That this called not only for lamentation and denunciation but for comprehension seemed to me obvious," comments Arendt (x). These few quotations from her essay seem even more relevant today than in 1951, when *Antisemitism* was first published.

To further consolidate the idea of Jewish autonomy (and hence responsibility), Arendt goes so far as to envisage the hypothesis that anti-Semitism also was the consequence of a "shift" in the Jewish perspective in the fifteenth and sixteenth centuries, when Jews "began to think 'that the difference between Jewry and the nations was fundamentally not one of creed and faith, but one of inner nature,' and that the ancient dichotomy between Jews and Gentiles was 'more likely to be racial in origin than a matter of doctrinal dissension'" (xiii).[20] According to Arendt, the fact that the European Jews began to cultivate their "alien character" at the time was "the condition *sine qua non* for the birth of anti-Semitism" (viii) and for their ulterior racialization. Although I consider Arendt's theory specious and historically unfounded from the standpoint of the Jewish world as a whole (at the same time, in Italy, there was an exceptional Jewish renaissance, integrated into the polity and communicating the treasures of kabalistic thought to Europe), I understand the logical and rhetorical necessity of the Arendtian demonstration. It is even possible to imagine that she drives the point home as forcefully as she can to counter Sartre's overly idyllic, Manichean outlook, as if she were saying, "The Jews are not the product of the gaze of others; they exist and may even be responsible for the catastrophes that happen to them!"

The circumstances of this historical genealogy (leaving aside the question of its veracity) show that what happened to the Jews happened as well to all European nations. This intellectual shift in perspective "occurred in Jewish self-interpretation first and at about the time when European Christendom split up into those ethnic groups which then came politically into their own in the system of modern nation-states" (viii). It could hardly be formulated more pointedly that the Jews are a people, and that their European destiny concurred with the destiny of all the other peoples of Europe, that began identifying themselves as closed groups, as "nations," through the exclusion of others, at a time when medieval universalism ("Catholicism") gave way to the nation-states.

The centrality of the Jews in such a central event for Europe as the Shoah ("There is hardly an aspect of contemporary history more irritating and mystifying than the fact that of all the great unsolved political questions of our century, it should have been this seemingly small and unimportant Jewish problem that had the dubious honor of setting the whole infernal machine in motion" [3]) does not therefore preclude the fact that Jewish destiny also resulted from a relationship of reciprocity with the environment. Arendt comments in this regard that the image that the Jews gave of themselves would not have been possible if it "had not been so oddly similar to what society expected of Jews" (83).

The Drama of the Jewish People's Eclipse

Arendt reevaluates the experience of the Emancipation on the basis of the criterion of the collective destiny of the Jews. In its genealogy she finds the causes of anti-Semitism and the warning signs foreshadowing the Shoah. There is no doubt that, to her, it was the "Jewish people" at the center of the catastrophes of the twentieth century: "Twentieth-century political developments have driven the Jewish people into the storm center of events; the Jewish question and anti-Semitism, relatively unimportant phenomena in terms of world politics, became the catalytic agent first for the rise of the Nazi movement [. . .] and finally for the emergence of the unprecedented crime of genocide in the midst of Occidental civilization" (x).

In fact, it was the Shoah that made this observation possible. "Only the horror of the final catastrophe, and even more the homelessness and uprootedness of the survivors, made the 'Jewish question' so prominent in our everyday political life. What the Nazis themselves claimed to be their chief discovery—the role of the Jewish people in world politics [. . .]—[has] been regarded by public opinion as a pretext for winning the masses or an interesting device of demagogy. The failure to take seriously what the Nazis themselves said is comprehensible enough" (3). Arendt's emphasis on the Jewish people as the target of anti-Semitism plainly contradicts the Sartrian thesis. After observing that the direct consequence of nineteenth-century anti-Semitism was Zionism, "a kind of counterideology, the 'answer' to anti-Semitism," Arendt adds the following: "This, incidentally, is not to say that Jewish self-consciousness was ever a mere creation of anti-Semitism; even a cursory knowledge of Jewish history [. . .] should be enough to dispel this latest myth in these matters, a myth that has become somewhat fashionable in intellectual circles after Sartre's 'existentialist' interpretation of *the* Jew as someone who is regarded and defined as a Jew by others" (xi). "Jewish dissociation from the Gentile world" (ix) weighed as heavily as Christian dissociation from the Jews, "for the obvious reason that the very survival of the people as an identifiable entity depended upon such voluntary separation and not, as was currently assumed, upon the hostility of Christians and non-Jews" (ix). Only for assimilated Jews did "anti-Semitism play [a] role in the conservation of the people" (x).[21] The "people" argument founds Arendt's historicist approach to anti-Semitism, which allows her to refute the twin doctrines of the "scapegoat" and "eternal anti-Semitism"—both vehicles in the naturalization and ahistoricization of an event that took place in history. "The history of a people without a government, without a country, and without a language" (8) is precisely what is at the center of the storm, and this people presents the anomaly of having had a historical project (it "began its history with a well-defined concept of history" [8]), but not a political one. Now, according to Arendt, the Jewish question is essentially a *political* issue: "It has been one of the most unfortunate facts in the history of the Jewish people that only its enemies, and almost never its friends, understood that the Jewish question was a political one" (56). This calls to mind Sartre's discussion of the paradoxical synergy of "anti-Semites" and "democrats." The Jewish problem is neither a social problem (to be resolved by the assimilation of Jews and the education of non-Jews) nor a humanitarian problem (calling for a rescue effort) but a problem of "peoplehood" in the Jewish condition as it was reconstructed in modernity (in the context of individual citizenship). The Jewish people seemed to have disappeared. Because "the old feudal estates and castes were rapidly disappearing into new classes" (63) with the advent of political modernity, "[o]ne concluded, very wrongly, that the Jewish people were a remnant of the Middle Ages" (63). But the "people" that the Jews formed before modernity did not vanish with the Emancipation, despite the official schema. Even in the eyes of the moderns, the Jewish people were a caste, "[a] new caste [. . .] of quite recent birth. It was completed only in the nineteenth century and comprised numerically no more than perhaps a hundred families" (63), banking families, to be sure, but because they "were in the limelight, the Jewish people as a whole came to be regarded as a caste" (63).

The analysis (typical of Durkheim's "social morphology") is interesting in that it establishes a parallel between the classes that developed with modern industrial society and the corporations and orders that existed under the ancien régime. The implication is that the old order assumed a new form in modernity, and that the Jewish people took on the form of a caste that no longer knew that it was a people. This conflation of modernity and feudalism had a negative impact on the "people" whose identity had become ambiguous. A degenerescence of the Jewish people took place in Jewish consciousness and in the Jewish condition. The Jewish people had been stripped of rationality and historicity and demoted to the rank of ethnic "tribalism." Studying in detail the case of Benjamin Disraeli, as exemplifying assimilated Jewry, Arendt notes that such "educated, secularized" Jews "lost that measure of political responsibility which their origin implied [. . .] Jewish origin, without religious and political connotation, became everywhere a psychological quality, was changed into 'Jewishness,' and from then on could be considered only in the categories of virtue or vice" (83). With remarkable insight, Arendt demonstrates the way in which a historical condition that would call for a rational approach was "perverted" and turned into "an innate virtue" (83), a fact of *birth*, a psychobiological reality, "a world of fatalities in which men find themselves entangled" (80–81). This is when the notion of the "Jewish condition" emerged. In short, the people came to be portrayed as having ahistorical, "natural" traits of ethnicity (as people say today) or of race (as people used to say). These two terms are, in fact, equivalent: ethnicity (at least in current French usage) is also infranational and hence infrapolitical, infrahistorical, and ultimately infrarational. To be sure, Arendt employs the term *chauvinism* and not *tribalism*. She underscores the paradox that, contrary to expectations, "Jewish assimilation engendered a very real Jewish chauvinism, if by chauvinism we understand the perverted nationalism in which (in the words of Chesterton) 'the individual is himself the thing to be worshipped; the individual is his own ideal and even his own idol.' From now on, the old religious concept of chosenness was no longer the essence of Judaism; it became instead the essence of Jewishness" (74)—that is, a conceited self-glorification, with Jews glorifying themselves as, in Disraeli's terms, a "chosen race," without the humanist, generous dimension inherent in the religious notion that sees chosenness as an obligation in the service of humanity and not a privilege. "Judaism, and belonging to the Jewish people, degenerated into a simple fact of birth only among assimilated Jewry. Originally it had meant a specific religion, a specific nationality, the sharing of specific memories and specific hopes [. . .]. Secularization and assimilation of the Jewish intelligentsia had changed self-consciousness and self-interpretation in such a way that nothing was left of the old memories and hopes but the awareness of belonging to a chosen people. Disraeli [. . .] was the only one who produced a full-blown race doctrine out of this empty concept of a historic mission" (73). In her lively, caustic style, Arendt lambastes "this conceit of the 'exception Jews,' who were too 'enlightened' to believe in God and [. . .] superstitious enough to believe in themselves" (74), which is what "tore down the strong bonds of pious hope which had tied Israel to the rest of mankind" (74).

The perversion into a "pathology" thus became the dominant trait of the Jewish condition in the eyes of Jews and Gentiles alike. The eclipse of peoplehood, even as the people persisted in spite of itself, ended up weighing on the minds and spirit of the Jews, whose private individual lives became the arena to which peoplehood had withdrawn, but this arena was not up to bearing the continuity of the people: it could only break or be distorted under its weight. It is not true, she says, that assimilated Jewry was alienated from Judaism. "Never did the fact of Jewish birth play such a decisive role in private life and everyday existence as among the assimilated Jews." The emancipated Jew hiding deep down inside the "secret of his origin, the secret of his people" had no idea anymore what it involved! In fact, writes Arendt, "such secrets did not exist and had to be made up" (66). In this way, the political problem of peoplehood in modernity was degraded to the idiosyncratic individual problem of emancipated Jews. "The majority of assimilated Jews [. . .] knew with certainty only that both success and failure were inextricably connected with the fact that they were Jews. For them the Jewish question had lost, political significance; but it haunted their private lives and influenced their personal decisions all the more tyrannically" (67). This is when "Jewishness" (83) emerged as a brute condition, a nonconscious, nonclarified, nondiscursive condition.

The impossibility of the people in the destiny of the emancipated Jew (whose emancipation was thus incomplete) condemned the people to a meaningless, absurd existence that found its way into all sorts of individual syndromes, as evidenced in the varieties of modern Jewish identity. "The Jewish reformer who changed a national religion into a religious denomination with the understanding that religion is a private affair, the Jewish revolutionary who pretended to be a world citizen in order to rid himself of Jewish nationality, the educated Jew, 'a man in the street and a Jew at home'—each one of these succeeded in converting a national quality into a private affair" (84), with the result that "their private lives became the very center of their 'Jewishness.' And the more the fact of Jewish birth lost its religious, national, and social-economic significance, the more obsessive Jewishness became; Jews were obsessed by it as one may be by a physical defect or advantage, and addicted to it as one may be to a vice" (84). Jewishness had become an irrational condition in the manner of a racial or congenital condition.

This process of converting the Jewish people into a racial or biological condition is what led to anti-Semitic racism. If Jewishness was a congenital quality and could be considered a "virtue" (an innate virtue), then anti-Semites could just as readily see it because of its innate character, as a vice, a biological stain. It was precisely for this reason that the salons began opening their doors to Jews and . . . to homosexuals. "The Faubourg Saint-Germain [. . .], as Proust depicts it, was in the early stages of this development. It admitted inverts because it felt attracted by what it judged to be a vice. Proust describes how Monseiur de Charlus, who had formerly been tolerated, 'notwithstanding his vice,' for his personal charm and old name, now rose to social heights," and Arendt to conclude that "[s]omething very similar happened to the Jews" (81). What made the Jews and homosexuals fashionable was the fascination exerted by the transgression of norms, but they continued to be regarded as "traitors" and "criminals." "[O]nly one's Jewishness (or homosexuality) had opened the doors of the exclusive salons, while at the same time they made one's position extremely insecure. In this equivocal situation, Jewishness was for the individual Jew at once a physical stain and a mysterious personal privilege, both inherent in a 'racial predestination' "(82). The admission of "exception Jews" into fashionable society—insofar as they stood out from other Jews who, for their part, were inadmissible—presupposed that they stood outside the norm (distinct from Jews because assimilated and distinct from non-Jews because they were Jews). This very fact, however, secretly but ineluctably prepared the way for their exclusion and their eventual eradication once their exceptionalness, the criterion of distinction for those who accepted them, ceased for one reason or another. (The revelation that Dreyfus was a manipulated victim, not a traitor, was therefore fatal to exception Jews, writes Arendt). "If it is true that 'Jewishness' could not have been perverted into an interesting vice without a prejudice which considered it a crime, it is also true that such perversion was made possible by those Jews who considered it an innate virtue" (83).

Hannah Arendt sees the emancipation paradigm as one of the causes of this perverted system. "Secularization [. . .] produced that paradox [. . .] by which Jewish assimilation—in its liquidation of national consciousness, its transformation of national religion into a confessional denomination, and its meeting of the half-hearted and ambiguous demands of state and society by equally ambiguous devices and psychological tricks—engendered a real Jewish chauvinism" (74). The demise of the collective condition, the end of the people, and the reconfiguration of Jewish existence in individuality produced a paradoxically regressive phenomenon. Far from prompting the assimilation and integration of individual Jews, it ferociously underscored their singularity. Repressed, the people came surging back up, but in a disfigured form.

This is understandable when you know that the people is an indelible fact in history, which is, in my opinion, solely the history of peoples. When the Jewish people (constituting, on principle, the avenue of Jewish access to humanity and to continuity in history) went through a period of "spiritual and religious dissolution" (28) after the Emancipation, instead of disappearing it withdrew into a form of "Jewish chauvinism." In an attempt to understand this development, Arendt examines the messianic paradigm in Judaism. Having lost all interiority in modernity, Jewish messianism broke down into two separate elements: chosenness and hope. Reduced to itself, the idea of chosenness opened henceforth onto "eternal segregation" (74), while messianic hope without chosenness "evaporated into the dim cloud of general philanthropy and universalism," as grandiloquent as it was empty. Arendt suggests that the historicity of the Jewish people is the condition sine qua non of Israel's spiritual and universal vocation, and that the basic attitudes of modern Jews derived from the dissolution of Jewish messianism—the secret heart of Jewish identity. We are in a position to understand then how chosenness, having lost its interiority, could prompt a sense of Jewish singularity gone awry. Assimilated Jews glorified their ethnic origin in its own right ("that fantastic delusion, shared by unbelieving Jews and non-Jews alike, that Jews are by nature more intelligent, better, healthier, more fit for survival—the motor of history and the salt of the earth" [74]), while regarding themselves as being just like others and alienated from

Judaism! Messianic hope, for its part, was to induce a number of Jews (the Socialists and Communists, of course) to believe in "final solutions of political problems which aimed at nothing less than establishing a paradise on earth" (74). Striving with all their might to be modern and to join in the chorus of praise for citizenship, the Jews persistently extolled the pettiest forms of their uniqueness, lacking the generosity that was the rule in classic Judaism. "The assimilationists [. . .] were more effectively separated from the nations [. . .] than their fathers had been by the fence of the Law" (74), which separated the Jews from the nations not on ethnic grounds, *sui generis*, but for moral purposes. "The enthusiastic Jewish intellectual dreaming of the paradise on earth, so certain of freedom from all national ties and prejudices, was in fact farther removed from political reality than his fathers, who had prayed for the coming of Messiah and the return of the people to Palestine" (74). Indeed, the modern Jew did not take into account the most naked reality of his position as an actor: his belonging to the Jewish people, which was an implacable strategic given in any Jewish position. Concerned with the universal, contemptuous of Jewish singularity and traditional beliefs and alienated from the Jewish people, the "Jewish intellectual," archetypal figure of modernity, thus emerged as the most unrealistic and utopian of figures, a source of catastrophes, because he abandoned reality for the sake of pipe dreams while pretending to be actively involved in the realpolitik of the real world and denouncing the "myths" of Judaism. And so despite themselves, modern Jews formed a people, and they alone did not know it. "Clemenceau [. . .] recognized and proclaimed before the world that Jews were one of the oppressed peoples of Europe. [. . . He] saw the Rothschilds as members of a downtrodden people [as] 'unfortunates, who pose as leaders of their people and promptly leave them in the lurch'" (118).

What I will retain from this striking portrayal of the Jewish condition is the process of transformation from the condition of "people" to that of a "race." Jewish identity lapsed into the "visceral" and the "biological," because the "people" was not recognized and the nation-state framework could no longer contain historical entities that were neither wholly territorial nor clearly definable, and this was the case of historical peoples. Biology, a new *political* category, came to be the criterion (with all its racist perversions) as peoples vanished into nations in the states. It was on this biological basis that the Jews were to find themselves persecuted and then destroyed in Nazism, without having the rational elements that would have enabled them to understand what was happening to them.

The Impossible Individual Destiny of Jews

The repression of the people in Jewish destiny governed the destiny of the individual Jew—the only one tolerated by political modernity. But precisely because of this contradiction, it was a paradoxical destiny marked by sharp contrasts. The *condition* of individuals could no longer be anything but the economy of the absent people. It was deployed according to the two-sided picture of modernity, with its two stages—social and political—upon which was enacted the drama of recognition/absence of recognition for individual Jews unable to assume their individuality because the people that sustained them was not recognized. "[T]hey always had to pay with political misery for social glory and with social insult for political success. Assimilation, in the sense of acceptance by non-Jewish society, was granted them only as long as they were clearly distinguished exceptions from the Jewish masses" (56). The description is somewhat reminiscent of Marx's remarks in *On the Jewish Question* on the gap between political categories in democracy and their implementation in society, between political emancipation, which makes all citizens equal, and the widespread inequality between the classes in society. Thus in nineteenth-century France the Jews were recognized as citizens with political equality but found themselves excluded in practice from social life. And when they were recognized in society, they lacked political equality, as was the case in the Germanic countries (in Austria, for instance).

Arendt explains this paradox with her theory of the "exception." It was because they were not like Jews that the first Jews were admitted into European society, by virtue of an exception that separated them from the Jewish people. In this sense, their individuality was founded on this exception that singularized them by disconnecting them from their people. The individuality that characterized Jewish citizenship was not, then, from the outset a status open to all members of the Jewish people. In the equal share that each individual received, there was always one share (that of the *people*) that was deducted. This is why, in stark contradiction to the principle of equality, "privilege" (the exception to the rule) became the avenue of Jewish admission to equal rights. Political recognition (of the individual) masked social exclusion (the people), yet the brunt of this exclusion fell upon the individual Jew. It is in this sense that Arendt locates the paradigm of Jewish emancipation in the privileges of the court Jews during the monarchical period rather than in the principles of equality of the French revolution. And this explains the suddenness with which equality could suddenly revert to exclusion in the anti-Semitic crisis. Behind equality stood privilege, hence exception, and hence inequality.

We can see in the hidden permanence of exclusion, despite the political equality, the sign of the people's continuity, which henceforth haunted the Jews who had become individuals. The destiny of the people was reenacted in the lives of individuals and ended up weighing upon them heavily: "Private life was poisoned to the point of inhumanity [. . .]when the heavy burden of unsolved problems of public significance was crammed into [. . .] private existence" (67). "Social discrimination, and not political anti-Semitism,

discovered the phantom of '*the* Jew' " (61); "henceforth, each one of them
had to prove that although he was a Jew, yet he was not a Jew [. . .] one
had to stand out—as an individual who could be congratulated on being
an exception—from '*the* Jew,' and thus from the people as a whole" (61).
The Jews "tried, therefore, 'to be and yet not to be Jews' " (56),[22] the "not
to be" targeting the people even though it was never recognized as such.
"It was by no means easy not to resemble the 'Jew in general' and yet
remain a Jew; to pretend not to be like Jews, and still show with sufficient
clarity that one was Jewish" (67). "This actually amounted to a feeling of
being different from other men in the street because they were Jews, and
different from other Jews at home because they were not like 'ordinary
Jews' " (65).

The Jew, in his individual condition, was driven to permanent self-denial
for the sake of civic "salvation." In distinguishing himself from other Jews—by
his exceptional character (genius, success, education)—he implicitly excluded
himself from the people, and hence he showed proof of his individuality to
gain access to citizenship. This means that the exception Jews needed to
set themselves apart from the backward masses (the people); in fact, it was
against "this background, so essential as a basis of comparison for social
success and psychological self-respect" (61), that the "wealth and education"
of the exception Jews "stood out so advantageously" (60). Emancipating the
Jews en masse (and hence as a people) would have had a negative impact
on exception Jews: the exception would not have mattered, and they would
have found themselves reduced to the level of the backward people. We
can understand, then, the extreme solitude of the emancipated Jew, who
had become a stranger in his own eyes, or to use Arendtian terminology, a
pariah: "The Jewish notables [. . .] stood, in a sense, as far outside Jewish
society as they did outside Gentile society" (62–63).

Faced with this situation, there were two possible avenues—surmounting the structural flaw or accepting its directive, although neither solution
could be frank and wholehearted. Surmounting this flaw by owning up to
it meant condemning oneself to a pariah condition, because the consciousness of reality (the fact for the Jew to be outside the norm in a norm-ruled
land) brought home the immense solitude of the Jew (and of every man)
in modernity. But accepting its logic and normativeness by overcoming the
handicap of solitude meant social success, to be sure, but also a bad conscience for having participated in the exclusion of Jewish historicity from
Jewish life. "[E]very Jew in every generation had somehow at some time to
decide whether he would remain a pariah and stay out of society altogether,
or become a parvenu, and conform to society on the demoralizing condition that he not so much hide his origin as 'betray with the secret of his
origin the secret of his people as well' " (66).[23] Pariahs and parvenus were

continuously dissatisfied and envied one another because each possessed a part of the wholeness that had been lost forever (truth without integration, integration through self-denial).

Whence the dichotomy between the "ordinary Jew" excluded from the salons and the "exceptional Jew" preferred even over non-Jews by these same salons because he was an exception from the ordinary Jew, that is, from the "Jew in general." Like Sartre's "authentic Jew" and "inauthentic Jew," the "pariah" and the "parvenu" are not free men. The pariah, who is conscious of the hiatus in the Jewish condition and therefore represents the more "moral" Jew, is a man who belongs nowhere, neither in society at large nor in the Jewish community. In this sense, the "authentic Jew" (that is, the Zionist), who enjoys Sartre's respect, meets with a similar destiny: despite his consciousness and his choice of autonomy, he continues to be determined by the anti-Semite's hatred. If this hatred ceases, then his identity vanishes. There is, however, a crucial difference between Arendt's pariah and Sartre's "authentic Jew": whereas the latter rests on nothing, both the pariah and the parvenu stand on the very real ground of a people that had become intolerable. "[T]he way of the pariah and the parvenu were equally ways of extreme solitude, and the way of conformism one of constant regret [. . .] Jews felt simultaneously the pariah's regret at not having become a parvenu and the parvenu's bad conscience at having betrayed his people and exchanged equal rights for personal privileges" (66–67).

On this basis, Arendt develops a typology of Jews according to the criterion of the people. "The Jewish notables wanted to dominate the Jewish people and therefore had no desire to leave it, while it was characteristic of Jewish intellectuals that they wanted to leave their people and be admitted to society; they both shared the feeling that they were exceptions" (64), and the rest of the Jews were relegated to the status of "backward masses," the last vestige of the denial of the "people." When bankers and Jewish notables "were attacked from all sides, they had a vested interest in the poverty and even backwardness of the masses because it became an argument, a token of their own security. [. . . T]hey were forced away from the more rigorous demands of Jewish law [. . .] yet demanded all the more orthodoxy from the Jewish masses"; the result was " 'the double dependence' of poor Jews on 'both the government and their wealthy brethren' " (62). The essay thus depicts the modern Jew as the loneliest of men, in utter exile on earth, even when he had become the darling of the salons. The Jewish condition lodged exile in the experience of modernity. Wherever he turned, even when he was recognized, the Jew was thrown back to the other pole of himself that lacked recognition.

Arendt insists a great deal on the perversion underlying the modern recognition of the Jews. The appeal of the Jews was based on a syndrome of attraction-repulsion: when bourgeois salons admitted them, it was precisely because they had nothing against mixing with the riffraff. She analyzes Proust's characters from this standpoint and shows how the Jew was admitted to these circles on the same basis as the invert. Jews were celebrated because they were suspected of being potential criminals, inverts, or traitors; this is what made their company so exciting and allowed the more fashionable houses to distinguish themselves from the stuffy monotony of ordinary bourgeois salons. In its relationship to Jews, high society was flirting with wickedness. This disturbing attraction to wickedness made it easy to switch overnight from a glorification of the Jew to anti-Semitism. Only in "transgression," in a condition experienced in the manner of a trespass, could Jews (like homosexuals) hold onto their "exceptional" and hence acceptable status. They could not escape this, because they could not achieve consciousness of their reality by themselves, so they were driven into either the most naive lack of realism ("the sons of Jewish millionaires inclined toward leftist movements precisely because their banker fathers had never come into an open class conflict with workers. They therefore completely lacked that class consciousness that the son of any ordinary bourgeois family would have had as a matter of course" [77]), or to an ill-considered pursuit of some abstract ideal: incapable of identifying with a people, the Jews identified with a "great cause" ("leftist movements in most countries offered the only true possibilities for assimilation" [77]). The two options could, of course, coexist.

Although her essay paints the tragic picture of a continual movement from bad to worse, it ends with the new prospect offered by Zionism. "The only visible result" of the Dreyfus affair ("the only episode in which the subterranean forces of the nineteenth century enter the full light of recorded history") "was that it gave birth to the Zionist movement—the only political answer Jews have ever found to anti-Semitism and the only ideology in which they have ever taken seriously a hostility that would place them in the center of world events" (120). That these are the words with which *Antisemitism* comes to a close says much about the importance of Zionism for Arendt. In light of the twentieth-century catastrophe, it appeared to her at the time as the sole position that would allow the Jews to rejoin a modernity that had crushed them until then.

The "Equivocalities" of Emancipation

Hannah Arendt's argument culminates in a theory of the anti-Semitic phenomenon as the paradoxical consequence of the emergence of the nation-state and the triumph of the idea of equality. "To the first contradiction, which determined the destiny of European Jewry during the last centuries, that is, the contradiction between equality and privilege (rather of equality granted in the form and for the purpose of privilege), must be added a second contradiction: the Jews, the only non-national European people, were threatened more than any other be the sudden collapse of the system of nation-states. This situation is less paradoxical than it may appear at first glance" (22). The system of political modernity and its two basic principles, equality and the nation-state, could hardly be defined more clearly.

Indeed, the principle of equality could be considered the absolute principle of modernity, since the "society" of nation-states is the expression of the *equal* right of each nation to its own state. Yet Arendt concentrates on the nation-state and offers no general reflections on political *modernity* and democracy as such: the latter concept is, in fact, barely mentioned in *Antisemitism*. Her critique of the nation-state opens onto international relations, that is, onto the system of nation-states since, in the framework of her trilogy, she follows her analysis of anti-Semitism with a study of "imperialism" (part two) and then "totalitarianism" (part three). Through these two variables, she examines the ambivalence, not to say the ambiguity, that characterizes modernity. It was as if it were structured by a paradox, as if there was a conscious, normative official schema of modern politics and an altogether different reality manifested in actual fact.

The Nation-State's Class

Take the nation-state. The actual condition of the Jews reveals the paradox that constitutes it (which Arendt does not analyze as such because she focuses her attention on the Jewish question). Arendt regards the nation-state as the backdrop for the birth of anti-Semitism: "Modern anti-Semitism must be seen in the more general framework of the development of the nation-state, and at the same time its source must be found in certain aspects of Jewish history and specifically Jewish functions during the last centuries" (9). The nation-state regarded itself as the "universal" state of the nation as a whole. "The breakdown of the feudal order had given rise to the new revolutionary concept of equality, according to which a 'nation within the nation' could no longer be tolerated. [. . .] This growth of equality, however, depended largely upon the growth of an independent state machine which, either as an enlightened despotism or as a constitutional government above all classes and parties, could, in splendid isolation, function, rule, and represent the interests of the nation as a whole" (9). It was for this reason that the Jews were emancipated: "Jewish restrictions and privileges had to be abolished together with all other special rights and liberties" (9), but it was for this reason too that their status as a "people" became intolerable (this intolerance for a "nation within the nation" is interesting, in that it shows how the "nation" was substituted for the "people" and how the "people" came to represent a danger for the exclusiveness of the "state," all of which took place in the framework of the state). "The full development of the nation-state" went with "its claim to be above all classes, completely independent of society and its particular interests, the true and only representative of the nation as a whole" (17). But this was precisely the problem, because the universality that the state sought was unworkable in practice. To achieve its purposes, the state needed a "class" to identify with it. "The failure of the absolute monarchy" at the end of the eighteenth century "to find a substitute [for the nobility] within society" (17) led the nation-state to set itself "above all classes," precisely because it could no longer be represented by a class. But such an abstract, universal state (emerging already under the absolute monarchy) led to "a deepening of the split between state and society upon which the body politic of the nation rested. Without it there would have been no need—or even any possibility—of introducing the Jews into European history on equal terms" (159).

The Jews were the ones who would become the mediators between the state and society, particularly in the economic field. They were the ones who would occupy the deepening gap between the two that Tocqueville analyzed so well: occupy it to fill it and thereby lend a semblance of coherence to what was in fact a structural flaw in political modernity. They were in a position to do so because they were not (or not yet) citizens and because they are still marked by their pariah condition. As outcasts of society, the state could rely on them specifically to act without upsetting the equality between the different parts of society and its formal universality. This universality, to be efficient, rested paradoxically on the singularity of the Jews as the state's "universal class." "Jews were, from the state's point of view, the most dependable element in society just because they did not really belong to it" (97). Economic necessity led the modern state to rely on the Jews; the very state that had emancipated them as undifferentiated, individual citizens turned to them because they formed a group, a class, a caste (in fact, a "people").

A similar idea surfaces from the revolutionary debate on the emancipation of the Jews. On February 24, 1790, the Assembly of Representatives of the Commune of Paris declared the necessity of "attaching to France a hardworking, mercantile nation that can only invigorate and foster commerce, and attract abundant wealth to the kingdom."[24] The bourgeoisie would not meet the needs of the state but chose instead "the way of private investment, shunned all state intervention, and refused active financial participation in what appeared to be an 'unproductive' enterprise. Thus the Jews were the only part of the population willing to finance the state's beginnings and to tie their destinies to its further development. With their credit and international connections, they were in an excellent position to help the nation-state to establish itself among the biggest enterprises and employers of the time" (18).

Arendt notes that when the state became an absolute power above society (starting from the absolute monarchy) and embarked upon large-scale ambitious economic enterprises, it found a crucial source of financial support in the Jews, who were in a position to raise the necessary capital on an international scale. "Investment of Jewish capital in the state had helped to give the Jews a productive role in the economy of Europe. Without their assistance the eighteenth-century development of the nation-state and its independent civil service would have been inconceivable" (98). The same situation continued—if in another form—after the collapse of the monarchies. In the Third Republic "the intermediaries between private enterprise (in this case, the company) and the machinery of the state were almost exclusively Jews" (96). This is what the Panama scandal revealed.

The fact that Arendt's discussion of the history of the nation-state covers both the monarchical and the revolutionary periods leads us to suppose again that her analysis does not specifically concern democracy. But it is also plausible that she considers, following Tocqueville, that the historical turning point occurred well before the revolutionary period. This, at any rate, is implicit in the idea that the emancipation of the Jews started well before the revolution: "It was, after all to these court Jews that Western Jewry owed its emancipation" (160). The services that they rendered to the royal families of Europe brought them privileges in a form of near-citizenship from which the Jewish masses did not benefit. They acquired this near-citizen status as exceptions, but it was granted to them insofar as they belonged to a group, because their affiliation to a group (and the international relations that went with it) is what put them in a position to fulfill an economic role on a European level. It was, then, as a "caste" that they acquired a foretaste of emancipation. "The Jews could remain a separate group outside of society only so long as a more or less homogeneous and stable state machine had a use for them and was interested in protecting them" (99). Thus Jews played the same role in modern politics as they had in the monarchical period: "Every political party had its Jew, in the same way that every royal household once had its court Jew" (98).

Arendt's approach here is in the spirit as much of Tocqueville as of Durkheim. If, as she asserts, the Emancipation after the revolution was cast in the mold of the ancien régime, and the equal rights of Jews as citizens reproduced their status as court Jews,[25] then this emancipation was an extension of the privilege granted to court Jews. This is powerful evidence of the fact that behind equality stood privilege; behind the individual status of citizen stood the caste, the group, the people; and behind modernity, the ancien régime, the former having moved into the latter's place. Morphologically, the turning point of the Emancipation is not, according to Arendt, as radical as most people think. She even considers that the continuation of the ancien régime in the democratic status was at the root of the Jewish question in modernity. The people continued to haunt the destiny of individuals, just as exception and privilege continued to torpedo individual citizenship.

We have here an initial definition of the paradox of the modern Jewish condition: the Jews were emancipated formally and ideologically as individuals but practically as a group or a caste. "Thus, at the same time and in the same countries, emancipation meant equality *and* privileges, the destruction of the old Jewish community autonomy *and* the conscious preservation of the Jews as a separate group in society, the abolition of special restrictions and special rights *and* the extension of such rights to a growing group of individuals" (12).

The rights of the Jews to equality and citizenship were recognized not as a consequence of the prior recognition of the rights of all men but as a privilege granted, exceptionally insofar as they were singularly Jews. At bottom, it was the condition of the court Jew that was extended to the Jewish masses, and this endangered, in turn, the very essence of equality. "Emancipation of the Jews, therefore, as granted by the national state system in Europe during the nineteenth century, had a double origin and an ever-present equivocal meaning. On the one hand it was due to the political and legal structure of a new body politic which could function only under the conditions of political and legal equality. Governments, for their own sake, had to iron out the inequalities of the old order as completely and as quickly as possible. On the other hand, it was the clear result of a gradual extension of specific Jewish privileges, granted originally only to individuals, then through them to a small group of well-to-do Jews; only when this limited group could no longer handle by themselves the ever-growing demands of state business, were these privileges finally extended to the whole of Western and Central European Jewry" (12).

This policy necessarily concurred with Jewish interests. "The nation-state's interest in preserving the Jews as a special group and preventing their assimilation into class society coincided with the Jewish interest in self-preservation and group survival" (13). "Under no circumstances could the state afford to see them wholly assimilated into the rest of the population, which refused credit to the state, was reluctant to enter and to develop businesses owned by the state, and followed the routine pattern of private capitalistic enterprise" (11–12). Yet the Jews did not "form a class of their own and they did not belong to any of the classes in their countries. As a group, they were neither workers, middle-class people, landholders, nor peasants. Their wealth seemed to make them part of the middle-class, but they did not share in its capitalist development" (13). In essence, the Jews were neither a class nor a caste; they were a people, even though they were not recognized as such: "their status was defined through their being Jews, [but] it was not defined through their relationship to another class" (13). Jewish access to democratic equality in the conditions of the nation-state thereby led, against all likelihood, to the silent reproduction in democracy of the segregation that had characterized the ancien régime. This was true morphologically if not ideologically or normatively, and paradoxically it was so within the framework of the universality of a democratic state, reputed to be above all factions.

The Privilege of Equality

Here is where we find Arendt's analysis of the two-sided picture of equality in democratic society. Equality was, of course, a constituent principle of political modernity. "Equality of condition for all nationals had become the premise of the new body politic" (12). Yet—modern paradox!—the hierarchy was surreptitiously reiterated: "while this equality had actually been carried out at least to the extent of depriving the old ruling classes of their privilege to govern and the old oppressed classes of their right to be protected, the process coincided with the birth of the class society which again separated the nationals, economically and socially, as efficiently as the old regime. Equality of condition [. . .] was at once replaced by a mere formal equality before the law" (12). Arendt observes "[t]he fundamental contradiction between a political body based on equality before the law and a society based on the inequality of the class system" (12–13), another dimension of the gap between political and social emancipation that characterized the Jewish experience of modernity. Surely one of the seminal images of this gap in the egalitarian and democratic postrevolutionary age is the restoration of noble orders by Napoleon I—an extreme manifestation of the deeper *invisible* recreation of hierarchies, this time on the economic plane. Within this hierarchical socioeconomic context under the formal cloak of political equality ("An insurmountable inequality of social condition" existed "side by side with political equality" [12–13]), the Jews stood out as the "only exceptions" to the system of classes. "[T]heir special services to the governments prevented their submersion in the class system as well as their own establishment as a class" (13). This amounts to saying that the Jews formed a "class" of their own in a society of classes to which they did not belong. This is, once again, a morphological perspective: the Jews participated as a group in a society in which the castes of the ancien régime had been recreated in the form of economical and political classes. As we have already seen, it was the "people" that had been excluded from political citizenship, and equality that was covertly revived in this way. From the standpoint of the principle of equality, this unrecognized "people" was necessarily regarded as an archaic "corporation," a caste, a vestige of a world gone by. The "Law relative to the Jews," adopted on November 13, 1791, revoked "all adjournments, reservations, and exceptions inserted into preceding decrees relative to Jewish individuals who will swear the civic oath which will be regarded as a renunciation of all the privileges and exceptions introduced previously in their favor."[26] Another text from the same period declared, "Our principles of liberty and equality have come to destroy all of the aggregations that separated citizens from one another in so many small nations within the nation itself."[27]

It was not, however, this political interpretation of the situation that prevailed, proof once again of the repression of the "people" and its consignment to the prerational and the unconscious. This objective and morphological discrepancy was to find expression, as we have seen, in racial terminology. Since the idea of the "people" remained an unthinkable taboo, the constituent hiatus of political modernity was translated into nonrational biological terms. If there was no reason, officially, formally, or ideologically, to deal with the discrepancy that characterized the experience of emancipated Jews (which, as we have seen, is itself an echo of the paradox or contradiction inherent in modernity), then it could only be the consequence of a "fatality." In her essay, Arendt undertakes a critique of the theory of equality as an impossible project that could only lead to a graver form of inequality than the one it was struggling to overcome. In her own words: "Equality of condition, though it is certainly a basic requirement for justice, is nevertheless among the greatest and most uncertain ventures of modern mankind. The more equal conditions are, the less explanation there is for the differences that actually exist between people; and thus all the more unequal do individuals and groups become" (54). If we follow her reasoning, then the modern principle of equality had an anti-modern effect: a reinforcement of the hierarchy. Equality, by nature, cannot tolerate differences. As one of the Jewish representatives to the Convention in 1789 tellingly said: "There can be no equality, where there are differences."[28]

Indeed, equality is necessarily premised upon equivalence and hence similitude or, at least, "substitutability" (only like things can be substituted), which thus becomes the true norm of equality. All those who fit this mold of equality conform to the norm: they are "normal." Equality is manifested in practice as a principle of normalization: differences that fall outside the norm and that cannot be otherwise are held to be "abnormal." And, according to Arendt, "there are ninety-nine chances that [equality] will be mistaken for an *innate* [emphasis added] quality of every individual, who is 'normal' if he is like everybody else and 'abnormal' if he happens to be different.

This perversion of equality from a political into a social concept is all the more dangerous when a society leaves but little space for special groups and individuals, for then their differences become all the more conspicuous" (54). Those who are different escape the norm and hence normality to the point that one is tempted to see in their difference an innate abnormality, inherent to their being, and therefore to convert it into a "natural," absolute, and physical difference, which is then doubly excluded: as a difference in relation to a norm and as an infrarational manifestation in a universe of Reason. But the fact is, there are natural differences. Not recognizing this and promoting equality on such a basis inexorably intensifies these differences. "And it has been precisely this new concept of equality that has made modern race relations so difficult, for there we deal with natural differences which by no possible and conceivable change of conditions can become less conspicuous" (54). Differences have been "racialized" and removed from the universal. Arendt maintains that the principle of equality prevents us from facing what constitutes an implacable reality in human beings and in the world—namely, difference—in any other way than through masking it, an illusory solution in any case, since no decree can alter a reality that will inevitably resurface again and again. This explains why theoretical equality triumphed in the political sphere while it collapsed to the point of carica-ture in the civic sphere. "It is because equality demands that I recognize each and every individual as my equal, that the conflicts between different groups, which for reasons of their own are reluctant to grant each other this basic equality, take on such terribly cruel forms" (54).

Among these cruel forms, racism holds a central place. "In such a society, discrimination becomes the only means of distinction, a kind of universal law according to which groups may find themselves outside the sphere of civic, political, and economic equality" (55). In the United States, she adds in a note, it is the Negroes who are victims of this discrimina-tion. The differences are converted into racial and natural traits because they cannot be stated in the language of equality. In the case of the Jews, the inexplicable "residue" from their "equalization" (admission to citizen-ship), namely, their Jewishness, their historical condition left undecided, was therefore understood in terms of biology and destiny (the Jews as a race and not a people).

Arendt's portrayal of fashionable salons provides a striking illustra-tion of the pressing search for distinction through the most unexpected means in a society where equality was a supreme value. The Jews, as we have seen, were admitted with mixed feelings to high society. Fashionable circles regarded them as "abnormal," and therefore dangerous, yet welcomed them—or at least those who stood out from their fellow Jews. They did so in an attempt to distinguish themselves from the rest of society and to endow themselves with a specific identity that the equality of chances did not permit. Mixing with an "abnormal" exotic category gave them a distinctive, out-of-the-ordinary character, at little expense. "[T]heir hosts [. . .] needed an ensemble of counterparts before whom they could be different, nonaristocrats who would admire aristocrats as these admired the Jews or the homosexuals" (85). The "Jews and the inverts" too had every interest in seeing this distinction persist, because they "felt that they would lose their distinctive character in a society of Jews or inverts, where Jewishness or homosexuality would be the most natural, the most uninteresting, and the most banal thing in the world" (85). "Both felt either superior or inferior, but in any case proudly different from other normal beings" (84). The exclusion of Jews thus became a fashionable source of compensation for an aristocracy longing to distinguish itself in the penurious system of prestige generated by the principle of equality. The repression of the people (the people as source of identity and sociality) in the civic condition manifested itself in this irrepressible urge for distinction and, at the same time, in the definition of the Jew as a stain or an exception.

The conclusion is paradoxical: as the equality of the Jews progressed, their differentiation grew stronger, and so did the feelings of resentment that necessarily went with it. Arendt discerns in this a rule of sorts: "Social pariahs the Jews did become wherever they had ceased to be political and civil outcasts" (62). We find here once again the contradictory two-sided picture of democracy: political and social. The indetermination of the Jews, subsequent to the repression of the people, led to a double bind: "What non-Jewish society demanded was that the newcomer be as 'educated' as itself, and that, although he not behave like an 'ordinary Jew,' he be and produce something out of the ordinary, since, after all he was a Jew" (56). The esteem that the Berlin salons showed Moses Mendelssohn went hand in hand with a profound contempt for his people. In this light, we can more readily identify the state of solitude and utter abandonment in which the emancipated Jew found himself or herself. "The great challenge to the modern period, and its peculiar danger, has been that in it man for the first time confronted man without the protection of differing circumstances and conditions" (54). If the Jews were faced with harsh adversity in the age of equality, then their destiny was, in fact, shared by all modern people.

A Universal Class within the Class Struggle

As far as the different classes and hence civil society were concerned, as in the political sphere, the Jews became the main target of social conflict. As a "caste," they had many points in common with the aristocracy (the primacy of the extended family with branches throughout Europe, loyalty to family before the nation, etc.), so much so that the liberal middle classes in their fight against the vestiges of the ancien régime "concluded that perhaps one could get rid of nobility only by first getting rid of the Jews" (31). This did not prevent the aristocrats, who "openly opposed the egalitarian nation-state" (32), from attacking the Jews whom they identified with the state responsible for their emancipation. The Jews were attacked for the same reason by the anti-Semites, who "aimed to destroy the political pattern of the nation-state" (39), and identified the Jews with the government.

The functional universality of the Jewish role in society is very much akin to its universality in modern politics in its nation-state form. Constituting an anti-class, the Jews were seen by all the classes as an unacknowledged caste that symbolized the most significant side of society as a whole. To attack the state and the prevailing social order was to attack the Jews. In politics, the state set itself up as an entity above all parties by taking on the Jews as a caste, while the anti-Semites attacked the nation-state by attacking the Jews, who were dissociated from citizenship, singled out, and reproached for their invasive universal presence.

The most striking feature of this system is obviously the paradox of the Jew as the simultaneous personification of absolute singularity (in the eyes of the liberal middle classes) and absolute universality (in the eyes of the anti-Semite and the aristocrat). In political modernity, the Jews thus found themselves acknowledged as a universal singularity, if not to say a singular universality. Maybe the Jewish sign played the role of indetermination and incompletion in political modernity. In equality, it was the factor of singularization that made it possible to step out of anonymity and nondifferentiation, the indivisible element in the equalization of conditions, the singular that did not fall in line with the norm of equality and that became, through force of circumstance, the pivot (the criterion) of equality. In politics and citizenship, the factor of universalization made it possible to go beyond singularities and hence the (necessarily singular) reactive element to the universal position. And yet we are dealing with one and the same being!

Knowing that behind the ambivalent figure of the Jews stands the people, the question changes: Why did the nation-state, that placed itself above all classes and repressed the people(s), need the Jews as a singular people to ensure its universality? Why did modern society feel equal and "normal" by comparison to the Jews, who were necessarily "abnormal" and "domineering"? Perhaps it is because—contrary to popular belief—equality and universality require a specific support to lean on. We are touching here on a concept of the universal and the singular that modern thought (especially in continental Europe and more specifically in France) has been incapable of forging because it is persuaded that the universal is obtained by eradicating singularities.

The indetermination of Jewish identity at the heart of society and the state puts the Jews (or, more precisely, the Jewish sign) nearly mechanically at the center. The Jew always personifies what is absent and at the same time overly present everywhere. This diffuse but empty presence contributes to turning the Jew into the focus of determination and identification. He personifies the common that is given to all to share and yet irremediably withdrawn from each and everyone in particular, while he himself is deprived of receiving his share and resembles a votive gift, a sacrifice offered for the salvation of the collectivity. I will return to this latter point, though not, of course, to fall back on the scapegoat theory, because, as the reader will have understood, we are not dealing here with an "eternal" anthropological propensity but with a process that took place in history, in the theater of modern politics and democracy. This is precisely what needs to be understood.

The People of All the European Peoples

Arendt outlines another theory based on the notion of communication that may provide a broader explanation for the Jewish condition than the dysfunctional logic of the nation-state's universality and the principle of equality. The nascent nation-states needed a vehicle of communication, a factor of international sociability at a time when the egocentric logic of modernity, of "every man for himself," prevented them from creating bonds with their European associates. The newly emancipated Jews had maintained sufficient family connections and collective ties in Europe and throughout the world to furnish a ready-to-employ international network that extended into the core of each of the European nation-states. The Jews found themselves playing a part that they had often played in history, the most well-known example being their role in the service of the Sublime Porte after the expulsion from Spain and Portugal in 1492, when they found refuge in the Ottoman Empire. The spread of Sephardic Jewry throughout Europe (and even as far as the Americas) put the Jews in a crucial position to serve as relays for Ottoman diplomacy with the European kingdoms. In the same way, the nation-state had an imperious need as much to preserve the continuity of Jewish singularity, indeed of the Jewish "people," as to emancipate the Jews individually—and necessarily as a privilege (outside the norm and outside equality), since the "people" had been surreptitiously maintained. The European Jews became the symbolic cement of Europe, because they were the only non-"national," non-"state" element in Europe, the only people left over after all the former peoples of Europe were converted into nations and states. "Without territory and without a government of their own, the Jews had always been an inter-European element; this international status the nation-state necessarily preserved because the Jews' financial services rested on it. But even when their economic usefulness had exhausted itself, the inter-European status of the Jews remained of great national importance in times of national conflicts and wars" (19). Arendt quotes Diderot: "Thus dispersed in our time [. . . the Jews] have become instruments of communication between the most distant countries; They are like cogs and nails needed in a great building in order to join and hold together all other parts" (23). The Jewish people was preserved for this reason, but also perhaps to serve as a covert souvenir, a memory of peoplehood for all the vanished peoples of Europe, expressing at once their deep hidden truth (the nostalgia for peoplehood) and what needs to be repressed (the people) in order to be modern. "The Jews could not only be used in the interest of this precarious balance, they even became a kind of symbol of the common interest of the European nations" (22). "It is still one of the most moving aspects of Jewish history that the Jews' active entry into European history was caused by their being an inter-European, non-national element in a world of growing or existing nations" (22). Arendt underlines in this respect the fact that it was two Jewish bankers who negotiated the Versailles treaty for France (Rothschild) and Germany (Bleichroeder). It was as if the Jews were Europe's "symbol"—symbol in the etymological sense, as the slate of clay broken in ancient Greece by two allies in memory of their alliance in case they would meet again and that served as confirmation of this alliance when fitted together. Simultaneously singular and spread all over (universal) the Jewish people was this "symbol," this souvenir of peoplehood, of the abundance of peoples everywhere overflowing the penury of the nation-state. It was the symbol that the Europe of nation-states gave itself to communicate, breaking the slate (the Jewish people) for this purpose; the universal born from this break in the singular, the universal recomposed only by perfectly matching every single detail of this break.

The symbol can only be a useful vehicle of communication when there is a will to communicate and a desire for union. When European solidarity was disrupted and Europe began flirting with war (and with total war, since the nation-states had nothing in common), the Jews lost their role. They reverted to a singular people, the one people too many in the European concert, consigned to destruction, because they reminded Europe too much of its forgotten community. "It is therefore more than accidental that the catastrophic defeats of the peoples of Europe began with the catastrophe of the Jewish people. It was particularly easy to begin the dissolution of the precarious European balance of power with the elimination of the Jews" (22). "It is not without historical justice that [the] downfall [of the Jewish role in European history] coincided with the ruin of a system and a political body which, whatever its other defects, had needed and could tolerate a purely European element" (62).

The Question of Man

Arendt's argument is a powerful one, insofar as it seeks the causes and prodromes of the destruction of the Jews in a global pattern. One cannot consider "the history of anti-Semitism as an entity in itself, as a mere political movement. Social factors, unaccounted for in political or economic history, hidden under the surface of events [. . .] changed the course that mere political anti-Semitism would have taken if left to itself, and which might have resulted in anti-Jewish legislation and even mass expulsion but hardly in wholesale extermination" (87). There is reason to believe that among the factors "hidden under the surface" the covert maintenance of the Jewish people by a modernity intent on emancipating only individual Jews played a crucial role. Thus political modernity is not directly responsible for the destruction of the Jews, but it led to it.

Arendt's essay is a big step forward when it comes to understanding the causes of the singularity of the Jews in the Shoah and the ambivalences of modern politics. She opens avenues at many points where Sartre's brilliant analysis led to impasses. But she provides less insight into a certain number of other aspects that were clarified by Sartre's discussion. The Arendtian argument is at once overly centered on the Jewish question—to the point that she overlooks the more global implications of the Shoah on modernity—and insufficiently so—inasmuch as she scarcely examines the concept of the "Jewish people" (cf. her mention of the Jewish people having "a well circumcised plan on earth" [8]). We rarely find in *Antisemitism* the kind of global judgment about the modern system that Sartre makes so powerfully. Perhaps this is because Arendt's aim is to examine totalitarianism rather than modernity, and to examine it politically rather than philosophically. It is by soliciting her text that I have endeavored to draw out the systematic dimension in relation to modernity that characterizes her analysis. Arendt actually sticks too closely to the historical circumstances and to the facts that she is studying.

What happened to the Jews—and this she acknowledges—happened to all Europeans, but not only because the Jews played a central role in political modernity, nor because they originally broke away from non-Jews for racial reasons. It was also—and this is my thesis—because Jewish destiny was a singular transposition of the common desire of Europeans. Let us take the example of the principle of "equality" faced with the reality of classes. The Jews formed a class without actually being one (a caste by birth?) in a society of classes that developed in the shadow of democratic equality. No doubt, as Arendt implies, this happened because they continued to be the people needed by the state but denounced by the republic. Yet it may also be that the very concept of class or collectivity (regardless of its nature) constitutes a real problem in political modernity. In an egalitarian society, people had a hard time being together. Their unity was a façade: behind it was a jungle where interests, competition, and hierarchy held sway. Let us take the example of the nation-state, modernity's political form par excellence. Was the reason the Jews did not find their place in it only, as Arendt suggests, because the nation-state needed their services as a group, and because it lacked both a territory and sufficient demographic concentration? Or was it rather because the nation-state was built on the destruction of peoples? The concept of the nation-state and its institution are the crux of the matter and not the "abnormality" of the Jews in relation to the norm of the nation-state. Perhaps it was not only the Jewish people that could not survive in the nation-state.

What this means is that Arendt's essay does not tackle the question of "peoplehood" and "modernity." Witness the Jewish case at the center of her investigation. One cannot understand the question of the "people" in the modernization of the Jews without looking at the premodern period when the people purportedly enjoyed a historical existence before being destroyed by the logic of the nation-state. However, Arendt never deals with this subject, except insofar as she draws on Jacob Katz's discussion of premodern Judaism to make a rhetorical (rather than a historical) point: the Jews can also be "mean," they are not eternal victims, and they too are actors in history. In fact, how could she deal with this subject when she posits from the outset (vii), and to some extent with good reason, a distinction between the anti-Judaism of the ancien régime and the anti-Semitism of the democratic era?—a distinction so radical that she can no longer conceive of the two together, and this despite the fact that she observes their objective synergy. "This superstition [the assumption of eternal anti-Semitism] has been strengthened through the fact that for many centuries the Jews experienced the Christian brand of hostility which was indeed a powerful agent of preservation, spiritually as well as politically" (7). Arendt defines the difference between the two forms of Jew hatred, but she cannot explain the transformation of one into the other, and she fails to understand that they may be two varieties of a single, more profound, logic. Before anti-Semitism ("a secular nineteenth-century ideology" [vii]), the Jews were the focus of the hostility of Christian Europe (7).

In light of what we have seen, it becomes clear that Arendt's difficulty in confronting the thrust and implications of modernization and analyzing it as a global system stems from the fact that she does not accept the idea of a connection between the modern and the premodern. The Jewish case in modernity, nationalism, and state imperialism could very well be the vestige of premodernity, paradoxically lodged at the very core of the highest modernity. But if this is so, it can only be apprehended by regarding modernity from the standpoint of premodernity: only by holding in view what precedes it can we fully comprehend the ins and outs of modernity, both manifest and latent.

Ultimately Arendt avoids the question that she brilliantly contributes to formulating. If Jew hatred continues when Jews have no power, and if it is not the expression of the archaic scapegoat ritual, and it is not the continuation of Christian society, then where does it come from? It can only come from political modernity. This question is a challenge to democracy, but Arendt does not answer it. She hastens to clear the nation-state of suspicion by shifting her analysis of the hiatus and the gap from the field of political society (modern citizenship) to the international arena and identifying the process that led to the catastrophe with the phenomenon of imperialism (the second part of *The Origins of Totalitarianism* after *Antisemitism*). According to Arendt, it was the decline of the nation-state at a time when imperialism was making its weight felt in all of the European states that led to the exponential rise in intra-European anti-Semitism.

Nevertheless, Arendt comes very close to clarifying the essential point at issue in the singularization of the Jews in political modernity (and in the Shoah): the question of Man, apprehended precisely in its dimensions of collective being in the polity (citizenship), in its relationship to power and in history, the transgenerational as it unfolds over time and in space (the "people"). Whereas Sartre admirably raises the question of man in democratic modernity, Arendt defines with more or less felicitous precision the social dimension of the concept of Man, as much in politics as in history and perhaps in culture, but she fails to unravel its tangled skein. "The great challenge to the modern period, and its peculiar danger, has been that in it man for the first time confronted man without the protection of differing circumstances and conditions" (54). These are wise words indeed! Man naked; man stripped bare in the state and in history under the impact of modernity's tabula rasa; man forgotten in modernity; man in exile in the citizen, abandoned to the forces of destruction.

Part 2

The Man-of-the-Citizen

CHAPTER 7

The Enigma of the Democratic Man

The very notion of "crime against humanity" forcefully underscores the fact that what was at stake in the Shoah was human identity. Memoirs written by survivors, such as Primo Levi's *Se questo è un uomo* (1947, *If This Is a Man*) and Robert Antelme's *L'Espèce humaine* (1957, *The Human Species*), testify to the reality of a tragedy that touched upon the limits of what is human. As Avishaï Margalit and Gabriel Motzkin have argued, the Nazis sought to humiliate the Jews before destroying them: "Humiliation requires [. . .] the victim [to] recognize that his tormentor is expelling him from the human commonwealth."[1] By humiliating the Jews, they deprived them of the "common identity that death imposes on"[2] all human beings; their death no longer resembled a human death. The Nazis did much more than cast the Jews of Europe out of citizenship. They excluded them from the human race, and in so doing they challenged the existence of a human race, even though they could not do without the idea of it. Excluding someone from humanity, even feeling the need to do so (this was the sense of the humiliation—which served no "technical" purpose—inflicted on the deportees before they were killed), is acknowledging the existence of this humanity in the very attempt to crush it. But the attention brought to bear on this humanity (damaged and lost in the "deprivation of individuality"[3] that characterized the deportee's experience) paved the way for a denial in recent years of the singularization of the Jews in the suffering of Jews (necessarily singular, since it is always a specific individual who suffers). Certain thinkers can in this way express a deep "concern" for humanity and have no qualms about negating the Jewish singularity, that is, denying the victim's individuality and identity. This is the case for Alain Brossat: "Concentration camp literature is one of the only 'genres' that uses the generic category of 'man' without further oratorical ado and without expressing the usual philosophical reservations about the vagueness and generality of the term. What we are hearing in titles such as *If This Is a Man* or *The Human Species* is not the old-fashioned tune of the ideology of man (Man). It was as if an incomprehensible brightness had been generated by the ordeal of absolute destitution, wherein man, divested of human qualities and conditions, became *more visible than ever*—as a man, precisely, as a human being [. . .] the indivisible nature of the human species, of the human condition."[4] There would be every reason to concur with Brossat's reasoning if it did not lead directly to a violent criticism of those he accuses of setting up a hierarchy of the dead by singling out the Jewish victims in the Shoah.[5]

As we have seen, focusing on the question of man is often a way of turning a blind eye to the question of the citizen; the heady lure of man's unfathomable nature, and the abyss that inhabits it, exempts us from considering the evidence of reality. However, raising the question of the citizen does not in any way drain the question of Man of meaning. We have seen that if citizenship failed in the case of the Jews, it was because the Emancipation had "left out," or rather denied, the Jew-of-the-citizen, and the Jew-of-the-citizen is precisely what made the Jewish citizen a man in concrete terms, belonging to a humanity that I have defined as "the people." And it is this particular, singular humanity and not human "nature" that is in question above all: the man-of-the-citizen. What makes for the humanity of man is that he is embedded in history and not "nature."

Democratic man has turned out to be an enigma in the destiny of the citizen where Man found himself eclipsed by the citizen. The Shoah put democratic man into question, fundamentally. If we can penetrate this enigma, then we will no doubt gain some insight into why the destruction of the Jew-of-the-citizen in the catastrophe and the contemporary crisis of the democratic citizen in general raise such crucial issues for future political thought. How could it be otherwise, knowing that the human, that "Man" (of the rights of man . . .) became a political "cause" in modernity? Man, who had been the focus until then of religion, philosophy, or poetry, became the prism and finality of political voluntarism. With the *Declaration of the Rights of Man and the Citizen*, Man is designated as a referent of politics, as an absolute value proposed to the polity, which is thereby summoned (all alone) to provide for the accomplishment of Man and to be the agency of his embodiment in the world. This ambition went far beyond the Aristotelian idea of man as "political animal" that was current in premodern political thought. Aristotle employs the term *zoon* to designate the civic "animal," a term that refers to *zoe*, or animal life, and not to *bios*, or the life of the person. Interpreted restrictively, we can infer from this nuance that if the rightful place of man (in the cosmic hierarchy) is in the polity, as the locus of language and justice that distinguishes man from animal, then his humanity (*bios*) cannot be wholly reduced to it. The polity corresponds to the intermediary being of man who cannot however fulfill his individuality and enjoy happiness outside of contemplative life, the activity of contemplation (the intellect) being the highest thing in man.[6] The civic condition of man would thus be the best state to which man can aspire, but only because ideal life cannot be attained in the concrete experience of men, and not because it embodies the epitome of his humanity. For Aristotle, if man naturally lives in a polity and in society, then the highest stage of the human condition exceeds these confines. In the Middle Ages, the economy of the temporal and the spiritual dissociated the order of the polity from that of the spirit, dividing Man between the terrestrial kingdom and the kingdom of heaven. But the modern ambition went infinitely farther than the universe of tradition which, springing from a revelation, always pointed somewhere else, somewhere beyond Man, namely, to God. In modernity, Man became the source of the law and the focus of the polity, but men in their singularity and their personality no longer inhabited it.

The Jew of the Man-of-the-Citizen

How did it come to pass that "Man," in whose name the Jews were recognized as citizens, became a factor in the exclusion of the Jew in the Jew's civic condition? The man-of-the-citizen repressed (into the unconscious) the Jew in the citizen. To understand this "dialectical mystery," we will have to return to the revolutionary debate on the Emancipation of the Jews and its highly enlightening discourse. The purpose of this look back at the past is archaeological not moral. The point is not to cast discredit a posteriori on the emancipatory intention of modernity's first democratic experience but to comprehend what it was in this experience (on an unconscious level) that made such aberrations possible.

And what do we find in the early stages of the Emancipation if not the "repression" of the Jew in the citizenship of Jews, implemented, moreover, under the best auspices of universal "human nature," in which the Jews, relegated to ghettos by the ancien régime, were to be given the chance to participate? Oddly enough, the Emancipation of the Jew as man went hand in hand with the rejection of man as Jew.

Partisans and adversaries of the Emancipation of the Jews clashed over the question of whether the Jews were men. This controversy is quite a good indicator of the status of man and the significance of "Man" in the modernity of the *Rights of Man and the Citizen*. Well before our era, when Sartre wondered, "Does the Jew exist? And if he exists, what is he? Is he first a Jew or first a man?,"[7] Abbé Grégoire declared that the Jews "are men like we are, and they are so before being Jews."[8] Anybody with a sound mind will hear in this affirmation—positive and generous, to be sure—an odd dissociation of the Jew and the man. Indeed, how can a Jew be a man other than as a Jew? It is in that capacity that he participates in humanity! Dissociating man from his identity is characteristic of mental illness (or of the analytic project of sociology and philosophy): the human is attached to and manifested in the identities of men. It is as someone in particular that I am a man. This dissociation, whose strangeness is worth emphasizing, is less the problem of Jews (to the extent that they are mentally sound, of course) than of the emancipators who challenged an old prejudice (and this was very much to their credit) yet remained very much under its influence. Eighteenth-century revolutionary consciousness defined the Jewish condition before the Emancipation (and outside the emancipatory relationship) as a nonhuman condition, one that was excluded from humanity. This hypothesis must not be accepted without questioning, because even excluded from citizenship (which was in fact no longer altogether the case after the *Lettres patentes* granted by Louis XVI or the status of near citizenship accorded to the Sephardic Jews of southern France), the Jews were nonetheless men. Even demeaned, even enslaved, a man is a man: humanity—and I will develop this idea later—is not a quality that depends on the recognition of men. It has (firstly and paradoxically for the moderns) a transcendent nature. We have here one of the first signs of the modern politicization of the human. The emancipators were in fact interpreting a political status as a matter of humanity (or inhumanity) when they claimed that those who did not benefit from citizenship were excluded from humanity. Limited specifically to the Jews, the assertion is all the more astounding when one considers that there were no "citizens" in France before the revolution, only "subjects." As a consequence, they should all have been considered outside of humankind! What this means is simply that for the Constituent Assembly and the emancipators, humanity was reduced to a matter of citizenship (the one they were granting), and that it was conceivable that the status of man (of the human) not coincide with the practical condition of man (the "animal" that stands, speaks, remembers, hopes, prohibits incest, and so on). Perhaps they imagined that there were men who were not human! This, at any rate, is what follows from Mirabeau's disturbing proposal: "In a government like the one you are setting up, it is imperative for all men to be men; all those who are not or who would refuse to become men must be banished from your midst."[9] And this conception is directly related in this same quotation to the Jewish question: "Now, Messieurs, is it because the Jews may not want to be citizens that you are not to declare them citizens?" Mirabeau's statement clearly demonstrates that to the revolutionary mentality the category of humanity was an exclusively ideological category, wholly dependent on the political authority.

This situation is to be considered in the context of the revolutionary project of "regeneration" that accompanied the emancipation of the Jews (and to which I will return). It was the first time in the history of mankind that man set out to create a new "regenerated" man solely by the agency of the government and to do so on a "tabula rasa," where tradition and initiation had been erased. The case of the Jews was to be exemplary. Their prerevolutionary subhumanity was emphasized all the more so that they could serve as a general symbolic example of the regeneration of men through citizenship. Hannah Arendt noted the extent to which the insistence in the eighteenth century on the Jew's foreign, exotic character served to establish a contrast with the new man-of-the-citizen that the old Jew was supposed to become. Depicted as the foreigners closest to Europe, theoretically excluded from mankind, the Jews were the personification of the Other, living proof of Europe's regeneration, thanks to the ideas of the Enlightenment. The new Jew would be the triumph of the "new Man." Arendt quotes Herder referring to the Jews as "new specimens of humanity," a "strange people of Asia driven into our regions."[10] The alleged radical foreignness of the Jews (who were as European as other Europeans) reinforced the spectacular project of their regeneration. If the most alien of men could become citizens, then the man-of-the-citizen could be regarded all the more strongly as universal. In the words of Lessing to Moses Mendelssohn, this universal citizenship was to be "the shortest and safest way to that European country without either Christians or Jews."[11] In the same vein, Herder expected the Jews to abandon "the old and proud national prejudices, customs that do not belong to our age and constitutions" in order to become "purely humanized"![12]

We can clearly see from this perspective that, under the virtuous banner of universality, the man-of-the-citizen remained closely (and unconsciously) bound up with political ethnocentrism. "If a tribal or other 'backward' community did not enjoy human rights, it was obviously because as a whole it had not yet reached that stage of civilization, the stage of popular and national sovereignty, but was oppressed by foreign or native despots. The whole question of human rights, therefore, was quickly and inextricably blended with the question of national emancipation; only the emancipated sovereignty of the people, of one's own people, seemed to be able to insure them."[13]

The most fervent advocates of the Jews' admission to citizenship had—in an unconscious yet altogether coherent manner—a negative appraisal of Jewish identity and agreed on the native degeneracy of the Jewish condition. Thus Mirabeau exclaimed, "Ah! Respect the appearance of humanity in these wretched people,"[14] and he observed the "corruption of Jews whose sole purpose is commerce. The only idol the Jews have is money."[15] Abbé Grégoire's numerous negative judgments on Jewish culture and religion include the highly derogatory statement that if the Jews "were but savages, it would be easy to regenerate them . . . but they have the acquired ignorance that has depraved their intellectual faculties."[16]

They saw this depravity expressed in every aspect of Jewish culture. Grégoire, the foremost advocate of the emancipation of the Jews, saw in Judaism nothing but "Talmudic reveries, a cesspit of human deliriums," a "rabbinic muddle," an "ample collection of twaddle and errors," a "chaos of Talmudic traditions," "burlesque traditions," "Cabalist and Talmudic reveries."[17] "A hundred of their writers have professed a hundred thousand and one reveries each more absurd than the other . . . as if credulity had appointed stupidity to write them,"[18] and he expressed his intention to produce works that would "ridicule the Rabbinism's mystical puerilities."[19] It would be only too easy to compile an anthology of quotations along the same lines by advocates of the Emancipation.[20]

How, then, did the emancipators justify the Emancipation of the Jews in moral terms? One of their arguments was informed by the logic of victimhood, whose history and origin are much older than most people realize! What the advocates of the Jews seemed to be saying was: "If the Jews are Jews, that is, if they are the fallen men, the non-men whom we see today in 1789, it is Europe's fault; it is Europe that drove them to this degeneracy. Let us free them from oppression and they will stop being Jews and become Men!" They considered, in fact, the Jewish being the very mark of opposition and alienation.[21] The Jew was recognized as a man because he was a victim (and not because he was a Jew). The second argument was based on the perfectibility of the Jews. This is a key principle in Enlightenment ideology, which is fundamentally a progressionist ideology. Since the Jew is perfectible (which is not the case, as we will see, of women or black men), despite his degeneracy, he can potentially become a man.

As to Europe's responsibility in the degeneracy of the Jews, there was no dearth of statements either. "The Jews have always been held in hatred and have seldom been able to rise to the level of others in human dignity."[22] "The height of injustice is to blame the Jews for the crime that we have forced them to commit."[23] "You are accountable for the universe of their vices or their virtues to come."[24] "Our contempt is what has tied them so strongly to their practices."[25] "Their religion is a refuge against the tyranny of government and against the injustice of men."[26] We should note that the Jewish representatives employed the same sort of language: "The Jews are strangers not by nature or by religion, but because they are unjustly regarded as such and cast out of society."[27] "Theocracy is the sole consolation of the wretched."[28]

On the subject of perfectibility and education (or rather "regeneration") the emancipators also spoke in perfect unison. "Let us rectify their education so as to rectify their hearts; for a long time we have been saying that they are men like we are, and that they are so before being Jews."[29] "Let us not pin our hopes on the adult whose habit is formed and will escape our grasp. Let us strike at the root of evil, and get a hold on the generation that will be born, the generation that has yet to reach puberty."[30] "The object that deserves the greatest attention is their children's education: it is an important enough task for the government to take all possible measures. Indeed, what fruit can we expect our efforts to yield if we let the Jews continue transmitting the same principles to their children upon which they themselves were raised, and making their children slaves to the same prejudices?"[31]

In this dialectical or ambivalent relationship to the Jew, the "Man" that underpins the emancipation necessarily refers to a humanity that is not consubstantial with Jewishness, that comes before it (or reaches beyond it, depending on the point of view), with Jewishness remaining the immutable sign of the degeneration of man for which Europe is responsible and guilty. It is because the Jews were men before being Jews, that is, before they were rejected by the Gentiles, that they can be "regenerated" and become men again in the future. It is by dissociating the Jew from the Man, that the Jew, restored to his dignity as Man and removed from his lack of dignity as Jew, is called upon to become a citizen, the personification of the regenerated man. That the few Jewish spokesmen of the period adopted the same lines of reasoning demonstrates the latter's structural reality and legitimating effectiveness. "It is as a French citizen and an ardent friend of humanity that I plead the cause of the nation whose vices were caused solely by the relentless hostility of its enemies," one Jewish representative exclaimed.[32] (Is it only as victims that Jews can challenge the moderns?) "Man" is thus defined as the absolute figure, the bare nature of all men, and all particular attributes (every man has a name and an address, and every man is the child of his parents, etc.) are purely incidental and secondary. Only Man among men is universal—the abstract model, unmarked by any contact with the accidents of history. "The *Lettres patentes* of the Jews are in Nature, and the stamp of nature is worth as much as the stamp of all the chancelleries of Europe. The Jews are not *naturally* depraved,"[33] "their customs and their characters are not naturally depraved,"[34] "the natural rights of man in society . . . argue in favor of the Jews."[35] "The Man, existing prior to the Jew, is natural, absolute, and universal Man. It is because this natural Man, this universal nature, is present in the degeneration embodied by the Jew, that the Jews are perfectible."[36] It is thus under the auspices of Nature, producer of Man, that the defenders of the Jews advocate the 'regeneration of the Jews.' "How can a nature, totally distorted and corrupted in the heart, be changed?"[37]

Very paradoxically, alongside this denigrating picture of the Jewish condition, the apologetic discourse in favor of the Jews also presented a moving picture of the touching humanity that the Jews had managed to preserve, despite their degeneracy, and that argued for their redemption. The myth of the "*bon sauvage*," entertained in Europe since Montaigne, took on specifically Jewish traits here: The men are "good husbands, good fathers"[38]; "After giving birth, their women still deign to recall that they are mothers"[39]; They are "sober and industrious."[40]

By the time the Jew reaches the end of his journey of initiation and becomes a citizen, his Jewishness will clearly have been eliminated, and he will have joined the (state) universal, of which his particularity was but a degenerate form. Thus behind the (universal) citizen stands the abandoned remains of the historical Jew. It was because the Jew was humanized (having become a man "statutorily") that the Jewishness in him was thrown into the storehouse of used accessories from the past, and so it was under the elevated auspices of the Human that the Jew was excised from the citizen—excised, abandoned, and, hence, left unthought, outside the confines of reason, without however disappearing in practice from the history of Europe, which he would henceforth haunt like an erratic ghost on the stage of anti-Semitism. No mental picture has ever actually changed reality. It was this Jew that Nazism was to take as a target, and it was by attacking him that Nazism reversed the conscious economy of the rights of man, "resuscitating" the Jew in the citizen and, hence, due to the modern logic's force of inertia (and of the unconscious), chasing the citizen from the Jew and rediscovering his "atavistic," "archaic" being. Indeed, it was not the Jew in the Man who was emancipated but the Man in the Jew. In line with the aim of modern rationality, the Jew in the Man was abandoned to indetermination, left to the jungle of the emotive and the instinctual; there was no place for the Jew as a Jew in the framework of political modernity. And it was upon this wanderer, lacking a clear awareness of himself (and therefore a strategy[41] or the ability to react, since you must know you are a target to dodge the blow aimed at you; you must know that you are Jewish to understand that Nazism targeted the Jew in you before the citizen), that the Nazi eagle was to swoop down. However, as the reader will have understood from part 1, even if the Shoah targeted the Jew in the citizen, it is the citizen who is the point at issue, much more so than the Jew. The tendency today to maintain the contrary (be it by advocating or condemning the "uniqueness of the Shoah") is a way of ignoring the failure of democratic citizenship and protecting it by placing the burden of the crisis on the Jews. But to understand the destiny of the Jew-of-the-citizen, one must understand the role of the Man-of-the-Jew (in this disturbing dissociation of Jew and Man), which sheds light on the man-of-the-citizen, on the very foundation of citizenship, and, hence, as we have just seen, on its structural instability and failure (this analysis is the purpose of part 2). The destiny of the Jews in the Shoah is, in fact, exemplary of the destiny of men in citizenship. It is due to their situation as universal outcasts throughout Europe that Europe's destiny was illustrated through them.

The other side of the question of the citizen is the question of Man, as "the rights of man and the citizen" gives us to understand, almost mechanically. The failure of citizenship manifested in the singularization of the Jews in the Shoah draws our attention to the feebleness of the articulation of man *and* the citizen. It was, in fact, the Man in the citizen who had to face adversity and his destiny naked.

A parallel could be drawn—although an exclusively formal one—between the removal of the Jews from citizenship by the Nazis and the dissociation of the Jew and (natural and universal) Man, which was the first step in the symbolic operation that underpinned their citizenship and their recognition as Men at the time of the Emancipation. I am not suggesting that there is a cause-and-effect relationship between the two dissociations, but that Jewishness—as an identity and a people—was isolated in a vacuum and left in a state of indetermination—politically and socially (generating anti-Semitism) as well as culturally (Jewish identity as a "mystery," a source of enormous perplexity), and that this lent itself to all sorts of perversions. The morphology of this dissociation was lodged at the core of the Jewish condition and exposed it, by force of inertia, to a potential distortion (outside of the emancipatory project of granting citizenship to the Jews). This explains why the Jewish condition carries, in European consciousness, what the repressed and the unconscious carry in any subjective consciousness. For this very reason, the structural dissociation that I am discussing here belongs to the category of the "unthinkable," for consciousness has not the wherewithal to apprehend itself by itself: it is at one with its being and the world, except when it totters on its foundations under the impact of an external event (this is what the Shoah let us see to a certain extent). In other words, it is in this (unrecognized) dissociation that Western consciousness considers the Jews and sees them.

Did the distinction between Man and citizen pave the way to Man's fall in the citizen? How can the citizen be part of the democratic order, while the Man is abandoned to virtual barbarity? Is it the destiny of Man—and no longer of the citizen—in democracy that is at stake after the Shoah?

Arendt and Sartre's Postwar Critiques of the Declaration

At the end of her essay on *Imperialism*, which follows the analysis developed in *Antisemitism*, Arendt undertakes a critical reappraisal of the politics of "human rights." The title of the last chapter, "The Decline of the Nation-State and the End of the Rights of Man," is as explicit as can be in this regard. "The very phrase 'human rights' became for all concerned—victims, persecutors, and onlookers alike—the evidence of hopeless idealism or fumbling feeble-minded hypocrisy."[42] "The survivors of the extermination camps [. . .] could see without Burke's arguments that the abstract nakedness of being nothing but human was their greatest danger."[43] What she identifies as the final crisis of "human rights" resulted not from an arbitrary return of barbarity, from the triumph of obscurantism over human rights, but to the contrary from the absolute extension of civilization, that is, of the political modernity derived from the rights of man. Being excluded from someplace at the time amounted to losing one's place in humanity as a whole and finding oneself outside of the confines of humanity. Others before Arendt, in the controversy over the *Declaration*, had drawn similar conclusions, in particular, regarding human rights as being nothing more than the rights of citizens.[44] On the basis of the experience of Jews, refugees, the stateless, and minorities (all rightless groups that emerged after the liquidation of the multinational states in Central and Eastern Europe), she observes "the constitutional inability of European nation-states to guarantee human rights to those who had lost nationally guaranteed rights."[45] The rift that separated man from citizen, by delivering man to total adversity, opened in the very place where the people disappeared. Arendt clearly adopts here the perspective of peoples with neither state nor nation, abandoned and left to certain death in the Europe of the Rights of Man and the Citizen. "[The] people without their own national government were deprived of human rights."[46] "True emancipation," she asserts, is impossible without "true popular sovereignty [which] could be obtained only with full national emancipation."[47] This comes down to saying that, in practice, the political nation, and not Man or the citizen, is the decisive criterion, a criterion repressed by political rationality.

Picking up an idea already formulated in the nineteenth century, Arendt demonstrates that the Human, approached and defined in terms of rights (the notion of "*rights* of man"), entails the intervention of an authority endowed with the sovereignty needed to enforce rights that are political and by no means natural. One cannot be a "man" and enjoy rights as a man without being a citizen protected by one's sovereign state, because only the state can guarantee the rights of man to the men who are its citizens. Similarly, any "right" is premised upon the existence of a court, and there is no judicial authority without an authority (the state) to enforce its decisions. Yet *all* men cannot possibly be citizens on the basis of the Rights of Man, upon which the universality of the democratic state is supposedly founded. History has shown, in the case of multiethnic states, that the abstract nakedness of citizenship does not suffice to guarantee human rights to minorities and the stateless, to nationals who do not belong to the dominant people and to non-nationals. It is the national and not only the democratic state that is in a position to guarantee these rights: "Only nationals could be citizens, only people of the same national origin could enjoy the full protection of legal institutions [. . .] the transformation of the state from an instrument of the law into an instrument of the nation had been completed; the nation had conquered the state, national interest had priority over law long before Hitler could pronounce 'right is what is good for the German people.' "[48] "[L]oss of national rights was identical with loss of human rights."[49] Because the man-of-the-Declaration was conceived and formulated in abstract terms with no support from an institution and an authority, anyone who relied exclusively on this concept (because he no longer enjoyed national rights) found himself projected into a rightless zone, delivered to savagery, driven to a decadent paradox, in which "a small burglary [would] improve his legal position," because "a criminal offense [became] the best opportunity to regain some kind of human equality, even if it be as a recognized exception to the norm."[50] "Only as an offender against the law can he gain protection from it. As long as his trial and his sentence last, he will be safe from that arbitrary police rule against which there are no lawyers and no appeals."[51] Strangely enough, it is by being an exception to the rule and transgressing the law that these men could hope to reestablish some sort of relationship to the rule and to the law. Unless, that is, they became men of genius and of exception, which was the other alternative. Arendt concludes from this state of affairs that Man cannot be a source of rights and emancipation for men and the citizen. Therefore it is suicidal (or illusory) to set up a polity and a status on such bases. And woe betide those who believe in these without the support of a state! "As mankind, since the French Revolution, was conceived in the image of a family of nations, it gradually became self-evident that the people, and not the individual, was the image of man."[52] "Man had hardly appeared as a [. . .] being who carried his dignity within himself [. . .], when he disappeared again into a member of a people."[53] This phenomenon was all the more damaging, insofar as it remained unconscious and unacknowledged. Indeed, it contributed to masking the issue of the political (the citizen) in the name of the natural (the man) and succeeded neither in safeguarding the latter nor in making it the source of the former and of the law! All in all, to Arendt, there is no efficient human rights policy and no way of founding the polity (of citizenship) upon human rights, which are, alas, evanescent in the political arena. Man and the citizen are in fact two expressions of a similar tautology, "a practical demonstration of the totalitarian movements' cynical claims that no such thing as inalienable human rights existed and that the affirmations of the democracies to the contrary were mere prejudice, hypocrisy, and cowardice in the face of the cruel majesty of a new world."[54]

The Shoah revealed man's actual nakedness. "The world found nothing sacred in the abstract nakedness of being human."[55] And, as we have seen, the survivors could not help but see "that the abstract nakedness of being nothing but human was their greatest danger,"[56] worse than slavery, since slaves, in spite of everything, still have "a place in society," which is a much more enviable status "than the abstract nakedness of being human and nothing but human."[57] Arendt imputes this nakedness to the idea of "nature" as formulated by Enlightenment thinkers and the repression of singularity contained in the universalizing abstraction of man. The Nature that was supposed to underpin the universality of the rights of man (and democracy) was a deadly illusion: "Today we are perhaps better qualified to judge exactly what this human 'nature' amounts to"; "nature itself has assumed a sinister aspect."[58] Indeed, there is no human *nature*: man is not attributable to nature. Nationality underpins humanity to a much greater extent, as it distinguishes men from savages, for "natural rights are granted even to savages"; "savages have nothing more to fall back upon than the minimum fact of their human origin,"[59] which is not enough to ensure life in civilization. In modern ideology's definition of Man, this eighteenth-century conception of nature was substituted for history. " 'Nature' took the place of history, and it was tacitly assumed that nature was less alien than history to the essence of man."[60]

What does this substitution, and reference to history, mean? Simply that "nature" was used in Enlightenment thought to repress the historical dimension of the people and, more specifically, its singularity: and this was rediscovered in the Shoah. "The fundamental deprivation of human rights is manifested first and above all in the deprivation of a place in the world which makes opinions significant and actions effective. Something much more fundamental than freedom and justice, which are rights of citizens, is at stake when belonging to the community into which one is born is no longer a matter of course."[61] Losing one's residence was tantamount to "expulsion from humanity altogether."[62] "Not the loss of specific rights, then, but the loss of a community willing and able to guarantee any rights whatsoever, has been the calamity [. . .]. Only the loss of a polity itself expels [man] from humanity. The right that corresponds to this loss and that was never even mentioned among the human rights cannot be expressed in the categories of the eighteenth century because they presume that rights spring immediately from the 'nature' of man."[63] That the rights of man ignored the people, and its avatar, which is the nation, could hardly be stated more plainly. The fact is, peoples and their identities are the product of their past, not the outgrowth of a rational abstraction: "Only their past with its 'entailed inheritance' seems to attest to the fact that they still belong to the civilized world."[64] "The human being who has lost his place in a

community, his political status in the struggle of his time, and the legal
personality which makes his actions and part of his destiny a consistent
whole is left with those qualities which usually can become articulate only
in the sphere of private life and must remain unqualified, mere existence in
all matters of public concern."[65] "It seems that a man who is nothing but
a man has lost the very qualities which make it possible for other people
to treat him as a fellow-man."[66]

It is this singularity—defined by the social place one occupies (and every
political community is premised upon a common space) and the singular
identity woven by history—that is seen as a threat by democratic universalism in its endeavor to promote a public sphere that supposedly transcends
particularisms. Singularity is qualified by Arendt as a "disturbing miracle":
"the fact that each of us is made as he is—single, unique, unchangeable."[67]
This whole sphere of the merely given (the singularity, the "people") relegated to private life in civilized society poses a permanent threat to the
public sphere, because the public sphere is as consistently based on the law
of equality as the private sphere is on the law of universal difference and
differentiation. Societies founded on equality "insist on ethnic homogeneity"
and try to eliminate "differences and differentiations which by themselves
arouse dumb hatred, mistrust, and discrimination," "because they indicate
[. . .] the limitations of the human artifice."[68] In Arendt's opinion, the Shoah
was proof of the failure of the modern idea of man, as well as the philosophy and political practices to which it led, particularly because they proved
incapable of conceiving, accepting, and handling, with responsibility, the
collective identity and singularity that make a man and that were abandoned,
in the exemplary figure of the Jew, to savagery and destruction.

The question of Man is also at the center of Sartre's discussion in
Anti-Semite and Jew. Through the destiny of the Jew, the philosopher also
shows, if in different terms, that Man is trapped as much as the Jew in a
tragic condition. Sartre employs the dialectics of the universal and the particular to demonstrate the impossible position of the Jew confronted with
the anti-Semite and . . . the democrat. And, paradoxically, the anti-Semite is
seeking the universal, or, more precisely, totality. "Anti-Semitism, a bourgeois phenomenon, appears therefore as a choice made to explain collective
events by the initiative of individuals."[69] As we have seen, the anti-Semite
regains a sense of unity and belonging to a nation through the exclusion
of the Jews. "The anti-Semite is a man who wishes to be pitiless stone, a
furious torrent, a devastating thunderbolt—anything except a man,"[70] and
this irrevocably positions the Jew (thus excluded and singled out) as the
man (the abstract modern man?) whom the anti-Semite does not want to
be because he rejects the revolutionary heritage of democratic universalism. The famous statement, "[t]he Jew is one whom other men consider

a Jew"[71] can, in this perspective, be understood as carrying an additional positivist meaning. The emancipated Jew would embody man in the eyes of the citizens (in fact, the "nationals" who see in him someone outside of the nation, a naked "man," outside of citizenship). He would personify the universal as expressed in the *Declaration*, because he has renounced his singularity. Sartre embraces this idea totally, since he denies that the Jews even have a historical bond. "Its twenty centuries of dispersion and political impotence forbid its having a *historic past*. If it is true, as Hegel says, that a community is historical to the degree that it remembers its history, then the Jewish community is the least historical of all, for it keeps a memory of nothing but a long martyrdom, that is, of a long passivity."[72] "The Jew is not yet *historical*, and yet he is the most ancient of peoples [. . .] he has wisdom and no history."[73]

The democrat's viewpoint runs counter to the anti-Semite's: he does not, however, recognize the Jew, since all he sees is the man in the Jew ("He recognizes neither Jew, nor Arab, nor Negro, nor bourgeois, nor worker, but only man—man always the same in all times and all places"[74]); " 'There are no Jews,' he says, 'there is no Jewish question.' "[75] The democrat's reasoning leads to an impasse ("His defense of the Jew saves the latter as man and annihilates him as Jew"[76]) and to a "policy of assimilation"[77] that proved to be a failure in the United States.

This, then, is the tragedy: the anti-Semite "wishes to destroy him as a man and leave nothing in him but the Jew, the pariah, the untouchable," while the democrat "wishes to destroy him as a Jew and leave nothing in him but the man, the abstract and universal subject of the rights of man and the rights of the citizen."[78] The singular is continually mythified and demonized: desired and excluded by the anti-Semite; glossed over and repressed by the democrat. Together these outlooks work to create the pariah condition inflicted upon the Jews (passively destined to catastrophe). "I agree therefore with the democrat that the Jew is a man like other men, but this tells me nothing in particular."[79] Indeed, the democrat has a tendency "purely and simply to suppress the Jew for the sake of *the man*. But *the man* does not exist; there are Jews, Protestants, Catholics; there are Frenchmen, Englishmen, Germans; there are whites, blacks, yellows."[80] "[W]hatever effort we made to reach to the *person*, it was always the *Jew* whom we encountered."[81] The Christians have had "the art and the audacity to pretend before the Jew that they are not *another race*, but purely and simple *men*."[82]

In this context, all the Jew himself can do is run away from his singularity so as to be admitted into the society of men, the very men who exclude him as a singular Jew. The Jew wants to be recognized as a man by other men, yet it is "among men that he feels himself lonely,"[83] because his humanity is disconnected from his Jewishness! This explains why the

Jew refocuses on his singularity and on his singular destiny and does not
see the extent to which his destiny exemplifies that of all humankind. "He
cannot perceive the loneliness of each man in the midst of a silent universe,
because he has not yet emerged from society into the world."[84] "The Jew
does not dream of [. . .] considering the condition of man in its nudity. He
is the social man *par excellence*, because his torment is social."[85] As a result,
no matter what he does, even if, at best, he opts for authenticity, he cannot
get out of the cage in which political modernity has put him.

Sartre gives here a new, subtler version of Marx's critique of liberal
democratic universalism. Naturally he denounces the "myth of universal
man,"[86] but despite his objective insight, he, like Marx, turns a blind eye
to the reality of the particular, which he defines as a "situation" resulting
from the failure of the universal (that remains the ultimate criterion of
judgment). When the class struggle, which is a struggle between particular
groups in a situation (the classes), has come to an end, and universal truth
has been established, the singular is bound to disappear. "[A]nti-Semitism
would have no existence in a society without classes and founded on collective ownership of the instruments of labor, one in which man, freed of
his hallucinations inherited from an older world, would at long last throw
himself wholeheartedly into *his* enterprise—which is to create the kingdom
of man. Anti-Semitism would then be cut at its roots. Thus the authentic
Jew who thinks of himself as a Jew because the anti-Semite has put him
in the situation of a Jew is not opposed to assimilation any more than the
class-conscious worker is opposed to the liquidation of classes."[87] In his criticism of human rights, Sartre proves to be incapable, despite his generosity,
of coming to terms with the singular as identity and collectivity (class or
people), even though he forcefully grasps the impasse of a democratic universalism that has unwittingly spawned nationalism and anti-Semitism (not
to mention social ranking), that has, in other words, produced singularity,
with the most savage irrationality.

The Failure of Democratic Universalism

The postwar debate about the capacity of human rights to serve as a foundation for the political security of the modern citizen, and hence of democracy,
came to a sudden end with the cold war and the evident need to stand up
for human rights against totalitarianism. It is only now, no doubt, after
the collapse of Communism, that this controversy has been put back on
the agenda. The lines of argument are not, however, altogether new; they
coincide in fact with the main lines of the controversy over the *Declaration
of the Rights of Man and the Citizen* that raged throughout the nineteenth

century. What was already at issue, then, in a central way, was the problem of historicity and its consequences on the status of collective and cultural identity and on the fundaments of law.

All of the peoples newly organized in nation-states (and a fortiori those without nation-states) shared the experience of the Jews who had lost their condition as a historical people when they were "elevated" from Jew to Man, in such a way that their identity was projected into a symbolic and political "no-man's-land." This was plainly evidenced in the irrational phenomenon of nationalism, which has yet to be explained, as well as in the pariah status of stateless peoples, regarded as "infra-national" (and who would be defined as "ethnic groups" today). Peoplehood (collective identity) thus informed the incognizant, irrational part of democratic sociality that, according to its own theory, was based on no "given" other than human rights themselves which, in revolutionary mythology, were one with "nature" and not derived from God or from a legislator (although we have no idea where this "nature" comes from and who sets out its laws).

A Look at the Historical Controversy

Looking back at the controversy over the rights of man, we can see that opponents and (often critical) advocates of the concept generally clashed along the lines of abstract universalism versus historicist empiricism, while trying to find a way to synthesize the two, and regularly failing to do so because both camps ineluctably fell back on positions on either side of the dividing line (universalism in Hegel's and Marx's case, and, "on the other side," particularism in Benjamin Constant's case).

Obviously the historicist argument weighed most heavily on the logic of the rights of man and the citizen. It challenged the very validity of the concept of Man. One of the most outspoken critics, Joseph de Maistre (1753–1821), declared: "The 1795 constitution [. . .] was made for man. But there is no such thing as man in the world. During my life, I have seen Frenchmen, Italians, Russians, and so on: [. . .] but I must say, as for man, I have never come across him anywhere."[88] His words hark back to the position of a theorist such as Edmund Burke (1729–1797) (cited by Arendt), who declared that he had more confidence in "the rights of Englishmen" than in "the rights of men." This school of thought does not believe that rights can be founded on the ahistoricity of man. Human "nature"—as implied by the naked, anonymous concept of Man—seems a dubious concept to them insofar as it makes a clean sweep of the course of history that forges the multiple identities of Humankind and underpins their corresponding specific laws. Basically, its argument pits History and Tradition (for Burke)—or

Providence for Maistre—against the abstraction of the *Declaration*. Burke maintains that mankind and nature are based not on reason and abstract universality but on the long course of history, "the great primeval contract of eternal society."[89] There is no nature, in his eyes, outside the long succession of generations. It is in history that human rights are forged and confirmed. The importance of the "people" emerges indirectly from Burke's considerations, where it figures as part of the eternal order of the world. "Our political system is placed in a just correspondence and symmetry with the order of the world [. . .] a stupendous wisdom, molding together the great mysterious incorporation of the human race." "Corporate bodies are immortal for the good of the members [. . .]. Nations themselves are such corporations." Nations are not "created," certainly not by an act of will; they are eternal givens. Maistre adds: "No nation can give itself liberty if it has not it already. Its laws are made when it begins to reflect on itself." "No assembly of men whatever can create a nation."

The strictly political purpose of the concept of man is often discussed by liberal critics (but also, as we will see, by Marxists). Maistre and Burke see in the rational abstraction that underpins it the source of an "unheard-of despotism" and a clandestine restoration of the very hierarchy that was banished in the name of equality but that any ruling power necessarily brings with it. The position of Benjamin Constant (1767–1830) diverges from that of Maistre and Burke. According to Bertrand Binoche, Constant argues that the "cause of the disaster [as manifested in the crises consecutive to the French Revolution] was not as much the ahistorical principle of the *Declaration* as its aim, namely, the absorption of man in the citizen."[90] In sum, man's fate necessarily depended on the citizen, and this despite the fact that the revolution had declared that man's natural rights were the source of the citizen's political rights.

Establishing law on the theoretical basis of a "social contract" inevitably leads to a paradoxical situation: man's natural rights can only exist if they rest on and are confirmed by the political rights of the citizen. In a similar vein, Jeremy Bentham asserts that such contracts are "pure fiction": "I consider the declaration, in the same way as Mr. Turgot, as the declaration of the rights of men who are in a state of citizenship or political society." This is the opinion that Arendt adopts after the Shoah. Man is nothing without the citizen; it is man who depends on the citizen, and not the other way around! Constant, for his part, opposes the individual to the man and maintains that it is the individual who enjoys eternal rights, and not man, and that these rights are grounded in history, not in nature.

Jurist F. K. von Savigny (1779–1561) advances a similar criticism: "Natural law is set up for the State more than for serious use."[91] The critics of the totalizing abstraction engendered by the concept of *man* often develop their arguments around the issue of law. As against the *Declaration*'s idea of man as the source of law, these theorists regard law as one of the "attributes" of the people, and they oppose singular people to an abstraction. In sum, they maintain that the singularity of the people, shaped through the course of history, is the only possible source of law and humanity. The conservative thinkers tend as a result to fall into the opposite excess, denying the principle of heteronomy that exists in the Law—a principle of great importance that ensures that Law is not merely a rationalization of the existing order, blind to the Other, to the alien in this case; a principle that guarantees that the Law is not founded on a fragmented concept of humanity. In their thinking, the singular tends to mask man, to the point that there is no more humanity, but only different species of men shaped by history. On the other side, the *Declaration* perspective sees only humanity and no peoples, except as modalities or as an infrahumanity, that is, as a biological "species" ("ethnic" groups). Savigny links history to the organic, the living organism, necessity, and law. "The substance of law is determined by the whole of a nation" and is not "the result of arbitrary decisions" but "emerges from the innermost spirit of the nation and its history."[92] This history is continuous: "Every period [. . .] is in an indissociable community with the whole of the past,"[93] which is what makes it implacably singular, in the sense that it is the opposite of the universal. History becomes in this way the arena in which the people unfolds as a singular "organism" in its relationship to other peoples and as a totality in relation to its members. But this organism can also age and grow senile, and, according to Savigny, the breakdown of the national identity of declining peoples ineluctably produces the universalist illusion, as they project their natural historical singularity onto the screen of the universal.[94] This is the symptom of a weakening in the identity of a people and the consequence of the reasoning behind the "rights of Man." One cannot avert the need to reiterate—even indirectly—the singular, national substance that the rights of man will not recognize and condemns. Without it, no society based on the rights of man can survive in historical reality. "There are people who hold their legal concepts and opinions to be purely rational simply because they ignore their provenance."[95] A relativistic sociological observation before its time!

In sum, I would say that behind the French Revolution's *Declaration of the Rights of Man and the Citizen* stood the French people in its national singularity, unacknowledged and hidden but omnipresent and decisive. This was evidently what a German at the time would have thought about the Napoleonic invasion to "liberate" the European peoples from the old regime and rule in the name of a power that was strictly French, not universal, to German eyes. The Napoleonic conquests led to the resurgence of nations and nationalism in Europe. German romanticism also paradoxically reacted against the legal universalism of the Enlightenment, as if a concept necessarily brings with it its counter-concept. Savigny consequently pitted the people against man and saw the source of law in the former. I will return to the highly problematical nature of this stance later; for the time being, suffice it to say that it is symptomatic of the unacknowledged impasse to which the philosophy of human rights had led and on which a good number of theorists insist: If man is the source of law (and the basis of citizenship), who if not the people, if not the assembly of sovereign people, is in a position to implement this production of law? When it comes to bringing law into actual effect, behind man unconsciously stands the people, which means that it is the people that defines man. Even if the people is thought of—in the best of cases—as a "civic nation," it nevertheless bears the mark of its singular history and identity. Modern, democratic, political communities may have claimed to be universal, but they were established on the basis of historical peoples. This collective singularity and identity (the "people" in my terminology), left out of human rights thinking, stand at the core of democracy's dark side and have been the source of modern catastrophes. To a certain extent, the mystery of this social unconscious became the focus of study of the discipline of sociology that emerged in nineteenth-century Europe with the resurgence of peoplehood in the form of nationalism and class struggles. It is only after having taken the analysis of this syndrome to completion that we will have sufficient grounds to tackle the definition of the "people."

This impasse is something that Hegel clearly perceived, and he tried to find a way out of it. In his conception, history and the existential condition of peoples are not solely an empirical matter. Rejecting the dilemma of the universal and the particular, he sees universal Reason, "the world mind," at work in the history of particular peoples; in his famous "dialectic," the particular and the universal are moments of a single whole. Hegel picks up Savigny's criticism of abstract rationality, but he also criticizes the nonabstract rationality that Savigny opposes to it with his *Science of Law*. Hegel seeks to reconcile the people and the law in the state that he sees as the entity in which the contradiction constitutive of modernity will be resolved. He believes that "the individual's destiny is the living of a universal life."[96] "The state of nature," as conceived by the Enlightenment, does not underpin civil society, which is pure fiction if it is not "altered" to form a state. Without the state, the people are but a mob, an uncontrolled, shapeless mass, an inert substance. Popular sovereignty is that of the state, not of the people. This is why the rights of the individual (and not of man) are grounded first in those of the state, and thereafter in those of the "world mind." Hegel opposes the individual to the Man of the *Declaration* not as an empirical individual but as a "determinate universality."[97] In Binoche's words, "If every man is a man, he exists only as a Jew, a Catholic, etc.—that is, as integrated in a network of mediations that defines 'the concrete life of the state.' "

But the opposite is also true: "A man counts as 'a man in virtue of his manhood alone, not because he is a Jew, Catholic, Protestant, German, Italian, etc. This is an assertion which thinking ratifies and to be conscious of it is of infinite importance. It is defective only when it is crystallized, e.g., as a cosmopolitanism in opposition to the concrete life of the state."[98] Thus at bottom, the singular is lodged in an economy of the universal that recognizes it in order to surpass it by uplifting it, and that uplifts it by negativizing it. But lifting it up into what precisely? Into the state that does not appear, as Hegel thinks, in transcendence and elevation (*aufhebung*), as the apogee of the world mind but as a universalization of the singularity. The people, hidden in the negative, are elevated into the apotheosis of the state, which forgets that it is a product of singularity and identifies henceforth with the world, with reason, and with the universal. Hegel's judgment about the French Revolution, that "it was a glorious dawn," but that it ended in a monstrous spectacle, could well be turned against his own vision of the state as apotheosis. Ultimately, the philosopher takes the reasoning behind the *Declaration* to its highest pitch, even as he condemns it. The state that Hegel defends is the state arising from the revolution that supposedly "integrated" its contrary, integrated the people within it, universalized the people and the singular identity in the state, instead of safeguarding the realm of the universal while recognizing the singular *in its place*.

Integrating the singularity of the people into the universality of the state is as problematical as defending the people against the state or the state against the people. It ends up universalizing and inflating singularity, instead of making it a moveable component of universality. This is exactly what Marx notes in his critique of Hegel, and the illusion of universality in a state that Marx regards as a screen concealing a liberal, "bourgeois democracy." Marx does not, however, revert to Savigny's organicism of the law or Burke's conservative outlook. To Marx, Man appears as an ideological screen concealing the pseudo-universality of bourgeois reason, but he does not find the people hidden behind the universal in the form of the state. What he discovers, on the other hand, instead of the people is the "class," the proletariat; this is, in fact, another way of thinking of historicity and the collective being, which had become inconceivable in the context of the *Declaration* with its conception of *man* as referent. Furthermore, Marx thinks of class in the context of history, of historical developments and class struggles: this is his theory of historical materialism.

Hence, Marx dismisses the people (conservatism) and the absolute state (Hegel) but brings in the notion of the class, which is another way of defining the "people" (the proletariat is portrayed as a genuine "people") not as absolute referent but as the vehicle of a process leading to a sort of state over and above the state: the Communist society that will emerge after the dictatorship of the proletariat, where singularity will ultimately be subsumed by the universal. It is easy to see the appeal of Marx's reasoning (refractory to the two opposing outlooks that divided Europe after the 1789 revolution) on the Jews who were being rejected by the nations of Europe because they were a people apart and were being admitted into the states on condition that they renounce their affiliation with this people, that is, admitted as individuals. But clearly the greatest enemy of the proletariat thus defined (a people invented from scratch, theoretically and practically, to serve as a referential principle) was the real "people" from which it came but which is supposed to reject it precisely because it is exploited, alienated, and deprived of identity by the dominant bourgeoisie. The (patriotic, national) invocation of the people appears to Marx to be the height of mystification. Collective identity and culture as a whole are pure fictions meant to cloud the mind of the proletariat and its awareness of its plight. The "people" is nothing but a false picture of the collective being and community whose future lies in the Communist society.

According to Binoche, Babeuf, before Marx, argued that "the 'man' of the Declaration can hide the bourgeois," and Marx held that "the 'man' of the rights of man is *always* a pseudo-universal,"[99] "for each new class which puts itself in the place of one ruling before it, is compelled [. . .] to give its ideas the form of universality, and represent them as the only rational, universally valid ones."[100] The bourgeois is convinced that he epitomizes man but in fact man is divided into classes, and among them the genuine man is the proletarian, whom Marx portrays almost as if he were the "suffering servant" of Isaiah who, according to Christian theology, personifies the suffering of mankind, so much so that the proletariat is raised from the rank of one class among others, to serve as the vehicle of the classless society to come. Marx's negative portrayal of the bourgeois as "egoistic man," as "man separated from other men and from the community,"[101] sheds light on his total conception of collective being. The Communist "community" is Marx's representation of the "people," but it is a community that will not put up with separation—that is, with singularity. Marx criticizes the separation between man and the citizen, in the name of the (Communist) community, but it is significant that he criticizes, in the same breath, Jewish singularity insofar as it is separated from all others (which is precisely what singularity is about). In this regard, the division between the private and public spheres that is the framework in liberal democracies for Jewish and civil affiliation strikes Marx in *On the Jewish Question* as the very paradigm of separation and illusion, since Marx sees in the Jew not a "people" but a "religion"; and, as we know, of course, he considers religion "the opium of the *people*" (emphasis added), the epitome of alienation, the locus of man's separation from his true self in humanity (projected onto a god because he cannot assume it himself). Binoche sums up Marx's position as follows: "The fact that I can be Jewish and a citizen at the same time proves that citizenship (political emancipation) does not free me in any way from religious alienation—which is henceforth a mere manifestation among others of legal alienation."[102] The criticism that Marx levels at the economy of human rights in its relationship to the Jew has nothing to do with the fact that the Jew as a legally recognized citizen does not really enjoy civic rights (in the manner of the proletarian, who does not enjoy property rights because he possesses nothing, even though the *Declaration* officially formulates these rights). He deplores the fact that it gives the Jew the right to be Jewish. And Jewishness, to Marx, is a congenital sign of alienation. The fact that citizens in the bourgeois democracy can be at the same time in their private lives Jews or Christians is the telltale sign of the persistence of alienation in democracy. According to Marx, the issue is not the state's emancipation from religion, which is the process that opens the civic sphere in the bourgeois democracy—with religion becoming a potential, private prerogative, like property rights, which are supposedly equal but are not necessarily in actual fact. It is not enough to have "rights" if they are not realized and incarnated. "The political emancipation from religion is not a religious emancipation that has been carried through to completion and is free from contradiction, because political emancipation is not a form of human emancipation which has been carried through to completion and is free from contradiction."[103] Marx sees Judaism (and Christianity) as an alienated state of the human condition. The Jew is not a man. The real issue to Marx is man's emancipation from the state. "The question of the relation of political emancipation to religion becomes for us the question of the relation of political emancipation to human emancipation."[104] "Only when the real, individual man re-absorbs in himself the abstract citizen [. . .] will human emancipation have been accomplished."[105] There must be no "separation" of human beings: neither Jew nor Greek, neither male nor female, as Paul would have said.

Marx sees the continued existence of the Jew in the citizen as evidence of the persistence of alienation in democracy. The citizen is a reverse illusion, the counterfeit flip side of man who is in reality the egotistic bourgeois; man is supposed to benefit from the universal and equality when he lives in the worst form of separation. This leads Marx too to conceive of the man of the *Declaration* as a hoax. Yet he does not attach any historical value to the paradoxical experience of Jewish singularity. And in this respect, in his own way, he shares the prejudices of the 1789 revolutionaries who saw in the Jew a degenerated form of humanity and hoped to release the Jews from this condition by admitting them to a humanity that would be universal and anonymous. Thus Marx accepts democratic universality totally, even as he criticizes it radically. This deep-seated contradiction in Marxism was to manifest itself later in world history, in the question of nations and nationalities, and in the question of peoplehood, that Marxist theory could not resolve. The socialist movement was consumed by this contradiction. If Communism was internationalist (and according to the *Communist Manifesto* "working men have no country," since they are without property and consequently deprived of the possibility of enjoying civic rights, which excludes them de facto from their own countries), then how could the class struggle be pursued, since it required the framework of a country and a nation? "For Marx, nations are not the content of revolutionary action; they are merely the forms inside which the only driving force in history—the class struggle—operates."[106] The international Communist movement was "poisoned by this question,"[107] because it was overwhelmed in the end by the resurgence of nations that it had denied in theory. But it is possible to regard the Marxist conception of the proletariat as indirectly reincorporating the nation: the members of the proletariat, excluded from all nations, are called upon to form an (anti-)nation, a nation that is like the negative of the nations from which they were excluded. In fact, the proletariat is destined, in the course of its expansion, to become coextensive with all of humanity and all nations. It is in this sense, by the agency of proletarian fellowship, that the advent of Communism will correspond to the advent of humanity, in the manner, here again, of a super-people: the community inherent to Communism is premised upon the people. By freeing man from his alienation, that is, from the singularity detached from the "universal," from the particularization that is the result of the division of labor and social classification, Communism will restore absolute humanity and abolish separation. From this standpoint, the people is obviously but an alienating ploy from which men need to break free. Paradoxically, despite his criticism of the democratic state, Marx sticks quite close to the absolute state, in a conception of an abstract "universal" humanity that is necessarily related to a similar, typically Hegelian representation. This may well be the repressed and unconscious source of the totalitarianism that Marxism was to engender thereafter.

The Savage Return of the Nation

The people resurfaced surreptitiously en masse (as much in theory as in actual fact) not only in the Communist movement that had set out to redeem the *Declaration*'s theoretical man but in every arena of democratic politics, with the collapse of the illusions represented by the Napoleonic empire—illegitimate child of 1789—and with the revolutions of 1848, the Spring of Nations. The repressed people returned, however, not as the people but as the "nation," a new entity that emerged under the influence of the French Revolution (and its ideal of popular sovereignty) and in the opposition to its warlike expansionism by the peoples of Europe.

With the *levee en masse* (mass conscription) in 1793, universal suffrage (which—to implement the principle of political equality—took the citizens as a single body) led to compulsive military service for all (thereby turning every citizen into a soldier). And it was in war that the people was transfigured into the nation, in war that the "nation" was forged not only in the country of the Rights of Man and of the revolution but also, in reaction, in all of the European empires that did not fail in the decades that followed to adopt universal conscription (if not citizenship).

The philosophy of human rights had not anticipated this national phenomenon, which came as a surprise and defied its rationality by acting like a pathological return of the repressed. The new age began under the banner of human rights and culminated in a brand-new phenomenon: a total war (that of 1914) that pitted entire peoples en masse against one another rather than the nearly private armies of professional mercenaries of monarchic potentates. It was as if war manifested the irrepressible return of the repressed in the serene, elevated discourse of human rights, a discourse that was unable to account for the peoples that were to fight one another to the death.

The people had been left out citizenship and could not be conceived in its framework. The historical ties binding together individuals in the people were replaced by state-controlled ties upon which the affiliation to the nation was based. The nation served as a vehicle for the return of the repressed people, for the uncontrolled persistence of the people in citizenship. Unthought, peoplehood came back under the auspices of the state in the form of nationhood. The nation is the people under the ascendancy of the state, finalized and instrumentalized by the state. The nation—even the republican ideal of the civic nation—testifies to this unthought (unthinkable) dimension of the rights of man; the universe of citizenship had been proclaimed, but at the same time a very particular form of collective identity (the nation) was forged that was inscrutable. Incapable of fathoming what made citizenship livable in reality (a society generated over the course of history), human rights thinking was even less capable of comprehending the identity of sociality, which is necessarily singular every time. The singularity (and singularity is always a matter of concrete, nominative history) remained unthought and prohibited in modern universality. The brute character of this unthought dimension found pathetic expression in the era of warlike, xenophobic nationalisms and imperial and colonial conquests to which the French Revolution gave rise (against its conscience). There is good reason to see this nationalism as a premonitory symptom of totalitarianism, of "totalitarian democracy" (to borrow the title of Jacob Talmon's book), a (mad) attempt to eliminate the contradiction in the nation and the citizen, in the hermetic overlay of the two, just as Marx set out to establish a community without separation. It may be argued that the conception of *rights of man* has remained incomplete because it engendered something altogether different than what was produced in history. In this phenomenon that witnessed the people reemerging, disfigured, in the brute violence of nationalism, we can see a process comparable (albeit on a passive mode) to the phenomenon that witnessed the Jewish people reemerging in the catastrophe of the Shoah, allocated to the tragic condition of victim. In fact, nineteenth-century anti-Semitism had already brought the Jewish people savagely and irrationally back up to the surface, disfigured as a race. It is highly significant that nationalism was regularly anti-Semitic and xenophobic.

Why was it that a civic, political, and hence rational, abstract, and universal community reduced to individuals needed an "identity" that, for its part, had never gone through the purge of Reason and was wholly sustained by the identity of the majority people upon which the nation-state was built? What is at stake in this syndrome is the social bond in political modernity and in the democracy of the rights of man and the citizen. This, then, is the setting of the greatest failure of political modernity, the source of its greatest dramas. Democracy has shown itself to be a system in which men have a hard time getting together and creating a community without provoking a catastrophe. The nation has turned out to be a vital "need" for the state, which has proven to be incapable of assembling its citizens on the sole basis of a constitutional civic bond with no sufficient charismatic power to aggregate individuals (whence the fact that sociologists of religion saw nationalism as a "civic religion").

The "Crime of Being Born"

The Obscenity of the Native Condition of Men

In Freud's symbolic system, the object of repression does not cease to exist simply because it is no longer overtly manifested. It continues to work in secret on the conscious mind that was unable to face it (which is why it was repressed). The people was thus removed from the rational, conscious thinking behind the rights of man and the citizen and came back in the disfigured, fantasized form of the nation, the "return of the repressed" people. Singularity and historicity, being impossible to conceive, were biologized, racialized, and naturalized.

The Project of "Regenerating" Humankind

As we have seen,[1] the source of the racialization of Jews, despite their status as citizens, can be traced to democratic political modernity's removal of the Jewish people from history. The (silent) persistence of Jewish existence, despite the anonymity of the citizen and the eclipse of the people, was plain for all to see. And because a rational explanation had become inadmissible, Jewish continuity could only spring from an atavistic condition, a biological given beyond the reach of human thought and action. It could only be a fatality.

The Nazi discourse that "zoologized" (to use Alain Brossat's expression[2]) the Jews, like the irrational anti-Semitism that preceded it, designated the Jewish *people* using the only available means of naming it in modernity: in the unthinkable and prerational terms of race and biology.[3] This biologization of the Jewish condition constituted the first step and the ideological prerequisite of the dehumanization of the Jews in the camps, where they were reduced to the level of the most primitive vegetative life so that, having been relegated to a state of utter insignificance, they could be exterminated.

But this biological category was already present in the emancipation's project of "regenerating" the Jews, which entailed rehumanizing them by elevating the singular to the level of abstract universality. The Jews were already seen at the time as a (human) "genus," a "species," a generic category. The regeneration project had two objectives: redeeming Jewry, whose nature had been corrupted (a species of humanity whose fallen state was due to persecution), and giving these alleged *"bons sauvages"* (which the Jews were considered to be in spite of all) access to the political condition of the citizen. The primary aim of the regeneration was to reverse the degeneration of the Jews for which Europe was blamed.

Regeneration is a very strong term, and it is more than just symbolic, since it englobes the body and the physical nature of human beings. The subtitle of Abbé Grégoire's, *Apologie des Juifs*, says as much, explicitly: "Essay on the physical, moral and political regeneration of the Jews." The use of the word "physical" may seem strange in this context. Why would the Jews, as victims of social and political ostracism, need to be "physically" transformed? The reference evinced their "naturalization," in the (highly significant) sense of receiving the rights of citizenship but also of having their rational, discursive, and cultural personality (which had become unthinkable) reduced to a natural phenomenon, a brute fact, a matter of genus and species. This project of regeneration was an innovation in political history. It actually concerned all men, for all men needed to be regenerated. They had to be "recreated" to meet the exigencies of "Nature," the new reference that had been substituted for God. The revolutionaries set out to recreate society and the social bond on the tabula rasa of history. Only this regenerated man could become a citizen. The "physical" dimension of the regeneration is heavy with meaning. Henceforth, the political was to include the physical: the bodies of men had become a political object for a state power that set itself up as the institutor of humankind. As I have already said, it was the first time in history that a civilization set out to create a new man and to do so counting solely on its own forces. And the state was the supervisor of this project. "Man" implicated the state because of the abstraction of Man (which suited the rationality of the state), and because Man had become the purpose of political action (only the state could produce Man on a universal scale).

That this Promethean, demiurgic ambition characterizes modernity has been borne out by all of the major political ideologies to our day. The *Arbeit Macht Frei* slogan over the entrance to the concentration camps was a strident manifestation of this ambition. And did not the Communist "reeducation" camps and the gulags aim at changing men by bringing the recalcitrant to heel? These two ideologies constitute extreme caricatural instances of this ambition, but they count nonetheless among the consequences of the Enlightenment project, for the "ethics" of "regeneration" implies sacrifices and eventual damages that are deemed legitimate and justified because they are for a "good cause." Putting opponents in work camps, extermination camps, psychiatric hospitals, and so on can make sense in totalitarian regimes from the standpoint of the "regeneration" of humanity.

In the case of the Jews, the regeneration participated in a policy of "enlightened despotism." It was decisive for their admission to citizenship, because "to maintain that Jews are incapable of fulfilling the duties of society is to maintain that they are Jews more than they are men."[4] "What conclusion are we to draw from what we've just read? That the Jews are to be banished or destroyed? No! This proves even more demonstratively how important it is to regenerate the people."[5] In their writing and speeches, the emancipators set forth a complete program with the aim of making "the Jews happier and more useful in France."[6] The first step was to make the Jewish population settle down by giving them the right to own land ("the right to buy landed estates will tie the Jew to the locality and to the homeland"[7]). Paradoxically, to prove the feasibility of this plan, the emancipators drew on the ancient establishment of the Jews in Palestine as a model (they thus fell back on a model of a politically sovereign Jewish people just at the time the Jews were expected to become individual citizens). But care was to be taken to make sure that the Jews were scattered throughout the country. Their community structures were programmed to disappear. "We can leave them their communities and their leaders for a short while still,"[8] but in the future there would be public sessions held "where they can be trained and watched"[9] and compulsive education in view of their rapid assimilation. Above all, they must be put to work, because "we have been deprived too long of the industry of a people that could have contributed to public prosperity."[10] A veritable plan for the economic integration of the Jews emerged; mention was made of settlement on uncultivated land, the construction of factories and, surprisingly enough, commerce, evoked particularly in the hopes of stemming the flight of Jewish capital to the English enemy! The idea was also entertained of taking advantage of the Diaspora's international network to strengthen the diplomatic relations of France. In short, the emancipators sought to "attach to France a hardworking, mercantile nation that can only invigorate and foster commerce, and attract abundant wealth to the kingdom."[11] Such lines of reform show the extent to which the conscious intention of regeneration contradicts the unconscious expectations that go with it: the aim may have been to make a new man of the Jew, but what is unconsciously expected of the Jewish citizen is modeled on the old paradigm of the Jew. One could hardly get closer to the core of the paradox of modern politics.

The Ambiguity of "Nature": The Biological Condition of Women, Blacks, and Jews

With the new man conceived in terms of "genus," the *regeneration* could only lead to the biologization of all those who fell outside the formal rationality of the rights of man. Henceforth, the conception of "Nature" was divided: it no longer referred to the abstract order of the universal (that underpinned the rights of man) but to the infrarational and the biological. As we have seen, Hannah Arendt analyzes this question in terms of the dysfunctions of the principle of equality. In a political culture where equality between men is a cardinal principle, she argues, it is likely that people who fall outside the norm (and it is inevitable that they do because they are different from one another, not "equal") will be considered "abnormal": an individual "is 'normal' if he is like everybody else and 'abnormal' if he happens to be different."[12]

The "perversion of equality from a political into a social concept" makes the differences between "special groups and individuals" "all the more conspicuous."[13] "And it has been precisely this new concept of equality that has made modern race relations so difficult, for there we deal with natural differences that by no possible and conceivable change of conditions can become less conspicuous."[14] Arendt argues that this concerns all citizens: "To all appearances new classes developed as groups to which one belonged by birth. There is no doubt that it was only in such a framework that society could suffer the Jews to establish themselves as a special clique."[15] "In such a society [the United States], discrimination becomes the only means of distinction, a kind of universal law according to which groups may find themselves outside the sphere of civic, political, and economic equality."[16] This concept of equality can neither accept nor conceive of difference (the "people," identity, gender, race, etc.), even though difference is what structures reality. As a result, such irreducible differences assume the appearance of something monstrous, excessive, and "abnormal." A "people" becomes an imaginary "race," demoted to the rank of a biological condition. We have already examined in detail Arendt's description of the ambiguous attitude toward the Jews in fashionable salons. It was because fashionable circles believed in the "exceptional" character (the genius) of some Jews that distinguished them from others that they accepted them as their equals. This difference founded on exception was thus very much like exceptions to the rule and exceptions to the norm (and hence to the transgression of norms in all forms), which is why the salon Jew found himself in the company of the homosexual. For fashionable circles, having prohibited relations with such riffraff provided them with a titillating occasion to distinguish themselves from their fellow creatures. Arendt's evocation of the Proustian figure of the homosexual clearly underscores the focus of attention on the corporeal, and in this case on the sexual. Jewishness thus found itself likened, by those who celebrated it, to a "perversion" of the body, outside the norm.

The mechanism of biologization is even more explicit in Sartre's essay. He argues at length that Jews are attracted to rationalism in order to escape from their own bodies: "They do not feel toward their bodies that complacency, that tranquil sentiment of property which characterizes most 'Aryans.' "[17] "The inauthentic Jew is deprived of his vital values by the Christian. If he becomes conscious of his body, the concept of race immediately appears to poison his intimate sensations."[18] "It is obvious that people introduce a great number of these biological values into the concept of *race*. Is not race itself a pure vital value?"[19] "In the very name of *universal* man, he refuses to lend an ear to the private messages his organism sends him: [. . .]. Universality being for him at the summit of the scale of values, he conceives of a *universal and rationalized body*. He does not have an ascetic's disdain for his body, he does not call it a 'rag' or a 'beast,' but neither does he see it as an object of veneration. Insofar as he does not actually forget it, he treats it as an instrument."[20] "[W]hat is the good of veiling a body that the gaze of the Aryans has denuded once and for all? To be a Jew in the eyes of the world—is that not worse than being naked?"[21] What an analogy! Being a Jew and being a naked man!

Oddly enough, Sartre broadens his picture of the condition of the Jew to cover that of Arabs, Negroes, and more especially women. "[T]he Jews—and likewise the Arabs and the Negroes," have the rights of citizens "*as* Jews, Negroes, or Arabs—that is, as concrete persons. In societies where women vote, they are not asked to change their sex when they enter the voting booth; the vote of a woman is worth just as much as that of a man, but it is as a woman that she votes, with her womanly intuitions and concerns, in her full character of a woman. When it is a question of the legal rights of the Jew, and of the more obscure but equally indispensable rights that are not inscribed in any code, he must enjoy those rights not as a potential Christian but precisely as a French Jew. It is with his character, his customs, his tastes, his religion if he has one, his name, and his physical traits that we *must* accept him."[22] By describing the Jewish condition and its relationship to the environment in corporeal terms and comparing it to the condition of women and blacks, Sartre is underscoring the fact that the Jew, the woman, or the black man is repressed in the citizen, in a way that is intrinsic to citizenship itself.

The comparison takes on added significance here, because we can deduce from it that those categories that manifest a difference (be they Jews, women, or blacks) are kept out of citizenship insofar as they are what they are. It was as if they could only enjoy civic rights if they denied their own identity, an identity that cannot be acknowledged and that certainly cannot be assumed in citizenship, because citizenship is not intended for such categories. It is for this reason that Jewishness, "femininity," or negritude was seen as racial, sexual, biological, natural, and nonrational (and today as manifestations of ethnic separatism or *communautarisme*). This is an ideological ascription, not a judgment based on fact: Jews, women, and blacks are "construed" as "others" who cannot be rationally and consciously apprehended and who therefore find themselves consigned to the infrarational, when it is not to a status of inferiority. Needless to say, the Jewish "race" does not exist, feminine identity reduced to gender is pure fiction, and negritude reduced to skin color is sheer stupidity. But one should be wary of concluding, on the basis of proof by contradiction, that we are dealing here with a model of citizenship that is purely and simply an invention by Christian white European males, as disciples of "gender studies" and other politically correct schools of thought are wont to do. That the altruism of Enlightenment philosophy was replete with triumphant ethnocentrism is an obvious fact, but there is a more abstract, more fundamental failure, a congenital flaw in political modernity that needs to be emphasized. Democratic citizenship was shaken by the "blow" of reality. It sought to promote an equality (restrictively political and legal, Marx would say) that could not be applied in the real world, because this equality could not bear the weight of everything that constitutes reality: there are, in fact, peoples, identities, surnames, women, men, blacks, Chinese, and so on. As such, all of these categories are barred from citizenship because their religious, cultural, sexual, or ethnical difference supposedly stands in the way of the "universal." It is a definition of man that is the point at issue. Perhaps the referent of equality is to be found elsewhere, and equality is to be promoted in another way? This is what I will be examining at the end of this discussion.

The history of democracy has shown the problematical character of the citizenship of the aforementioned categories of citizens. We have looked at the case of the Jews during the revolution, but this was also true for women and blacks. The historical facts are plain to see: the revolutionary men were not planning on granting women access to citizenship. In 1804, the Civil Code reasserted the total legal incapacity of married women, and it was not until 1944 that French women acquired the right to vote and hold office! The fact that gender parity and quotas of equal representation for men and women in government are still topical issues today attests to the persistence of a de facto discrimination. As for blacks, the National Assembly meeting to discuss the French colonies and the status of slaves decided against allowing slaves and people of color (around 1 million people) to benefit from the rights of man but granted citizenship to the whites in the colonies, thus confining the rights of man to Europeans only. It was not until 1793 that the Constitution condemned the "*Code noir*" of 1685 that regulated slavery in France (and that considered slaves merchandise), and not until 1794 that slavery was abolished. But Napoleon reestablished the *Code noir* in 1802. The blacks (in Guadeloupe) regained their rights forty-six years later, thanks to the struggle of Victor Schoelcher. And let us not forget the case of the United States: one of the greatest democracies in the world made do with a system of racial segregation until 1954, and this moral stain did not seem to otherwise impede its "normal functioning." Even today, Afro-Americans suffer from a discrimination that is a social structural reality despite legal and political efforts to combat it. In this regard, some of Tocqueville's comments in the nineteenth century are not without present-day relevance: "I do not imagine that the white and black races will ever live in any country upon an equal footing." "And it may be foreseen that the freer the white population of the United States becomes, the more isolated will it remain."

The Europeans "first violated every right of humanity by their treatment of the negro and they afterwards informed him that those rights were precious and inviolable. They affected to open their ranks to the slaves, but the negroes who attempted to penetrate into the community were driven back with scorn"; "The negroes may long remain slaves without complaining; but if they are once raised to the level of free men, they will soon revolt at being deprived of all their civil rights; and as they cannot become the equals of the whites, they will speedily declare themselves as enemies."[23]

Blacks Outside the Confines of Humanity

Even before examining the historical developments, a look at the emancipators' discourse concerning women and blacks throughout the eighteenth century evidences the same problematical outlook that we have seen in relation to the Jews. How can one fail to notice that the subject of "emancipation" itself is exclusively focused on Jews, women, and blacks, and, generally speaking, slaves? The debates of enlightenment luminaries and revolutionaries on the colonial question and whether "the rights of man could be extending to an extra-European area reveals a developed discourse"[24] on the natural inferiority of the blacks who, due to their origins, are declared unfit for citizenship. Paradoxically (and therein lies its ambiguity), the same Nature that supposedly underpins the right of all men to citizenship is invoked as grounds for refusing citizenship to blacks. "This nature becomes [. . .] the referent that authorizes and justifies the exception."[25] It is the basis of a doctrine of natural determinism: "Each people has its own peculiar nature, its own distinctive character [. . .] it is mad enterprise, a pointless philosophical dream to try to change it."[26] "We have reason to doubt that our new Constitution can be applied to distant regions. The difference in climate is reason enough to check our enthusiasm for humanity."[27] "It is to be feared that too much haste will only delay the happiness of our colored brethren; feeble eyes must be prepared for the flood of light that is about to strike them."[28] Ascribing the inferiority of the blacks to their tropical environment, Mirabeau concluded that "their insouciance, their laziness, their aversion to work are natural."[29]

The influence of Montesquieu on such political climatology is patent. "But as all men are born equal, slavery must be accounted unnatural, though in some countries it be founded on natural reason; and a wide difference ought to be made between such countries, and those in which even natural reason rejects it, as in Europe, where it has been so happily abolished."[30] Montesquieu is basically arguing here that the universality of the principle of equality does not stand up to the diversity of climates. This quotation clearly evinces the shift in the sense of "Nature" from a supposedly universal concept and a source of ethics to a matter of biology outside the sphere of the universal. In his major work, Montesquieu delivers a whole series of very negative cut-and-dry judgments about "inferior" peoples in the world.[31] The author of the entry on Negroes in the *Encyclopédie* agrees with him about the condition of blacks: "Their nature demands that they be treated with neither too much indulgence nor too much severity." Because of this congenital inferiority due to the climate in which they live that has modified their very nature as human beings (a claim that is supported by French zoologist Buffon's studies[32]), blacks are not perfectible by nature. They cannot even be reeducated, and regeneration cannot be applied to them! Like animals ("Negro women," Voltaire declared, "transported to the coldest countries still produce animals of their own species"[33]), they cannot escape the laws of nature. Blacks were often positioned on the borderline between animality and humanity and the question of whether they are really men came up with even more insistence than in the case of the Jews. In *Observations on the Feeling of the Beautiful and the Sublime*, the illustrious philosopher Emmanuel Kant (who had never left the place where he was born and never had a relationship with a woman—the very same philosopher who advocated "the euthanasia of Judaism") maintained that "[t]he religion of fetishes so widespread among [the Negroes] is perhaps a sort of idolatry that sinks as deeply into the trifling as appears to be possible to human nature."[34] And elsewhere, he approvingly cites Hume as asserting "that among the hundreds of thousands of blacks who are transported elsewhere from their countries, although many of them have even been set free, still not a single one was ever found who presented anything great in art or science or any other praiseworthy quality"![35] Significantly, it is around the question of their perfectibility that the defense is organized by partisans of their emancipation. "Aren't they as capable as whites of improvement in the sciences and the arts?,"[36] cried one emancipator. And Victor Schoelcher ironically commented: "As far as I am concerned, it has been demonstrated to me that the negroes are a variety of a species of animal called man, and for the single reason that they are men, they are free by right."[37]

Like the Jews, the degraded state of the Negroes (and on this point everyone agrees) is not their fault. Their advocates ascribe it to slavery. Diderot and Raynal complain: "You've neglected nothing when it comes to degrading these wretched people, and then you reproach them for being worthless."[38] "In other words, the African became what the white man wanted him to be."[39] Condorcet illustrates this attitude to perfection. Negroes "have become incapable of fulfilling the function of free men"[40] as a result of their state of enslavement for which their masters are responsible, not nature. This incapacity is very deeply embedded in their psychological makeup, which is why they will have to go through a period of "preparation" before assuming civic responsibilities. They will have to be "subjected [. . .] in the initial period to severe discipline regulated by laws"; the "task of guiding them" will be confided to "firm, enlightened, and incorruptible" men.[41] These men are the colonists who are to educate blacks to freedom during a period of time set at seventy years.

Like the Jews again, the anticipated outcome of this process will not be the recognition of the reality and identity of blacks but racial blending, with the black diluted among the whites. "There is no room in this framework for accepting the Other as someone different [. . .]. Once his strangeness is abolished, he will be [the philosopher's] equal, because he will be exactly like him in every respect [. . .] his future as a free, reasonable man depends on freeing himself from everything that characterizes him as a black man."[42]

Women Outside the Confines of Citizenship

"Nature" is also invoked as grounds for barring women from citizenship. This exclusion seemed so self-evident to the revolutionaries that they made few declarations on the subject. Only after a woman's revolutionary club, the *Club des citoyennes républicaines révolutionnaires*, was founded on May 10, 1793, did the revolutionaries feel the need to react. Fabre d'Eglantine mocked these women as "adventuresses, female knights-errant, emancipated girls, and amazons."[43] The club was suppressed by the government, and Olympe de Gouges, its guiding spirit, was guillotined. A feminist from the early days of the revolution, de Gouges was keenly aware of the blindness of the

Declaration concerning women. On September 14, 1791, she published her *Declaration of the Rights of Woman and the Female Citizen.* The first article states: "Woman is born free and equal to man in rights." Article two states that the purpose of "political association is the conservation of the natural and imprescriptible rights of woman and man," and article three declares that the nation is "nothing but the union of man and woman." The "postcript" to her declaration starts with the words: "Woman, wake up!"

Saint-Just, for his part, defended a republican morality in which the role of the woman was to procreate for the benefit of the republic, which has the obligation to step in and separate childless couples who do not fulfill their duty to the state (one more example of the exercise of state power over the body!). Robespierre assigns to women the role of "giving birth to heroes" ready to die for their country. The whole era was under the influence of Rousseau's ideas on the role of women as formulated in *Émile ou De l'éducation*, which was a main source of inspiration for the anti-feminine ideology of the period. Once again, it is "Nature" that was said to oppose the equality of the sexes. Women are predestined to the private sphere and to a strictly moral life because of the specific physiological reality that is theirs (pregnancy, nursing, etc.). Since one cannot change the facts of nature, this is a biological fatality. A woman who knows her nature and therefore her duty is better than a learned woman: "If there were none but wise men upon earth [the learned woman] would die an old maid."[44] There is no reason to alter nature's decree: "This inequality is not at all a human institution, or at least it is not the work of prejudice."[45] This is the ground and the principles upon which women must be educated, because respect of this inequality protects women, whose capacities are often limited, and works to preserve the proper order of society. In the same spirit, we have Kant maintaining that "a woman at any age is a minor civilly, and the husband is her natural guardian [. . .]. These creatures cannot defend their rights or take care of civil affairs by themselves anymore than they can go to war."[46] Mirabeau agreed that women have a "delicate constitution" that predestines them to "perpetuating the species and attending with solicitude to the perilous moments of infancy."[47]

As for the defenders of women, they proceeded in the same way as for Jews and blacks. Condorcet, who was exemplary from this standpoint, pitted against the supposedly "natural laws" the force of habit that pushes democrats to refuse equality of rights to women. Women were unable to develop their capacities because they had been confined to the duties of wives and mothers by men. Condorcet thought that men were responsible for the degenerate condition of women, but he did not deny that women were in a state of degeneracy. To him, the refusal to grant citizenship to women was a sign of a return to the elitist aristocratic morality against which the revolution fought.[48] The principle of women's inferiority was in keeping with the spirit of the ancien régime and incompatible with the spirit of the *Declaration*. But Condorcet failed in his day to gain recognition for women as citizens.

The Unthinkable Native Principle

What exactly is at issue in this biologization that puts categories of human beings outside the pale of rationality and citizenship (women and blacks fundamentally and from the outset; Jews sporadically, under the Third Reich and Vichy)? It is tempting to respond in reference to the alterity, difference, and otherness embodied by these categories, but such a response, assuredly justified, only scratches the surface of the question. We are dealing here with a much broader problem, one that concerns political modernity as a whole and not merely one aspect thereof.

It reflects a structural contradiction that can be pinpointed by comparing the strange notion of creating a new man (the "regeneration") with the idea stated in the first article of the *Declaration of the Rights of Man and the Citizen*, that "men are born and remain free and equal in rights." If the fundamental rights of man (liberty and equality) are derived from mere birth, from the prosaic (and eminently passive) fact of being *born*, then how are we to understand the project of "regeneration" and especially the act of "declaring" rights on the basis of the authority derived from humankind? The declaration actually implies that it is an assembly of Humanity that is the source of these rights and that creates the new man. Once again we are faced with the ambiguity of the concept of Nature that we have already discussed: at once abstract and universal (the "human nature" and the natural order of the world that exists independently from the individual and that is the source of the *Declaration*) but also an empirical reality (birth is the prerequisite for citizenship, and every birth is unique). The term *naturalization* is revealing in this respect because it designates both the acquisition of a nationality, and hence of citizenship, and also the act or process of bringing something down from the sky of ideas to empirical reality. And empirical reality has everything to do with the principle of particularization, detail, and the singular, and not with universalization conceived as an abstraction of the particular.

We have here the symbolic construction that explains the terms of the Jews' admission to citizenship: Nature dictates that they are born men—and they were acknowledged as such by the emancipators—but citizenship dictates that they renounce the very conditions of their birth, namely, their Jewishness. Civic naturalization supersedes natural birth, despite the fact that natural birth is stated in the *Declaration* to be the source of citizenship. The paradox, if not the contradiction, between rights and empirical reality that Marx denounced is manifest here. The Jews are citizens because they are born men (when in fact they are born Jewish), and because they are citizens, they are no longer Jews.

The least we can say is that we have here much less of a problem of recognition of others and hospitality than a problem of birth, of the native principle of man that remained unresolved and unthinkable in the symbolic system of the *Declaration*. The latter is wholly grounded in the very native principle that it so skillfully represses. The first three articles of the Declaration of August 26, 1789, are telling in this respect.

> Article 1. Men are born and remain free and equal in rights. Social distinctions can be based only on public utility.

> Article 2. The aim of every political association is the preservation of the natural and imprescriptible rights of man. These rights are liberty, property, security, and resistance to oppression.

> Article 3. The source of all sovereignty resides essentially in the nation. No body, no individual, can exercise authority that does not proceed from it in plain terms.[49]

But from where does this nation come as if by magic? What on earth could possibly found this nation other than the state? Although it is true that the term *nation* etymologically means birth, it is not because one is born that one belongs to a nation. Birth has to be confirmed and construed by the state. Thus the state would be the source of the *Declaration* and the source of the natural rights of man. That this is the case we have already seen from the postrevolutionary ideological controversy and the Arendtian analysis. We can grasp here the full force of the contradiction: it is because men are born that they are sovereign, but without the power that confirms this birth, without the power that embodies the authority derived from nature, nature remains null and void.

This is substantiated by the fact that men (and therefore peoples), as Arendt says, who do not benefit from the protection of a state do not in fact benefit from "[t]he Rights of Man, supposedly inalienable [but which] proved to be unenforceable—whenever people appeared who were no longer citizens of any sovereign state."[50] It is pointless to say that people have human rights, if these rights are not confirmed and supported by a state. Such peoples are merely "born." They have only birth for legitimacy. Theirs is an empirical not a theoretical nature. Arendt observes that to protect them there were only humanitarian organizations and not the society of states, and "When the Rights of Man became the object of an especially inefficient charity organization, the concept of human rights naturally was discredited a little more."[51]

The passage from birth to nation via the state masks the meaning of the native principle (which is manifested in the condition of people) and obfuscates the nation (which manifests the native principle through the prism of the state). Because the native principle at work in civic naturalization is neither acknowledged nor unraveled, it has lent itself to being "biologized" (via empirical naturalization) and relegated to the domain of the irrational, the singular, the particular. Because it was unthinkable, improper use could be made of the state and the nation (totalitarianism and nationalism). The nativity of man has thus remained the greatest mystery of political modernity. It is what stood in the way of full equality for Jews, women, and blacks and was an obstacle in the recognition of foreigners (not recognized as citizens, even though they were men[52]). No one knows how to deal with birth in democracy, and this means that no one knows how to deal with real men.

When we say today, after André Frossard,[53] that the Jews were exterminated solely for "the crime of being born," we are referring to all of these problems without knowing it. Throughout history, and even today, (Jewish) citizens have been reproached for remaining Jewish in their citizenship, because they were in fact born Jewish, and all of their pathetic efforts could do nothing to remove this "indelible stain." It is the citizen insofar as he is born a Jew who poses a problem. Citizenship could not annihilate the Jew's birth. As far as the blacks were concerned, their skin color all too blatantly called to mind a natural condition that clashed with "universal" (meaning uniform) civic naturalization. And women had a different sex; worse, this sex symbolized temporality and change (through the menstrual cycle) and generative power (through childbirth). Each of these three categories was then, in its own way, too reminiscent of empirical nature, of the fact of being born, for all those who believed in a theoretical nature springing not from God or the natural order but from man (actually the state, as we have seen), and all those who adhered to an abstract human discourse that disregards the fact that man is a being that is born (and that is born from a woman to boot).

We thus see that empirical nature, henceforth biologized, irrationalized, ahistoricized, and particularized, was to be seen as an obstacle to ideological nature—that sublime value underpinning the democratic order—, an obstacle to the Promethean and demiurgic ambition of political modernity as the midwife of total man, under the empire of the state. "Man appeared as the only sovereign in matters of law as the people was proclaimed the only sovereign in matters of government. The people's sovereignty (different from that of the prince) was not proclaimed by the grace of God but in the name of Man, so that it seemed only natural that the 'inalienable' rights of man would find their guarantee and become an inalienable part of the right of the people to sovereign self-government."[54] Everything that was held to be a fact of nature appeared henceforth as a challenge to the power of human political association. Everything that was passively received—identity (which is always collective at the start), sex, or skin color—lost all constitutional dignity and was written off as detrimental to equality.

But that was precisely the problem. How could these irreducible differences, inherent in humanity, which is structured by them, be admitted in a world of equality and liberty? Such manifestations of nature had supposedly ceased to exist, so they became the object of repression, but they continued to "work" secretly on the very foundations of democracy, opening the way to all of the miscarriages. As the synthesis of all of the natural prisms, peoplehood became especially problematical. The people was no longer recognized as a given in the real world, with which one had to "make due." Instead, it took the form of a construct reinvented by the state, namely, the nation, that mysterious entity in which the violent return of the repressed was manifested. Since the nativity of citizens was acknowledged only by civic naturalization, it came back massively in the form of nationalism and racism. The construction of humanity that was the project of political modernity was thus tautologically structured like a magical circle excluding anything that could remind modern citizens that they were born, and that their sovereignty could not be absolute and total or that, at the very least, totality was not the principle of sovereignty.

Total Man and the End of Heteronomy

The magic circularity of birth and the nation, of theoretical nature that replaces empirical nature while becoming identified with it, draws our attention to the will for autonomy, and hence the refusal of heteronomy that characterizes the philosophy of the *Declaration*. In the universe of total man—who is all at once the source, the theater, and the actor of power— there is no exteriority, at least not avowed and recognized as such, as an interaction with alterity. If we return to the nineteenth-century controversy over the rights of man we can see the exact terms in which this problem was formulated. Again and again two questions were implicitly raised that highlighted what was judged to be the impasse in the conception of the universal. These questions may help us shed light on the circularity of total man. The ambition of universality was systematically faced with the questions of exteriority (or negativity) and anteriority (or historicity), which were two ways of challenging the tautology of the political as its own source.

Let us look, for instance, at Jeremy Bentham's (1748–1832) criticism of the inconsistency in the wording of the *Declaration*. Why declare property a universal right when it cannot be exercised by those who do not own property? If the first article declares that all men are equal in rights and the second that property counts among these rights,[55] then men should be equal in property, therefore, the national property should be divided into equal shares. The fact that there are still propertyless people means that the rights stated in the *Declaration* only legitimate actual property and the inequality that exists in reality. Thus the declaration of universal equality leaves someone out (the propertyless): someone is absent or is there only by default. We could apply the same reasoning to the dialectic of man and the citizen that we have been examining. All men are equal, but all men are not citizens. Foreigners, for instance, are not citizens. So the rights of the citizen that are declared to apply to all men and are grounded in the universal rights of man leave men out; they are absent by default (or in absentia).

To a certain extent, Marx develops the same reasoning as Bentham: "the so-called rights of man, the *droits de l'homme* as distinct from the *droits du citoyen*, are nothing but the rights of a member of civil society—i.e., the rights of egoistic man, of man separated from other men and from the community."[56] This *separation* materializes in his eyes the absence of *all* men in the man as citizen. The absolute citizen disregards the social characteristics of man, since all men are deemed equal, regardless of their social attributes. But here too, in civic as in economic terms, these positive attributes end up determining the fate of equality. The question of exteriority (the "absence") comes up in Marx's argument too, and he condemns it as the quintessential sign of alienation. Likewise, Marx considers the fact that the citizen can also be "Jewish" as evidence that (religious) alienation is lodged within citizenship, and this suffices to delegitimate it. In the conception of man, what remains in the negative, in absentia within the positivization of the citizen, is interpreted as the symptom of abstraction and illusion that man projects on the crude and "egoistic" reality of the citizen.

This negativity, highlighted by the critics of the rights of man, is often raised by the liberal, conservative current as a problem related to the source and legitimacy of rights in the *Declaration* as coming from man and not God or tradition. If man is the source of the citizen (guardian and actor of this humanity), then what is the source of man? Where does he spring from? The tautological circularity of the *Declaration*—and its impossibility, at once theoretical and practical—is taken to task from this standpoint. Burke observes, in this regard, that the sovereignty upon which the government is founded and of which civil society is divested cannot proceed from man and an assembly of people, since the very existence of this civil society implies that sovereignty has been withdrawn from them (what makes civil society is the fact that it has conferred the power to judge upon someone in particular). "The moment you abate anything from the full rights of men, each to govern himself, and suffer any artificial, positive limitation upon those rights, from that moment the whole organization of government becomes a consideration of convenience,"[57] which means of convention. Unlike the critical current, the conservatives approach the *Declaration* not from the negative of man in the citizen but from the positive of the citizen in man. If, as Burke states, "No man should be judge in his own cause,"[58] then the source of sovereignty must be outside of man, and consequently sovereignty and authority cannot spring tautologically from man himself. They are based on convenience, tradition, and heritage. "The rights of men are in a sort of middle, incapable of definition, but not impossible to be discerned."[59] Unlike Marx, Burke regards the indetermination of the rights of men as giving tradition and history its legitimacy as opposed to the Contract. The real rights of nature are not natural rights (that would precede entry into citizenship based on the Contract) but rights proceeding from the continuity of generations. And the rights of man are outside of nature. Burke basically rejected the break that political modernity represented, insofar as it conceived of natural rights (rights of man) as transcending the rights of the citizen and governing them (Burke demonstrates the impossibility of this by his critique of sovereignty).

Joseph de Maistre develops a similar line of argument. Whereas the rights of the people (of citizens) can be fairly well determined by looking back at the course of history, the historical genealogy of sovereignty is lost in the mists of time. "The rights of the people, properly speaking, start fairly often from a concession by sovereigns, and in this case they can be established historically; but the rights of the sovereign and of the aristocracy, at least their essential rights, those that are constitutive and basic, have neither date nor author."[60] The people is absent from and exterior to sovereignty. It cannot be its own source, nor can it be the source of legitimacy. The people refers back to an authority outside of itself: the sovereign (or God for Maistre). Hence the people cannot be the source of rights as the revolutionaries believed: "The 1795 constitution, like its predecessors, was made for man. But there is no such thing as man in the world." Unlike a Frenchman, an Italian, or a Russian, man is a pure abstraction: "Thanks to Montesquieu, I even know that one can be Persian; but I must say, as for man, I have never come across him anywhere; if he exists, he is completely unknown to me."[61] In his critique of democratic representation (of the necessary delegation of power to a representative, since men must renounce being their own judges and rely on a sovereign power), Maistre wittily describes the absence of the people from the sovereignty that remains irremediably outside it and that forms the basis of its humanity. "Through bad faith or inattention, it is fairly often assumed that a proxy alone can be representative. This is an error. Every day in the courts, children, the insane, and absentees are represented by men who derive their mandate solely from the law. Now the people unite to a high degree the three qualities, for it is always a child, always foolish, always absent. Why then can its guardians not dispense with its mandates?"[62]

Benjamin Constant sought to situate the exteriority in the eternal "rights of the *individual*" to avoid reducing man to the citizen. He too noted that the natural rights of man have no basis in reality without the political rights of the citizen. Constant maintained that the fundamental rights of the individual (and not man) were not natural but historical and preconstitutional, "independent of social and political authority" and "existing prior to any structure designed to secure them."[63] But the problem persists, because the exteriority that Constant sought while rejecting the fact that man precedes the citizen is an illusion, since it is defined by the immanence of history, and history is changing by nature.

In the same vein, Auguste Comte claimed that the universal will be accomplished in history with the advent of the positive spirit. When positivism triumphs during the final stage of humanity (after the theological and the metaphysical stages), duties will replace rights. The individual can never pay back his congenital debt to all of the generations of humanity that have made him what he is. Similar to God, humanity is an "immense organism," a Great Being, which, animated by its own evolutionary movement, constitutes the sole source of rights for man who is thus caught in the tautology of immanence without anything outside himself to lean on, anything to found his permanent rights. Swallowed up by the humanity that spawned him, he is left with nothing but duties toward it.

Such a totality (but this time differentiated for itself) is also found in Hegel's thinking. Despite the distinction between them, the singular and the universal are in a relationship of mutual lack and call for the synthesis that is the third stage in the dialectical development of the world mind. In this synthesis the singular always remains a determination of the universal and the universal the accomplishment of the singular.

As we can see, the question of exteriority and, more generally, that of the reference to the origin were regularly raised by all of these thinkers in relation to the rights of man. This exteriority could be condemned in the name of the unity of existence, of theory and practice, of the people and the individual, or due to its impossibility or its deceptive and alienating character. It also could be sought as a basis for the rights of man, not in nature but in history, in tradition, or in God, by those who opposed the idea that man (insofar as he is exterior to the citizen) or nature (insofar as it is exterior to history) can be the source of rights and freedom for man and the citizen. This controversy shows that it was the critical and revolutionary current (notably Marx and Hegel) that condemned the principle of exteriority in the foundation of the rights of man and that advocated the tautological circulation of being, whereas the liberal, conservative current championed this exteriority and consequently accepted, against all expectations, the principle of a split between man and citizen that characterizes the revolution, but in the place of man, they put the divine, hypostatized history, or the individual (in Constant's case). This may very well be the criterion that separates totalitarian democracy from liberal democracy.

All of these theorists take up the issue from the standpoint of the source of rights. If man is the source of rights, then how can such rights constitute an obligation for men? Can rights be abstract and rational? Do they proceed from "nature," or do they have their origin in the lives of peoples? Are the rights of man a hoax and man just a bourgeois? These theories all revolve around the nature of legitimate power and its eventual source. All of these thinkers note the exteriority, the "alterity," of legitimate power to sociality, whether it is to deplore it (Marx), to analyze it (Burke), or to go beyond it (Hegel). They thus raise the much deeper question of the fundaments of the political (of the collectivity, of rights, of authority, etc.) and more broadly the question of origin (of the natural and of identity). This is the question that we will be taking up now, for it subtends the question of what is "given"—prior to reason and choice—in the rights of man and the citizen: the "people" that escapes the grasp of the declaration.

The question of anteriority—and hence of historicity—is also discussed by all the protagonists in this controversy. Maistre is the most explicit on this point. "Although written laws are always only declarations of anterior rights, yet it is very far from true that everything that can be written is written; there is even in every constitution always something that cannot be written, and that must be left in a dark and impenetrable cloud on pain of overturning the state."[64] Thus authority, the state, and law have fundaments that are beyond the powers of a human declaration. Savigny argues that the codification of law based on reason results from an obliteration of origins that can only happen to "senile nations" in the process of losing their peculiar characteristics. When the identity of nations breaks down, its legal remnants are projected into an abstraction. Maistre considers the nation one of those "things that must be left in the dark and cannot be subjected to human legislation."[65] Behind the unreal, abstract concept of man stands the reality of individuals determined by national affiliations. The sources of law are therefore anterior to their declaration; they can be said to be "natural" in the sense that they escape the confines of the political. To Burke, there is a natural side to law that is an outgrowth of the order of the world, and nations are immortal, "corporate bodies" participating in the order of the world.

The historical evolutionism adopted by these theorists, be they conservatives or "revolutionaries," leads them willy-nilly to the question of origins and to the discrepancy between what results from the past and projects for the future. There is a suspicion running through Savigny's critique, and often Burke's, that behind the universal lurks a singularity that is as "senile" as it is ambitious. Since natural law is grounded in nothing, the only way to give it a content is to draw on the singular, or, to use Savigny's terms, on the "given." What happens then is that "the given is dressed up as the universal."[66] Now "it is impossible to reject the given; it ends up dominating us. We can fool ourselves, but we cannot change it. Those who mistakenly imagine that they are exercising their own free will in cases when only this superior freedom is possible are renouncing its noblest titles."[67]

Arendt further develops the idea of an irreducible given that did not give way under the weight of the Enlightenment's faith in the human will, what she calls "the merely given." She describes "this whole sphere of the merely given, relegated to private life in civilized society" as "the disturbing miracle contained in the fact that each of us is made as he is—single, unique, unchangeable." "The dark background of mere givenness, the background formed by our unchangeable and unique nature, breaks into the political scene as the alien which in its all too obvious difference reminds us of the limitations of human activity—which are identical with the limitations of human equality."[68] This "mere givenness" is bound up with the nature of each person; it is "mere existence [. . .] all that which is mysteriously given us by birth and which includes the shape of our bodies and the talents of our minds."[69] These qualities that belong to each person (or to each human family) lie outside the confines of reason and democratic universality, which they threaten because they cannot be absorbed by them. Natural givenness cannot be absorbed by modern politics, which is incapable of dealing with it. It belongs to the sphere of differentiation, and thus it poses a threat to equality, as we have seen, because equality "is not given us, but is the result of human organization insofar as it is guided by the principle of justice. We are not born equal; we become equal as members of a group."[70] The politics of equality strives to reduce these differences that threaten its stability and "arouse dumb hatred, mistrust, and discrimination, because they indicate [. . .] the limitations of human artifice."[71] But the "merely given" is indelible: "wherever public life and its law of equality are completely victorious, wherever a civilization succeeds in eliminating or reducing to a minimum the dark background of difference, it will end in complete petrifaction and be punished, so to speak, for having forgotten that man is only the master, not the creator of the world."[72] But the opposite is also true, because men are in mortal danger in the democratic polis whenever they are thrown back on "their natural givenness, on their mere differentiation [and] lack that tremendous equalizing of differences which comes from being citizens."[73] In that case, they lose their humanity. "If a Negro in a white community is considered a Negro and nothing else, he loses [. . .] his right to equality [. . .]; all his deeds are now explained as 'necessary' consequences of some 'Negro' qualities; he has become some specimen of an animal species, called man." This is what "happens to those who have lost all distinctive political qualities and have become human beings and nothing else."[74]

The paradox is thus absolute: democratic politics cannot take into account the "given," the origin (collective, individual, or family) that is the passive lot of each person and that cannot be denied. When democratic politics forgets this, it becomes petrified or perverted. But when men are reduced to this given and lose their civic rights as citizens, they are removed from humanity and doomed to certain death. This is another way of saying that although the "given" is present in modernity (in its unconscious aspect), to the point that it cannot be eradicated without destroying humanity, political modernity (in its conscious aspect) still has no room for it. In sum, we arrive at the same conclusion once again: humanity has still not found a place for itself in modern politics whose center and ultimate aim is Man.

The Auto-Foundation of the Universal and the Foreclosure of Origins

At this point in the analysis, I would argue that what is at stake in the relationship between the singularity of the Shoah and the universal is the question of origin. I have arrived at this conclusion after looking at a number of analytical hypotheses: the question of people, of difference, of alterity, of nativity, of exteriority, of heteronomy, and finally, of origins. In what way does the notion of "origin" englobe the others? What makes it a significant criterion? If we examine the myth of the "tabula rasa" and of "auto-foundation," we can see the degree to which modern humanity strove to be its own origin. Its identity is, in fact, ineluctably bound up with a denial of origins (necessarily "natural), a denial of the anteriority from which man draws his being (the "people" is the heritage of an immemorial past, the individual is the child of parents, and every person passively inherits a psychological and physical makeup), the ineluctable given in life that is imposed upon man and to which he must adapt. We are in a position now to grasp the relationship between this notion of origin and the native principle, one that induces a genealogical perspective. The individual's origin is his birth: the individual's parents are the actors in and witnesses to this birth. But modern man cannot bear the fact of being born, of having parents, of being preceded by someone else. Everything in him refuses this inescapable ("biological") given that he regards as an insufferable infringement upon his imagined, boundless freedom and an attack on the gratifying, narcissistic myth of self-generation. Among the contemporary modalities of the contemporary loathing of birth, witness the disappearance of death from the public eye (mechanical deaths tucked away in hospitals) and in vitro procreation and cloning. It also becomes clear, in this light, why psychoanalysis became modernity's most popular science, and why its models are so useful to us in understanding the two faces of modern politics. There is a modern consensus that only psychoanalysis has the legitimacy to speak about these things that seem odious on an ethical plane, since they hold out to modernity an unflattering reflection of itself. The unconscious (of democracy) is not "democratic," and only the psychoanalyst has the right to identify its presence in the minds of the moderns. It was as if it bore witness to the permanence of the "archaic" in the "modern." This is what Claude Lefort is saying when he observes that democracy is based on "the power of words": "The symbolic was effective only in traditional societies."[75] But the reality runs deeper. Construed as a nation under state supervision, the repressed people withdrew into the lives of individuals. Individuals became, perforce, the seat and ultimate source of identity, which is always collective at the start. "Peoplehood" took refuge in the "private" sphere, and individuals carried it (consequently, the Nazis searched for the Jewish citizens in their private homes to get hold of them as a people). Contemporary individualism has thus inherited "peoplehood." Yet the individual, despite contemporary illusions, cannot be the source of identity: a person's identity is always the (free) reconstruction of bits and pieces of collective identities. Psychoanalysis has taken on the task of studying the individual (in whom the collective is hidden), but it is hardly qualified to study the collective, which is the vocation of sociology.

The idea of the tabula rasa went hand in hand with a conception of modernity as the "advent" of truth and its total disclosure. Nothing was to escape the grasp of Reason: no more secrets and no more taboos, except perhaps by common consent. That reality could be in any way beyond reason seemed impossible. Everything was supposed to be manifest. This modern materialization of what had been regarded as a potential or a virtuality until then turned origins into an act of power and of will (as per the Rousseauist myth of the social contract, which defines political power as proceeding from an original act of consensus by an assembly of citizens), an act taking place in the total exposure of the light of Reason that could not fail to continually bring the origin back to mind. Political power tried to take hold of the origin and incorporate it into itself, without realizing that there is always an element of secrecy, indetermination, and prohibition in the origin. And political power must always refer to an other (an ancestor, God, a principle, the people, etc.) to establish its legitimacy.

In the Freudian narrative, the Oedipus and castration complexes act as so many veils over the origin to help the child separate from the parents and construct an identity. In Genesis, divine creation is hidden behind the *tohubohu* and the dark "abyss" (*tehom*) that came in its wake. In contradistinction, political modernity brought the origin out into the cold light of day in order to gain control of it. But the more modernity projected the origin outside, with nearly obscene materiality (in terms of "biological" birth), the less capable it became of confronting it in thought, no less in real life. This exposure was actually a form of repression, since the light of the origin was too strong for the eye to sustain. What happened could be defined as a *foreclosure*, in the legal sense of the term, as it was picked up by psychoanalytic theory,[76] meaning a procedure that "shuts out," an "externment." Seen in terms of foreclosure, the origin would be omnipresent in a strongly corporeal form in modernity, but totally invisible and unthinkable. This is what is at the root of contemporary hyperrealism. The mechanism of "biologization" serves to manifest that which has been radically repressed in reality as an exclusively "natural" phenomenon, one that is objectively highly present due to its physicality. This repressed element of the origin, divested of rationality, exists henceforth only in its corporeal dimension (whose obscene presence is in fact a disguised absence).

In a way, this "externment," this site of origin's foreclosure, is the site of the Jewish signifier in the contemporary era: omnipresent, as we have already seen, to the point of obscenity but at the same time radically hidden from view. The presence of the Jew in modernity was reduced to its corporealization (atavism, ethnicity, the victim's corpse, singularity, community, people, destiny, etc.), which means to its absence, its removal from the pale of meaning, rationality, and intelligibility. Anti-Semitism exorcises the return of that which was repressed in the Jew (the origin) and which comes back to prey on the modern mind like a ghost with no interiority (the Jewish "body"). "The now classic statement of foreclosure, that 'what was banished from the symbolic reappears in the real,' is open to two interpretations. Does the foreclosed signifier reappear like an erratic signifier in the real or is the reappearance of the foreclosed the reappearance of a pure reality?"[77] Now being that the real is inconceivable in the perspective of foreclosure, "isn't it then in the sense that it has become 'real' that the foreclosed signifier reappears in the real,"[78] that is, that it slips out of consciousness?

Seen from this perspective, the imprisonment of the Jews in camps was meant to circumscribe the origin (the body or, in this case, Jewish nativity), to expose it in the "real" in order to be free of it and reduce it to nothing. Incomprehensible to modern rationality, the biological and the corporeal seem to call irresistibly for containment (or rather "externment," exclusion from a "thinkable" inside to an "unthinkable" outside). We are touching here on the very "economy" of foreclosure. What is barred from consciousness is "cast outside into the darkness,"[79] never to be found again, leaving no trace (because it is corporealized and reified), and no memory. "What will take the place of a trace, will be strangeness and heterogeneity."[80] Foreclosure is the result of a dual movement. The repression feeds the unconscious and at the same time produces externment (containment outside), which means a manifestation in the order of the "real" that escapes the "symbolic." The subject will no longer be able to formulate it in words (the biological and corporeal are held to be inert, massive, and archaic). The repressed object (the origin) vanishes from the pale of reason and language to reappear as an inert thing bound up with biological nature, "race," "ethnic group," and "singularity." The only echo of the origin left in this inert thing is its aura of strangeness, of something nonhuman, elemental, and monstrous. Thus everything that pertains to the "natural," to what is "given," everything that the subject has to passively accept because he or she cannot do otherwise (one can run to the ends of the world, but one cannot change one's parents!), has been removed from the realm of intelligibility and divested of meaning by modernity. Confronting such things means raising the question of the anteriority and origin of the given, a typically religious question that has become the exclusive domain of psychoanalysis in modernity. The modern mind has contented itself with using science to examine the quiddity of the origin and has glossed over the issue of finality (the farthest the modern mind has gone in this regard was Heidegger's conception of man as "being-toward-death," but who ventured to conceive of man as "being-toward-life"?) It is by way of a detour that the other face of modern thought (embodied by such thinkers as Marx, Freud, and Nietzsche) approached the question of origin as such and sought to appropriate it and bring it under control. The origin remained the final obstacle to a power searching for total control. If men in their own immanence are the source of authority, then what is to be done with this irreducible "given"? If men are equal, then what is to be done with the concrete differences that constitute them? The modern state thus sought ascendancy over the body (insofar as it represents difference and givenness escaping the boundaries of political reason) in order to bring it under the control of rational norms. The Fascist and Nazi states, and totalitarian states in general, illustrated to the point of caricature the political ambition of governing the physical dimension of the human being (through physical education, health, civil status, etc.). The race for Olympic medals in the former "popular democracies" was a telltale symptom of such a project.[81] Through the "hyperrealist" symbols of the corporeal, the state was in fact trying to measure itself against the origin.

On the one hand, all of these elements externalized, or "externated," the repressed people. On the other, the nation manifested the return of the repressed people (henceforth unthinkable due to its "naturalization") in a way that turned peoplehood into a thing of objective and instinctual nature. But in keeping with the workings of foreclosure, the nation was bound up with the state, the conscious entity that represses, while the biological had to be continually held at bay and contained. In this regard, we can distinguish two forms of the nation: the "civic nation," under the dominion of the state and belonging to the conscious sphere, and the nationalist nation, under the rule of the biological and belonging to the repressed sphere.

All of the categories that crystallized and materialized this "origin" in one way or another—the stateless, foreigners, Jews, women, blacks, and so on—met a similar fate in modern politics. But it is clear that certain categories, because of their proximity to the national phenomenon, were the privileged victims and witnesses. The Jewish people is the paradigm in this respect, even though all peoples without a state suffered the same fate. More than women or blacks, Jews became the vectors of the "biological" and of the "body." Because, unlike women, Jews are a people (Jews include women, but women do not include men), heirs to a long history and present in the heart of a divided Europe of nation-states. The desired-denied paradigm of Christianity, Jews summed up the destiny of the unthinkable and refused origin. It is because there was foreclosure of the origin that those who were objectively too close to it and who did not fit into the norm were exposed to total adversity. Nothing in the rights of man provided for its recognition and protection. By excluding Jews, racial laws, racism, and intolerance excluded the biological and rendered what was lurking behind it—the origin evidenced in the people—unthinkable.

The "people" can be understood as the product of generations, the product of the filiation of fathers and sons, born of mothers, who transmit the heritage of an origin, the memory of an immemorial anteriority, that is not necessarily historical, and in any case not historically verifiable. This filiation escapes the hold of the political (until modern times, it was the church, not the state, that had dominion over birth, marriage, and death registries), and it is bound up with the very structure of historicity. It is the structure of human groups, each of which abides by codes prohibiting incest and by rules of matrimony whose function is to continue the name of the origin. Pierre Legendre has underscored in his work the political implications of the genealogical principle. "Filiation is the first principle of institutional systems for humanity as a whole. Filiation's horizon includes survival, life, expansion and death in the human species."[82] Its purpose is to "institute [man], by the dogmatic procedure that ties the biological, the social and the unconscious together. This dogmatic procedure [. . .] always answers the same need, that of founding the Interdiction and of ensuring that this discourse produces the desired normative effect, what we in the West call the law. [. . .] The focus of this construction, which is tautological by nature, is the principle of filiation, whose concrete translation is the genealogical order, an inexhaustible storehouse from which individuals draw the identity baggage they need to live [. . .], the basic categories of their identity, that, before becoming the effective baggage of their lives, pass through intermediary hands, through the hands of the parents who are the makers of identificatory images."[83] The group created by filiation institutes the Interdiction, the stake of which is to make the individual enter into ties and become a speaking being. "There is no subject who is not held within limits, instituted as a sexually differentiated and mortal being. This fact is clearly evinced by the *état civil*, which places the subject in a genealogical chain: birth, sex, son or daughter of . . . ending with death."[84] The figure of the father (the "Name of the father" in Lacan's words), plays a central role in this process. It is important "to understand that the name is in a *necessary relationship* with a representation of the Father."[85] Its "structural significance" is "to make present for the subject the relationship to the species, the horizon that exceeds every subject, a representation of the mythical Father, that is to say the logical instance of a founding Third [*le Tiers*], which in this case founds the name."[86]

Legendre sees the modern myth of self-foundation as a catastrophe: "The parade of the self-founded subject is the liberal counterpart to totalitarianism, imposing upon new generations the terror of an image that is impossible to assume. The price of bypassing the processes of identification is desubjectivation and, for many, a despair from which they find no issue, save through self-murder."[87] "[I]ndustrialized societies of West European tradition" seem to think that they are "capable of freeing themselves from the mythical constraint, [. . .] from the logic of the founding Third,"[88] "substituting for the prospect of new beginnings, the belief in the absence of limits and giving rise to unheard of institutional manipulations founded simply on the principle of pleasure. As to the effects of the political reign of this fantasy of absence of limits—an ineradicable fantasy in humanity—, Nazism provided a demonstration that [. . .] has not been examined carefully enough."[89] Legendre denounces the "dogma of modern times, not recognized as such, according to which the person chooses his order of allegiance and founds himself by himself [. . .], sets himself up as a mini-State, that is, as a sovereign body, legislator and judge of taboos."[90] The state in our industrialized regime "is in the position of this legal Third, because it is the Author of the founding discourse of filiation with all its legal consequences; from the standpoint of this discourse, the State as Author can be said to be the monumental or absolute Subject, in the manner of the Torah, the law-maker God of the Christian canonists, or the Koran."[91] What happens is that "every subject is put into the position of being its own state. Society then turns on the subject, and requires the subject to found itself, and to do so in the genealogical sense, meaning to be its own absolute Reference."[92]

The role of the people, I might add, is to carry "all of the complexly interrelating conscious and unconscious interpretations revolving around the enigma of the Interdiction."[93] The Interdiction is "the imperative of differentiation that civilizes murder and incest by transposing the stakes into the universe of words."[94] The role of the people is to "institute life by instituting the subject,"[95] to be "the guarantee point of human lives: the supporting framework of the speaking species, the montages of identity."[96] "What we know for sure about life, as living-speaking beings destined to die, is a representation; it is knowledge about parents."[97] The question of origins is vital for us: "Outside of the question of origins, humanity has nothing to say. Against a backdrop of despair at being born, the human being enters life by elaborating a representation of origins, which is, to begin with, a representation of the Abyss. The question of how the Abyss can be represented in a livable way, in a way that serves life, is precisely what is at stake in the system of filiations."[98]

According to Legendre, the Nazis attacked the very principle of this system of affiliation.[99] The logic behind "the act of killing the Jew, that is to say the son of Israel [had an] institutional value."[100] The Nazis were attacking "the principle of filiation as such, the genealogical idea as an institutional principle [. . .], the very idea of law. [. . .] The ultimate justification of what we call Law for humanity is nothing other than the notion of filiation."[101] The Nazis perverted the law, making sure that the extermination of the Jews was conducted within a "legal" framework, indeed, with exaggerated legalism (the Nuremberg laws, the *Statut des Juifs*). Nazism attempted "to rethink the idea of filiation on a new *legal* basis, [. . .] for a new Humanity, rid of the Jews"[102] and hence of the principle of filiation. "The Hitlerian recourse to Science in the extermination of the Jews corresponded to a rejection of the Reference, or more precisely, to the impossibility of sustaining the bond of filiation, firstly for the Nazis as subjects in the human species." As a result "there was no more father or son, the montage of the Reference was smashed to pieces, and hatred was disguised as a scientific service rendered to this new Humanity."[103]

Henceforth, under the banner of science, there was no need for a montage of discourses and metaphors to deal with the problem of murder in the father-son relationship. "[T]he value of truth dissolved into brute physicality, that of scientifically observable meat. The Reference was dead. We had entered the domain of sheer physicality."[104] "The Hitlerian acting out operated a reversal, dislocating the laborious constructions of European casuistry, Jewish and non-Jewish, by staging filiation as pure physicality. A leap had been taken from the body as vehicle of access to interpretation (the circumcision) to the body as argument in the suppression of the interpreter (racial biologism)."[105]

Like Arendt, albeit on a psychoanalytical plane, Legendre relates Nazi madness to the modern state, and even to human rights. "The Shoah was conceived in terms of human rights, on the basis of a legislation that set down racist purification, in the words of Hitler himself, as the one holiest human right (*ein heiligstes Menschenrecht*)."[106] The modern state, "master of the body and sovereign interpreter,"[107] insofar as it claims to be the Reference and absolute legitimation, with power over genealogy and the institution of the subjects, is in danger of perverting sociality ("the State means a certain state—or status—of the founding Reference of filiations, and hence a certain state of the idea of the Law based on the transfer of the power to interpret to the State"[108]). "[T]he threat of perverting that which is in essence untouchable—the founding Reference—hangs over Western humanity. Anthropologically, the State remains a fragile defense against the risk of destruction of the idea of Law and filiation by madmen or crooks who have occupied the supreme locus of power."[109] "[W]ith the invention of the State, something brand new appeared that altered the system of texts and interpretations. State modernity rests on this basis: power over the body was transferred to the State, which was invested with a sovereign power of Interpretation. At the price of a definitive dis-embodiment of the relationship to the text, the relationship to authority, that is to say to the Law and to filiation, took an irrevocable turn in the West."[110]

For all of these reasons, Jewish destiny came to embody the destiny of the origin in modern consciousness and more especially in politics. Something *archaic* (from *arche*, beginning, principle) took place through it. The Shoah attacked Jewish singularity, its body, its historicity, its collective condition, its difference. It attacked the "people" and in so doing it "revealed" (or rather "concealed," as we have seen, through foreclosure) the "zero point" of modern consciousness, the reality of the modern condition (biologiza-tion, on the one hand, and repression, on the other, the very syndrome of foreclosure) and the failure of political modernity—the immense hole, the lack of words,[111] the human abyss that inhabits it. Legendre maintains that the Shoah interests humanity because it raises "the principle of life in the human species."[112]

CHAPTER 9

The Hidden Religion of Modernity

The refusal to recognize and accept the primordial givenness of human existence (birth, filiation, peoplehood, etc.) is a characteristic trait of the modern value system. Until modern times, religion "managed" the question of the origin, not only in reference to God but also and especially in rituals that served as cyclical reminders of the origin over time.[1] And religion was also and very significantly in charge of the institution of filiation and genealogy (registry of births, marriages, and deaths). But modernity went beyond the delegitimation of religious authority, to reject "tradition," the imperative of transmission, and the "passivity" of reception. It posited instead a morality based on a "tabula rasa," along with a faith in the power of human action and will. Reason was pitted against religion; everything, including man, was to be recreated ex nihilo, on a rational basis. This, as we have seen, was the basic project of modern politics, called upon to eradicate the "genealogical" order in its attempt to recreate human nature and achieve total ascendancy over the human condition.

This was the *conscious* "contract" of modernity. But, as we have seen, an extraordinarily powerful unconscious force, as powerful as the repression that had engendered it, preyed upon and undermined modernity, as it came to the surface again and again in a variety of forms, including collective hallucinations. Democracy had reproduced the religious, but without traditional religions. Instead, it created religions that did not see themselves as such. The idea that secularization has removed religion from human destiny once and for all is a widely held modern belief that needs to be reexamined and revised. Even the foremost theorists of secularization, such as Durkheim and Weber, had equivocal thoughts on the matter. Man was repressed in citizenship, removed from the realm of rationality, foreignized, and circumscribed within a gigantic black hole (for he is born and hence lodged in a filiation that escapes his control no matter what he thinks). Citizenship could do without him, and he became the object of a diffuse, unacknowledged, hence, savage and tragic, religion: the hidden religion of democracy.

203

The Taboo of Man

Modernity recognized itself in "the cult of Man"[2] yet never has the destruction of men taken a more terrible toll than in modernity, when the concern for the real man was replaced by the glorification of abstract Man. The apotheosis and eclipse of Man is not incoherent, nor is it an artificial paradox. We are dealing here with a system of totem and taboo, which is known in all of the social sciences to be a dialectical system: the principle that attracts, repels at the same time, eliciting also the desire to approach the desired object and its rarity. One of the authorities in the field, Émile Durkheim, even built his analysis of society entirely upon this principle, formulated in terms of a dialectic of the sacred and the profane. In his writings in particular we find the scenario of the poignant drama of political modernity: the glorification of Man leading to his eclipse. The early sociologists were for the most part powerful witnesses to this process. Well before Durkheim, Saint-Simon and August Comte "introduced and developed the idea of the religion of humanity in France and in modern society"[3] as the source of a "spiritual bond"[4] indispensable to the existence of any collectivity. Saint-Simon posited a "new Christianity" and Comte a "cult of the Great Being of Humanity," destined to take over from Christianity. These utopias seem remote to us today, but it would be a mistake to see them as insignificant pieces of folklore. They embody the spirit of modernity that needed this "cult of Man" to constitute and define itself. Durkheim sought, for his part, to introduce morality into the secular Third Republic because he was convinced that no society, not even a secular one, could survive without religion or the sacred. "There is no human community without some form of common creed."[5] His whole theory is founded on the premise that societies develop from a collective, religious ecstatic experience that generates a "sacredness," which he defines as a formal, morphological reality without intrinsic substance. A collective energy is released in the effervescent moments of demographic concentration that produces a representation of the assembled group, making its members aware that their gathering has meaning and an identity. This meaning, according to Durkheim, is always religious at the start: the "collective representation" that society produces of itself always seems to its members to come from the outside, in the manner of a god. In short, the idea that a society has of itself and that enables it to develop as a society is the idea of God. From this perspective, then, society is divinized in order to exist as a human society. The "sacred" is that which is not profane, the result of a demarcation or a dissociation, introducing heterogeneity into the world and into the collective life around which society is organized and ensuring the continued existence of society which time is ceaselessly eroding. The sacred gives rise to a religious temporality that safeguards society by allowing its members to relive the experience of their community's founding moment again and again in the cycle of rituals. According to Durkheim, the sacred is a very real principle of organization, but it is devoid of content and determination. The circle of sacred things is not limited once and for all, for sacredness can be attached to anything. Thus Durkheim had no problem conceptualizing the idea of a "secular sacred"; indeed, he could not imagine for a moment that modern society, having cut its ties with religion, could survive without the "sacred." For a while he entertained the idea of Science replacing Revelation, but mainly he strove to develop a secular morality.

Sociologists, veritable theorists of modernity, thus placed Man on a sacred pedestal in a universe governed by the Declaration of the Rights of Man. Man (and his society) was regarded as the source of the sacred, the supreme value of civilization and politics, the highest embodiment of "Nature." The substitution of Man for God is patent here. In Durkheim's words, "Man has become a god for men."[6] "One of the fundamental axioms of our morality—perhaps even *the* fundamental axiom—is that the human being [. . .] merits the respect that the faithful of all religions reserve for their God."[7] "Durkheim was a neo-Kantian who accepted Kant's abolition of God by turning man into God—an operation which was built on notions of conscience, personal judgment and reason."[8] According to Kant, duties to God are to be understood as duties to men. Such a morality is, in Durkheim's terms, "a religion in which man is at once the worshiper and the God."[9] Durkheim argues that "[t]he human personality is a sacred thing; one dare not violate it nor infringe its bounds, while at the same time the greatest good is in communion with others."[10] "[T]he fundamental axiom is that the human being is the sacred thing par excellence [. . .]. We ourselves express this when we make the idea of humanity the end and raison d'être of the nation."[11] "Certainly I will maintain the sacred character of morality. I base my opinion [. . .] upon the facts. It is impossible to imagine that morality should entirely sever its unbroken historic association with religion without ceasing to be itself [. . .]. Morality would no longer be morality if it had no element of religion. [. . .] This characteristic, sacredness, can be expressed, I believe [. . .] in secular terms."[12]

But what is the nature of Man thus sacralized? Durkheim's description of sacredness as such gives us some insight into the matter. Sacredness is a defined place, separated from the profane, which it excludes and circumscribes, yet the two separate realities have no intrinsic or essential substance. "The sacred being is in a sense forbidden; it is a being which may not be violated; it is also good, loved and sought after."[13] How can one reconcile the sacredness of the human being, the idea of the human being as the very site of sacredness ("one dare not violate it nor infringe its bounds"[14]), with the fact that this human being "is (also) the distinguished object of our sympathy," and that "the greatest good is in communion with others"? How can Man be revered by men? How can the sacred be respected and approached at the same time? J.-C. Filloux underlines the inherent contradiction of a line of reasoning that is dialectically "well oiled" yet without practical applications in reality: "The person is thus both ideal and real, forbidden and loved for the actor who experiences his sacred character."[15] Filloux regards Durkheim's inability to tackle amorous relationships, especially in the form of sexual union, as an illustration of the impasse to which the sacralization of Man leads. Since the Man exalted by Durkheim is characteristically masculine and feminine, the perfect man can only be manifested in the amorous union of the couple, brought to a head in the sexual act. Pushing his reasoning to the end, Durkheim notes that the sexual act violates the sacred bounds of the other. "There is a form of profanation in not respecting the boundaries that separate people, in violating the bounds, and penetrating unduly into another person." This profanation reaches an exceptionally intense pitch in the sexual act, because the two persons lose themselves in one another. From the perspective of individualist morality, there is the seed of "fundamental immorality" in this "oddly complex" act.[16] And yet love alone can move the "cult of man" (characterized by the desire for the sacred thing, which is eminently appealing). In a rhetorical issue to this dilemma, Durkheim maintains that the profanation of the human caused by the sexual act is offset by the fact that it provides the occasion for a communion between the two people. Over the course of the marriage, this union will have done no more than shift the sacred bounds of the individual person. "We find ourselves in an impasse whenever it is a matter of concretely applying the principle of sacralization: the dialectic of distance, prohibition, and love; taking into account the abstract "human" in the relationship to a singular individual."[17]

This example of the love relationship could be transposed from interindividual relations to the relationship of man to man within the framework of society and citizenship. While Man is held up as sacred to citizens, it may very well be that relations between men in citizenship cannot escape profanation and sacrilege, that they cannot avoid a violence similar to that of the sexual act that violates the bounds of the person. Too much singularity, too many material details, and too much concupiscence would sully these relationships, with regard to man's sacredness. Or is it that, as with the analogy of sex and marriage, this profanation would give rise to an even greater unity that offsets the violence: the unity of the total society and the absolute nation? One could hardly devise a more theoretical way out of the logical impasse to which the abstract idea of man leads. The whole tragedy of political modernity is contained in this Durkheimian nutshell.

The Man without Qualities

To Durkheim, society is the source of the sacredness of man "Man has no innate right to this aura that surrounds and protects him against sacrilegious trespass. It is merely the way in which society thinks of him, the high esteem that it has of him at the moment, projected and objectified."[18] Thus what ties us to others is not specificity, identity, or singularity but merely and exclusively what makes us human. And this humanity is in fact society: "When the social ideal is a particular form of the ideal of humanity, when the type of citizen blends to a great extent with the generic type of man, it is to man as such that we find ourselves bound,"[19] which basically means that what is being respected in the sacredness of the (private, individual) person is society, Man in general, not necessarily the person in particular. "What binds us morally to others is nothing intrinsic in their empirical individuality; it is the superior end of which they are the servants and instruments."[20] As Filloux notes, Durkheim declared already in *Suicide* that "man, as thus suggested to collective affection and respect, is not the sensual, experiential individual that each one of us represents, but man in general, ideal humanity."[21] Entirely in keeping with the spirit of the revolution, it is the individual who is summoned to abnegation, to sacrifice his singularity—without which he is nothing—on the altar of society. There is no individual in particular in the sacred person, in the so highly exalted Man. There is only the individual as an interchangeable part of a whole—society—in which there is nothing in particular. Exalted Man has no real existence. He refers back to society, and society refers back to absolute Man, the product of society. "The dignity of the individual that is conferred upon him by the 'religion of humanity' does not concern the 'individual' characteristics, the 'particularities' that distinguish him from others but the fact that he has 'something of humanity' in him."[22] Exit the singular! Exit humanity as a specific being, since it amounts to nothing more than sociality; it has no substance beside sociality! This Mystery is enacted on the parvis of a cathedral built to the "religion of humanity"!

The individualism that Durkheim defends is thus ambiguous and the source of illusions. It masks the absence and impossibility of any positive individuality and identity in man. It is an "ethical individualism" whose focus is not "the singular individuality in the individual" but rather "humanity" and even the "human condition of the concrete individual."[23] Durkheim identifies this individualism directly with the individualism that "the Declaration of the Rights of Man attempted, more or less happily, to formulate."[24] He is aware of the contradiction in his conception but sees no other response than in the tautological reasoning discussed earlier. The cult of the "person," of man as a "sacred thing" but a thing devoid of interiority and identity, is the sign of "the minimum amount of collective consciousness necessary for the cohesion of modern society,"[25] characterized by the individualization necessary for the division of labor. The emptiness of man thus emerges as that which makes it possible to transcend the individualism engendered by the modern economy. "The person who on the functional level of the division of roles and tasks is summoned, as it were, to find fulfillment, is on the analytical level of integration of common values, the object of respect, similar to God."[26] And so, whereas the human person in practical and social reality is divided and dispersed, on the level of principles, the human person is one, but an absolute negative one. Man is, of course, "an individual by definition," but what is respectable about him is not his singularity, his own individuality; it is his "humanity in the abstract."[27] "The cult of Man" is addressed "to the human person wherever it is to be found, and in whatever form it is embodied. Impersonal and anonymous, such an aim, then, soars far above all individual minds and can thus serve them as a rallying point."[28]

Man is thus the effigy, the representation of society, and does not exist outside it. "The respect for man in general, for the humanity in each man finds its basis in the collective character of the very 'mind' that formulates it."[29] "The inalienable character of the individuality and singularity of the self is forged in social interaction."[30] And it is around this Man in general that society unites, since "the sacralization of the person is not only social in origin and expression but also [...] the only moral conviction that can unite men in modern society."[31] We have come full circle. This circular reasoning explains why man is abstract, "empty," without qualities, and without determination. The center of the collectivity is empty: the factor of unity transcending particularities is the sacred, prohibited man who has no empirical existence. Durkheim finds no way out of this impasse but to resort to another universal dimension in the form of an absolute totality that is impossible to dismember, namely, society. We find here again, albeit formulated differently, the idea that the man of the *Declaration* is nothing without the society and the state of which he is supposedly the source.

Hence, at the core of society we find man, but at the core of man lies a void. "What constitutes the dignity of man, is what is most impersonal about it."[32] This impersonal aspect is "the soul of the group. In fact, it is this which constitutes the very substance of individual souls. Now this is not the possession of anyone in particular: it is a part of the collective patrimony; in it and through it, all consciousnesses communicate."[33] It is related to the universality of reason ("reason is that which is most impersonal within us"[34]). "Thus, we make our way, little by little, toward a state [...] where the members of a single social group will have nothing in common among themselves except their humanity, except the constitutive attributes of the human person in general."[35] "[A]bove the changing torrent of individual opinions [. . .] nothing remains which men can love and honor in common if not man himself."[36] This is, once again, a purely negative, restrictive definition of Man: Man as what is left when all singularities have been removed, taken out of the common! The common is defined therefore as what is left over after the subtraction of singularities. The ensuing vacuum of singularities is identified with a whole that excludes otherness and exteriority. Man as an empty abstract category constitutes the sole bond between men, and since there is nothing other than Man, since there is no exteriority to humanity ("the cult of man has as its primary dogma the autonomy of reason"[37]), and Man is nothing in particular, the whole amounts to nothing.

The emptiness of Man that results from his sacralization opens onto a totality that is identified with society. This emptiness is what sustains citizenship and the capacity of men to be citizens. But since it refers back to society, we can conclude that society alone gives credence to the idea and the reality of Man, yet Durkheim tells us nothing about the fact that all societies are endowed with singular identities. Or, rather, he tells us only indirectly, in a way that shows to what extent he is the true unrivaled thinker of the rights of man. Indeed, we find in his theories the problem of the corporeal and the biological discussed earlier, for the humanity and dignity of man can only be attained in his eyes after deducting the corporeal. He regards the person as the product of two factors: an impersonal factor (the spiritual dimension, the soul of society which the individual enters through socialization) and an individuating factor that he identifies with the corporeal dimension. The body has a crucial role in the making of society. "As bodies are distinct from each other, and as they occupy different points of space and time, each of them forms a special centre about which the collective representations reflect and color themselves differently. The result is that even if all the consciousnesses in these bodies are directed towards the same world, to wit, the world of ideas and sentiments which brings about the moral unity of the group, they do not all see it from the same angle; each one expresses it in its own fashion."[38] In this way Durkheim develops his famous sociology of knowledge (and more broadly his social morphology), seeing the fabric of sociality in the process of collective representations. Now all these "determinations of corporeal origin have the effect of enslaving"[39]; "passion individualizes, yet it also enslaves. Our sensations are essentially individual; yet we are more personal the more we are freed from our senses and able to think and act with concepts."[40] And since "what makes a man a person is that by which he is confounded with other men, that which makes him a man, not a certain man,"[41] "the only way we have of freeing ourselves from physical forces is to oppose them with collective forces,"[42] that is, society or man in general.

Just as Man does not exist without the society that produces him (but why does it produce him as an Englishman, a Frenchman, or a Spanish man?), rights of citizenship cannot be implemented without a state to establish and defend them. The state's "vocation henceforth is to guarantee the very existence of a society united by the common religion of Man,"[43] and democracy is "the political form through which society reaches the purest self-awareness."[44] Nowhere does Durkheim state more clearly that the religion of Man is the religion of democracy. And the latter is the site of emptiness and indetermination, because Man, even exalted, is home to no one in particular.

The Democratic Abyss

The emptiness of Man is thus deployed in a major way on the stage of society, and sociological analysis naturally recognizes it as one of sociology's intangible principles. The most erudite theories of religion and society seem to have a structural blind spot when it comes to the mythical point of origin and have been unable to address it in rational terms. The founding fathers of sociology all grappled with the enigma of religion, which they saw as the origin of society, but not one of them took up the origin of religion, other than as a fictional narrative or theoretical myth. For Durkheim, collective effervescence (the "corrobori") was the source of the founding representations of the social group. Marx saw alienation underlying the human condition and went looking for its source first in politics and then in economy, but without analyzing its social origins. Max Weber took no interest in the origins of religion, even though he was totally absorbed by the study of its consequences and its mechanisms. Freud developed the myth of the primal horde. Modern thought has remained silent on the subject of the origin. Worse still, it has turned its silence and ignorance into the very basis of its most sophisticated, rationalist theories, which therefore stand on quicksand.

How can we account for this strange phenomenon that confirms the inability of modernity to grasp, consciously and rationally, the significance of the indetermination of Man in democracy?

The Significance of Democratic Indetermination

What is the nature of this vacuum that haunts democracy, of this absence of Man in the institution of Man? The reader will have understood that I identify it as the stage of the modern tragedy, the place where the abyss opened up where Jewishness was first produced as a singularity just when it was attaining the summits of citizenship and universality before sinking with all hands. But prior to examining the process (which, may I remind the reader, I have posited to be unconscious and "savage") that enabled such a perversion of political modernity's conscious project—the glorification and liberation of Man—, we must consider the positive and normative interpretation of the democratic void, regarded as the very emblem of democracy, as the hope for and condition of Man's freedom.

Claude Lefort's work best exemplifies this approach. Classic critics of the rights of man, from Burke to Maistre and Marx, had indicted (if for different reasons) the inconsistency and indetermination of man in the *Declaration*, but the identification of a *void* in the abstraction of the universal was something altogether new in political philosophy. Claude Lefort's examination of the subject raises a problematic of body and void that puts us on the path of an anthropological explanation and thereby brings us closer to what we are trying to understand. "The legitimacy of power is based on the people; but the image of popular sovereignty is linked to the image of an empty place, impossible to occupy, such that those who exercise public authority can never claim to appropriate it. Democracy combines these two seemingly contradictory principles: on the one hand, power emanates from the people; on the other, it is the power of nobody. And democracy thrives on this contradiction."[45] "Once the rights of man are declared, there arises, so it is said, the fiction of man without determination. [. . . A] number of our contemporaries continue to sneer at abstract humanism. Now the idea of man without determination cannot be dissociated from the idea of the *indeterminable*. The rights of man reduce right to a basis which, despite its name, is without shape, is given as interior to itself and, for this reason, eludes all power which would claim to take hold of it [. . .]. Consequently, these rights go beyond any particular formulation which has been given of them; and this means that their formulation contains the demand for their reformulation."[46] Throughout Lefort's work, indeterminacy and the void emerge as factors of freedom. In a dichotomic perspective, he depicts the body, fullness, and absolute determination as the alternative to the void. His thinking insistently swings back and forth between an analysis of this painful void and its totalitarian temptation, because to his mind getting away from the void necessarily entails corporealizing it, freezing a space that would otherwise be open to movement. "Democracy thus proves to be the historical society par excellence, a society which, in its very form, welcomes and preserves indeterminacy, in sharp contrast to totalitarianism which, built under the banner of creating the new man, is set up in reality against this indeterminacy and claims to possess the law of its organization and its development."[47] Democracy, he admits, can give rise to a desire for totalitarianism: as a vacuum draws fullness, so democracy has in it a potential for totalitarianism. "In my view, totalitarianism can be clarified only by grasping its relationship with democracy."[48] Totalitarianism emerges as the temptation to fill the void through the corporealization of democracy in "the image of the people-as-One."

> It does not matter that, for a while, the people is confused with the proletariat; the latter is then conceived mythically as the universal class into which all elements working for the construction of socialism are absorbed; it is no longer, strictly speaking, a class [. . .] it has become the people in its essence and notably includes the bureaucracy. This image is combined with that of a Power-as-One, power concentrated within the limits of a ruling apparatus and, ultimately, in an individual who embodies the unity and will of the people. These are two versions of the same fantasy. For the People-as-One can be both represented and affirmed only by a great Other [. . .] that great individual whom Solzhenitsyn has so aptly called the *Egocrat*. But the same image is also combined with the image of the element alien to the people, with the image of its enemy [. . .]. The definition of the enemy is constitutive of the identity of the people. And, from this point of view, the metaphor of the *body*, which was current even in the time of Lenin, demands attention. [. . . T]he integrity of the body depends on the elimination of its *parasites*.[49]

But there is reason to wonder whether Claude Lefort has really thought through the question of the void, other than as a binary opposition between emptiness, on the one hand, and fullness or the body, on the other. From his analysis, democracy emerges as a problematical intermediary stage in a long historical process premised upon the principle of corporeal determination. As we have seen, democracy is endangered by the prospect of a totalitarian "body," and it follows in the wake of the corporealization of society that characterized the ancien regime in which, according to the theory of Ernst Kantorowicz (extensively quoted by Lefort), the king's own body was coupled with a mystical body, embodying the people. "[T]he society of the *ancien régime* represented its unity and its identity to itself as that of a body—a body which found its figuration in the body of the king, or rather which identified itself with the king's body, while at the same time it attached itself to it as its head [. . .]. The image of the king's body as a double body, both mortal and immortal, individual and collective, was initially underpinned by the body of Christ. [. . .] long after the features of liturgical royalty had died away, the king still possessed the power to incarnate in his body the community of the kingdom, now invested with the sacred, a political community, a national community, a mystical body."[50] The beheading of Louis XVI emphatically inaugurated the age of the void in which the collectivity was referred not to a "body" but to an empty place whose occupants were anonymous and temporary.

> The *ancien régime* was made up of an infinite number of small bodies which gave individuals their distinctive marks. And these small bodies were fitted together within a great imaginary body for which the body of the king provided the model and the guarantee of its integrity. The democratic revolution, for so long subterranean, burst out when the body of the king was destroyed, when the body politic was decapitated and when, at the same time, the corporeality of the social was dissolved. There then occurred what I would call a "disincorporation" of individuals [. . .] entities who would have to be counted in a universal suffrage that would take the place of the universal invested in the body politic. [. . .] The idea of number as such is opposed to the idea of the substance of society. Number breaks down unity, destroys identity [. . .]. The modern democratic revolution is best recognized in this mutation: there is no power linked to a body. Power appears as an empty place, and those who exercise it are mere mortals who occupy it only temporarily [. . .]. There is no law that can be fixed [. . .] no representation of a center and of the contours of society [. . .]. Democracy inaugurates the experience of an ungraspable, uncontrollable society in which the people will be said to be sovereign, of course, but whose identity will constantly be open to question, whose identity will remain latent.[51]

There is also reason to wonder whether Lefort has really thought through the question of the body. By presuming that the "body" is necessarily a sign of totalitarianism or of the ancien régime's "corporatism," he is perpetuating the very modern reduction of positive existence to the biological and the corporeal, excluded from the sphere of democratic rationality, which is glorified as a void. On the other hand, he does have the perspicacity to note that this void almost inevitably triggers a fascination with the "body." Basically one could say that he is aware that Man, as a "body" (an identity, a people, a sex, etc.) incarnated in history and reality, is in a situation of "externment" from democracy where Man's place, the throne that democracy built for him, is empty. "[A]nalyzing modern democracy [. . .] reveals a movement which tends to actualize the image of the people, the State," and this "movement is necessarily frustrated by the reference to power as an empty place and by the experience of social division. [. . . W]hen society can no longer be represented as a body and is no longer embodied in the figure of the prince, it is true that people, state, and nation acquire new force and become the major poles by which social identity and community can be signified. But to assert, in order to extol it, that a new religious belief takes shape is to forget that this identity and community remain indefinable."[52]

It is this permanent, dialectical ambivalence—profusely underlined by Lefort—that makes me challenge his constant defense of the state of indeterminacy in democracy. First of all, it is untenable from the standpoint of political morality. If it were a question of an existential or metaphysical condition,[53] of the emptiness inhabiting the human condition, then it would be intellectually and ethically acceptable. But we are dealing here with a system of power that governs men's destinies. The example of the Shoah and the other atrocities of the democratic era should make us think twice about accepting as inevitable or good what I understand to be a flaw in democracy. And it could be superseded in ways that are not necessarily totalitarian, as Lefort fears. Overcoming this flaw in democracy could be a cardinal step forward for politics in the twenty-first century, an additional stage in what Tocqueville called the democratic *process*, which began with the French Revolution and is still in progress, for democracy is an ongoing process. But I also consider Lefort's position ultimately untenable on the theoretical plane. If democracy is defined as an interlude between two corporealized systems (the ancien régime and totalitarianism), then the void that it institutes is not a durable reality, since the political situation that the void creates is continually haunted by a desire for the One. And, according to Lefort's outline of the dilemma, it can only be a totalitarian One, which is a mockery worse than the corporatist society of the ancien régime. Had Lefort ventured beyond this unstable void, in its opposition to the body, he would have been compelled to invent a new age in democracy. In other words, as he expressly recognizes, the void is inhabited by the fantasy and the phantom of the body.

Logically this points to the implicit permanence of the religious in modern politics, not surreptitiously but as its structuring factor. Lefort advances the hypothesis of the "democratic essence of Christianity or the Christian essence of democracy."[54] Admittedly, the theory of the king's two bodies is of Christian origin. In the same way that the church is the head of mystical body of Christ, the king is the head of the national body of the kingdom. Lefort interestingly sees therein a model of "the relationship between the *particular* [*singulier*], which is still inscribed within the limits of a body, of an entity which is organized spatially and temporally, and the *universal*, which is still related to the operation of transcendence."[55] Based on the conclusions he draws from an analysis of Michelet's theories, Lefort asks whether it would be "appropriate to posit the view that a theologico-political *formation* is, logically and historically, a primary datum [. . .] and to see in the oppositions it implies the principle of an evolution [. . .], detect how certain schemata of organization and representation survive thanks to the displacement and transference on to new entities of the image of the body and of its double nature, of the idea of the One, and of a mediation between visible and invisible, between the eternal and the temporal. We would then be in a better position to ask whether democracy is the theater of a new mode of transference, or whether the only thing that survives in it is the phantom of the theologico-political."[56]

And this is precisely what is problematical about Lefort's theories. What is the nature of the void to which he is constantly, almost obsessively, returning in his discussion of democracy? Lefort describes the "permanence of the theologico-political" as "the irreducible element,"[57] which is exactly what is at issue. One can hardly content oneself with an abstract, aesthetic observation if one is to come to grips with the modern tragedy. The idea of "irreducibility" points to a mystery and saves one the trouble of delving further into the reality of the democratic era and its perversions. The perversion of democracy in totalitarianism may have a deeper origin than Lefort imagines, one that necessitates exploring the enigma of this "irreducible element," of this "theologico-political" that rises like a king in its bosom, an origin that may help us explain both totalitarianism and the democratic void by allowing us to get out of the fatality of their antagonism. What is at issue is precisely that the religious (manifested here in the search for the mystical body—the nation or the people, incidentally and not intrinsically perverted in totalitarianism and nationalism) was perpetuated in a violent, savage, and unconscious way in an age when it was supposed to have disappeared but was actually structurally reproduced without rules or checks. If this is the case, then it is impossible to think through democracy without thinking through the nature of the void and the indeterminacy that characterizes it *in its very principle* and not as a residue of the past or an inexplicable irreducible element. How can we rethink modern politics *together with* this unexpected religiousness that disfigures the face it consciously presents on the outside? It is this savage, deadly religiousness, a symptom of the flaw in the system of the rights of man and at the same time a betrayal thereof (according to the conscious-unconscious model), that must be acknowledged and identified as an altogether modern phenomenon, wherein we will find an explanation for the murderous lapses of modern politics. This unknown religion was consubstantial with modern politics, with modernity as the apotheosis of Man without substance or identity, of Man exalted on the condition that he sacrifice his singular existence, the very foundation of any existence.

Indetermination and the Void as Questions of Limit

Perhaps the question of the void and its strange religiousness, as well as the question of the body that Claude Lefort raises so aptly, should be reexamined from the perspective of the immanence and autonomy that characterize modernity. This is what I have tried to do in emphasizing how little was left of any notion of exteriority or anteriority in modernity's self-defined Man and how it had been replaced by the messianic illusion of an already accomplished present. The radical autonomy of Man and the tabula rasa of the past presiding over the modern opus raise the question of limits (a variation on the question of exteriority), through the agency of which we can gain insight into the savage religiousness of democracy. And they raise this question in the terms of democracy itself, that is, before any evocation of the morphological continuity of the religious. In establishing Man as the source of himself and as the source of law, political modernity ineluctably wrote off the very notion and possibility of limits in human identity and political life. In basing equality upon a principle of absolute sharing (within the political arena for liberalism and within the social and economic arena for utopian socialism), democracy induced a perspective of totality (*all* must be shared, hence, "the all" must be posited) that reduced Man in the citizen to a state of total exposure, with nothing left in the "shadows" and no possibility of finding shelter. It reduced Man to total immanence. Modern theories premised upon the death of God are explicit in this regard. But does this schema, which reflects the manifest, apparent reality of modernity, correspond to reality?

In terms of the psychology and political sociology of identity, one can hardly imagine an identity being forged without establishing a relationship between an inside and an outside. Consequently, democracy witnessed the recreation of a transcendence in its midst, generating what sociologists have variously described as "political religions," "civil religions," or "metaphorical religions," a transcendence with no God and no instituted religion, a transcendence wholly contained within immanence.

The great political ideologies that accompanied totalitarianism, such as Communism and nationalism, have been interpreted as religious phenomena that foster social cohesion by compensating for the atomization characteristic of individualistic and abstract democratic societies. Thus there would be a perverted and perverse religiousness in Nazism. All of the sociological theories outlined earlier integrate, sometimes unwittingly, this dimension, which is paradoxical in the framework of their theoretical project of understanding society by itself, in radical immanence. The fact of the matter is that they could not construe a theory of social cohesion without falling back on the collective category of exteriority. As we have seen,

Durkheim argues that it is upon moments of effervescence and demographic densification—when individuals removed from the routine and dispersion of their quotidian are seized in a religious ecstasy (the "corrobori")—that society is founded at the same time as religion. Max Weber, in his idea of charismatic authority (which provides a relevant description of the modern experience of political power), conceives of the possibility that power in modern bureaucratic societies can come from a source outside of the confines of utilitarian rationality. He also clearly demonstrates in his theories of political sociology that all political collectivities, as all political powers, are based on the principle of exclusion ("the originary exclusion" dear to anthropologists), if only because the exercise of power requires a territory, a circumscribed area of jurisdiction delimited by a boundary that puts the subjects who do not come within its competency on the outside to obtain a monopoly of legitimate violence on the inside. Combining Durkheim's and Weber's theories, Victor Turner[58] shows that societies go through phases of effervescence when new values are generated, the *communitas*, and phases of rigid institutionalization, the *societas*. Last but not least, Freud himself thought of the unconscious as being outside of consciousness and not subject to its control, and of the reality principle as an instance of exteriority that imposes its law upon the pleasure principle and determines the identity of the self. Is not one of the earliest experiences of transcendence the realization of the subject that it cannot return to the origin (to the mother) and hence regress into immanence (which it must abandon in order to constitute itself, through the paternal and social prohibition of incest)? What are all of these thinkers saying if not that exteriority is the determining principle of identity and singularity? They are reintroducing transcendence in the language of immanence, not genuine transcendence but a morphological, mechanical transcendence wholly focused on immanence.

And so transcendence (immanentized this time) was stealthily reintroduced into modernity, in theory as in practice, without anybody knowing it and with everyone persuaded that it had been banished. In this sense, a savage religiosity manifested itself at the core of modern rationality through the reintroduction of exteriority and the recreation of a totally mythical form of anteriority: all ideologies produce myths about the origin, the "golden age," of the groups they exalt, and all rewrite their mythological past in view of an imagined future. We have here the occasion to verify the extent to which these two aspects—exteriority and anteriority—are characteristic of transcendence. Whatever the case was in reality, transcendence was (consciously and declaratively) experienced in modernity as immanence, unaware of itself as transcendence. The key question is to understand what made the practical recreation of transcendence "necessary" when everything pointed to its disqualification. Why was the religious recreated in modernity?

I have already discussed the impasse of modern consciousness concerning the question of origin and the "externment" (the exclusion) of the corporeal and the biological that constitutes it. The ignorance of the principle of origin implied by the aspiration to be All, including one's own origin (Man as source of himself), also can be interpreted as a refusal of limits, because the relative dependence that the anteriority of the origin entails and the restriction of the self to the inside that exteriority supposes go hand in hand with the existence of a limit and hence the impossibility of the totality. Identity cannot be recognized as an identity nor mastered without the recognition of a limit. Upon this depends the recognition that there is an Other present beside the self, which leads in turn to a sense of responsibility. Faced with the presence of someone else, we are brought to weigh our acts and to adapt our behavior with regard to the other. It is because one recognizes one's own limits that one can feel *obliged* to someone else. It is impossible to imagine the existence of a society without such a principle of obligation. The relationship to the law is premised upon it, as is the civil obedience that goes with responsible civic freedom. In a democratic society where all citizens are supposed to be individually equal, what can oblige them to abide by a law that comes not from God but from the collective decision of the citizens, from the "people"? How can the sovereignty of the "people" be exercised upon citizens who are its source (divisible and countable by virtue of the system of *universal* suffrage)?

The seminal theorists of the democratic idea tackled this cardinal "practical" problem, which raises the question of the viability and implementation of democratic universality. Spinoza and Rousseau both concluded that individualism, even rational individualism, could not provide sufficient grounds for founding a principle of obligation, that such a principle could only originate from a superior being, powerful enough to impose an authority upon men who consider themselves absolutely equal.[59] They thus proposed to reintroduce religion into the democratic state (indeed, it is not easy to find a supreme power superior to God!) but this time as an agency of the state, under its direction, for the purposes of setting up the system par excellence of socialization to obedience. So right from the outset, theorists of the democratic idea programmed the return of the religious to a political sphere that had just gotten rid of it, but this time the religious was to be under the directive power of the political and integrated to it. The invention of a "civil religion" (the term is Rousseau's!) went hand in hand with the establishment of a democratic state separated from religion. Instituted religion was dismissed, and a civil religion took its place that did not call itself a religion and that brought transcendence down to the sphere of power and men.[60]

The preamble to the *Declaration of the Rights of Man and the Citizen* (August 26, 1789) betrays this immanentized transcendence. The "natural, inalienable, and sacred rights of man" are declared on the basis of the idea that Man or Nature is the source thereof, but this is done in "the presence" and "under the auspices of the Supreme Being" ("the National Assembly recognizes and declares, in the presence and under the auspices of the Supreme Being, the following rights of man and citizen"), and hence of an anonymous transcendence, to what purpose, we do not know, since "men are born free and remain free and equal in rights." Unlike God in the American democracy whose presence is still felt (witness the use of the motto "In God We Trust" or the mention, "under God" in the Pledge of Allegiance), this Supreme Being was to have no future in French political culture. Nevertheless, this odd mention of a Supreme Being bears witness to the need of the Constituent Assembly to assert a form of transcendence, even a totally abstract, conceptual transcendence forged by the hand of Man, at the very moment when Man was proclaiming his rights.

The identity of Man built on an interiorized (immanentized) form of transcendence exposed itself to all sorts of perversion due to the loss of the reality principle, the principle of exteriority. Thus modernity unconsciously spawned a mechanism that recreated transcendence, which is at the origin of the secret religion that inhabits it, as if proof had been delivered that one cannot escape a foundation extrinsic to the political sphere, and that it is the religious (be it instituted or savage) that takes charge of this function in the economy of social existence. The totalitarian monstrosity was a paroxysmal expression of this fact.

Sacrificial Exclusion

The reproduction of a boundary in immanence (the "immanent transcendence") could be obtained only through a mechanism of *exclusion* that dissociates forms of immanence by creating an illusion of elsewhere. As we have already seen, total Man was born from the exclusion of the corporeal, the biological, and the particular, an exclusion that presupposed a sacrificial outcome. It did so theoretically, since the singular (the people, identity, etc.) had to be sacrificed to achieve the universal, but also in practical terms, since the paragons of the corporeal (i.e., women, Jews, and blacks) were destined to accomplish this sacrifice for others in a manner that was admittedly abstract and commonplace, but also paroxysmal, on the occasion of "sacrificial crises," to borrow René Girard's expression. As the reader will have understood by now, this exclusion produced a sacralization; it recreated an empty (prohibited) space in the fullness of immanence, but the moderns were unable to come to terms with this phenomenon, since they continued to deny exteriority.

The theorists of ethnology have delved the farthest into exteriority from the standpoint of the originary exclusion, of the murder of a surrogate victim. The sacrifice of the *pharmakon* in Ancient Greece often has been seen as the supreme paradigm of this theory. Girard, Derrida, and Vernant are counted among the many recent thinkers to rely heavily on the *pharmakon* as an explanatory model.[61] The modern democratic mind is justifiably fascinated by this annual Athenian rite, the purpose of which was to get rid of the "blemish" through two *pharmakoi*, one for men and one for women, selected from the lower classes and prepared for a year to be sacrificed. In remote antiquity, the two scapegoats were probably stoned to death, their corpses burned, and their ashes dispersed. This exclusion restored the internal equilibrium of the city-state that had been destabilized as a result of excess or anomie. The term *pharmakos* itself, meaning both drug and poison, clearly points to the ambivalence and duality of a system in which good (the city's salvation) and evil (the murderous sacrifice) are inextricably intertwined.

What is at issue in sacrificial exclusions or expulsions is the status of the other. The other can be alien, abnormal, or inferior but also superior, be it a god or a human with too much power, as was the case of the "tyrant" in ancient Greece, expelled because his excessive excellence endangered the stability of the city. This expulsion of the other is absolutely indispensable to the renewal of the city, because society needs to set a boundary to establish its identity. "The fundamental feature of the whole rite is that something is thrown out of the social body."[62] But what matters most is not so much the purifying, cathartic aspect of "transferring that which the individual or the community finds unpleasant or harmful within itself to the outside, onto a thing, an animal, or a man which then serves as an intermediary."[63] It is not by "transferring evil"[64] onto a scapegoat that the community's health can be recovered but rather, in my opinion, by recreating a limit and an exteriority, morphologically to begin with, without which the human group cannot be maintained (and Durkheim saw this but was unable to unravel its meaning).

René Girard's version of the scapegoat theory is interesting in this respect. His theory of mimesis[65] in itself is less important, I think, than what it implies about the mechanism of differentiation and hence of identification (since identity always involves placing what is different on the other side of a boundary). "The universal spread of 'doubles,' the complete effacement of differences, heightening antagonisms but also making them interchangeable, is the prerequisite for the establishment of violent unanimity."[66] In the sacrificial exclusion of the scapegoat, a boundary is being sought in order to reintroduce difference in a group that is threatened for one reason or another by nondifferentiation and massification. A scapegoat, who is supposed to stand out symbolically from the mass, must be sacrificed for all individuals, substituted for all individuals (despite their differences and despite the surrogate's own difference and individuality), to break the massification and the nondifferentiation and recreate identity and hence difference.

In the scapegoat, it is the substitutability that is being sacrificed as much as the substitute, and this is what restores difference. When difference "has been effaced, purification is no longer possible and impure, contagious, reciprocal violence spreads throughout the community,"[67] unless the community can find a surrogate victim to bear the violent lack of differentiation that threatens the community, to become under the effect of mimesis the double of each person in the community. By removing a victim from the group, the group makes room for recreating social order. But the prior identity of the scapegoat must lend itself to the process; there must be some trait, real or imaginary, that makes the victim stand out from others and personify in the collective mind the fantasy of power that it is supposed to possess and that accentuates its abnormality and monstrosity so that the sacrifice can go ahead with no regrets and no moral guilt. "The good scapegoat [. . .] is the weakest link in the hierarchical structure"[68] but also the one that seems to be the most powerful and whose exclusion makes it possible to reconsolidate the structure.

The different mechanisms, such as exclusion and scapegoating, that serve to produce exteriority are sacrificial by nature. First they produce a sense of the "sacred," the venerable, and the uncanny, of things beyond the pale of thought that arouse a feeling of obligation and obedience because they point to something mysterious above and beyond the individual and human reason. Victor Turner's *communitas*, from which a new social order derives its revitalized inspiration, is one such mechanism. But all of these mechanisms are merely outlets for a preexisting violence, inherent to the social order before the "sacrificial crisis." The myth of the total Man, of the self-originating Man, does violence to the human condition itself, and it does so necessarily and congenitally. This is something that we are now in a better position to understand. We have seen that it is the lack of differentiation that leads to the sacrificial crisis and to the murder of the scapegoat. This means that the denial of the principle of boundaries is murderous, and that it is so not only for the scapegoat, whose exclusion, excision, or extermination automatically recreates a boundary, but for the murderer as well. The total Man has proven to be a profoundly suicidal project for humankind, for Man in general.

The close relationship between the experience of boundary denial that characterizes the fantasy of a total, abstract universal and the desire to put others or oneself to death is brilliantly analyzed by Pierre Legendre. In an essay on the suicidal act, Legendre argues that suicide is a way for the subject to give himself a boundary that he was not given by the person from whom he descends and whose place he is destined to take, to wit, the father. The suicided person's death creates a limit for the "suicider." Indeed, the suicidal act (which is a homicide by definition, since a man is killed) involves two people—the perpetrator of the murder and the victim. It so happens that in this case, they are, of course, the same person, whence Legendre's question: What could it "mean *to be two*, in the case of the human subject?"[69] and turning to the father-son relationship, he argues that "the person who kills himself commits a parricide."[70] Now since the father is obviously "physically" absent in the suicidal act, it is the father's image, as the very figure of Interdiction (of incest), that the son strikes dead. And he strikes it dead precisely because the Interdiction that it represented was not effective enough. The staging of the Interdiction serves to "act out the structural imperative of differentiation in the human species."[71] This is the role of the father as "guarantor of the differentiation that must be imposed on the human subject in relation to [. . .] the mother."[72] The Interdiction figured by the Father is what renders "humanly representable" "the death that is necessary to life, the subjective separation from the mother under the auspices of the third instance, namely, the paternal instance."[73] Striking down the image of the Father is the savage, ultimate limit that the son sets for himself, with the aid, notwithstanding, of a father whose authority was insufficient. But in doing so the son really kills himself! This is because, as Legendre explains, the father is also firstly the son of his own father, "a son who relinquishes his place to his own son,"[74] which means that he relinquishes his (unconscious) request as a child (addressed to his parents) to his own child, who can thus subjectively assume his status as a son and take his place in the filiation, which can be defined as the "symbolic permutation of places."[75]

But relinquishing one's place requires an awareness of one's limits. This is the role of the paternal Interdiction in relation to the mother who stands for a lack of limits to the child due to the original symbiosis between the two. It is the father, on the outside, who separates the two. It is the father who represents exteriority. Having received from his father the boundaries that allow the son to become a differentiated subject, he in turn passes them on to his own son. This, at any rate, would be a successful example of filiation. But when the father fails, when the Interdiction is not effective, the son lacks the boundary needed to build a separate identity. The son's inability to get out of the nonlimited relationship with the maternal figure has dramatic consequences. "Suicide reveals the tragic riddle with which the subject is confronted in the process of humanization."[76] It is the answer that the subject gives himself (and the subject, as we have seen, is two) in his attempt to solve the riddle of the origin. When separation fails to come from the father through transmission, the subject tries to give himself a limit. All experiences of limits contain an element of death, of separation with the self. In this case, the death is no longer a symbolic death inflicted from the outside, and so it becomes a reality. In killing himself, or rather in killing the (insubstantial) father in himself, the suicided person materializes the boundary that will allow him to institute himself as a son. He becomes his own father, but because his father is a product of his imagination and he is his father's son, the death and separation that should be symbolic become real! By killing himself, he is finally "born" as a son! The limit that was lacking is set up through sacrificial self-destruction. "[A] suicide is a human sacrifice that stands as testimony to the failure of differentiation in the genealogical logic."[77]

Legendre thus underlines the deep-seated significance of the sacrificial act for the subject: setting a boundary, providing the occasion to lose something so as to develop as a separate, differentiated identity, capable of meeting others. The sacrificial act may involve the loss of something or someone else (an animal, an object, or a human being) or of the self (through self-sacrifice, when the symbolic or ritual mechanisms are ineffective). Legendre maintains that there is an economic relationship between generations, a principle of payment. Each parent must relinquish his or her own unconscious request (referring back to the status of the Father in each parent's family) in order to "enter filiation subjectively."[78] When this does not happen, when words cannot "metabolize" the question of the Father, the intergenerational "payment" cannot be made. The child is the creditor vis-à-vis the representation of the father. The father is the titular debtor. He owes his son what he himself received from his father: a payment that takes the form of imposing a boundary, of symbolically instituting the son as a subject separate from the mother."[79] The suicide is payment for the father's unpaid debt: the imposition of the boundary, or otherwise put, the principle of the Law embodied in the principle of castration that separates from the mother. The son pays for his father, in his father's place, in order to institute himself at last as a son! We have here a form of "genealogical justice," with sons indeed paying their fathers' debts. This idea, which is found in biblical discourse (remedied through repentance) and in Greek tragedies (ratified through fate), is unthinkable in our democratic culture, except in the context of psychoanalysis.

Legendre's discussion of the sacrifice involved in the suicidal act helps us understand the deeply sacrificial nature of modernity's instinctual, savage attempt to reproduce boundaries and exteriority in immanence. This model of the subjective psyche can be applied to the overall economy of the spirit of modernity, which is characterized, as we have seen, by the autonomy and immanence of the human subject and a denial of exteriority and anteriority.

Such a transposition from the existential case of the individual to the global social referent is all the more significant insofar as society is founded on the principle of differentiation. "No one escapes the law of separation. The concrete father, himself the son of a mythical mother, can assume this responsibility only in reference to his own father and, beyond that, to the separating principle: the image of the Father as imposed and transmitted by the social discourse of the Reference in the culture."[80] No human reality can escape the trial of separation. Modernity consciously denied the necessity for it but unconsciously sought and recreated separation, perforce in a sacrificial, suicidal manner. And since it refused to deal institutionally with the question of origin and transmission, the invention of a surrogate could only be an unwilled, uncontrolled process. It recreated separation in immanence and, hence, it reproduced immanence in a monstrous way: by producing a transcendence adulterated in immanence, with inevitable sacrificial fatality. Man, having become God for Man, was doomed to self-destruction, in a process similar to the suicidal relationship of the father and the son. Exteriority could be recreated in immanence only by means of a sacralizing exclusion, by making pariahs of categories and groups considered "alien," by the denial of difference and hence of alterity. This is why the sacrificial death inflicted upon others to restore the differentiation so necessary to collective and subjective identity is never very far from the self-inflected death of the individual subject or collectivity that must die to compensate for the boundary that it did not receive from outside in order to be born at last! The democratic experience premised upon the idea of Man without limits, the idea of Man-as-God, swings back and forth between these two extremes: between different types of social and political alienation that are constitutive of it (despite its conscious principle of political equality, hierarchies are continually resurfacing in it) and different types of totalitarianism of murderous and suicidal intent ("*Viva la muerte!*").

The Hecatombs of Modernity

There is, then, a sacrificial principle at work in modernity. It is a necessarily violent way of reintroducing an experience of giving and doing good deeds in an egalitarian world that set out to eliminate them as radically as possible in the name of absolute total sharing, which left nothing out and no room for the gratuitous. The entire history of modern politics illustrated the bloody, murderous nature of this uncontrollable violence. And it was in the modern era that this violence reached hitherto unimaginable heights. War and persecution have always been part of human history but never on such a scale, with so many millions killed and such radicality in the extermination.

The root of this violence is to be found less in the modern techniques of destruction as in the flaws in the very spirit of political modernity that the Shoah threw into relief with such vivid crudeness that it is impossible to avoid confronting them anymore.

Right from the start, with the French revolution, this unexplained violence was already manifested in the bloody massacres of the Terror, perpetrated in the name of freedom! It is very interesting in this regard to examine Claude Lefort's highly symptomatic rereading of Edgar Quinet's thesis in *La Révolution* on the phenomenon of the Terror, which "becomes intelligible only if it is placed within its political and religious context."[81]

> According to [Quinet], when the revolutionaries retreated in the face of the task of making a religious revolution, they found themselves faced with a spiritual void. In that sense, the Terror appears to be a substitute for the one action which could have united the revolutionary actors in one faith and which could have revealed to them [. . .] the identity of their enemies, the nature of their own cause and the nature of their own identity. In the absence of that creative action and of its guiding idea, the distinction between self and other or between the people and its adversaries no longer had referent in reality. It was impossible to locate the enemy, who became one with the suspect, and the revolutionary himself lost the criterion of his own morality. He sought it in the imaginary, in the ability to assume the risk of death in the service of the Revolution. [. . . T]o use Quinet's own terms, "The revolutionaries were afraid of the Revolution." And they concealed their fear behind a mask of heroism which meant only this: overcoming death, with the fear of the other and the death of the other as their guarantee.[82]

Quinet thus sees the Terror as the result of a congenital flaw in the Revolution itself, which turned to it as "a substitute for a religious revolution" that it dared not undertake. The revolution had granted freedom of worship, but Catholicism was so deeply rooted in society and permeated reality so thoroughly that "in such conditions [. . .] to grant freedom of belief is to grant nothing."[83] The bloody ferocity of the revolutionaries compensated for their "timidity"[84] when it came to dealing with the established religion. They beheaded the king but dared not attack the "theological principle," incapable of seeing its "profound interdependence" with the monarchical principle.[85] The recourse to Terror appears, then, as an extreme form of compensation. Commenting on the revolutionaries' short-lived attempt at de-Christianization through a cult to the "goddess of Reason," Quinet ironically notes their "inability to see the religious revolution as something more than a feast for the eyes and a *coup de théâtre*."[86] But this "first cult at least represented pleasure; the cult Robespierre dedicated to the Supreme Being was based upon fear, and he had to crush the iconoclasts [. . .] in order to keep the people inside the doors of the former church and to prevent them leaving, the terrorists forced them to stand between scaffolds."[87]

I do not subscribe to Quinet's explanation of the Terror as the result of a revolution that was not taken to completion in the religious sphere, but what I would like to highlight in his argument is the idea that Terror was related to the repression of the religious which then returned with paroxysmal violence in the political arena. Lefort paraphrases Quinet's argument in the following terms: "The revolutionaries were afraid of the Revolution [. . .] and they made an idol of it [. . .]. By deifying it, they petrified it, because they were afraid of being carried away by a movement that might have destroyed the basis of their old beliefs. By [. . .] making it an abstract being, they avoided the task of setting everyone free [. . .]. The Terror is a sign of their inability to break with the past in either the political or the religious realm."[88]

It is odd, if very significant for our purposes, to find Quinet comparing "French Terror and Hebraic Terror"[89] as systems "applied to the regeneration of a people." Moses led the Hebrews out of slavery and forced them to wander in the desert "in fear and trembling for forty years," in what was "indeed a government through fear" intent on tearing them away from their old habits of servility. But unlike Moses, "the revolutionaries failed to perform the first task required of any lawgiver: they would not institute the people on a religious basis. If Moses had acted like them, if he had consecrated old idols 'stained with the blood of the twelve tribes [he] would now seem execrable to posterity.' "[90] We find in this respect the concern of Spinoza and Rousseau, mentioned earlier. The principle of freedom of worship "contained the seeds of counter-revolution,"[91] and the energy that could have been used against the adversaries of the Revolution was turned back against the revolutionaries. "The revolutionaries were being self-contradictory when they reverted to the old law of terror and, at the same time, safeguarded the rights of their enemies. And that contradiction inevitably destroyed them."[92]

Quinet considers, however, yet another source for the Terror as being in the idea of Man formulated by the *Declaration* that, by its abstraction, led to a negation of the individual. At the "origins of revolutionary voluntarism" is the "scorn [of the revolutionaries] for the individual, that sad legacy from the oppression of old. 'Be like nature,' said Danton. 'She looks to the preservation of the species and is not concerned with individuals.' If the so-called terrorism of nature is applied to human affairs, it becomes necessary to behead humanity itself."[93] "From the outset, we turned the Revolution into an abstract being like nature, into an idol which we deified and which needed no one, which could, without any danger to itself, swallow up individuals one after another and wax strong on the annihilation of all." Lefort comments that this "fiction combines with another, which does more to explain the mechanisms of the Terror: that of the original goodness of man, which is borrowed from Jean-Jacques Rousseau. 'Who would believe that philanthropy itself could also lead to Terror?' exclaims Quinet."[94] The seeds of the Terror are to be found in the superlative definition of Man. Quinet argues that the revolutionaries "began by putting 'man is good' on the agenda and, when they encountered difficulties in establishing justice, they concluded that they were caught up in a vast conspiracy, and failed to see that in most cases it was things themselves that conspired against them."[95]

In a way both of Quinet's explanations of the Terror, as resulting from the incompletion of the revolution or from excessive certitude (the revolution as "idol"), attribute the bloody events to the crisis consecutive to the destruction of the very principle of limits.

Sacrifice and the Morality of Victimhood

The religious and sacrificial dimensions thus appear to be central to democracy. According to our paradigm of the unconscious, they are not, of course, generally expressed clearly and directly. Sometimes they even manifest themselves, very paradoxically and contradictorily, in their opposite, that is, via an identification with victimhood, with the condition of the victim in the sacrificial drama, be it in reality or in fantasy. Sacrifice is desirable in the democratic ethos! In fact, the only morality that democracy recognizes is identified with victimhood. Sartre remarks in his portrayal of the democrat (whom he pits against the anti-Semite) are highly pertinent in this respect: "It is as if [the democrat] were fascinated by all who plot his downfall. Perhaps at the bottom of his heart he yearns after the violence which he has denied himself."[96] The democrat always sees himself as persecuted, because he refuses to assume responsibility for the violence whose seeds are contained in democracy too. He cannot recognize this without putting his own virtue into question. In the democratic conception of morality, those who endure suffering (in fact, the last ones to suffer) are always right. How can we account for such a strange twist of mind? What makes the vanquished necessarily right? There are victims who are responsible for the course of events they endure and victors who illustrate the triumph of justice. Justice is independent of the condition of the person being judged, even though this condition must be taken into consideration (particularly in the case of people who are suffering). It sometimes happens that the righteous defeat their enemies! Is that reason to pronounce them guilty? The moral stance that always identifies justice with suffering and power with injustice and amorality informs the principle of responsibility in the democratic ethos. The glorification of and identification with the victim betray an identification with the suffering side of the democratic ideological system and a refusal to face, no less assume responsibility for, its persecuting side. It was in nationalism, as we will see, that offering oneself up in sacrifice, even onto death (in situations of war) was raised to the rank of a supreme value. The possibility of having such a morality of victimhood in democracy derives from the latter's dual conscious and unconscious nature, which dialectically enables its value system to stand on moveable ground. The moral position of the Left criticizes the conscious face of democracy in terms of values derived from the consequence of phenomena—phenomena of a persecuting type—themselves due to the forces of the unconscious face of democracy. The victims raise democracy's self-consciousness: they carry the emblem of democracy's veritable morality. Thanks to them, democracy can always identify itself with a moral stance and need not come to terms with its responsibility. In the current crisis of democracy, the role of victim is played by what the French call "*les exclus*," literally the excluded, or all those who, for one reason or another, live on the margins of society. We identify with them and with their lot, work to improve their condition, and basically recreate social cohesion around them. In so doing we disregard the responsibility of the system that produced them, for which we are accountable and from which we, unlike *les exclus*, benefit.

But democratic identification with the victim, as the condition of morality, has deeper roots. Democracy, as a universe of absolute equality and hence of total sharing, engenders willy-nilly a tendency to amorality. No one can be compelled in this individualist universe to feel duty-bound to anyone else. Everything is supposed to be equally divided between equal citizens: there are no "shares" remaining to be divided, save perhaps the irremediably ungraspable emptiness of what was shared. Good deeds and giving in general have no place in this universe. They are no longer valued. And if there still be any need for them, then it can only mean that the sharing has been unequal. Since everything is owed (as shares) to equal citizens, giving can only be a sign of questionable morality. Socialism set out to politically rectify a system of sharing that it deemed unequal and not to challenge the very idea of total sharing. It is, then, through the agency of the victim's experience (the one who is not equal) that democracy rediscovers morality, a morality that is necessarily bound up with sacrifice and victimhood. The victim allows individualist citizens to enjoy a sense of moral indignation, to make a show of compassion that they would surely not have for their equals, and thereby rediscover morality. From that point on, even if one is not a victim and is not suffering, one must identify with the victim to show moral rectitude and share in the recognition from which the victim benefits. In a universe of total equality, nobody sees anybody else. When all has been shared, there is nothing in common but emptiness.

We can now understand the reason for the absolutely sacrificial nature of democratic morality. This nature is ambivalent: in producing exteriority to identify with, democracy removes a share from its total sharing and consecrates it in an act of absolute giving so as to reconsolidate itself. In so doing, it produces a victim with which it identifies and which, by taking its place, restores its identity. All of these mechanisms are clearly meant to generate a sense of commonality and obligation that no longer exists and to provide a foundation for authority and law in a relationship between equals who refuse them.

The line of argument used by liberal thinkers and critics of democracy can be reread in this light. All recognize the permanence of the sacrificial. "Marx [. . .] insists on the fact that the production of surplus value (obtained by paying subsistence wages) is the worker's sacrifice to society, a sacrifice imposed by the Bourgeoisie."[97] This modern sacrifice is the alienation imposed by general or dominant interests. Durkheim sees "social constraints" as a form of sacrifice or renunciation. Even utilitarian liberalism did not put an end to sacrifice. In fact, "Utilitarianism is intimately related to the sacrificial order."[98] After all, according to the principle of efficiency "if a social transformation is such that some must win and others lose, who is there to stand in its way?" "What appears on the surface to be the most anti-sacrificial doctrine, the one that holds or seems to hold that only pleasure and happiness count, and that there is nothing that does not proceed from calculated self-interest, turns out to be the most altruistic of doctrines, the most hungry for sacrifices."[99]

The morality of sacrifice that had prevailed after the Shoah was supplanted in the 1980s by the morality of victimhood, particularly in the period following the collapse of Communism, with the rise of "humanitarian causes" and "human-rightist" policies. Democracy found a source of regeneration in victims, who became the saints and martyrs of human rights, rediscovered and pitted against totalitarian (but also democratic) states, in the name of an apparently stateless moral universalism. But the "humanitarian crusade" that refused to see anything other than individual subjects in the victims—beyond inter-*national* dimensions—soon found itself confronted with the national dimensions of wars and the *national* dimensions within itself. Humanitarian parties (nationals of specific countries) could be taken for intruders and themselves become victims or aggressors, caught up in a spiral and compelled to engage in reprisals (be it in Somalia, in Irak, or in

Bosnia, where a blue helmet was killed), and these reprisals cause victims
of another sort. "In this confrontation (between peacekeeping forces and
the partisans of armed nations), the former take into account only the
victims who are supposedly passive and ignore willing victims,"[100] that is,
willing martyrs. Attacked by the latter, "they have no other choice. They
can only take up the challenge and fight them, even if it means that they
themselves become victimizers [. . .]. All they can do is arouse a spirit of
supreme sacrifice in their own ranks [. . .] or abandon the victims to their
fate."[101] In either case, the morality of victimhood cannot survive, "for it
lacks a sacrificial determination, which is the prerogative of specific nations
[. . .]. The cause of Man depends perhaps on the capacity of its advocates
to submit to sacrifice,"[102] which means, in this case, assuming the political
responsibility inherent in the national condition. The morality of victimhood,
as an ascetic attempt to get beyond the sacrificial morality, finds itself pulled
back into the sacrificial drama, which is its deepest underlying principle.

The Unanimous Nation: Filling the Sacrificial Abyss

Until the 1980s the prevailing form of democratic morality was based
on sacrifice, not victimhood. What emerged from the democratic abyss
was more often the (positive) phenomenon of the nation ("dying for your
country") than the (negative) phenomenon of victimhood. The nation had
proven to be something more than an assembly of citizens united to make
decisions about political affairs (article 3 of the *Declaration* states that the
"source of all sovereignty resides essentially in the nation"). Most often it
was under the banner of some mysterious, age-old collective identity that
the nation managed to unite the men who had become individual citizens,
so equal that they had nothing more in common (since, as we have seen,
the principle of equality induced a principle of total sharing that threw
everyone back onto their own individuality). This can be read from the
very terms of the *Declaration*. Article 3's statement, that "no individual can
exercise authority that does not proceed from the nation in plain terms,"
contradicts the assertion in article 1, that "men are born free and remain
free and equal in rights." The one asserts the transcendence of the nation,
as the source of all authority over individuals, and the other the irreducible
freedom of the individual (which proceeds from nature) as the source of
sovereignty. The national phenomenon and its nationalist corollary prospered in the gap between these two principles. In the nation, individuals
become interchangeable, mere emanations of the sovereign nation, seen as
something greater than the sum of its citizens. "The big unit can only be
an undivided whole if is made up of identical units," Sieyès declared. The
individual units are the citizens. But the men who are citizens also have an

irreducible, individual, and transgenerational singularity. This singularity, as we have seen, was to reoccupy, in an unconscious way, the nation, the great empty body of citizens in search of an identity. Thus the nation, "one and indivisible," took the place of the king's body that united the collectivity in the ancien régime. As Marcel Gauchet has observed, the revolutionaries "actually liberated the signifying energy accumulated over the centuries in a magnetic term [he cites Sieyès: "What is a Nation? A body of associates living under a common law"], which would end up driving them more than they were to make use of it. They detached the Nation from the King only to take up the position that the King occupied vis-à-vis the nation."[103]

In the years following the proclamation of a disidentifying universal form of politics, an unexpected phenomenon occurred: the massive revival of communal identity. Here was the nation again, no longer the (conscious) "civic" nation but the (unconscious) "national" nation which, this time, transcended the rationalist categories of the modern project of citizenship in a straightforward, triumphant affirmation (nationalism) of collective singularity. The emergence of democracy "was accompanied by the appearance, for the first time or in an altogether new light, of the state, society, the people, the nation. And one would like to conceive of each of these forms in the singular, to defend it against the threat of division, to reject anything that flaws it as a symptom of decomposition and destruction, and, since the work of division seems to be unleashed in democracy, one would like either to curb it or to get rid of it. But state, society, people and nation are indefinable entities in democracy. They bear the imprint of an idea of the human being that undermines their affirmation, an idea which seems derisory in face of the antagonisms that tear apart the world, but without which democracy would disappear [. . .]; [T]he desire for revolution [. . .] serve[s] the cult of unity, the cult of an identity found at last in the singular."[104]

Democratic life thus turns out to be driven by an irrepressible desire to compensate for and fill the void of citizenship. The longing for unity and totality reflects the unbearable depths of the abyss beneath democracy. The search for totality and the experience of the abyss structure the "hidden religion" of democracy. Its sacrificial syndrome aims at totality. It is an attempt to recreate an undivided whole through loss, removal, or exclusion (the "sacrifice"), to give society an exteriority that prompts it to define itself as unified in reaction to an outside rather than in relation to itself and its countless divisions. The element "externed" in the sacrifice fosters the unification of the civic nation. This unity is imperative, since political equality is premised upon the interchangeability and fungibility of the man without qualities. Hence, the totality is massive, compact, and lacks differentiation (and in this respect I disagree with René Girard, who argues that the sacrificial act restores social differentiation). Differentiation of society as a whole (as an identity vis-à-vis the world) exists, to be sure, but not differentiation of society in relation to itself (that is, in terms of classes, functions, hierarchies, etc.). All totalities are sacrificial. They require each person to make sacrifices for the good of all. The democratic idea of the "general will" implies such sacrifices: "invoking the general will raises, *ipso facto*, the altar of holocausts. The social whole is an implacable divinity that demands its share of victims whenever it is named or represented."[105] And these victims are justified because their sacrifice is for purposes of "public utility." In fact, totality is always a "unanimity minus one," minus the excluded, sacrificed element, which is removed from the total count and thanks to which a transcendence is recreated that enables the collectivity to see itself as a whole, even though it is dispersed and divided throughout. "Because of the victim, insofar as it seems to emerge from the community and the community seems to emerge from it, for the first time there can be something like an inside and an outside, a before and after, a community and the sacred."[106] This is the sacrificial moment. "The mechanism of victimhood, the unanimity found in the common hatred of a surrogate victim, is actually a unanimity minus one; but the excluded person is so radically other that he does not count among the members of the community and never did."[107] We can see from this once again that totality is by no means unity, or rather it is a mock unity: the unity of all is achieved by the expulsion of the one, one against all, one in place of all, and it is upon this condition that the one is reflected in the whole. "It is precisely because the elements of the social whole can be substituted for one another that some can be sacrificed for the whole."[108] Substitutability therefore underpins the whole, which is the opposite of singularity: the one is achieved by its expulsion from the totality. The one of the whole is not to be confused with the one of the singular. Alain Caillé quotes in this regard Gusdorf, who wrote that one of the foremost aims of sacrifice was "to obtain salvation for the whole by giving up a part [. . .] the sacrificer offers the part for the whole."[109] Caillé also cites Saint Augustine: "This is the sacrifice of Christians: we being many, are one body in Christ."[110] By exchanging a victim for the reunion of all, the sacrifice shows that the "substitutability of each individual for all, and hence the indifferentiation and the disidentification of singular individuals, is 'what allows the universal communion in the Great Whole.' "[111] In this sense, the Whole calls upon the individual to sacrifice himself, to surpass himself in a new condition of being that transcends him (namely, that of the citizen) and that exceeds his own forces. This is what Durkheim calls the "sacred," but for Durkheim this sacred was the social whole.

Thus in democracy sacrifice makes possible the sole collective being that seems to have any basis in reality, and that is the nation much more

than the political community of citizens, which is an abstract legal institution without interiority or desire, since it ignores people in particular
along with their historical and transgenerational substance. But at bottom
this political community also may have a sacrificial nature. In the *Social
Contract*, Rousseau describes the process involved in the constitution of
sovereignty by which each individual gives up (sacrifices) an (equal) share of
freedom for the good of all, that is, for the common good. It is from the
pooling of these individual renouncements that the collectivity is formed.
The "contract" itself can even be seen as advocating a model based on
the expulsion of a surrogate victim (the individual share given up for the
common good). Hobbes develops the idea of a process of "contagion" that
gradually makes every member of the social body abstain from violence and
ultimately leads to the election of an individual endowed with the power
and the right to kill, a right that is eminently reversible, as illustrated by
certain archaic cultures where the chief becomes the surrogate victim who
guarantees the salvation of all.[112] We know from experience that citizenship
without the "nation" is but a pious dream: it turned out to be the privilege
of a (singular) nationality, and its universality proved dubious. The sacrificial
mechanism is at work then in both citizenship (the civil nation) and the
nation (the national nation), though unrecognized as such, and even denied
in democratic discourse and consciousness. Once again, we can see that the
making of the democratic universal is structurally sacrificial in its conscious
process (citizenship) as in its unconscious reality (the nation). The surreptitious reproduction of a sacrificial principle of giving (including of oneself)
in a universe premised upon nature and reason ineluctably led to major
perversions at the origin of the great tragedies of the last two centuries.
Modernity recreated transcendence without admitting it, so that this purely
imminent transcendence, this religion without a name, gone berserk, was
cruel and murderous under the guise of total innocence.

   The nation was the main protagonist of this drama, on the inside,
in turning against its minority populations or against foreigners, as on the
outside, in turning against other international players. It sometimes even
turned against a part of itself: this was the case during the revolutionary
terror with the Vendée massacres that Gracchus Babeuf characterized as a
"populicide" and that can be seen as the prototype of the modern genocide.
The wars in the twentieth century, when the world had shrunk in the wake
of the nineteenth-century colonial conquests, became the stage of gigantic
bloodbaths, starting with the First World War. The wholesale murder of
the Armenians was the first occurrence of a contemporary genocide. This
sacrificial bloodbath was hardly an accident or a fluke in modernity. To the
contrary, it was the expression of an unrecognized but deep-seated aspect
thereof. And this is something that cannot be ignored after the Shoah,

which, in this respect, constitutes the point of no return for modernity. We can no longer be content with simply setting modernity back on its feet as if it had experienced a temporary setback (one among many whose importance is relative). We must pave the way to a new era in history and humanity, a new age in democracy, after doing a "soul accounting" of the modern adventure.

Wherein We See the Term Holocaust *in a New Light*

It is not among the least surprising outcomes of an analysis that set out to "deconstruct" the explanation of the persecution of the Jews based on the scapegoat mechanism to see it cropping up again in all its splendor. The sacrificial figure of political modernity that emerges from my analysis is, to be sure, altogether different from the ahistorical, anthropological, and abstract figure that enjoys widespread currency. I have, in fact, taken great care to examine the observable particularities of modernity, as much declarative as real. We have seen that, parallel to its overt discourse, an unacknowledged religiousness persisted, springing from a flaw in modernity's conception of Man, which because it was unconscious cracked right through its entire structure starting from its very foundations.

The role of victim played by the Jews in this hidden sacrificial religion is obvious. I have tried in this respect to demonstrate the historical and very precisely modern relativity of the destruction of the Jews. It is not the result of an accident in history that could be explained, outside of any historical context, by the scapegoat theory. Quite the contrary. I have stressed the fact that such a theory lacks any basis in reality. I have based my approach to the sacrificial tendency inherent in democracy on an analysis of modern political discourse and practice by relating this syndrome to a precise historical reality—namely, modernity. That democracy unconsciously rediscovered such a mechanism as the *pharmakon* raises the question of the real workings of modern society, which, on this point, is not as remote from traditional society as is generally imagined. That the Jews fit the part is to be explained less by metaphysical causes than by historical factors. The failure of their emancipation had predisposed them morphologically for the role, as had the fact (in a context of regression to tradition) that they had long played the part of absolute referent in the Christian matrix of Western identity.

And so as we near the end of the analysis, we can say that, without losing sight of all the conditions discussed earlier (and that completely overturn the usual perspective), using the term *holocaust* to qualify the destruction of the Jews is neither absurd nor excessive in a certain sense. The word expresses at bottom a hidden, ignored reality in modernity—namely, its

sacrificial tendency. Sartre and Arendt were well aware of this but did not
realize its implications. Arendt, as we have seen, excelled in her analysis of
the historical and political conditions that made the Jews fit the part they
played in the drama. She showed how the Jews embodied the indeterminacy,
the void, and the abyss inherent to democracy. "In contrast to all other
groups, the Jews were defined and their position determined by the body
politic. Since, however, this body politic had no other social reality, they
were, socially speaking, in the void."[113] She also pointed to the Jews' position in modern society as the weakest link in the social chain: just as "the
French people hated aristocrats about to lose their power more than it had
ever hated them before,"[114] as Tocqueville so aptly noted, so "antisemitism
reached its climax when Jews had similarly lost their public functions and
their influence, and were left with nothing but their wealth. When Hitler
came to power, the German banks were already almost *judenrein* [. . .]." "The
same holds true for [. . .] the Dreyfus Affair [which] exploded [. . .] when
Jews had all but vanished from important positions."[115] One could add that
anti-Semitism was born precisely when the dissolution of the Jewish people
was pronounced. The Jewish signifier was sufficiently strong symbolically
for all to unite against it, vague and uncertain enough to sustain all sorts of
projections of the imagination, and not powerful enough in reality to resist
exclusion. It could thus play the *pharmakon* of modernity and become "a
kind of symbol of the common interest of the European nations."[116]

Whereas Arendt clearly understood the historical conditions that
led to the Jews' status as pariahs, Sartre was the one who more forcefully
grasped the religious, sacrificial character of the modern exclusion of the
Jews (although he failed to see the religious, sacrificial nature of democracy itself). He saw in anti-Semitism "a rite of initiation which admits [the
anti-Semites] to the fireside of social warmth and energy. In this sense
anti-Semitism has kept something of the nature of human sacrifice."[117] The
Jews are a "variety of men" that "serve as a scapegoat," a "species that bears
witness [. . .] destined from the start to either inauthenticity or martyrdom."[118]
A series of sacrificial terms marks Sartre's description of this *pharmakon*.
"[T]he situation which he has to lay claim to and to live in is quite simply
that of a martyr."[119] "[H]e cannot choose not to be a Jew. Or, rather, if he
does so choose [. . .], it is precisely in this that he is a Jew."[120] "[T]he Jew,
an intruder into French society, is compelled to remain isolated. If he does
not consent, he is insulted."[121] "This perpetual obligation to prove that he
is French puts the Jew in a situation of guilt,"[122] which Sartre compares to
the situation depicted by Kafka in *The Trial*: "Like the hero of that novel,
the Jew [. . .] does not know his judges, scarcely even his lawyers; he does
not know what he is charged with, yet he knows that he is considered
guilty."[123] "It is we who constrain him to choose to be a Jew [. . .] there is

not one of us who is not totally guilty and even criminal; the Jewish blood that the Nazis shed falls on all our heads"[124] Sartre paints a striking picture of the Jew as democratic citizen and pariah that is very unlike the portrait given by Arendt. "He knows that he is one who stands apart, untouchable, scorned, proscribed," an archaic exception that also applies to the anti-Semite who "looks upon himself as a sanctified evildoer [. . . in] a sort of inversion of all values, of which we find examples in certain religions—for example, in India, where there exists a sacred prostitution."[125] Sartre sees in this evidence of the archaic remnants of premodern society, of "a still prelogical community,"[126] characterized by "mechanical solidarity," to use Durkheim's terms, wherein the individual is drowned in a mass of fungible, interchangeable units without individuality. These individuals form a mass and unite in their hatred and persecution of the Jews: "All they have to do is nourish a vengeful anger against the robbers of Israel, and they feel at once in possession of the entire country. True Frenchmen, good Frenchmen, are all equal, for each of them possesses for himself alone France whole and indivisible."[127] "The society that the anti-Semite conceives of is a society of juxtaposition" and "he has [. . .] an imprescriptible and inborn right to the indivisible totality of the country."[128] It is very clear from Sartre's analysis that the nation unites and consolidates its bonds through anti-Semitism, through making a pariah of the Jew. The anti-Semite "wishes to destroy him as a man and leave nothing in him but the Jew, the pariah, the untouchable."[129] It is standing on the brink of the abyss of the Jewish sign that the nationalist anti-Semite grasps his identity. But the democrat "wishes to destroy him as a Jew and leave nothing in him but the man, the abstract and universal subject of the rights of man and the rights of the citizen."[130] Sartre attributes this situation to the Christian heritage: "To know what the contemporary Jew is, we must ask the Christian conscience. And we must ask, not 'What is a Jew?' but *'What have you made* of the Jews?' "[131] It is because of the accusation of deicide that the Jew was "taboo," because he was "a murderer or the son of a murderer" and therefore inspired "religious horror" that "the anti-Semite has chosen the Jew as the object of his hate."[132] "Thus it is no exaggeration to say that the Christians *created* the Jew in putting an abrupt stop to his assimilation and in providing him, in spite of himself, with a function in which he has since prospered."[133]

The pariah condition of the Jews—separate and alone, execrated but necessary to the very substance and continuity of society, doomed to bloody sacrifice or reprobation—reflects upon modern Europe as a whole and betrays something of its innermost substance. Described as a "holocaust," the Shoah points to one of the deepest traits of political modernity. Only a deep repression of very powerful truths could prevent us from seeing this.

CHAPTER 10

The Memory Controversy as a Decoy

The perspective that I have been developing necessarily disrupts the conventional way of thinking in the debate on the singularity of the Shoah. The controversy is marked by contrast. Neoleftist discourses evince a tangible reality, but they disfigure the question this reality addresses to contemporary political consciousness. So whereas they deserve credit for confronting the real issues of the postwar period (the meaning of the singularization of Jews and the crisis of democracy), they are to be criticized for distorting them. This is a debate, however, that remains confined to intellectual circles. It is an altogether different matter with the debate on "memory," which has recently reached a paroxysm that tells us much about the logic of the unconscious. Far from being the sign of a return of the repressed, it may very well reflect a massive repression of the central question of the late twentieth century, a repression in the guise of an unbridled return of the repressed. We may very well be dealing here with another case of foreclosure; the more it is discussed, the more repressed it actually is. The excessiveness and "obscenity" of the focus on the Shoah would in fact mask its repression, and the superposition of its Jewish dimension would be comparable to the trees that prevent us from seeing the wood.

In light of the problematics that I have been discussing, one can see that the controversy over memory and its "abuses" is a decoy distracting attention from the real subject of debate and focusing it on a fixation abscess or a fetish of sorts that takes the place of reality and thereby masks its presence so that one need not confront it. This extremely subtle ideological system established in recent years eliminates the subject of debate while raising the debate itself to a pitch that is as grandiloquent as it is hollow and groundless and that inevitably arouses doubt and suspicion.

It is not so much that "memory" is being threatened by oblivion or by history, as if all that mattered was to keep alive a memory of the past that was in danger of being erased or negated, or to write the henceforth academic history of a drama that is over and done with. The problem is not the hysterical or self-interested use that the Jews supposedly make of it or the amnesia of European countries, even though all of these constitute aspects of reality. The two responses to these false debates are the "duty to remember" versus the critique of Judeo-centrism, and they both beg the question.

I have defined the question in terms of the Jew's singularization in the body of democratic citizenship, a process that started in the nineteenth century with the birth of anti-Semitism and culminated in the Shoah. The Jews were targeted in their specific quality, in their absolute singularity, because they had been set apart from other citizens and "singularized" in the civic nation. Due to the unique character of this condition, their singular destiny ineluctably reflected the nature of the civic condition and the fate of the singular human being in the democracy of the Rights of Man. The Shoah forcefully demonstrated that the singular was doomed to disaster precisely because it had remained unthought and unacceptable, prohibited in democratic consciousness and practice. It is this singularity—that is, the singularity within citizenship—that must be addressed if we are to clarify the full significance of the Shoah and other contemporary tragedies and see what lessons we can draw from them for the future.

The impasses to which the contemporary controversy leads become all the more apparent as a result. The focus on the singularity of the Shoah paradoxically masks the real question that it raises. Advocates of the Shoah's absolute uniqueness are correct up to a point, but they see it as a *terminus ad quem* of Nazism and the fate of the Jews as the ultimate fate of all humankind. On the other side, those who criticize the Jewish singularization of the Shoah from the terrible panorama of contemporary genocides focus the debate so much on this singularization, limiting it to the Jews, that they lose sight of the overall fate of singularity. Indeed, they scorn it in the name of universality and humanity when they do not actually demonize it as an expression of egocentrism and political self-interest. They are not wrong to call attention to the universal horizon, but they use it as a pretext to avoid addressing the crux of the problem—namely, singularity in universal citizenship. They end up reviving the old rhetoric of modernity and resurrecting the figure of "Man" that died in the camps, as if nothing had happened and things could be picked up where they left off, even though such thinking is belied day after day by the fact that the modern hecatomb continues. In this light, it is easy to see why the continued existence of the Jews disturbs them. It testifies to the obsoleteness of an ideological outlook that is a mere façade, be it civilized and distinguished, occulting the real fate of human beings. The result is paradoxical: defending third world victims of genocides against the centrality of the "genocide" of the Jews, they prove unable to examine the nature and implications of these genocides in political terms and end up surreptitiously reproducing the same ethnocentrism, but this time with the self-righteous veneer of moralists above passions, while the burden of ethnocentrism is shifted to the Jewish referent. The fact that I have been concentrating my discussion on the significance of the Shoah for political modernity does not mean that I contest the validity of other ways of looking at it. However, I believe that confronting the failure of modern politics is the necessary prerequisite to the many other possible approaches to the matter. At any rate, it is the one that is most urgent, because it conditions the clarification of the fate of Man in the political world at the end of the twentieth century, as illuminated by the dark light of the Shoah.

The Psychology of the Shoah's Singularity

The focus of the controversy on "memory" does, however, evidence some elements of the real. Pitting memory against oblivion is a roundabout way of taking up the question of origin, whose importance to our understanding of the impasses of modern humanity was discussed earlier. Pitting memory against history is a way of saying that the concrete experience of individuals (in this case, of Jews) does not correspond to their consciousness of it. It is a way of saying that there is a gap between the Shoah in public discourse and in reality. The major problem with the memory argument is its derealizing psychologism and the depolitization and ahistoricization it induces. Another problem, recurrent in all of the writings on the subject, is that it focuses less on collective consciousness than on the Jewish referent, as standing for what Tzvetan Todorov calls "the abuses of memory." In this way, the "memory" argument pushes the failures of democratic citizenship and political modernity out of the picture. It leads to a psychologization and corporealization (in the collective body of the Jews, since the Jews are corporealized as an "ethnic group") that allows theorists to avoid peering into the bottomless pit of anxiety that the Shoah has opened in the consciousness and fate of modernity.

In *The Vichy Syndrome: History and Memory in France since 1944*, Henry Rousso significantly entitles his chapter on the rise of the controversy over the Shoah "Obsession (after 1974): Jewish Memory." In what is, in many respects, an admirable and important book, the historian analyzes the "reawakening of Jewish memory"[1] and the reaffirmation by the Jewish community of "its identity within French society,"[2] yet apparently at no moment does he feel the need to scrutinize in detail the specific history of French Judaism since the 1950s—if only to meet methodological standards to which he otherwise subscribes. He quotes Raymond Aron and Claude Lévi-Strauss, yet he makes no attempt to examine currents of thought within

the Jewish community; Rousso seems to adhere to Aron's highly ideological and (uncharacteristically) scientifically unfounded opinion that there is
no such thing as a Jewish community in France, despite the fact that his
discussion is posited on its existence. He admits that "Aron's views were
hardly typical of Jewish opinion in general"[3] (and I would be tempted to
add, even less of Jewish history). One can only conclude that for Rousso
the Jews have no history of their own.

     This does not stop him, however, from making two blanket assertions.
He maintains that after 1967 the Jews became "French Jews rather than
Jewish Frenchman,"[4] and that they found themselves isolated because of
their support for Israel in a period marked by the debate on decolonization
and the development of the third world. He also claims that "[e]lements
within the Jewish community also appealed to history to bolster their own
claims to authority and to silence opposition from Jews reluctant to grant
Israel unconditional support."[5] He puts forward these suppositions in the
guise of an analysis without ever examining their morphological and social
underpinnings,[6] which is ordinarily the first step in any analysis of ideological currents in epistemological sociology. Maurice Halbwachs, one of the
greatest theorists of social memory, based his entire approach on the method
of social morphology that simultaneously considers social facts and ideas.
Here it is impossible to separate the ideas that were the subject of debate
within French Judaism from the morphological situation of Jews in French
society after the Shoah, after their individual status as citizens had been
overturned and with it the entire edifice of the Emancipation. Ultimately,
Rousso lapses into specious psychologism (he writes of an "obsessional
phase"[7]). Because he treats opinion phenomena solely as mental constructs,
he loses sight of their social dimension. He approaches Jewish memory as
a collective phenomenon to be explained by the psychology of identity and
not by social facts, as if the Jewish condition was all in the mind, and for
that matter in a disturbed, sick mind, divorced from reality. "The duty to
remember cannot for long run counter to the duty to seek the truth. In
fact, hypermnesia, or too much of the past, is as worrisome as amnesia. To
avoid either, I agree with Paul Ricœur that we have to replace the 'duty
to remember' with the 'work of memory.' "[8] But this sort of "work" is not
what the historian does when he studies the history of French Judaism.

The Ethnicization of the Shoah's Singularity

The memory discourse is thus systematically related to the reconstruction in
France of a Jewish identity, that is, to an affirmation of belonging to a Jewish
collectivity. The idea that an ethnic affirmation subtends the invocation of

"memory" and the defense of the Shoah's "uniqueness" has gained widespread currency. As we saw earlier, there is some truth in this, but it must not be understood as a process that concerns Jews only and that would therefore be something unusual. Yet that is what Rousso is suggesting when he explains the birth of this Jewish identity by the arrival of "Sephardic Jews," who "uprooted from their native lands, fought hard to preserve the distinctive features of their religion and culture. In this respect, they resembled other *pieds noirs* (repatriated French citizens from North Africa) but differed from the more assimilated Ashkenazy Jews."[9] These newcomers (the majority of whom, Rousso seems to have forgotten, were Algerian Jews and hence French citizens since 1870, well before the Jewish immigrants from Eastern Europe) are held responsible for driving *from the outside* the affirmation of a Jewish identity and the "ethnicization" of the French Jewish community. In a similar vein, Pierre Nora asserts that the memory of Vichy took hold in the collective consciousness partly as a result of "the development of a specific Jewish identity," and he argues that the Six Day War marked the onset "of the gradual rediscovery by the Jews of France of a religious, cultural, and historical continent that had been obliterated by French-style assimilation," but he goes on to say that "the ground was prepared [. . .] by the massive return of Algerian Jews starting in 1962. The arrival of these North African Jews, who were much more in touch with Jewish practices and traditions, even contributed to providing a real sense of 'community' to a collectivity that had no community identity before, and broke in this way with consistorial Judaism's conception of being a Jew in the synagogue and at home but not in the street or in public life. Furthermore, on the level of collective memory and imagination, the Algerian Jews may have poured back into Vichy the sense of abandonment by France that they had good reason to feel as French citizens of Algeria."[10] Thankfully Nora takes care to specify that this thesis "is improvable though not improbable." In this way he too ignores the crisis in French political identity caused by the Vichy interlude, and without this, it is impossible to understand the development of a Jewish identity and community in France, which can be traced back to the establishment in 1943 of a new body representing the Jews to the political authorities in the Resistance.[11] He too forgets that the Jews of Algeria were full-fledged citizens, in what was then one of the departments of the French Republic, and that the Consistory had long been titled the "Consistory of Israelites of France and Algeria." Finally, the traditionalism of these Jews is more an image than a reality: when the uprooting from Algeria took place, North African Judaism was well on its way down the path of assimilation.

The purported ethnicity of this identity, which is no longer religious or individual, is thus advanced as one of the main explanations for the memory discourse and its abuses and is systematically ascribed to outside causes.[12] This ethnicity usually provides analysts with the occasion to morally stigmatize the Jews, accused of self-absorption and ethnocentrism, and lambasted for donning the virtues of victimhood to achieve their own aims.

All of the writers discussed earlier (Brossat, Todorov, etc.) adopt this perspective. They all pit this ethnic identity against elevated ideals of universality and a concern for the other. I have already responded to this line of reasoning but have yet to take up the argument based on the "self-interested" character of the identity-based memory discourse in political and social (not to mention financial) terms. The idea of a pathological hypertrophy of memory in addition to excessive identitarianism crops up regularly in the writings of the more radical theorists.

That memory came to dominate Jewish institutional discourse in the 1980s and 1990s is clearly the case. It could even be said that a politics of memory developed that supplanted the identification with Zionism. Indeed, collective identification in the Jewish community in France with political Zionism, which had constituted a "civil religion" of sorts in the 1970s, was superseded by the "religion of the Shoah," which fulfilled the same functions. Because the Shoah was associated with a sense of moral obligation in collective consciousness, Jewish institutions drew legitimacy and a power of confirmation from it. This led to a number of abuses that were, by and large, the work of self-styled spokesmen of the Jewish community trying to compensate for a veritable lack of moral authority and not the outcome of a concerted strategy. But what reason could there have been for Jewish identity to become so exclusively tied to the memory of the Shoah, knowing that reducing Jewish identity to this oppressive memory endangered the very survival of the Jews whose identity could not remain alive without hope or a creative project?

Objectively we cannot help but note that this "memory politics" corresponded to a global situation that exceeded by far the bounds of the Jewish condition, otherwise it would have been unproductive, if not suicidal. Few analysts have thought in these terms, because they are obnubilated by a Jewish dimension conceived in exclusive terms. Two explanations are possible in this regard. If Jewish institutions and self-styled spokesmen derived prestige, authority, and even power from the memory discourse, then it was because their surroundings were willing to grant these to them; after all, prestige, authority, and power do not exist outside of a social framework. The Jews could never have acquired these by themselves. And the reason that society at large was willing to grant them the prestige they were seeking through the memory discourse was because it too invested anything that touched on the Shoah with a moral force and hence an authority. Without this prior attitude, things would not have taken this turn. But, on a much deeper level, no one has asked why the Jews felt obliged to use such a roundabout means to assert a necessarily collective identity, nor why, prior to that, the identification with Zionism had become a civil religion of sorts. Why identify with the state of Israel or with Auschwitz in order to assert a collective identity? No doubt because there were no elements in the symbolic codes of the collective unconscious in France, and in democratic countries in general, to nurture, sustain, and confirm an assertion of Jewish identity as such. And so they were sought in external arenas and in registers apt to arouse compassion. The identification with the victim was a way of apologizing for the existence of the identity assertion and soliciting the comprehension of the surroundings, rendered responsible for its existence, even guilty of it, and hence compelled to accept it. As far as the Shoah is concerned, this is obvious. But it also was the case for the identification with Israel until 1967, because the state of Israel was threatened with total destruction. Most analyses of this situation have focused on the idea of a Jewish manipulation and a greed for power when it may very well constitute, to the contrary, an awkward apology for one's own existence.

By falling back on the victim-based rationale of the memory discourse, what were the Jews doing if not adopting the morality of victimhood that characterizes the democratic ethos, which, as we have seen, places the sacrificial vocation above all. Moral legitimacy is typically associated in this ethos with the condition of victimhood. Democracies have always found the moral courage and legitimacy to go to war or to fight for a cause when they are victims of an aggression. But there may well be something subtler involved: the demand for recognition of Jewish *collective* identity through the agency of victimhood may be a way for Jews to participate once again in the most traditional form of democratic citizenship, the one that leads to their disappearance as a collectivity. None of the critiques of the "rivalry of victims" has entertained this possibility. Only Sartre, with typical brio, points us in the right direction in two insightful passages. Noting that even the "authentic" Jew depends on opinion (and hence, in the final analysis, on "recognition" from others), and that when this Jew opts for authenticity, it does not mean that he is willing to shut himself up inside a ghetto. He goes on to write, "The choice of authenticity can, in fact, lead to conflicting political decisions. The Jew can choose to be authentic by asserting his place as Jew in the French community, with all that goes with it of rights and martyrdom; he may feel that for him the best way to be French is to declare himself a French Jew. But he may also be led by his choice of authenticity to seek the creation of a Jewish nation possessing its own soil and autonomy; he may persuade himself that Jewish authenticity demands that the Jew be sustained by a Jewish national community. It is not impossible that these opposing choices might be reconciled and made complementary as two aspects of Jewish reality."[13] Sartre regards Jewish "authenticity," asserting one's Jewish identity in face of adversity, as inseparable from martyrdom, or what we would call "victimhood" today. The Jew must constantly "prove" that he is not the foreigner whom he is accused of being, but he is the last one to know it because "he belongs to the very class of people who reject him."[14] "In vain may he argue about his culture, his accomplishments; it is a Jewish culture; they are Jewish accomplishments. He is a Jew precisely in that he does not even suspect what ought to be understood."[15] Because of his situation in the present, not the past, authenticity for the Jew "is to live to the full his condition as Jew; inauthenticity is to deny it or to attempt to escape from it. Inauthenticity is no doubt more tempting for him than for other men, because the situation which he has to lay claim to and to live in is quite simply that of a martyr."[16] Thus asserting a Jewish identity is spontaneously placed under the banner of martyrdom—one is guilty even before asserting one's identity. "This perpetual obligation to prove that he is French puts the Jew in a situation of guilt. If on every occasion he does not do more than everybody else, much more than anybody else, he is guilty."[17] In this respect, authenticity is not to be seen as an end in itself. The authentic Jew in Sartre's conception demands only to be recognized, that is, to dis-appear. Once he is accepted and anti-Semitism is defeated, the conditions behind his assertion of authenticity disappear. After all, "the authentic Jew is the one who asserts his claim in the face of the disdain shown toward him."[18] The inauthentic Jew "admits with [the anti-Semites] that, *if there is a Jew*, he must have the characteristics with which popular malevolence endows him, and his effort is to constitute himself a martyr, in the proper sense of the term, that is, to prove *in his person* that there are no Jews."[19] This paradoxical process consists, for the Jew, in asserting himself, gaining recognition in order to disappear as a Jew: "It is not the man but the *Jew* whom the Jews seek to know in themselves through introspection; and they wish to know him *in order to deny him*. With them it is not a question of recognizing certain faults and combating them, but of underlining by their conduct the fact that they do not have those faults."[20]

The Need for Recognition as a Fallacious Explanation

Sartre's discussion shows how the demand for recognition of singular memories can paradoxically lead away from ethnic and identity-related assertions. This is not, however, the argument that has widespread cur-rency today. The psychologism inherent in the contemporary approach to memory situates the problem in a logic of *recognition* for an identity stung by the dehumanization of the Jews during the Shoah.[21] Exemplifying this outlook pushed to excess is Jean-Michel Chaumont's book *La Concurrence des victimes*, in which the author makes extended use of Todorov's theories. Chaumont situates the search for recognition by the Jews, and firstly by survivors, in a sequence of humiliation, shame, and revenge. "By and large, the identities demanding recognition are identities that have suffered from and often been deformed by the stigmatizations endured throughout their relationship with mainstream identities."[22] Not only was the suffering of survivors unrecognized on their return from the camps, but survivors were, in fact, regarded with opprobrium and covered with shame. "The difference in status and in 'public recognition' separating 'racial deportees' and resistants imparted a formal, legal dimension to this discrimination."[23] Instead of fighting against such a situation, the Jews internalized the refusal of society at large to recognize that they suffered as Jews. (And Chaumont, who quotes Sartre, understands this perfectly: "The Jews were not fooled by a homage that, because it did not name them, could not reinstate them as part of humanity in the same terms and for the same reason that they had been excluded,"[24] to the point that they felt ashamed of their state and their identity.) "The explanatory factor for the shame" resides in "the internalization of the tormenter's judgment"[25]; it is the shame of the "vilified body."[26] The debasement that the Jews suffered at the hands of the Nazis is thus paradoxically imputed to them, which makes it easier to avoid facing the hiatus in political modernity and citizenship that Vichy and the Shoah represented. Everything could continue as before: the Jews could reassume their place again as if nothing had happened, at least as long as they were persuaded that there was no other alternative. It was the Six Day War that provoked a change in values and mentalities: "The sense of shame for being a victim was turned against the world that had inflicted it."[27] Chaumont traces this about-face to a symposium organized in New York on March 26, 1967, by the journal *Judaism* and specifically to the role that Elie Wiesel played in it. I will not dwell here on the absurdity of turning a handful of thinkers into the mouthpiece of the Jewish world. The crux of the matter is that Chaumont sees this cycle of humiliation, shame, and revenge as being responsible for a search for recognition that far exceeds the restoration of the dignity of Jewish identity. He goes so far as to raise it to the rank of a quasi-economic system that he denounces as an economy of prestige. "The central conflict is over this rare and precious resource that traditional sociology calls prestige that counts among the famous three P's of American sociology: power, property, and prestige."[28] Prestige is "used in the manner of a rare commodity, identical to other sources of power. In this context, the prestige that some earn amounts to a loss, at least relative, for others."[29] Chaumont makes extensive use of banking terminology: he writes of "mechanisms" of recognition, "unpaid debts," "interest," "the huge bill that the formerly underprivileged group presents to the paying authority," "exhausted credit," "bad payers," and "depreciating the authority from which recognition is demanded."[30] Such terminology is particularly unwelcome when addressing the subject of Jews. "To see groups competing for the title of greatest misery is an unsavory sight [. . .]. The competition for the status of the victim par excellence can be reduced to a vain search for a displaced prestige."[31]

What is at stake in this recognition, as we have seen, is "an identity assertion addressed by the different sectors of the Jewish community to the rest of the world."[32] Behind the defense of the uniqueness of the Shoah, it is "the uniqueness of Jewish identity" that the Jews are defending. The author coins the strange expression "memorial singularity" to define the "transcendent unicity" that expresses the fact that an experience is always absolutely unique for the person who lives through it. Any memory is singular, absolute, and unique. The problem with the discourse on the uniqueness of the Shoah is that to defend the uniqueness of Jewish identity its advocates selfishly monopolize the category of genocide and deny or downplay other genocides in the process. The reader is given no insight into what lies behind this ethnic Jewish identity that is at the center of his discussion. The author occasionally refers to himself as a sociologist, yet he never asks himself in sociological terms exactly who are these Jews he is discussing. What is the morphological nature of the group that they supposedly constitute? What light can their objective condition cast on their identity? We do not know upon what bases he relies to establish Jewish opinion, yet he often evokes "the" Jewish community (the inverted commas used to question its oneness—and judiciously so—do not suffice to clarify the concept) and implicitly supposes that there is international Jewish unity when he sees Wiesel's comments and a conference in New York as a watershed in the attitude of Jews all over the world. He even seems to regard the Jews as a people, since he compares the "Judeocide" to "ethnocides" (the "destruction of regional communities in Britanny, etc."), like those that the emergence of nation-states provoked after the French Revolution.[33] In all likelihood, Chaumont is aware that collective identity belongs to the realm of the unthinkable in modernity; he admits that "we find the idea that individuals can be prisoners of a given collective identity unbearable."[34] But it takes more than an acknowledgment of "a very distinct Jewish character"[35] to understand the "memorial singularities" that seem to hover in the air like so many pure psychological and symbolic forms without real substance. And only this comprehension could ground Chaumont's approach.

In his analysis, Chaumont, who is otherwise well intentioned and not always misguided, lets himself go to a moralizing argument that employs concepts of guilt, self-overcoming, and comprehension, which are completely inadequate when it comes to answering the question that the Shoah addresses to democratic citizenship. As a result, he all too promptly rejects the concept of uniqueness and does so in grotesque terms: "It is high time to put an end to it [. . .] to tuck away the elements in the debate on uniqueness in one of those houses of horrors that they used to have in fairs. It is as macabre, useless and offensive as the monstrosities that used to be displayed there. It should be sealed away in a jar of formaldehyde."[36] But if singularity is at issue, then it is so not only for a sick Jewish identity but also for democratic Europe, where it was left without protection, where modern Man and the citizen were reduced to naught. The meanders of the development of Jewish identity serve here to hide the democratic abyss, and the recognition argument prevents us from finding a remedy to the crisis of democracy, and thereby a way to avoid other catastrophes that may bring about the total eradication of democracy this time.

The book ends, not surprisingly, with a defense of multiculturalism. With stung identities as a common denominator, the Jews are likened to homosexuals, transvestites, "unemployed persons,"[37] and "raped women,"[38] and Chaumont proposes to turn what he calls the "Shoah fortress" into a "Shoah asylum." The purpose of multiculturalism becomes clear in this light: through the negation of difference and identity inherent to modern citizenship, it creates a place *in situ* for those bodies that were once excluded by the principle of universality and that are now recognized but only as "bodies" (and ethnic groups are necessarily corporeal, since they are infrarational and atavistic), which means as a function of an unchanged logic based on a misunderstanding of alterity. Chaumont admits that Auschwitz should "break down any semblance of certainty, in theory or practice, upon which we thought we could count,"[39] but his analysis does not bear out this intention. The explanatory hypothesis of recognition that underpins his discussion lacks a rational, objective basis (by which I mean a historical and political basis) and prevents even his most interesting point (the focus on collective identity)[40] from leading to anything more than a moralizing posture.

As we have seen, the question of the singularization of the Jews in the Shoah concerns all of political modernity. The Jews were the main vehicles of this crisis, and it is precisely their singularity and specificity that constituted the central issue. What is the significance for political modernity of the singularization of the Jews? That is the real point at issue in the Shoah's "singularity." Far from obstructing comparison with other genocides, far from establishing an absurd hierarchy of suffering and martyrdom between exterminated peoples, the analysis of this singularity should throw some light on all of the genocides of modernity, because in the very discourse of modernity more than in their own, no other group experienced the failures and impasses of modern politics with such paroxysmal violence. The fate of modern humanity resonates in their experience as in a sound box. It is by comparing the avenues of their singularization and singularity that we can gain insight into this fate.

The Second World War represented a hiatus that cannot be integrated into our memory as long as we have not taken the confrontation with its concrete reality through to the end, and done so in the very political and historical terms in which it was formulated. How can we speak of memory, not to say of commemoration, when there has been no bereavement, because we the living simply have not faced the yawning gap, the abyss, that the victims left in our midst, at the very core of modernity?

Part 3

❦

The Jew-of-the-Man

The Singular and the Democratic Universal

In the singularization of the Jews that occurred during the Shoah (and that had been at work ever since the admission of Jews to rights of citizenship and the birth of modern anti-Semitism), it was, of course, the singularity of the Jews in citizenship that met a catastrophic fate. The tragic fate of this singularity became the litmus test of all singularization in democracy, of which it was the paroxysmal experience. This is why it has a practical significance that far exceeds the bounds of the moral and historical reality of the Jews and has universal value. I have shown how mythicizing and sacralizing this singularity, on the one hand, or denying it in the name of universality and generosity, on the other, are ways of covering up the abyss that was opened by the Shoah at the core of modernity, ways of denying what it really was and what it represents at bottom. They are all unconscious mechanisms that serve to avoid looking at the Sword of Damocles hanging over modern politics since the Second World War.

But, if the Jewish condition was the dangerous "laboratory" of modernity, and if what happens to the Jews must be explained by what happens to the moderns, then when it comes to understanding why the Jews were the ones who embodied the fate of singularity one cannot ignore the *sui generis* reality of Jewishness.[1] Could there be something in the nature of Jewish sociality that attracted such an exemplary experience? If what happened to the moderns is elucidated by what happened to the Jews, then could it be

249

that Jewishness was what was problematical in modernity? We are touching here on the crux of what I have set out to examine. If we were to keep strictly to Hannah Arendt's analysis, then we would be staying within the confines of modern politics. According to Arendt, the Jewish people was a pariah because it did not have a state and a territory that would have allowed it to survive in the concert of European nation-states. This perspective takes the criterion of political modernity as the unsurpassable horizon of humanity. This is neither totally false nor totally true, because modernity is not the end of human history. History is pregnant with a future, and not only a regression, after the decline of modernity. Moreover, this conception implicitly assigns an exclusively passive role to Jews, seen as the recipients and eternal victims of historical developments, whose only option is to conform to the nation-state norm (which is what Zionism did). In sum, Arendt portrays history as if it were exclusively driven by the logic of the nation-state, and anything that falls outside of it as ineluctably and eternally a pariah. According to this reasoning, the Jews are the inert symptom of the failure of modernity and not active agents in the events.

Perhaps this perspective can be reversed and Jewish singularity, which has been excluded from modern logic, reconsidered as an active element in its own right, charged with a depth of meaning that could cast light back onto the modern logic. Perhaps it is only in modern logic that Jewishness assumes the form of a singularity, only in the light of the democratic universal that it stands as the paradigm of singularity. What—besides the lack of a land and a state—could account for the fact that the Jews became the pariahs of political modernity? In trying to answer this question, I will be elucidating both the positive dimension implicated in the modern problem and my own conception of singularity. The supposition is that there is an intrinsic substance and freedom in being Jewish, Sartre's opinion notwithstanding.

Indeed, I have not set out in this analysis to defend singularity as it has been conceived (and repressed) by modernity in opposition to democratic universality. I have endeavored to see the modern logic through to its end, and this logic cannot take us farther than this explanation based on singularity. The point, then, is to get beyond this very logic. This intention is the bedrock of my efforts to understand modern society. Singularity as conceived by modernity is not my guiding moral principle.

CHAPTER 11

The Enigma of Jewish Singularity

In trying to answer such a question, there is a great danger of lapsing into the aporias of the rhetorical Jew.[1] A number of theorists, psychoanalysts in particular, have explained Nazi hatred of the Jews by the fact that the Jews represented the Law. Jews may have embodied the Law in the Christian imaginary (though not necessarily in the modern imaginary), but relying on this as an explanation is still a form of mythification, of the same symbolic operation that underlies the Nazi vision (the Jews as the personification of evil), an abstraction that obstructs any consideration of the real existence of Jews. (Do Jews embody the Law, for instance, even when their behavior runs counter to it?) We are still dealing here with the West's fantasy of the Jews and not with the Jews. Nonetheless, the figure of the Law is not altogether misleading. It puts us on the track of the strongest trait of sociality of the Jewish *people*, "the People of the Book"—to wit, the centrality of the Bible, the Book of Books. With or without a land and state of their own, and even scattered over the face of the earth, the Sinaitic book held Jewry together, at least until the late eighteenth century and perhaps the middle of the nineteenth. This was more than just an imaginary tie; it was as concrete a social reality as can be. I have analyzed elsewhere[2] how even the most divergent social currents of Jewish society were structured by a relationship of identification to the Book, with each social group belonging to and drawing its legitimacy from a specific hermeneutics. When the Nazis burned "Jewish" books in public autos-da-fe, they were attacking this social structure. This was already the case for the autos-da-fe of the Talmud in the days of the Spanish Inquisition. It was because this sociality governed by the Bible opposed a sociality that was purported to be totally governed by the state that it became the pariah of modernity. This situation is often mistakenly understood in terms of an opposition between the diaspora and the state, as if Jewish exile personified the anti-state. This is a misconception that fails to come to grips with the phenomenon. The centrality of the Book was at work throughout ancient history as much in the experience of state power (the Jewish kingdoms of ancient Israel) as in the diasporic experience. Admittedly, it was manifested more strongly in the Diaspora, to the point that the Book assumed the role of a surrogate "land" (though the Book's centrality could not have been what it was without the land, as a reality or a messianic promise). This diasporic period also corresponded to the end of prophecy, which shows us the extent to which it was prophetism that assumed the centrality of the Book in sociality during the period of settlement on the land and in the framework of the logic of state power. The absence of prophetism today is no doubt at the source of the drama of contemporary Jews' in their relationship to the reestablished land. What characterizes this form of sociality?

First, its nonautochtonous nature. Unlike Athenian citizens, the citizens of Jerusalem sought their foundation not in relation to the soil from which they sprang but in relation to the Book from which they came (and which tells them that they came from the wilderness). The Book is thus the (empty, abstract) center of the body politic (the Temple houses it in the Ark of the Covenant). It is not, as romantic diasporists believe, a figure of anti-polity, anti-sedentariness, nomadism, and absolute exile (the aesthetico-nihilistic view of Jewishness). The Book is not the anti-state; it is something different than the state, which can lay the foundation of a polity and the exercise of political power. The second characteristic could be called "unidentity," not the opposite of identity but something different, an identity that goes through a release from itself. This identity is to be understood in terms other than an identification with the identical, because if the reference is the Book and not the land, then it is a changing, shifting, effervescent reference, with identity being made and unmade in the multiplicity of references (hermeneutics) to the Book.[3] We have thus seen the emergence throughout history of complex Jewish identities, combining the Book with cultures outside of it, but drawn to it by some of their creative potentialities.

During the nation-state era, when a dominant people and a *national* territory were conflated, Jewish sociality became a problem, an obstacle to the establishment of what was supposed to be total absolute power, since it was the "power of the people," not because the Jews had no national territory or state, but because they relied on the Book and on an awareness of the exile that inhabits human beings, even when they have settled on a land. (One might define the prophetic consciousness in these terms, as it was continuously reminding the Hebrews, tempted by power and sedentarism, not to forget the desert covenant.[4]) By their Book, the Jews escaped the control of the state. This was not the first time: they had already escaped the control of the first absolute figure of the state—the Church, born from its fusion with the Roman Empire after the conversion of Constantine. The

Jews then obstructed the universal transparency of "catholicity": their Book was identified with and reduced to the "letter" to exclude it from the more valued realm of the "spirit."

In modernity—when the Empire of Reason and the absolute power of rational discourse embodied by the state were being proclaimed (a rational discourse grounded in statistics, that is, in a mathematized "real")—the narrative (the Book) of the people[5] around which Jewish sociality was forged was impossible to sustain. Many methods were used to counter it, from Napoleon's Sanhedrin—whereby the Jews forsook the historicity of the Book, meaning the narrative of their origins, and retained only the legal dimension of the text—to nineteenth-century biblical criticism that undertook to dismember the biblical account (notably its narrative dimension) by divesting it of its coherence or relating it to autochtonous mythical narratives from Babylonia, Phoenicia, or Egypt. The "Science of Judaism," which developed in early nineteenth-century Germany, set out to accomplish the same purpose from inside the Jewish world.[6] Thus for modern politics, the Jews embodied the narrative of the Book at the heart (of the discourse) of the state. They were living testimony to the fact that the state was not the absolute condition of a people's existence, that power, authority, and the source of the law did not emanate solely from the state, that human beings do not draw their identity from the state, and that the narrative of origin cannot be replaced by the discourse of reason, which can only ever be the discourse of the state. The nation-state tried to bring the natural human diversity in line with an absolute normative model, that of domination and power. The Book, on the other hand, generates a diversity of interpretations, a scattering of identities, and the birth of individuals, but it does not abandon these individuals to their wandering; it federates them around its centrality, even disputed (and it is in this sense that the Book is the source of a polity and does not evince a diasporist nihilism). Does this Book not speak of one thing only, namely, the Covenant, and hence the union of the one and the many? The sociality of the Book is not sectarian and monolithic as the discourse of Reason likes to think. Since it does not need the power of the state (unlike the Church, which reduced the centrality of the Book), the Book has no empire.

I will not delve into the philosophical implications of these questions, which I have examined elsewhere,[7] but we can gain some insight into what constituted Jewish identity until modernity through Paul Ricœur's concept of "narrative identities." Ricœur's analysis is enlightening, even though he disregards the political dimension of narrative identities along with the hiatus between traditional and modern societies and pays insufficient attention to the difference between the narrative of the Book and modern national narratives. According to the philosopher, the identity of an individual or a community is constituted as a narrative marked by a relationship to time in which there is permanence. "Unlike the abstract identity of the Same, this narrative identity, constitutive of self-constancy, can include change, mutability, within the cohesion of one lifetime."[8] "To answer the question 'Who?' as Hannah Arendt has so forcefully put it, is to tell the story of a life."[9] "[T]he narrative identity of an individual or a people [stems] from the endless rectification of a previous narrative by a subsequent one."[10] This narrative requires a "plot,"[11] a notion that Ricœur sees as elucidating the Greek *muthos*, "the organization of [. . .] events (into a system)."[12] Ricœur recognizes that he drew inspiration for his theory from the "people narrative" constituted by Judaism: "It was in telling these narratives taken to be testimony about the founding events of its history that biblical Israel became the historical community that bears this name. The relation is circular—the historical community called the Jewish people has drawn its identity from the reception of those texts that it had produced."[13]

That society is inextricably bound up with the Book is, in fact, a very old idea in Jewish philosophy. Medieval Jewish philosophers formulated a considerable body of theory concerning the sociality of the Book.[14] Maimonides developed a theory of polity and power grounded in the division between narrative and reason. Generally speaking, it is Reason that is the guiding criterion (this reason being that of the "philosopher-prophet," the soul of enlightened government), while narrative (meant for ordinary people held in the sway of myths and the imagination) is the instrument of the government. Spinoza later adopted this scheme wholesale. The Scripture, he argued, was meant for the "common herd" to ensure the obedience of the masses, "only bound to know those histories which can most powerfully dispose their mind to obedience and devotion."[15] The practice (by the state) and mastery (by the prophet) of allegory became the foundation of the exercise of power to Maimonides: only the prince, philosopher, and prophet can understand and master the ambivalence of the Book, whose narrative increasingly becomes a mere tool of government power, capable of taming the whimsical imagination of the masses. I need not emphasize the extent to which this doctrine is lodged at the very origins of the modern autonomization of the political. With this outlook, we have clearly abandoned the politics of the Book and embarked upon the politics of the state. Maimonides can thus be regarded as one of the founding fathers of political modernity alongside Spinoza.

It is worth noting, at this point, what distinguishes my approach from Ricœur's. The Book of Books is composed of more than just narrative; in fact, it contains as much law as narrative. Ricœur recognizes as much when he cites Gerhard von Rad's *Theology of the Old Testament* in a note.[16] But he denies the specificity of the legislative dimension, arguing that it has been "narrativized" in the story of the giving of the law. For this reason, what

I mean by the "Book" is not what Ricœur understands by "narrative identity." It is precisely this combination of law and narrative that enables the Book to lay the foundation of the polity, for if we can understand how the Law lays the foundation of a political order, then we can less readily grasp what role the narrative can play, since it lacks a normative thrust. Ricœur keeps his analysis to the collective imagination and the literary register and programmatically overlooks the political order. Admittedly his work participates in the tradition of literary criticism and cannot be expected to tackle political realities. The Book, which is greater than the narrative and which sustains a polity, contains an empty space, an elusive something apart, that the narrative "(non)represents" in relation to the order of the polity. In this void (and I am confining myself here to a morphological approach[17]), Judaism hears "God." The democratic state, as described by Claude Lefort, contained a similar empty space (which only lends weight to the idea that we are faced with two competing models: the Book and the state), but it was "dealt with" in a totally different way[18]: regarded as intolerable, it was filled, as we have seen, by the nation, which drew even greater power from it. At bottom, the modern nation occupied the empty space that God "occupied" in the sociality of the Book.

In *Elementary Forms of Religious Life*, Durkheim brilliantly describes how sociality and collective (national) identity emerge from the projection of identity in immanent transcendence, that is, through the emptying of the materiality of the original crowd that becomes a nation in the process: the group's self-image, which arises from this projection into the void, comes back to it from the outside in the form of a god. The "Book," in contrast, does not fill the emptiness that it carries with it and that summons individuals and the collectivity to come into being and to embark upon an interpretative journey based on the exercise of intelligence and the faculty of reason, which calls into question the place where one is and calls for peregrinations and mobility. It is impossible not to see that, for the moderns, the Jewish *people* were the vehicle of this disturbing, gaping void that has to do with the origin and the human group and that terrified the nations that had Jews in their midst. All of the images of the Jew—wandering, stateless, ugly, contaminating, cosmopolitan—derive from this experience, as does the singularization of the Jews, the approach to them through the agency of singularity. These images express the anxiety of the moderns and not the reality of the Book.

Yet it is worth noting that even though (or precisely because) they were excluded by the discourse of the state and of political modernity, these images played an important role in the identity of a European identity. In fact, this exclusion played an important role in the capacity of the Europeans to build an integrated European identity. This is obvious insofar as nationalists and anti-Semites were concerned. The repulsive figure of the Jew helped them forge an identity based on the assertion of a positive fullness that was pitted against this emptiness. It was on the edge of this void—that reiterates the experience of the origin (escaping control)—that the assertion of their identity was raised in a refusal to face the elusive origin and uncanniness (the "unconscious," "God," etc.) in the being-there of human identity. Without delving into this emptiness here, it could be compared to the burning bush whose flames do not consume the letters of the Book—a flame at the heart of being, alight in its creative withdrawal.

The Nazis turned this luminous burning into a destructive, consuming fire, and in so doing they turned the empty space of a coming into an abyss of nothingness. The burning of Jewish books was a prelude to the burning of the people of the Book and to Europe's self-destruction.

The Man-of-the-Jew in Question: The Limits of Postwar Jewish Singularity

With the model of the Book as a reference, we can assess the process of "normalization" that modified the Jewish condition after the Emancipation and that culminated in political Zionism. Emancipation brought with it the privatization of the Book and its retreat from the polity. The narrative, severed from its companionship with the Law, assumed a mythical dimension that lent itself more to fictional constructs than to real life. To put it in colorful terms, books by Jews began taking the place of the Book. With auto-emancipation, the state of Israel (definitively?) deposed the Book from its central position among the Jewish people and took its place as the federating principle of the people, henceforth, more and more a "Jewish nation" than a "Jewish people." In the era of the state that began then, the Book of Books was turned into an archaeological guidebook that served to prove and provide the foundation for the autochtony of those who increasingly saw themselves as Israeli rather than Jewish. The fact that even Ahad HaAm (1856–1927), the advocate of "spiritual Zionism" who refused the centrality of the state so dear to political Zionists, distanced himself from the civilization of the Book evidences the across-the-board agreement of all Zionist tendencies in their relationship to the Book. Ahad HaAm denounced the "people of the book" in favor of a "literary people" "whose life and literary creativity are in harmony, with literature developing in response to the needs of each generation and each generation abiding by the spirit of literature."[19] The "literary people" are part of a continuum between life and the written word, with the latter playing a cardinal role in the former. In contrast, "the People of the Book is a slave to the Book. Its soul has deserted its heart and been dissipated in the written word," so much so that the Book paralyzes the people: every idea and every act has to artificially obtain the approval of the Book instead of being inspired by it. The people no longer evolves; it becomes hostage to an inert book. It is no longer the "heart" that influences literature but the written word that imposes itself by force on the heart. The "love of Zion," in Ahad HaAm's version of Zionism, must change the center and purpose of Judaism from the Book and the written word to "the heart's vital aspiration to the nation's unity, its resurrection, and its free development in accordance with its own spirit, on universal human foundations." Zion may not obliterate the written word and the Book, but the latter must no longer be at the center of Jewish life.

This substitution of the state for the Book is crucial to an understanding of the crisis that rocked Jewry as it began getting back on its feet. It was, in a way, the end of rabbinic Judaism. The same process can be seen at work in all of the developments that we have been witnessing, particularly since the Six Day War. The problematical relationship between the Synagogue and the state stems from the conflict between the Book and the state and its implications on the nature and government of the Jewish *people*. Its consequences can be seen in the state's bureaucratization of Judaism (a state religion in the Napoleonic fashion) but also in the diminished creativity of the Scriptures in all areas of culture as well as in the autochtonization of the Book in religious Zionist irredentism—a dramatic strategy for inject-ing the Book back into an Israeli society that rejects it—or in the insidious refusal of ultra-orthodoxy to respect the authority of the state and an Israeli nation governed by the state.[20]

The "bureaucratization" of the Jewish people after the Six Day War was grounded in an ideology that gave pride of place to the *state* of Israel in Jewish life. This was one more form of bureaucratic centralism, rely-ing, in this case, on the Jewish Agency to thoroughly politicize the lives of the Diaspora communities. All of the characteristics of political Zionism, and notably its project of forging a "new man" from the old Jew in exile (a variation on the "regeneration" of the Jew), are proof that the Jewish national response may well have been an adequate response to the chal-lenge of political modernity, but it in no way departed from this same modernity. Political Zionism achieved the remarkable feat of restoring the Jewish condition at the very locus where there was no place for it anymore. In this respect, it was a living challenge to the modern logic with regard to the Jews but also, and paradoxically, its most unmitigated expression. The Israeli experience thus marks the explosive encounter between the disappearance and the reinstatement of the historical Jew (which was, for this reason, incomplete). The problematical developments around the "new historians" demonstrated the extent to which this experience no longer dominated the situation and found itself submerged by a return of the repressed. The experience of Israeli singularity was a success and at the same time a failure, at least when it came to finding a solution for political modernity's incapacity to accommodate singularity (Jewish singularity, but also—since there is a state—the singularity of others, and in this case, on a regional scale, that of the Palestinians). Elsewhere I have described this condition of being as one of "inner exile," in the context of a historical relativization, wherein the "small return" (political Zionism) and the "small exile" (contemporary Diaspora) form the weft and woof of a period that is no longer wholly in exile but not yet in a return, the first moment of the "great return" that is still but a promise.[21] The assumption of Jewish singularity by political Zionism, important as it may be, is not where my argument has been leading. Political Zionism is not the end of the road. My purpose is not to defend particularism against universalism but precisely to get out of this false dilemma. I do not mean by this that the state or the relationship to the land of Israel is situated outside of the Jewish vocation, but rather that there could be a relationship to sovereign power and to the land that would not eradicate the centrality of the Book in Jewish sociality. Admittedly, such a relationship has yet to be invented (in fact, the future of Judaism is tied to this invention). Therein lies a cardinal principle in my analysis: the history of the Jews was not the experience of a congenital "abnormality" that made of them pariahs in their souls, never to benefit from a land of their own. There is a "life" for peoples outside the confines of the nation-state and a future for humanity after modernity; people can free themselves from modern politics. This principle could be described as one of hope. What it promises is far from clear, but it opens the horizon to the future. We can see in the case of the Jews that Judaism must be an issue for the Jews themselves rather than a pro domo plea. It is a critical reflection on Jewishness that I am undertaking here.

The diasporic singularity that leans on that of Israel bears out the same conclusions. We have already seen the way in which postwar diasporic identity remained unclarified. Since the 1980s, it may well be undergoing a radical crisis. The École de pensée juive de Paris excelled in analyzing the philosophical and metaphysical significance of Jewish singularity but had difficulty grasping its political implications. The Six Day War thus swept away a good part of the heroic ethics that the Paris school had built up, because it could not face a historical turning point that confronted it directly with the State in Judaism. One of its major failures was that it took for granted the restoration of Jewish singularity and the persistence of democratic universality in its conception of the access of Jewish consciousness to metaphysical universality without thinking through their political consequences. But how could singularity be celebrated without clarifying the nature and *political* implications of its expression? The difficulty was obvious with such thinkers as Léon Askenazi and André Neher, who opted for emigration to Israel and found themselves caught in the ideologico-political impasses (religious irredentism) of a meteoric engagement with Zionism, inspired by a generous metaphysics. But the thinking of Emmanuel Lévinas, who did not choose to move to Israel, is susceptible to the same criticism, insofar as life in the Diaspora is concerned. Did he succeed in formulating the "philosophy of singularity" for which he had called?[22] If we examine the implications of his philosophy in terms of Jewish singularity, then there are grounds for perplexity. In universalizing the concept of "chosenness" (and this is the thrust of his Talmudic essays), he did not help contemporary Jewish consciousness perceive the practical limit that separates the singular (a specific Jewish existence) from the universal. This limit is the prerequisite for humility; it underpins the altruism of singularity and prevents its limitless hubris, which we may have seen at work in the 1980s and 1990s (Judaism presented as an absolute morality and experience for all of humankind without the stringent standards toward oneself that must accompany it; without this, altruism leads to eliminating the limits of the same and becomes susceptible to all sorts of perversions). Lévinas's accurate analysis on the plane of moral conscience becomes highly problematic when transposed to the political and historical plane, and this transposition is inevitable, because no matter what Lévinas says, there is every indication that he draws his inspiration from historical Judaism.[23]

Once Jewish singularity had become a concrete historical and political condition, it became imperative to clarify the concept of "chosenness" (if only to renounce it, even if this amounts to renouncing Judaism) in its relationship to Jewish historical reality and thus necessarily to develop a critical political philosophy, equal to the universal ambition. Lévinas may have taken the status of the singular (literally referring to Jewishness) too much for granted, so he did not feel the need to elucidate the concept, which was one of the main tasks of classical Jewish philosophers confronting singularity with universality.[24] That chosenness be extended to encompass all human beings without "thematization," that is, without relating it to one person in particular, is philosophically understandable from the perspective of Judaism, because the election is "a being divesting itself, emptying itself of its being,"[25] but the conception is problematic on the historical plane, that is, applied to the Israel of historical Judaism, where Lévinas drew it. It takes a good deal of critical sense and political insight not to avoid a misunderstanding. Singularity can only be a vehicle of the universal when it stays rigorously disciplined in relation to itself.

The optical illusion is thereby at its height: all men are supposed to be Jewish, but there are no more Jews. And what about the (henceforth) "sociological" Jews? "Each time Israel is mentioned in the Talmud, one is certainly free to understand by it a particular ethnic group [. . .] but [this is] to forget that Israel means a people who has received the Law and, as a result, a human nature which has reached the fullness of its responsibilities and its self-consciousness."[26] What is Israel? The Israel of messianic times? Sociological Israel? All of humankind? We can measure here the full weight of Lévinas's silence about the political and historical dimensions. What could be regarded as heroic and grandiose in the post-Shoah period (because it involved asserting that the singular fate of the Jews had been the fate of all humanity and refusing withdrawal) was insufficient once the Jews had assumed their singularity, especially in the politics of the nation-state.

The ideas developed by the Paris school are profoundly admirable, but they cannot meet the challenges that face the Jewish people at the end of the twentieth century. The malaise today with regard to the singularity of the Shoah (the uneasiness over the boundary between the Jewish specificity of the Shoah and its implications for all of humanity, with Jews maintaining both without elucidating their interrelationship) comes from a similar lack of clarity, which is characteristic of our times. Evidence of this, or at least a sociological symptom thereof, can be seen in the debate that took place in the United Stastes in the 1990s. In a highly controversial critical article on Elie Wiesel's work,[27] Naomi Seidman compares an earlier draft of his major novel, *Night*, first published in 1956 in Yiddish (and thus for a Jewish public) as *Un di velt hot geshvign* (And the World Remained Silent), to a second French version, one quarter of its length. The latter was greatly influenced by François Mauriac, who launched the young author and advised him. Whereas the Yiddish-speaking central character, Eliezer, seeks vengeance and tries to break down the wall of indifference, the French-speaking survivor, Elie, develops the theme of silence, mystery, and the absence of God, the "scandal of the dead" rather than the "scandal of the living." Seidman presents documents to support her claim that Mauriac and publisher Jérôme Lindon were behind the Christological theology of the Shoah manifested in the French version in the theme of the unspeakable, which stands in marked contrast to the Yiddish draft's emphasis on vengeance and judgment that would have brought Wiesel's work closer to Solzhenitsyn's at his return from the Gulag.

Thus Wiesel would have paved the way to today's prevailing discourse about the Shoah as "unthinkable" instead of assuming Jewish singularity in a more pugnacious spirit. The sacrificial Christological theme of the Holocaust would have developed from the eclipse of the political and historical dimensions of an event that took place first and foremost in the history of human beings and in modernity. Whether the thesis in this essay is fair or not, the archaeology that it proposes of the terms used in the debate on the Shoah is interesting in its own right: it rests on the hypothesis of an unresolved conflation, which leads to confusion, of the motifs of the Shoah's singularity and universality.

As a general rule, intellectual invocations of "Judaism" have been divested, over time, of their historical weight and substance, to figure in the circumlocutions of the "rhetorical Jew," promoted this time by the Jews themselves. The so-called "new philosophy" current in the 1980s may have been one of the consequences of this trend, along with the all-embracing ethics of "human-rightism," but also the insularity of some sectors of Jewish opinion, which are, in a manner of speaking, the illegitimate children of the misconception (and, it must be stressed, only the misconception) of the École de pensée juive de Paris.

Jewish consciousness became so inward looking that it tended to lose contact with the exterior, even when, in the case of Lévinas, it was wholly directed toward the latter and not specifically concerned with the singularity of Jews. We have been experiencing something of an eclipse of the great spiritual vocation of Judaism ever since this very intellectually creative period. Witness the highly provincial character of Jerusalem, a city that has risen from its ruins. The creative postwar tension generated by the search for the universal in the national or collective phenomena has been relaxed. A "civil religion" has supplanted this search, initially based on the state of Israel and, hence, the state principle and the nation—on the *refound* people—and thereafter on the memory of the Shoah—on the *lost* people. Thought has given way to ideological discourse and advocacy. What was a factor of awakening consciousness and creative effervescence became a fashionable convention. But it also is the very concept of "community" that has shown its limits, based as it is on a malfunctioning system of "representativeness." That is because a "community" in a democratic system can only maintain its legitimacy by remaining relatively "dormant," more symbolic than activist. Having no democratic basis, since universal suffrage is the prerogative of government bodies, it cannot "go too far." But on a number of occasions in the 1980s and 1990s, it went overboard in ways that put into question the sociopolitical viability of the postwar model of community identity[28] by highlighting its ill-considered aporias. There can be times when the affiliation that ties individuals to a "community," over and above citizenship, becomes a hostage to institutions whose only authority derives from their purported representativeness, but that transgress—for all sorts of reasons—the tacit agreement that is the source of their legitimacy. In this case, the community, which was a way of restoring the citizenship of the Jews, would ruin their enjoyment of democratic rights.

All of the limits discussed earlier regarding the revival of postwar Jewish singularity call on the Jewish world, which addressed the question of the Jew to Man, to address the question of Man to itself and the world at large. The Jewish question, in the final analysis, is the question of Man that the Jews address to all men. This reversal of the now-proverbial statement, that the "Jew is one whom other men consider a Jew," certainly did not occur to Sartre. The book to come will be titled "The Man-of-the-Jew." It will mark the start of a new era.

CHAPTER 12

The Enigma of the "People"

The relative vagueness in which I left the concept of people—which may have given the impression that I advocate the prevailing forms of communal identity (on the model of nationalism)—was necessitated by my analytical method. The "people" (and its identity) has remained the undefined and incomplete ingredient of political modernity and democracy in particular. I have used it as an open-ended category that still needs to be understood, contrary to what most people believe. Picking up on Paul Ricœur's ideas, I would say that the problem of peoplehood in modernity was the problem of the narrative in the abstract universalism of rights and that of literature in the dominant mathematical language of rationality. In the modern period, it was in the abyss of the people that the political was instituted. Despite the moderns' will to power, they could not subjugate the "uncanniness" that the people carried with it. Nazism was, no doubt, the most powerful and most violent experience of a people (the *volk*) instituting itself in the state by destroying the nation and meeting the impossible people in modernity—to wit, the Jewish people—in the impossible place of peoplehood that is modernity.

The Modern Saga of the "People"

A people is regarded today as identical to a nation, when in fact these are two distinct figures of collectivity that have to be dissociated. Modernity was a very hard time for peoples, with the expansion of nation-states and their inevitable territorialization. With their indistinct and mobile boundaries that are human rather than spatial, peoples had difficulty adapting to the totalizing, self-determining project of the nation-state. They were always spilling over the nation-state's boundaries and challenging its efforts to achieve absolute sovereignty. Life can never be wholly fitted into preestablished categories; it always brims over in a gratuitous way. This is the "in-finite" dimension of humankind. All of the conflicts of the past two centuries have resulted from the borders of nation-states that no longer corresponded to the "borders" of peoples. The European wars, but also the many conflicts in third world countries with abstract borders determined by colonial nation-states, were the consequence of this disparity between peoples and nation-states. Before modernity, there were no borders based on identity, as we understand it today; the borders were the political of monarchies. The singularity was assumed by the king who thereby released society of this burden (at the price of their subjection to a flesh-and-blood monarch whose sole distinction was to have been born, the passive heir to his predecessor). In a kingdom, several peoples, even those geographically noncontiguous or only partially so, could pledge allegiance to a king who assumed the singularity of the whole political entity. When the singularity is assumed by a nation at one with a singular state (instead of a king), there is a risk that the identity and allegiance of other peoples, who are subjected to the rule of this state, will be alienated, because a civic nation always relies on a majority people, necessarily singular and therefore absolutized, since it knows no more limits. This is the logic that the nation-states pursued through tough policies of national integration that would not suffer the affiliation of individual citizens to indeterminate peoples transcending the strict boundaries of the state. The nation that the state ineluctably generated came to identify with the majority people, which had supposedly disappeared.

Today the nation-state is everywhere on the wane, and an awareness of the personality of peoples is emerging, but no sooner do the peoples resurface that they are conjured away again: the general opinion is that nations are returning as part of a resurgence of nationalism and fundamentalism. In addition, any form of "identity" is seen as a form of fundamentalism. A new hierarchical classification has appeared. The "people," which is rejected, is categorized as an "ethnic group," with the implication that it is a subnation or an archaic nation, below the supreme stage of rationality (the state), and hence below the political threshold. The ethnic group is seen as related to biology, instinct, and pathos, not rationality. This is actually just a more sophisticated way of referring to what was known as "race" in the nineteenth century! This notion of "Jewish ethnicity" (always decried) has a long future ahead of it. The unanimous condemnation of identities is, in fact, the final convulsion of the false consciousness of the moderns (who thought themselves "universal"); it is the expression of their confusion and decline because, as we have seen, this is not what is happening at all. It is easy to see in this light why the singularity of the Shoah is regarded as an insurmountable obstacle, a challenge all the more unbearable insofar as the Jews have produced one of the strongest "narratives" of a people in the world. A new ideology, perhaps what is called "postmodernism," is taking hold that endeavors to rationalize and legitimate globalization. The New

Left would thus be adopting the globalization discourse that regards peoples and nations as obstacles to the flow of the market—thereby setting up the objective grounds for what could become a new form of anti-Semitism.

It is in the same light that we can grasp the triumph today of a new theory of the nation that provides globalization with its "scientific" complement. I am speaking of the theory that posits the nation as an imaginary construct, an "imagined community," a narrative of origins. The bible of this current of thought is Benedict Anderson's *Imagined Communities*, which defines the nation as "an imagined political community—and imagined as both inherently limited and sovereign."[1] But Anderson is not alone. Eric Hobsbawm speaks of "the invention of tradition,"[2] and Danièle Hervieu-Léger (picking up Pierre Legendre's concept of "genealogical reference"[3]) speaks of "reinvented traditions" to describe the return of religious belief.[4] These conceptions draw directly on Ricœur's "narrative identity," but they take it in a sociopolitical direction that was not his. This is not the place to undertake a sociological criticism of this theory.

We have already seen it at work in the discourse of the "new historians" in Israel. It is inscribed in the framework of deconstructionism, a distant philosophico-literary outgrowth of the constructionism developed by Durkheimian sociological theory to analyze the way in which societies "construct" their reality and their identity. Such constructions can then be "deconstructed" for purposes of understanding. From the theory of narrative as the absolute source of collective identity, the new sociologists jump to the conclusion that all forms of collective identity (and not only the nation) are artificial inventions, language constructs that stand in opposition (implicitly at least) to a concrete reality.

This idea silently reiterates Marx's denunciation of the ideology and artifice of all cultural structures. But what differentiates the new sociologists from Marxists (and makes them post-Marxists and postmodernists) is that, unlike Marx, they no longer believe in the real (which for Marx is economical). Their conception thus leads to the "dandyish" nihilism of an individualism in tune with the ideology of globalization. There is something truly naïve about their heuristic astonishment at (re)discovering the national "imaginary." They seem to be unaware that the real for human beings is as much a matter of language as it is of economy or biology, otherwise they would not be so surprised that the "people" is a "narrative."

By "people" I understand a reality that is much "greater" than the nation, one that harbors the enigma of the origin, the basis of humanization, and that is always characterized by singularity. As Ricœur aptly observes, "There is no plot of all plots capable of equaling the idea of one humanity and one history."[5] Humanity exists only through peoples and their narratives. It is congenitally a plurality of singularities. Peoplehood is always a singular experience. The people is the framework that allows individuals to receive and experience identity and form their own personality. It carries the principle of differentiation and alterity, because it escapes control and is the source of exteriority and heteronomy in the human condition. Peoples are the face of humanity whose history is through them.

The Limits of the "People's" Indetermination

A consideration of "peoplehood" cannot, however, exhaust the political sphere, because the "people" is precisely what is below the threshold of the political (and constantly surpasses it everywhere); it is what the political should not handle. I am not therefore an advocate of the superlative exaltation of the "people." The people carries the political with it, but the opposite is not the case (which it is for the nation). Nevertheless, it has a place, a delimited place, in the edifice of sociality. It was because the people was repressed that it lent itself to perversions. The question is what is its place in relation to the state and citizenship?

The amazingly modern ideas of Joseph Albo, a fifteenth-century medieval Jewish philosopher, may provide some insight into the place of the "people" in the political process. Analyzing the relationship between the Law of Moses, that binds the Jewish people in a covenant with God, and the Law of Noah, the source of the covenant between the nations and the Creator of the Universe—and thus the relationship between the particular and the universal—Albo theorizes that there are three types of law: natural, conventional, and divine,[6] with the latter category including the laws of Noah and Moses. Each type of law has a different function.

Natural laws are based on the "nature" of human beings. To satisfy the material needs of human beings, they must join forces on a permanent basis. Man is a "political animal" who needs a body politic and public order. The fact that it is possible to live as a hermit far from the society of men only demonstrates that political nature cannot be reduced to physical nature. The former has more to do with satisfying the psychological need for security (and securing the satisfaction of such needs on a permanent basis). The human *species* and the human *group* are thus always political. "Natural law" stands at the junction of basic vital needs: the psychological need for security and the need for legal order in society.[7] It is the formal condition for the constitution of any type of human society. Natural law confers moral coherence and humanity upon human society, and this is as important to human beings as their physical condition. The criterion of this moral coherence is distributive justice (based on the principle of an equal share to each individual), and its end purpose is to make possible what is just and eliminate what is vain. Thus all political systems (that meet the need of security) must protect individual rights.

Natural law is the necessary but not sufficient condition for the establishment of a body politic. To be more than just an abstract system, a particular society needs a concrete act of promulgation and of constitution based on the consent of its members. Natural law must thus become a convention if it is to be an accepted standard of justice and legitimate the exercise of coercion to secure its application. This coercion is the counterpart of the freedom and responsibility of the members of the body politic, which are the two principles of conventional law. One might say that what human beings need is not a society in general but a society in particular—what I would call a people—so that natural, universal law will be observed. Natural law has an exclusively negative thrust (its purpose being to eliminate evil and injustice), and it cannot by itself promote a positive form of human fulfillment. The latter is only possible in a concrete society, defined in its teleology and its sense by the historical culture of a people and not by nature. Only a real political community, necessarily singular, can allow us to see to it that our freedom and desirable goals are achieved. These goals cannot fly in the face of the needs of natural law (the order needed to guarantee the security of human beings). Conventional law is not based on natural law, but it is limited by it. Its end purpose is not distributive justice (to each an equal share) but the satisfaction of desire and the avoidance of the undesirable. Desire is thus its principle, inseparable from its cultural identity. Conventional law does not spring from the political nature of human beings but from their cultural nature, from "public opinion." In this sense, Albo regards it as being superior to natural law, because it gives justice its practical conditions of application. It is appropriate to the condition of human beings. Whereas natural law is the same for all humans in all places, conventional law depends on place, time, and the nature of the people that it governs, and this nature is lodged in history and singularity. This singularity is the sign of its excellence, because it particularizes abstract natural justice and makes its application possible. But if conventional law is based on consensus, then it is not absolutely democratic. It implies a hierarchy, because it lays the foundation for a power of coercion to secure its application (within the bounds of natural law). It undergirds the legitimacy of the wise man, the legislator of social order and convention.[8] Hence, equality (distributive justice) is not sufficient for achieving a society's concrete goals. There must be power, the cause of inequality: certain people are at the helm, while others are not.

This leads us to the need for a third level of law, and that is "divine law." Conventional law is relative, uncertain, and impermanent. A prisoner of opinion, place, and context, it cannot offer reliable criteria for what is desirable, and desire is changing. There is one more step in the order of law needed on the path to truth and justice. Only what Albo calls divine law can lead us to a knowledge of true goodness and evil. For this reason, divine law harbors true happiness and the possibility of attaining true goodness. The human mind (conventional law) and physical nature (natural law) cannot by themselves lead to this. Such criteria of desirability and undesirability can only be revealed by an event and a tradition that pass them on and perpetuate their memory. The purpose of divine law is not to directly govern political society—conventional law suffices for this purpose—but to guide individuals to "human perfection."[9] What gives it this capacity? It is addressed to neither man in general nor to a given people but to man as a concrete individual, providing the individual with criteria to delimit and govern individual acts. It is addressed to each person in particular, and it is because it takes into account this particularity that it is infinitely superior to the universal law of nature. Divine law is the apotheosis of universal law. It constitutes the human as subject. It inspires judgments that mete out punishment and reward on the basis of the condition of the responsible person and the context of the act (for example, one cannot apply *lex talionis*, and demand "an eye for an eye," from a one-eyed person). The capacity for adequation, or appropriateness, is what distinguishes a true judge, who is attentive to the singular case, from a law professor, who is attentive to legal mechanics and principles. The legal system thus leaves the realm of abstraction and recognizes individual people, the individual subjects of law. According to Albo, divine law comprises all elements and all dimensions of the person's human situation.

Albo arrives in this way at the idea that in the universal it is singularity, not indifferentiation, that has the highest degree of merit. The universal that Greek philosophy regards as superior is seen as inferior in the Jewish philosophical outlook. Singularity is placed at the summit of human accomplishment and becomes the very face of the universal. All three types of law are necessary. Each adds to the other without superseding it. The singular is manifested over and above human nature and the people and as a fulfillment of their promise. The individual is the accomplishment of the singular. The "people" (conventional law), limited by natural law and the uncertainty of the "desire" that animates it, cannot constitute the "end of the road," the finality of the human condition (which is subjectivation). But without its mediation, a political society cannot be established, and subjects cannot be born in nature, since natural universality is but a pious wish. The "people" both relies on nature and is dissociated from it (through the polity and culture); natural law must limit it and force it to "separate" from itself,[10] and this is logically consistent with the idea that there can be no people without a law (a conventional law limited by nature). The separation to which I am referring here leads not to anonymity and indifferentiation but to individualization, singularization, and subjectivation. The whole problem of political modernity is that whereas the third level of law has disappeared, the need that the polity has of it is just as strong. The state made up for its absence by taking its place, not in addition to the people but by appropriating the people and thereby demolishing it to become the nation. Although the people had no place anymore, it did not cease to exist. It was cast into the realm of the unthought and the unthinkable, where it continued to work on the nation-state in the subterranean manner of the unconscious.

CHAPTER 13

Toward a New Age in Democracy?

From the standpoint of the singular, thus defined, state universality necessarily appears as a total universality in which the singular is but a cog, an inert "body," an instrument in the service of a whole, with no room left for human beings as they are, one plus one plus one. State universality purports to transcend particularities, subsuming and elevating them in citizenship. Hegelianism gave an ideological version of this that borders on intellectual and political totalitarianism. Today, state universality is increasingly the object of criticism. Pierre Bourdieu lambasted "the 'universalist' hypocrisy of branding all nonpolitical demands as 'particularist' or 'communautarist' breaks in the universalist ('Republican') pact." "It is paradoxical," he wrote, "to see symbolic minorities called to universal order specifically when they rally together to demand the universal rights that are being withheld from them."[1]

Léo Bersani, a theorist of homosexuality, sees "the characteristic trait of a highly particular identity in French universalism. And when a society that is as culturally homogenous as France feels threatened by heterogeneity and finds itself confronted by a recalcitrant alterity, we see how easily a certain language of universalism is used as a defensive weapon to protect its particular identity."[2] In the same critical vein, Sylviane Agacinski maintains that "[o]ne of the greatest weaknesses of abstract universalism is precisely that it substitutes a concept of universal undifferentiated 'man' for differentiated human beings."[3] "According to the principle of the excluded third, abstract universalism always tends to identify the human or the subject with *one of the two terms* of the difference it claims to ignore [. . .]: the 'man' in the 'rights of man' was a citizen of the male sex."[4]

In a way, it is the indetermination of democracy that arouses this limitless Promethean and hegemonic desire for totality, which may seem generous and hospitable on the surface but which actually divests itself of particular men and women and welcomes only "persons," meaning no one in particular. Claude Lefort discusses this point at great length. This is the catastrophic dimension of universalism, and this is what has been shaken

271

by the logics of singularity over the last two centuries and especially over the last fifty years. Sartre's words, some fifty years ago, made sense from this point of view, when he commented that the singular man was lost in the universalism of citizenship. The democrat, he observed, "affirms that Jews, Chinese, Negroes ought to have the same rights as other members of society, but he demands these rights for them as men, not as concrete and individual products of history."[5]

The paradox of state universality can be explained as the consequence of the will to self-sufficiency in a democracy that abandoned transcendence for immanence but that could not content itself with that (whence the mythical cast given to the universal and the state). Man had to be remade, reeducated in view of becoming a total man, the citizen, but he had no face. The people of universal suffrage became the source of law, but their voices were not counted as a function of their particularities and interests. In this sense, the universal expresses the viewpoint of the state and not that of the men and women in the citizens. And yet it is by their experience that we can reassess its value, it is by what it repressed that it must be judged, in light of its historical failures. This is how Sartre's surprising statement relating the universal (and particularly French universalism) to the singularity of Jews is to be understood: "Not one Frenchman will be secure so long as a single Jew—in France or *in the world at large*—can fear for his life."[6]

State universality thus carried with it the transcendent projection of immanence constitutive of democracy and citizenship, by means of which the state "normalized" men until the mid-twentieth century. To put it otherwise, in view of our discussion, state universality was the apotheosis of a suppressed collective singularity that left no room for any of its direct manifestations; the nation-state eliminated the people and collectivities as much as individuals. The "civic nation," the "community of citizens," to borrow Dominique Schnapper's expression,[7] welcomed populations from other historical peoples—and there is good reason to be thankful for this—but it did not always know how to defend them in situations of adversity (anti-Semitism, the Dreyfus affair, and the Shoah are telltale signs of this failure), and it did not accept—at least not before the war—the legitimacy of their sense of specific belonging that came in addition to their citizenship.

In truth, only France really qualifies as a "civic nation." Under the banner of the universal (the "rights of man"), it was the aim of the French Revolution to establish a citizen nation, that is, a people that would be a nation spontaneously (and hence a state), transcending all affiliations and defining itself solely as an abstract entity (in which all singularities are erased). It is a unique case in contemporary politics in which the model of abstract universalism was assumed to the hilt in the paradigm of "*la*

République une et indivisible." This is why I have found in the ideologico-political (and cultural) history of modern France a remarkably exact mirror of modernity. Even though the disaster of the twentieth century was more limited in France than in Germany, it was French Jacobinism that embodied the most total and abstract form of political universalism. Revolutionary France fell into the totalitarian trap from the outset, with the extermination of the Vendeans, which Babeuf defined as a "populicide,"[8] and which constituted the nonindustrial prototype of modern genocide. Its purpose was the extermination of the Vendean population (cf. the decision by the Convention on October 1, 1793), 15 percent of which was in fact slaughtered. All the basic characteristics of a genocide were there: the rational and efficient system of extermination, the "antechambers to death," mass drowning, the "ovens" into which women and children were thrown, the burning of women's bodies to collect their "fat" for utilitarian purposes, the tanning of the victims skin, and so on.

But the state's universalism had a brighter side to it, and this is the one that is usually given pride of place. The best of this aspiration to undivided totality was later materialized in secularism, but it was perhaps more an ideal than a reality, because the "people" always escape the determination of the state and cannot be reduced to its rationality. This "civic nation" liked to think of itself as an abstract, universal republic, but it spoke French, followed a Catholic calendar, recalled "our ancestors the Gaulois" and the baptism of the Frankish king Clovis, and so on. The secularism was the legal framework of and condition for French pluralism, but it could not provide a self-sufficient identity that would compensate for the historicity and singularity of a people. The secularist aspiration was most strongly embodied by the Third Republic and its "École de la République," whose aim was to forge the civic nation. But what is left of this aim today? The system corresponded to a strong repression of specific identities in France and to French colonial expansion. The history that was taught in the Republican school turned the history of France since "our ancestors the Gaulois" into the story of the chosen people in modern history. Secularism has surely been an essential factor of social peace and respect for the other, but it still does not speak Esperanto, nor does it follow the calendar devised by the French Revolution in its attempt to break away from Christian time, and it by no means relinquishes its French historical heritage. It would be inhuman if it did. Once again, it is clear to see that the Republican "civic nation" is based firstly on the majority people, setting the tone for the nation's culture and lifestyle, which is altogether natural and inevitable.

The French nation thus includes several peoples whose individual members are citizens of the state and part of the "civic nation," the foundation of which remains the French people. Secularism is first, in practice, the hospitality and generosity that the majority people extends to other peoples who share its life. In other climes, where French secularism was unknown, "civil religions' assumed the task of compensating for the vertiginous hiatus between the different peoples and the nation of the state. These "religions" were intended to religiously celebrate the unity of the civic nation and the sacredness of its affirmation beyond the peoples that ineluctably compose it. The nationalism to which these civil religions led was a mystical form of ecstasy that exceeded the requirements of patriotism, since its purpose was not so much the defense of the homeland as the fusion of all parts in a single body. In the French nation, the peoples or communities—and even the French "people," in theory—lost their significance. As a result, they were demoted to an infrarational status, and their memory was appropriated, in the worst of cases, by antidemocratic currents (the extreme Right) and, in the best, by religion. The nineteenth century (with the feverish clash over the Dreyfus affair) best exemplifies the conjunction of these two currents, pitting the majority people against the nation-state and the citizenship that characterized it and included members of minority peoples (in this case, the Jews). The same pattern can be seen with the current resurgence of the extreme Right and of religions, at a time when civil religions are on a seemingly irremediable decline, and the identity-based diversification of nation-states has been resurfacing (like a reminiscence of the former peoples.) In France, regional reform revived the old monarchic provinces that the theoretical division of the French Republic into departments had not eradicated and endowed these regions with quasi-parliaments. The *loi Pasqua*, a directive law on territorial planning and development, which took effect on February 4, 1995, established *pays* that are roughly coextensive with the old historical counties. No matter how hard the state endeavored to ignore all but its citizens, the reality of peoplehood could simply not be eradicated.

Is it possible, then, to share Schnapper's enthusiasm in promoting the "civic nation" as an ideal for today, as if this idea had not two centuries of problematic history behind it? To be sure, Schnapper is fully aware of the gap between this ideal and the already accomplished reality, even though she does not address the issue directly. She does, however, rightly underscore the exemplary character of the French experience of state universalism, which was the most paroxysmal experience of its kind in the world and which, precisely for this reason (and together with the model of open secularism that has developed since the Second World War), may very well contain the seeds of universalism in the social rather than political sphere. In this case the legacy of Republican universalism would be not so much the "civic nation," to which Schnapper attributes a sacred value,[9] but the secular system, which by virtue of a benevolent neutrality would prompt social actors and the state to adopt a minimal form of identity in their relationships with one another. Yet state universalism, which went hand in hand with this secularism that blossomed as the state grew weaker, seems doomed to international decline with the emergence of big blocs (the European Union is one such bloc), relativizing the importance and function of the nineteenth-century nation-state (now in its death throes), while powerfully reinforcing the search for identity on the part of peoples and collectivities that these developments have released (witness the upsurge of collective identities, be they regional, ethnic, religious, sexual, etc.). Are we then to advocate singularism and "identitarianism" against universalism?

The Limits of Identity Politics

Multiculturalism is presented today as the way out of abstract universalism. Is it a manifestation of the return of repressed singularity to the public stage? Our period is indeed characterized by an exponential rise in identity-based affirmations, because in addition to the traditional identity of historical peoples (regardless of their geographic or numerical importance), sexual groups (homosexuals, feminists) are now asserting separate identities. This phenomenon, which upsets traditional categories, is very significant for assessing the validity of multiculturalism, if the latter is seen as comprising "sexual" (especially homosexual) and not only historical identities. First, it shows in no uncertain terms how great was the nudity of abstract man, a nudity that became even more blatantly obvious after the Shoah, and that drove people to define themselves in terms that were as close as could be to their personal experiences, in this case to their sexual experience, even though this is shared by all identities (there are homosexuals in all identities, but there is no homosexual *people*).

The impetus behind this new identity construct (seen through the sexual prism) derives not so much from a historical condition as from the condition of oppression experienced, in all identities, by a given sexuality or gender. The identity, insofar as it is collective, stems from victimhood and ultimately from the history of this condition. In light of our discussion, the fact that the referent for sexual identities is the corporeal, and even the biological (some maintain that there is a homosexual gene), suggests that they occupy the place of the repressed (the body), as if to actualize it in the face of a shaken principle of repression. As we have seen, this is the very place of foreclosure. If this is the case, then these sexual identities would paradoxically be an integral part of the very logic of modernity that they contest but that they, in fact, adapt to their purposes, which would mean that we are still in a logic of particularism, and hence—dialectically—of state universalism, even if the latter has been declared totally bankrupt.

The multicultural paradigm to which these identities belong does not implement what I have called singularity. Ultimately all of these identities are interchangeable: they constitute a disparate set of endless variations on a single modality of identity. This type of multiplication of singularities leads less to pluralism than to a uniformity that is so deeply entrenched that there is no possible relationship between them. They have become modalities of the same reality. The "difference" that they so noisily profess has no significance, since it does not open onto the other. Paradoxically, in this multiculturalism, there is no relationship anymore. We find ourselves once again in a system of equality based on total sharing and interchangeability, and the fact that it is grounded this time in the particular rather than in the universal does not make it any better. Individuals pass into the hands of their communities, becoming hostage to them. Communities and their leaders behave like "proprietors" of their individual members. A good case in point was the way in which Act-Up activists blackmailed a French deputy in 1999, threatening to reveal his homosexuality if he did not conform to their political stance. Seen from the perspective of Joseph Albo's theory about conventional law that characterizes communities of desire (the "people"), multiculturalism can be said to revive this intermediary level, but as an end in its own right, whereas Albo would have argued that communities must be restricted on one side by natural law (ensuring the security of individuals) and on the other by a superior law, that is, by divine law (the law that permits the emergence of subjects).

The chaotic plethora of identities and affiliations, with nothing in common other than their objective juxtaposition, condemns them, in the multicultural paradigm, to total relativization and neutralization. Since they have no universal horizon (even though their unending serialization presupposes such a horizon), what they have in common can only be conceived by the agency of separate negotiations each time. But singularity is not inscribed in a series, which is why I think today's multiculturalism is merely the passive response to the crisis of the universalist state and to its incapacity to compensate for the enormous abyss that separates it from its citizens. Multiculturalism recreates intermediary groups between individuals and the state. The problem is that whereas the state is no longer functional, it is still thought to be actively against the constitution of these intermediary identities that state universalism used to consider unacceptable.[10] At bottom, nearly all political ideologies have tried to compensate for this abyss. This is particularly true of Marxism, which conceived of the classes as "mediators" between individuals and the state, but also of nationalism, which placed the nation in a position of mediation between peoples and the state. Both, though, still had state universalism as a horizon: the abstract citizenship of the "civic nation," in one case, and the classless society, for the other (if via the dictatorship of the proletariat). Today, multiculturalism inserts in the position of mediation behavioral group identities, more pragmatic than historical because of the deactivation of the state pole. The whole difficulty is that there is nothing left to mediate, since there is no state anymore, and so multiculturalism ends up paradoxically recreating and perpetuating a state pole (or the illusion thereof) in order to develop its own economy. It forcefully opposes the imperialism of state universalism, but it does so from the very position that state universalism sets for it, and thus it remains wholly embedded in the logic of state universalism.

Identity as Additional

In stressing singularity, I have not been arguing in defense of particularism but rather trying to get out of the vicious circle of state universalist reasoning, of universalism as embodied by a leveling power that demolishes the identity of human beings who are summoned to don the neutral uniform of abstract citizenship and abandon the reality and substance of their lives. Only the singular is born, lives, and dies; only the singular has its place in historical time.

    With singularity I am referring to a dimension of human experience that is irreducible, that cannot be exchanged for another, and that will always remain radically alien to the norm. The will to take only Man into consideration has led to negating an irreducible reality, recalcitrant to all forms of totalization. What is at stake with singularity is establishing a common place for all singular and unique differences, not by negation or suspension but through acceptance and dialogue. The real problem that the modern polity has to address is how to live with this irrepressible fact and not how to eliminate, mask, or bury it. Because it is irreducible, not facing it and not recognizing it is leaving it open to adventurism and decomposition. Hannah Arendt very aptly commented in this regard, "There are ninety-nine chances that [equality] will be mistaken for an innate quality of every individual, who is 'normal' if he is like everybody else and 'abnormal' if he happens to be different. This perversion of equality from a political into a social concept is all the more dangerous when a society leaves but little space for special groups and individuals, for then their differences become all the more conspicuous."[11] When advocates of abstract universalism today condemn the "differentialism" of "symbolic minorities" (these are Pierre Bourdieu's terms) and conflate it with the sophisticated racism of the French New Right, they are providing a clear illustration of the perversion criticized by Arendt.

    It is from this nonappropriable, irreducible, and unique dimension of each individual and each group that the indetermination of democracy comes. And this is precisely what it is unwilling to recognize and examine for the best reasons in the world—that is, in the name of a total, democratic sharing among one and all. The problem is that total sharing comes up against singularity, and singularity is an unshareable share, and this is what prevents the enterprise of universalization from creating a vacuum and producing the universal. Contrary to the view of state universalism, this unshareable share is not the vehicle of particularism, finitude, or sameness. To the contrary. Because it opposes the enterprise of totalization—which is one of closure and total control—it is the vehicle of infinity and nonstate universalism. Because it cannot be shared and hence escapes the enterprise of sharing, it expresses the infinite dimension of humanity. The sharing can never be total. There will always be something left over that constitutes the bedrock upon which the community is built. It is this singular share that is the source of commonality, a commonality that people can never appropriate for themselves and that throws them back to their singularity and not to the vacuum of state universalism. This is already a sign that singularity is not related to sameness, that it carries inside it the singularity of the other.[12] Democratic equality is only desirable or attainable once this irreducible share has been removed from the sharing and set aside. There will always be something nonappropriable in humanity, something irreducible in the polity. Only when this unshareable share is recognized can equal sharing begin. We can then enter the political theater based, in democracy, on the principle of equality.

This empty space that cannot be appropriated is not of the same nature as the emptiness described by Lefort or the sacred as defined by Durkheim. Both Lefort and Durkheim ascribe an element of mystery and irrationality to this empty space. Singularity, as I conceive it, is not dissociated from the universal. It is not the "remainder," the raw, meaningless leftover that results from the universal operation. Rather, it is what comes in addition to the universal and exceeds it in all respects, what is over and above it, because it pertains to bounty and wealth, while the state principle and democratic power have to do with scarcity. Being-a-given-someone rather than an undifferentiated, abstract human being does not take anything whatsoever away from collective being. But this being-a-given-someone rather than someone else should not be apprehended—in its affirmative stage—as a fixed determination (and hence as that from which state universalism would offer release). The singular does not belong to the order of nature, as modern dogma maintains; it is what humankind has conquered against the nondifferentiation of nature and biology. It belongs to the order of culture. To see it this way involves a radical reversal of perspective. Identity is the movement par excellence of human specificity in the face of nature's blind determinism.

Singularity, in this conception, is the apotheosis of hominization. It is what differentiates man from animality. And it is for this reason that it escapes control, unlike the Enlightenment's abstract nature, which is the dream of a negating totality, since it eliminates all singularities. In this respect, singularity is to be distinguished from singularization, which always involves a massification, a negation of identities, the uncontrolled consequence of modernity's repression of singularity. Singularity is what stands in the way of the constitution of a mass. Turning singularity into the focal point extricates us from the centralizing logic, because singularity is out of the center by the principle of strangeness that informs it, although it is not necessarily at odds with what state universalism is seeking (in a warped way). What we need here is a change in perspective, an analysis that would posit abundance and a multiplicity of singularities as a starting hypothesis rather than scarcity (and the idea that there is not enough room for all of these singularities, and hence they must be eliminated). Adopting this hypothesis would lead to rethinking commonality as that which is added onto identities, and even overflows them in every respect, before and after, and not that which takes away from them.

Or, conversely, from the standpoint of state universalism, the singularities would be beyond the scope of the political, as that which overflows its bounds in a beneficial abundance. The identity that the nation-state considers a leftover, a remainder of the universal operation is, in fact, something extra. It is this opposition between remainder and extra that must be reexamined in order to reestablish and renew democracy today. In short, singularity would be at once outside the political and that upon which it is founded.

Identity in its different modalities needs to be understood in terms other than "differentialism," with its rejection of a universal horizon in the name of separate differences. It is precisely an approach based on singularity, or identity, that can get us out of the binary opposition particularism/universalism, differentialism/universalism. First of all, we must shift the focus to multiplicity, abundance, and polycentrism and not be afraid of existence if we are to get out of the simplistic antinomies inherent to political religions. One can be oneself without rejecting others or withdrawing into oneself! The human condition is about meeting the other on the basis of an identity (mine and the other's). Allowing for this coming together necessarily involves some sort of "sacrifice," which consists in an offering of the unshareable share, in taking singularity out of the computation, out of the controllable. This sacrifice is by no means a self-sacrifice, which would be but a pretense, at any rate, since heroes and saints are rare. The principle of giving is at the heart of this relationship. Identity must always be conceived in relation to the other, as a gift and not an appropriation.

The concept of identity has been greatly misused, demonized, and belittled in the name of altruism. People have forgotten that it presupposes, at its very core, the presence of the other—whom it can ignore, but beneath whose gaze it ineluctably develops. What makes a father's identity is his son and his condition as the son of a father. It is in the relationship that identity is forged. An utterly isolated identity, of the desert island type, does not exist in real life, although it may be a fascinating fantasy for the subject. Marx defined this "hollow" at the core of identity in terms of social (economical or political) relationships (the "relation of human being to human being is the relationship of man to woman), which amounts to saying that at the core of identity is a passage toward the other and beyond the self. But to him, this was a negative condition and the cause of alienation. Collective identity illustrates this even more: it is the passage of all passages (of individuals), it is what makes the passage of individuals through the world possible. The "community" is thus etymologically the place where one passes with others, "passes (*meo*) with (*cum*)" others. And to pass, one must paradoxically create a place where the world "narrows." This is identity. There is no passage through an undifferentiated desert, only wandering. A city with its narrow streets, on the other hand, is a place of passage, a place of identity par excellence. The world is anonymous, neutral, and indeterminate. One cannot enter into it. The narrowing (identity) that people create in it when they come together helps them out of the undifferentiation to which nature reduces them. You have to pass down a street to be hailed by name. It is in this narrowing, this singularization, that man "passes" through the world and thus acquires a singularity, the essence of which is the proper noun, the specific name. And calling a name requires someone other than oneself. When a human being is called, he or she is detached from the massification of nature. Identity is held in the calling of one's name, it is born out of it, for being called by name is not a matter of being "recognized" but of being "birthed," being truly "born," being intrinsically "known."

Ours is a very different perspective than that which Charles Taylor, following Hegel, defines as "recognition."[13] The latter is centered on sameness and the identical, while here it is the other that is at issue. It is the relationship that carries singularity with it, which means that the other is embedded at its core. It is no longer a matter of surpassing sameness but of giving birth to alterity. This is what I have called "abundance." The name designates the singularity, and the passage through which the singular emerges is the universal, one could say. The community is a singular, hospitable refuge that enables each person in particular to pass through the exteriority of the world.[14] This gesture is the process of non-state universalism.

Defined in this way, identity presupposes a difference that is thus completely opened to the other. Emanuel Lévinas strikingly describes this difference as "a non-in-difference in which the other—though absolutely other, 'more other,' so to speak, than are the individuals with respect to one another within the 'same species' from which the *I* has freed itself—in which the other 'regards' me, not in order to 'perceive' me, but in 'concerning me,' in 'mattering to me as someone for whom I am answerable.' The other, who—*in this sense*—'regards' me, is the face."[15] This "non-in-difference" goes hand in hand with "the goodness of responsibility." "The rights of man manifest themselves *concretely* to consciousness as the rights of the other, for which I am answerable."[16] In short, assuming singularity lays the foundation for moral responsibility. "In responsibility, which is, as such, irrecusable and non-transferable, I am instituted as non-interchangeable: I am chosen as unique and incomparable."[17] Thus Lévinas focuses his discussion of the rights of man on the "rights of the other person," knowing that it is impossible to conceive of human rights without the condition of justice, that is, the boundary that the rights of the other man imposes on human rights. Although it is not clear from this text whether Lévinas considered the citizen the form of this limitation on man, he does specify that justice, "the formalism of universality,"[18] does not suffice to guarantee human rights. Indeed, human rights cannot be understood by a negative (the need for justice) but by the idea of goodness upon which the veritable humanity is founded. "To limit oneself, in the matter of justice, to the norm of pure measure, or moderation, between mutually exclusive terms, would be to revert to assimilating the relations between members of the human race to the relation between individuals of logical extension, signifying between one another nothing but negation, additions or indifference. In humanity, from one individual to another, there is established a *proximity* that does not take its meaning from the spatial metaphor of extension of a concept."[19] In fact, contrary to the perspective I have been developing here, Lévinas does not seem far from thinking of identity in the same terms as Durkheim, as "[a] uniqueness beyond the individuality of multiple individuals within their kind. A uniqueness not because of any distinctive sign that would serve as a specific or individuating difference. A unity prior to any distinctive sign [. . .]. The rights of man manifests the uniqueness or the absolute of the person, despite his or her subsumption under the category of the human species, or because of that subsumption."[20] But unlike Durkheim, Lévinas regards this void intrinsic to the person not as the locus of society but as a divine presence, "the coming of the idea of God on the basis of the patency of the rights of man."[21]

In sum, counter to the commonsensical use of the term, I understand identity as the very experience of nonautochtony, irreducibility to exchange, and abundance sustaining multiplicity. It is beyond computation and beyond state universalism. It is the pivot of difference without differentialism. It is the echo of the vacuum and thus opposes the totality that fills it. We can think of the singular community as being not so much something less than the universal and the public arena of the political but as something additional, something that pertains to the symbolic and the cultural spheres for which the state is not the guarantor. The universal is out of the reach of the political. Communities cannot and should not be lodged within the state, but the state cannot and should not deny them.

The Meaning of the Separation Between Man and Citizen

With the multicultural model, we arrive at the caricatural, opposite effect than the one to which state universalism leads, yet the very principle of the latter does not disappear and continues to exert a decisive impact on the semblance of autonomy of the "multicultural" collective identity. The Promethean dream of total immanence has an even stronger hold in this paradigm; it is simply not played out this time in the theater of state transcendence. And, as we have seen, this immanence, insofar as it is responsible for the totalization of social and political life, is precisely what is at work in the failure of political modernity. The elimination of political transcendence (unconsciously reiterated) in the multicultural model does not fundamentally alter the problem of immanence. The ambivalent denial of a pole does not abolish the relationship of polarity.

The way that multiculturalism has of looking like one thing and being another raises a deeper question. Why did a multicultural paradigm, wholly embedded in immanence, need to surreptitiously reintroduce the very transcendence it denied by continually positioning itself in opposition to the state and its universalism? This may indicate that there is something irreducible about transcendence in the economy of social existence. There is then a typically modern trait in the "postmodernism" of multiculturalism. It is because modernity consciously refused to accept this transcendent dimension that it unwittingly perverted and reproduced it in other forms (political religions, the "hidden religion" of democracy).

As we have seen, the cardinal problem of modernity was that of limits, that of limiting itself and accepting its finitude. The question of origin represented one form of this problem. And as we have noted, the key characteristic of totalitarianism is the abolition of limits. It was this same limit that was abolished in state universalism, although in a way that was not as obvious due to the dissociation between individual and collectivity, the particular and the universal, man (the private) and citizen (the public). Having arrived at a critique of political transcendence and at the same time an acknowledgment of the irreducibility of a principle of transcendence in life, I must now take up from a different standpoint the dissociation of Man and Citizen in the Declaration that I have criticized up until this point. Theoretically, it introduced a separation into immanence, since Man is supposed to transcend the citizen and be the source of civic status and rights. But we have seen that things did not happen that way in practice. The universal became associated with the pole of the citizen in relation to men, and the citizen came to personify the transcendence of singular men, to the point of emptying Man of all substance. This is what follows from the idea of a "civic nation." Was this a departure from the spirit of the Declaration, and, if so, why? By giving pride of place to the citizen as the embodiment of the universal, political practices that drew inspiration from the Declaration put Man in the position of total dependence on the state. This is what Arendt observes when she states that the rights of man amounted to nothing without a state. In separating man from citizen, the Declaration of the Rights of Man and the Citizen of 1789 (very different in this respect from the American Declaration of Independence) put the universal in a position of total dependence on the state, precisely because it dissociated the universal from Man, left in the haze of an abstraction, to the point that it was the state that ended up instituting the universal. This situation could only lead to totalitarian excess (the first modern example of which was provided by Jacobinism). The rights of man thus followed improperly (in moral terms) from the rights of the citizen. The citizen came to define Man. Yet this citizen was subject to the power of state, and even to the henceforth-total power of a state whose universality was inevitably a misguided illusion *ad intra* (there were different components in the nation) and *ad extra* (there were other "foreign" nations). This is precisely the point at issue in democracy since the Shoah: it is not up to the state to institute man or to embody the human universal. The polity is not the be-all and end-all of man. It cannot institute the human (the eventual monstrous consequences of this enterprise can be seen in the potential uses of genetic manipulation and cloning that scientific progress has made possible today). In psychoanalytical terms, this project borders on madness, because it eliminates the bar separating the symbolic and the real.

This separation between the real and the symbolic has a long history behind it. Until political modernity, religious transcendence instituted the symbolic disjunction in the economy of social existence. In destituting it, the state seized this role for its own use, to the point of ascribing to itself the benefit of self-establishment and self-sufficiency. The symbolic fracture was so thoroughly absent from the scene of political modernity that it was reintroduced through the agency of a hidden religion, whose morality of sacrifice and victimhood has caused extensive damage. Lacking a bar of separation, the subject becomes the bar and the separation by offering himself up in the act of suicide. The dissociation of Man and Citizen in the Declaration could have reinstituted the fracture in the symbolic operation, with Man posited as over and above the citizen. But the opposite took place, and this is the source of the failure of political modernity. To put it in paradoxical terms, I would say that its failure arose from its relationship to the religious, because it is the religious that is at issue, the "sacred" to use Durkheim's term, the place of the remainder-surplus of the universal operation. Elsewhere I have coined the term *augret* from *augment* and *retrait* (retreat or withdrawal) to describe this dimension.[22]

One must be clear on this point: separation is a necessary "founding" principle. It is the source of language and communication, of the operation of symbolization that enables the subject to develop a relationship with the real and with others, without conflating dream and reality, inside and outside. This separation leads the subject to bereavement, to accepting the loss of a world that would materialize dreams and desires, a world of immediacy and fusion (which could be a definition of madness). It institutes what Freud called the "reality principle," a separation that is difficult to accept and that requires a detour by way of law and heteronomy (that is, transcendence). Accepting my own strangeness in the world is the condition for recognizing the other and for acting in and on the world, which is irremediably exterior to me.[23] At the source of this experience is the awareness that there is something in life that will always escape the grasp and power of man, even an assembly of men, no matter how strong in numbers they may be. There is a secret, shadowy part that constitutes man's deepest identity and that can never be disclosed. It is this secret (the "*augret*") that state universalism tried to seize. And this form of universalism is total, because its transcendence masks absolute immanence (even if it requires a theater of transcendence).

The political cannot be the agency of separation (that opens identity to the other), and only the agency of separation can institute the social. The instituting agency cannot be the agency of political power. The political cannot seek its origin in itself. The origin escapes (and must escape) its control; the institution of the social must fall outside of the domain of the political and the state. The origin is in charge of the Human; it is the matrix of individual and collective identity, and it implements the operation of symbolic fracture. It is the agency of singularity, of the share removed from the sharing, in the very act of sharing (which comes under the responsibility of the political), the share left out or the unshareable remainder from the operation of sharing, the one that cannot be divided in two, what is over and above the sharing (it is this elusive, ambivalent character as an object of desire, because it is out of reach, that explains why it was held to be "sacred" throughout history). Democratic equality is possible only after this "share" has been withdrawn from the sharing, in such a way that it institutes the commonality, a commonality that can never be totally shared. The problem is that the democratic ethos today refuses such sharing. This share (which is another way of indicating transcendence) carries with it the principle of giving, bounty, and generosity. This is why democracy unwittingly rejects the relationship of giving that is the only one that can "deal with" this experience. The irreducible "given" of life cannot be the object of sharing. Only the relationship of giving can meet the challenge, but this relationship, contrary to what democratic theory assumes, can by no means structure the political or it risks spawning tyranny. It must precede the political and sustain it but stop at its threshold. In return, the political must recognize its limits in relation to it. Democracy needs to rediscover in its foundation the gesture of giving, in the full thrust of its uncertainty.

Contrary to what many liberation theorists (following Marx) continue to believe, liberation is not a matter of tossing out the "Rights of Man *and* of the Citizen" so that citizen and man become one. This is what Sartre is hoping for when, according to a Marxist paradigm, he sees an end to anti-Semitism "in a society without classes [. . .], one in which man, freed of his hallucinations inherited from an older world, would at long last throw himself wholeheartedly into *his* enterprise—which is to create the kingdom of man."[24] The "and" is the symbolic bar. The point is to secure, not to eliminate, the distinction it instituted but which it did not safeguard because the citizen in political modernity engulfed Man and left him in a state of indetermination. This essay opens a field of speculation and analysis that can only be outlined here. Indeed, if man cannot be reduced totally to the immanence of the earth and is always in some respect a stranger on earth, then the "alienation" that characterizes life (to be alienated is to be the other—the stranger—to oneself) is irreducible (something that Marx could not admit, even though he had, significantly, thought of alienation in religious terms before doing so in sociopolitical terms). The irreducibility of the other in identity exists in the sphere of collectivity as well, with the result that the idea of the absolute immanentization and naturalization of man (which is the very soul of modernity) is nothing less than utopian. Man escapes his own grasp and refers to a plane that he does not master. And it is on this plane that identity and the social are instituted. We have called this dimension "the people." The political can only intervene afterward, as a secondary reality.[25]

From the standpoint of the political, there is an irreducible heteronomy. The political cannot seek its foundations in the political body itself without giving rise to a monstrosity. Rousseau's theory of "general will" needs to be reassessed in this light. The discrepancy between his theory (rational and generous) and practice has evidenced its limits. It is a myth that no reality could embody. The will can never be absolutely general, because in the *universal* suffrage that follows from this idea, there is always a minority whose will is not taken into account. What is more, the partition between the majority and the minority is dependent on uncertain contingencies: no one can predict what will happen during an election, and so consulting the general will is less a rational operation than a "magical" one, a lottery of sorts, that orients the decision. This is even truer today, when public opinions have become impenetrable and opaque. General will can never produce more than "conventional law." Purported to institute the self-establishment of the state by the political community, it was more a mythical construct than a fact. Antonio Negri put his finger on this problem in *Insurgencies: Constituent Power and the Modern State*.[26] He asks from where the norms that characterize a political and social order come, norms that necessarily preexist legislative, executive, and judicial power in the form of an "originary" power, which he calls "constituent power," that regulates and governs them. What, then, is the source of this power that, manifesting itself clearly in times of crisis and revolution, institutes a new order but seems to rise from nowhere? Negri maintains that this founding power may be unfounded, that it may be "the absoluteness of an absence," "absolute and unlimited procedure," "all-powerful and expansive, unlimited and unfinalized"[27] (akin, perhaps, to the divine?). We find here again a reiteration of Lefort's democratic void. "[A]bsence, void, and desire are the motor of the politicodemocratic dynamic as such."[28] Negri entertains a variety of possible "subjects" adequate to "absolute procedure" (in fact, the "revolution"): the nation, the people, and lastly (as one might expect from a Marxist theorist) "living labor"[29]—none of which brings anything new to an otherwise useful reassessment of the question that we have seen at work since the inception of democratic theory with the problem of a basis for obligations in a value system that refuses transcendence.

The Nonpolitical Institution of the Social

If the limitation of the political is the cardinal problem of political modernity, then the key question we must ask ourselves today is, what form could this limitation and separation possibly assume, knowing that the religious has always played this role in the past? Maybe what is being decried today as a "return of the religious" is a sign that the "postmoderns" are looking away from the political in their search for a limit by way of which a faltering identity could be reconstructed. It is clearly the question of religion in the political that is being raised here or, to put it in more sophisticated terms, the question of a limitation of the political and of a confrontation with the irreducible transcendence that remained in immanence.

How important this question was to early theorists of the democratic idea seems to have been totally forgotten by democrats in the first place. Every one of them, without exception, had recourse to the principle of an authority of the religious type to construct the symbolic economy of the democratic idea. It may be useful to pick up our analysis starting from there. Rousseau was the most explicit in this respect. He realized that it takes more than the love of one's country to produce the sense of obligation without which there is neither law nor morality.

Having thereby acknowledged that the source of law cannot be immanent, he argued that the legislator will have to "have recourse to an authority *of a different order* [emphasis added] capable of constraining without violence and persuading without convincing."[30] And, as if to underline the religious and national (the people) framework of this authority, Rousseau adds: "This is what has, in all ages, compelled the fathers of nations to have recourse to divine intervention and credit the gods with their own wisdom, in order that the peoples, submitting to the laws of the State as to those of nature, and recognizing the same power in the formation of the city as in that of man, might obey freely, and bear with docility, the yoke of the public happiness." In the draft chapter of *Social Contract*, "The General Society of the Human Race," left out of the final published version, Rousseau acknowledged the incapacity of the "general will" to produce the transcendence upon which the political relies.

> It is false to assert that, in the state of independence, reason leads us to contribute to the common good through a consideration of our own interests. Far from being allied, private interest and the common good are mutually exclusive in the natural order [. . .].
>
> The proof that enlightened and independent man would have reasoned in this way [in defense of their private interests] is that this is precisely how any sovereign society reasons when it is accountable for its conduct to no one but itself. How can one reply convincingly to such arguments without bringing in religion to aid morality and making the will of God intervene directly to bind men together in society? [. . .] So let us leave on one side the sacred precepts of the different religions, the abuse of which causes as many crimes as their use can spare us from. Let us leave to the philosopher the examination of a question which the theologian has never treated except to the prejudice of the human race.[31]

Rousseau has the philosopher answer the theologian and say "it is to the general will that the individual must address himself to know how far he must be a man, a citizen, a subject, a father and a child, and when it is fitting for him to live and when to die."[32] Then he puts the following words into the mouth of the independent man: "I admit that I can clearly see there the rule that I must consult [. . .], but I still do not see the reason why I should be subject to this rule." He concludes, "No one, indeed, will disagree with the view that the general will is, in each individual, a pure act of the understanding which reasons, when the passions are silent, about what a man can ask of his fellows and what his fellows have the right to ask of him. But where is the man who can thus *separate himself from himself* [emphasis added]? [. . .] to impose on himself duties whose relation with his own individual constitution he cannot see?"[33]

It is, therefore, as a logical necessity that Rousseau reintroduces an "authority of a different order" as the (separating) principle of general will and political society and finds himself facing an aporia. He objects to religion and religious authority but observes the need for such an authority to undergird the principle of obligation, which he naturally assimilates to religion, because it is the sacred in religion that has been the source of the greatest experience of "separation." And so he is led to advocate a religion with "neither temples, nor altars, nor rites, [. . .] confined to the purely internal cult of the supreme God and the eternal obligations of morality," a "civil religion" (these are his own terms) that would pick up the rites and ceremonies of traditional religions but place them under the authority of the state. He submits religion—which is necessary to democracy—to the power of the sovereign to protect society from the abuses that go with it. Rousseau turns the aim of religion into securing the cohesion of the state and legitimating its authority and extends the role of the state to exercise jurisdiction over religion, religious beliefs, and rites. Following this line of reasoning, we can see how this transcendence was denied in theory but came to be reintroduced in *extremis* and totally immanentized.

In fact, Rousseau appears to be restating Spinoza's conception of religion[34] as an educational instrument for the political: "Moses desired to admonish the Hebrews in such a manner, and with such reasonings as would appeal most forcibly to their childish understanding."[35] "We all know what weight spiritual right and authority carries in the popular mind: how everyone hangs on the lips, as it were, of those who possess it. We may even say that those who wield such authority have the most complete sway over the popular mind. Whosoever, therefore, wishes to take this right away from the sovereign power, is desirous of dividing the dominion; the Divine right, or the right of control over spiritual matters, depends absolutely on the decree of the sovereign, who is its legitimate interpreter and champion.

[. . .] Therefore the true ministers of God's word are those who teach piety to the people in obedience to the authority of the sovereign rulers by whose decree it has been brought into conformity with the public welfare."[36] This outlook was not only that of the first theorists of the democratic idea, it was still current in the Third Republic, when Jules Ferry advocated a Republican morality that would take over the role of religious authorities: "We must find a definition, no matter how succinct, of duties toward God."[37]

We have here, in a nutshell, the scenario of the tragedy of modernity. Rousseau is exemplary of this syndrome that witnessed the reintroduction of religion in the (secularist) negation of religion in order to lay the foundation for modernity. Democratic thought has not yet truly confronted this aporia rationally. Having failed (from its own standpoint) to find "an authority of a different order," it took the easy way out and "recycled" religion to establish a form of transcendence, which ultimately turns out to be absolutely necessary, in its professed immanence. It will be the task of democratic theorists in the twenty-first century to tackle this issue.

The Future of Political Transcendence and the Safeguard of Men

The issue can be clearly formulated. The moderns can no longer hide from the secret religion that inhabited democracy. They will have to face up to the (monstrous) reintroduction of transcendence in political immanence and hence confront a reality that appears to run counter to the conscious spirit of democracy. If we admit that this surreptitious reintroduction was the source of totalitarianism, that it was at the origin (in the term's deepest and most distant sense) of all the major contemporary catastrophes, then we can no longer accept the idea of leaving the "democratic void" untended and even of finding, following Lefort, an advantage to it. The alternative is not between the "void" and totalitarianism. It is, rather, this void that because it is an unavowed transcendence can become an abyss into which the political sinks, because the political (immanence) is ineluctably drawn to it, to fill and gain ascendancy over it. And it is this void that must be preserved from the political and instituted as a separate sphere: this is the only way of avoiding the sacralization and religionization of the political. Ultimate purposes (the "sacred") must desert the political and develop outside of its confines. The political must by no means embody a collective ideal (the "people" posited as a "nation") and even less a system of values (an ideology). It should restrict itself to the material management of the most trivially concrete matters. The political absolutely must remain a secondary reality and not a primary, foundational force. The agency that institutes the political and the social has to be separated from the agency that exercises political power. The symbolic must be separated from the political.

This instituting agency that I have qualified as transcendent is the matrix of individual and collective identities. By its transcendence, it can assume the role of the symbolic bar in the formation of identity, and for identity to emerge, it must take up the challenge of separation (from oneself) and face the empty space (which harbors the other) that it carries within it and the passage of the being that traverses it (the passage of generations, of filiations, of time, etc.). Indeed, if identity is the condition of responsibility for and recognition of the other, then this recognition can only be effective if identity overcomes its own inertia, its harmonic fascination with itself, and separates from itself. Peoplehood is the condition of humanity, not its end purpose. In this sense, the universal of humanity is still a horizon for peoples. The challenge of transcendence for individual or collective identity is also the challenge of the universal.

But it is not up to the state to oversee the trial of separation that underpins identity. The formation of the subject must take place outside of the political, and even prior to it. It is the "people" who prepare for it. This is why the universal cannot be attained in the political (that is, in a necessarily violent, totalitarian way). It must be outside of the political, which means that it cannot be formalized within citizenship, because citizenship designates a status of affiliation to a particular state (that is, to a system that civil society gives itself to serve it and that embodies nothing but this service), even if this citizenship provides the framework in which all affiliations enjoy equal rights and duties as singular groups that are not required to deny their singularity to benefit from this status. If openness to the other has already been achieved before the political stage through the trial of transcendence, then there is no need for self-denial, no need to sacrifice one's identity to gain entry into civic status.

In sum, man must take precedence over but not supplant the citizen, and man himself must undergo the trial of separation within his identity (to avoid doing so in the condition of citizen), insofar as this separation must be posited and instituted for there to be recognition of the other. As we have seen, the confusion between transcendence and immanence, between (unavowed) "religion" and politics, was at the origin of contemporary tragedies. It is as monstrous for the state to gain an exclusive hold on ultimate purposes as it is for the Church to have an exclusive hold on political power. The unconscious collusion between these two once-separated powers has always been a danger for democracy. The autonomization of the political did not suffice to secure the freedom of individuals, because religious power did not disappear; it merely fell into the hands of the state. This is the origin of democracy's "hidden religion," the mystique of the nation and the mystification of the political sacralized in its triviality. If "religious" experience is indeed irreducible, and "peoplehood" cannot be "handled" by the state, then democracy can no longer avoid facing transcendence. It must confront this challenge on new terms.

The problem is how to separate the instituting agency (the religious, the people) from the political agency and how to concretize the former in democracy; this is something with which democratic theory has never grappled. To whom could such a task be entrusted today? One can hardly imagine it devolving to the churches and religions that fulfilled this role until the establishment of the democratic state, even though they may be readier now after two centuries of secularization than they ever were before. Their elites would have to undergo a cataclysmic upheaval for such a thing to be feasible, because they were, as Rousseau maintains, at the origin of so many perversions and excesses. The difficulty is that it is impossible to imagine the existence of a religious body with neither church nor clergy, that is, without engendering secondarily a strategy of power that always leads to the abolition and delegitimation of the political. Moreover, not all religions are apt to take on such a task. I see no existing institution currently capable of fulfilling this role. Would one have to be invented, and could the future of democratic theory depend on such an invention? Neither the state nor religion as they are today could meet the requirements of a model in which transcendence is removed and dissociated from the political sphere. The search for such an agency must be inspired, of course, by a democratic principle. If one day the religious is to be the vehicle of transcendence in identity, it can only be so in a way that is passive and inert, with transcendence activated solely by conscious individual choice, as if the universal were a source that only flows when an individual comes to draw from it. The multiplicity of religions would stand as proof of the authenticity of the universal, which is thereby prevented from becoming totalitarian. Democracy must now address the question of the "sacred" in altogether different terms.

Such a theoretical invention would suppose that democratic thought draw on a different model than that of Athens, elevated to an ideal by nineteenth-century thinkers determined to ignore its shortcomings (the exclusion of women and foreigners from citizenship, the negation of the dignity of work, the omnipresence of an irrational religion in politics, etc.) in their effort to pit it against the religion of the Bible. In fact, more than the Athenian model of autochtony (the myth of the City born from the soil), the model that could rejuvenate democratic thought is that of the Exodus from Egypt and the journey across the Sinai Desert (supremely ignored by the modern political tradition of [a formerly Roman Catholic] Europe, even though it evinced an original conception of democracy founded on the "covenant"). The Sinaitic model, prior to any theological construct, is determined in relation to an experience of estrangement. The collectivity is founded in exile and not in its rootedness (and thus it turns its back on the principle of autochtony), but its aim is to settle in a land. In addition, the Sinaitic revelation is an experience of transcendence and heteronomy of the law establishing a democratic and an egalitarian relationship to ultimate values (with Moses as merely an intermediary between God and the political collectivity), along with a collective being whose substance is drawn from the interrelationship between immanence and transcendence (and not from land or memory). This paradigm shift is not as radical for democracy as one might think. It has generally been forgotten today that the early theorists of democracy focused a great deal of attention on what was called the "Republic of Moses," or the Hebrew Republic: this was the case for the Protestant utopists in their opposition to royal absolutism but also for the likes of Spinoza (*Tractatus Theologico-Politicus* is a study of the Mosaic state) and Rousseau (his *Considérations sur le gouvernement de Pologne* contains a vibrant defense of the body politic created by Moses). Perhaps this is the vein that democratic theorists could mine in an attempt to revive the virtue of permanent creativity with which Tocqueville credited democracy.

The "archaeology" of political modernity that I have undertaken in this work participates in the democratic project of freedom for human beings. Rediscovering singularity and identity is pointless if it does not help us confront the challenge of living together and of recognizing human beings in Man; it is meaningless, in sum, if it does not help us invent hospitality in the Rights of Man. It is the stranger and strangeness that are at issue in the problem of transcendence inherent to state universalism.

Hospitality involves welcoming somebody to one's home, someone in addition to the members of the household, and receiving this individual by name, because it is not anonymous people who gather together in a household but people with proper names. Such hospitality is possible because the host is willing to make a place in his or her midst, to open up to more than the self. Everything revolves around whether the host regards this place as "subtracted" or "added." If this empty place is defined as the citizen's, the place made in the "people" and by the people, then what comes in addition is the identity that—because it welcomed the other—also becomes collective identity. Welcoming the other is no longer experienced as a lack in terms of identity. Such a demand for hospitality, grace, and charity that citizenship alone (the "universal" law) cannot provide—but of which it is the test—can be observed today in all democracies. The decline in democratic institutions and the concomitant rise in "humanitarian" themes and the politics of "human rights" can be understood in this light (though we have seen that there can be no such thing as a *politics* of human rights). The powerful search for identity that characterizes all families on earth, and that is especially manifest in democracies, answers this quest. The contemporary need for "community" is a need for hospitality in the empty, cold world of citizenship that has lost its collective spirit and discredited the very experience of the collective because of the catastrophes that it engendered. The democratic universal, thus attained in the alliance between identity and hospitality, would be released from the grips of state power and the temptation of totality, and Man—who has suffered in the past century the worst tragedies in human history, those that he inflicted upon himself—will be born at last in the fate of men.

> *Everything that has been written in these lines illuminates and at the same time hides what burns in the furnace of the Shoah. What analysis could ever reach the bottomless bottom of the abyss that is man?*
>
> *Humankind now hovers over this empty space that has opened up at the core of civilization. Why then must we strive to understand? So as not to let the dead bury the dead. So that the memory of those who are gone is kept alive in the society of the living, thus perfected by their testimony, the silence of which ceaselessly resounds in the words of men.*

Notes

Introduction

1. See the inventory drawn up by Jean-Michel Chaumont in "Connaissance ou reconnaissance? Les enjeux du débat sur la singularité de la Shoa," *Le Débat* 82 (November–December 1994).

2. Cited by M. Berenbaum and J. K. Roth, in "What If the Holocaust Is Unique?," *Holocaust, Religions and Philosophical Implications* (New York: Paragon House, 1989), 5.

3. George Steiner, "The Long Life of Metaphor; An Approach to the Shoah," *Writing and the Holocaust*, ed. Berel Lang (New York: Holmes and Meier, 1988), 159.

4. Claude Lanzmann, "De l'Holocauste à *Holocaust* ou comment s'en débarasser," *Les Temps Modernes* vol. 34, no. 305 (June 1979): 1897.

5. Paul Ricœur, "Le temps raconté," *Temps et récit III* (Paris: Seuil, 1985), 273. This term is also used by F. Bédarida in *La Politique nazie d'extermination* (Paris: Albin Michel, 1989), 323.

6. Alain Brossat, *L'Épreuve du désastre. Le XXᵉ siècle et les camps* (Paris: Albin Michel, 1996), 398. [TN: In Europe "liberal" stands in opposition to "socialist" and not to "conservative" as in the United States. Europeans basically see liberals as adherents to laissez-faire economic policies.]

7. Tzvetan Todorov, "The Abuses of Memory," trans. Mei Lin Chang, *Common Knowledge* 5 (Spring 1996): 24.

8. Ibid., 15.

9. Brossat, *L'Épreuve du désastre*, 321.

10. [TN: A phenomenon to be distinguished from communitarianism or multiculturalism, in that its connotations are wholly negative in France, where it designates ethnic or religious solidarities and allegiances that threaten to override the republican ideal of a single national community of individuals.]

11. *Mission d'étude sur la spoliation des Juifs.*

12. Jean Mattéoli, *Le Temps* (Geneva: March 5, 1999).

13. Cf. Shmuel Trigano, ed., "Penser Auschwitz," *Pardès* 9–10 (Paris: Le Cerf, 1989).

14. Brossat, *L'Épreuve du désastre*, 266–67.

15. Emphasis added; thus there would be a democratic manipulation of genocide comparable to Stalinism.

16. Louis Janover, *Nuit et brouillard du Révisionnsme* (Paris: Méditerranée, 1996), 51.

17. Ibid., 89.

18. Cf. Jacob Talmon, *The Origins of Totalitarian Democracy* (Boulder, CO: Westview Encore Editions, 1985 [1952]).

19. Todorov, *Face à l'extrême* (Paris: Seuil, 1991), 304.

Chapter 1

1. "Observation pour les Juifs d'Avignon à la Convention nationale" (signed by Aaron Revel, *chargé de pouvoirs*, and A. David Milhaud), cited in *La Révolution française et l'émancipation des Juifs*, vol. 5 (Paris: EDHIS, 1968), 13. We will quote a lot of these texts in the coming chapters (especially chapters 7 and 8). They were reprinted in an eight-volume facsimile by the Editions d'Histoire Sociale (EDHIS) under the title *La Révolution française et l'émancipation des Juifs*: vol. 1, Mirabeau *Sur Moses Mendelssohn, sur la réforme politique des Juifs*, 1787; vol. 2, Thiéry *Dissertation sur cette question : existe-t-il des moyens de rendre les Juifs plus heureux et plus utiles en France ?*, 1788; vol. 3, Grégoire, *Essai sur la régénération morale et politique des juifs*, 1789; vol. 4, Zalkind Hourwitz, *Apologie des juifs*, 1789; vol. 5, *Adresses, Mémoires et Pétitions des Juifs*, 1789–1794); vol. 6, *La Commune et les districts de Paris. Discours, Lettres et Rapports*, 1790–1791; vol. 7, *L'Assemblée Nationale Constituante. Motions, Discours et Rapports. La Législation nouvelle*, 1789–1791; vol. 8, *Lettres, Mémoires et Publications diverses*, 1787–1806.

2. "Speech on Religious Minorities and Questionable Professions" (December 23, 1789), cited in *The French Revolution and Human Rights: A Brief Documentary History*, translated, edited, and with an introduction by Lynn Hunt (Boston, MA, and New York: Bedford/St. Martin's, 1996), 88.

3. Abbé Gregoire, "Motion en faveur des Juifs," *EDHIS*, vol. 8, 24.

4. Diogène Tama, "Collections des procès-verbaux et décisions du Grand Sanhédrin convoqué à Paris" (Paris: EDHIS, 1807).

5. Letter to Herr Gemlich, September 16, 1919, in Eberhard Jäckel, ed., *Hitler. Sämtliche Aufzeichnungen 1905–1924* (Stuttgart, 1980), 88–90. Translation by Richard S. Levy: http://www.aldridgeshs.qld.edu.au/sose/modrespg/jews/adold1.htm.

6. Raul Hilberg, *The Destruction of the European Jews* (New York and London: Holmes & Meier, 1985), 28.

7. Père Jean Dujardin, "Réflexions sur la Shoa," *Bulletin du secrétariat de la conférence des évêques de France* 3–4 (February 1989): 18.

8. Avishai Margalit and Gabriel Motzkin, "The Uniqueness of the Holocaust," *Philosophy and Public Affairs* 1996 (25): 65–85.

9. One of the most violent discussions on this subject can be found in Brossat, *L'Épreuve du désastre*, in particular, in part 2, chapter 2 (pp. 272–94), where he

delivers a virulent attack against Yves Ternon's attempt to clarify the concept of genocide in *L'État criminel, les genocides au XXe siècle* (Paris: Seuil, 1995).

10. Raphaël Lemkin, *Axis Rule in Occupied Europe: Laws of Occupation, Analysis of Government, Proposals for Redress* (Washington, DC: Carnegie Endowment for International Peace, 1944), 79.

11. See Catherine Coquio, "L'extrême, le génocide, l'expérience concentrationnaire, productivité et apories de trois concepts," *Critique* (May 1997): 349.

12. Georges Wellers, *Mémoire du génocide, un recueil de 80 articles du Monde juif, revue de Centre de Documentation Juive Contemporaine*, in *Monde Juif*, ed. G. Wellers, S. Klarsfeld (Paris: CDJC/FFDJF, 1987).

13. Simone Veil, "L'extermination des Juifs a été banalisée," in *Chronique du procès Barbie. Pour servir la mémoire*, ed. P. Gauthier, 475 (Paris: Le Cerf, 1988).

14. Annette Wieviorka, *Déportation et génocide* (Paris: Plon, 1992).

15. Annette Wieviorka, "Indicible ou inaudible? La déportation, premiers récits (1944–1947)," in Trigano, ed., *Pardès 9–10* (Paris: Le Cerf, 1989).

16. Jean-Paul Sartre, *Anti-Semite and Jew*, trans. George J. Becker (New York: Schocken Books, 1948), 71.

17. Ibid., 71–72.

18. Henry Rousso, *Esprit*, no. 181 (May 1992): 16.

19. The forerunner of today's CRIF, which is now an acronym for *Conseil représentatif des* institutions *juives de France.*

20. Annie Kriegel, "Pouvoir politique et expression communautaire: Le CRIF," *Pardès* 3 (Paris: J.-C. Lattès, 1986), 205.

21. I have elsewhere suggested that the community could be seen as an "overall framework of collective sociability which finds expression through a variety of networks running through all spheres of civil society and structured in a set of common representations [. . .]. It is from the top (and not the bottom) that the 'community' brings together people who otherwise belong to all sorts of structures and networks in society at large [. . .]. It is something of a 'common home' whose occupants pursue their own lives and keep their windows open to the outside, an abstract house whose walls are made of symbols and common collective representations." See Trigano, "Le concept de communauté comme catégorie de définition du judaïsme français," *Archives européenes de sociologie* 35:1 (1994): 61–62.

22. See note 10, p. 295.

Chapter 2

1. *Night* (1958), *Dawn* (1960), and *Day* (1961), first published as *The Accident*.

2. Cf. Francine Kaufmann, "La naissance d'un discours littéraire juif, autour de la Shoah en France et en Israël," and Alan L. Berger, "La Shoah dans la littérature américaine: Témoins, non-témoins et faux témoins," in Trigano, ed., *Pardès*.

3. It is found in the prophetic texts (for instance, Isaiah, 47:11 and 10:3), the Psalms, Job, and the Proverbs, where it signifies "devastation," as from a hurricane or a storm.

4. *Hurban*, meaning destruction, was the term used to describe the massacres during the First World War (including the pogroms during the civil war in Ukraine); Shoah, meaning "catastrophe," was reserved for World War II.

5. The term was apparently popularized by Arno Mayer.

6. It was born in the French Resistance as a school of Jewish Scout Leaders (somewhat on the lines of the Christian Uriage School). For more details, see Trigano, ed., "L'École de pensée juive de Paris," *Pardès*.

7. Cf. Trigano, *Un exil sans retour ? Lettres à un Juif égaré* (Paris: Stock, 1995).

8. The Centre Communautaire Laïc Juif (CCLJ).

9. Yair Auron, "Jewish-Israeli Identity among Israel's Future Teachers," *Jewish Political Studies Review* 9: 1–2 (Spring 1997): 105.

10. Cf. *Documentation chrétienne* ("Les grands textes"): "Le Carmel d'Auschwitz. Les pièces majeures du dossier," Supplement no. 1991 (October 1, 1989): 37.

11. Ibid., 28.

12. Jean-Marie Lustiger, "Singularité de la Shoah," *Études* 3881 (January 1998): 73–79.

13. Cf. Menahem Friedman, "Les Haredim and the Shoa," in Trigano, ed., "Penser Auschwitz."

14. Among the various interpretations, we find a Jewish "death of God" theology that conceives of God as Holy Nothingness. For more about these questions, see R. L. Rubenstein, "Alliance et divinité. L'Holocauste et la problématique de la foi," in "Penser Auschwitz," 59.

15. Pierre Vidal-Naquet, "A Paper Eichmann (1980): Anatomy of a Lie," in *Assassins of Memory*, trans. Jeffrey Mehlman (New York: Columbia University Press, 1992).

16. Todorov, "The Abuses of Memory," 14.

17. Illegal, undocumented immigrants, literally "without papers."

18. The CORIF, or Conseil de réflexion sur l'islam de France.

Chapter 3

1. In discussing what he called "the ambiguity of the sacred," Durkheim argues that there are two kinds of religious forces, those working for good and those working for evil, and that these are seen in notions of purity and impurity. In other words, things can be sacred and pure or sacred and impure. Cf. *Les Formes élémentaires de la vie religieuse* (Paris: PUF, 1985), 584–85.

2. Cf. Robert Redeker, "Les Dédoublements du négationnisme. De la négation des chambres à gaz à la négation de la singularité de la Shoa," Conference "Les Beaux lendemains de l'antisémitisme," held at the Collège des études juives de l'Alliance israélite universel, December 14, 1999.

3. Cf. Limor Yagil, "Holocaust Denial in France, 1945–1994," in *Holocaust Denial in France*, ed. Pierre Vidal-Naquet and Limor Yagil, 21 (Tel Aviv: The Project for the Study of Anti-Semitism, 1994).

4. Nadine Fresco, "Les Redresseurs des morts. Chambres à gaz: la bonne nouvelle. Comment on révise l'histoire," *Les Temps Modernes* 407 (June 1980).

5. Louis Janover, *Nuit et brouillard du révisionnisme* (Paris: Méditerranée, 1996), 123.

6. Brossat denounces the "appropriation of the patrimony of the extermination of the Jews in the camps," *L'Épreuve du désastre*, 323.

7. Paul Rassinier, *Le Drame des Juifs européens* (Paris: Les Sept Couleurs, 1964), 323.

8. Maurice Bardèche, *Nuremberg ou la Terre promise* (Paris: Les Sept Couleurs, 1948).

9. This is the title of Thies Christophersen's pamphlet.

10. Janover, *Nuit et brouillard*, 172–73.

11. Rassinier, *Le Drame des Juifs européens*, 129.

12. Janover, *Nuit et brouillard*, 111.

13. "Auschwitz: The Big Alibi" was originally published in 1960 in *Programme Communiste* 11 and reprinted in the international Communist Party bimonthly, *Les Prolétaires*, as a supplement to issue 276 in 1979. Bordiga proposes "to expose the real reasons for the extermination of the Jews, which have nothing to do with ideas and everything to do with the capitalist economy and the social conflicts it engenders." He explains that "capitalism had no more room for the Jews," that the petty bourgeoisie, seeing itself in danger, "sacrificed one of its segments," the Jews, before the liquidation of the proletariat. Another recurrent theme in this text, which is also found in Brossat's book, is that the Shoah acts as a smokescreen to hide other horrors engendered by democracy: "The corpses of Jews are exhibited to cover repressions in Algeria, to make the proletariat appreciate true democracy and forget the horrors of our lives. Using the corpses of the victims of capital to try to bury this truth, to make the corpses serve to protect capital—surely this must be the most infamous exploitation of all." Another omnipresent idea in this text is that both Fascism and anti-Fascism are bourgeois ideologies.

14. Janover, *Nuit et brouillard*, 111.

15. Ibid.

16. A fact that Louis Janover deplores (ibid., 82), because it obliges the ultra Left to profess a democratic engagement and accept democracy by refraining from its necessary criticism.

17. Brossat, *L'Épreuve du désastre*, 292, emphasis.

18. Shelby Steele, *The Content of Our Character* (New York: St. Martin's Press, 1991), 118. Cited in Todorov, "The Abuses of Memory," 13.

19. Ibid., 24.

20. Ibid., 14.

21. Ibid.

22. Ibid., 15.

23. Ibid.

24. Ibid.

25. Ibid.

26. Ibid., 23.

26. Ibid., 17.

28. Could this indicate, in a subliminal way, a connivance between the Jewish victims of Nazism and the Bolsheviks and Stalinists, as Hitler claimed?

29. Todorov, "The Abuses of Memory," 20.

30. Ibid., 24.

31. Ibid., emphasis added.

32. Brossat, *L'Épreuve du désastre*. To cite two telling examples, among many others, Brossat writes that "the aporia" of a "reterritorialization of Auschwitz in the absolute singularity of Jewish history ultimately brings the Shoah into the sphere of calculations and interests" (321) before proceeding to enumerate in detail the economic traffic to which he is alluding; elsewhere, in speaking of "the renowned intellectuals" who maintain the "uniqueness of the Shoah," he declares, "we can only hope that *they know not what they do*" (306, emphasis added).

33. The rhetoric about the Shoah's singularity "is inseparable from the illegitimate violence exercised by the State of Israel against the Palestinians" (327).

34. "It would be more appropriate to describe the Shoah as an ethnocide: the Jews being in a sense a 'people'—at least, at any rate, more so than they are a race" (286).

35. Ibid., 287.

36. In this regard, Brossat has the following memorable comment to make: "[In the modern political constitution] the Jewish difference is visible and sayable only insofar as the Jew is recognized as a same [*sic*] and not as a supposed specimen of some immemorial *ethnos* (*genos?*)" (289). So basically he exists without existing!

37. Ibid., 292.

38. Nothing less than the entire substance of reality!

39. Ibid., 285.

40. According to Brossat, it is standard practice for hangmen to "naturalize the living beings they intend to kill" (284). Elsewhere he speaks of the Nazi "zoologization of human questions" (285).

41. Ibid., 285–86.

42. Ibid., 289.

43. Ibid., 324–25.

44. Ibid., 284.

45. Ibid., 288–89.

46. Ibid., 398.

47. Ibid., 298.

48. Ibid., 339.

49. To borrow the title of Stéphane Courtois's introduction in Courtois et al., *The Black Book of Communism: Crimes, Terror, Repression*, trans. Jonathan Murphy and Mark Kramer (Boston, MA: Harvard University Press, 1999).

50. Ibid., 9.

51. Tzvetan Todorov, *L'Homme dépaysé* (Paris: Seuil, 1995), 33. Cited in Courtois, *The Black Book*, 747.

52. Ibid., 15.

53. Ibid., 9.

54. Ibid.

55. Ibid., 14.

56. Ibid., 16.

57. Ibid., 740.

58. Ibid., 18.

59. Ibid., 19.

60. Stéphane Courtois, "Crimes communistes: le malaise français," *Politique internationale* (Summer 1998): 372.

61. Ibid., 17.

62. Ibid., 23.

63. Ibid., 17.

64. Ibid., 23.

65. Cf. Annie Kriegel, *Le Système communiste international* (Paris: PUF, 1984); Aryeh Yaari, *Le Défi national* (Paris: Anthropos, 1979); and Abraham Léon, *La Conception matérialiste de la question juive* (Paris: Edi, 1991).

66. It is no accident that in laying the theoretical foundations of the main current of Zionism, Socialist Zionism, Ber Borokhov adapted a Marxist theory of nationalities to the case of a Jewish nation.

67. Cf. Ilan Greilsammer, *La Nouvelle Histoire d'Israël. Essai sur une identité nationale* (Paris: Gallimard, 1998).

68. Yosef Grodzinski, "Combattre la sionisation de la Shoa," *Haaretz* (July 15, 1994).

69. See also the study and collection of texts by Dan Michman, ed., *Post-Zionism and the Holocaust: The role of the Holocaust in the Public Debate on Post-Zionism in Israel (1993–1996)* (Ramat-Gan: Arnold and Leona Finkler Institute of Holocaust Research, Bar-Ilan University, 1997).

70. Boaz Evron, *La Shoah—Un danger pour le peuple*, Iton, fasc. 21 (May–June 1980), and *Haheshbon haleumi* (Tel-Aviv, Dvir, 1988).

71. Cf. Uri Ram, *The Changing Agenda of Israeli Sociology: Theory, Ideology and Identity* (Albany: State University of New York Press, 1995).

72. As the revolution liberated and emancipated universal humanity, foreigners were excluded from the political arena (i.e., from citizenship) by decree. Cf. Sophie Wahnich, *L'Impossible Citoyen. L'Étranger dans le discours de la Révolution française* (Paris: Albin Michel, 1996).

73. Amnon Raz-Krakotzkin, "Exile within Sovereignty: Toward a Critique of the 'Negation of Exile' in Israeli Culture" (in Hebrew), *Theory and Criticism. An Israeli Forum* 4 (1993): 23.

74. Dina Porat, "L'Historiographie israélienne sur le Yichouv à l'époque du génocide," in *Les nouveaux enjeux de l'historiographie israélienne*, ed. F. Heymann, 84 (Jerusalem: Centre de recherches français, 1998).

75. Evron, *Haheshbon haleumi*.

76. Cited by Greilsammer, *La Nouvelle Histoire d'Israël*, 32.

77. The intellectuals in the Canaanite movement that emerged in the 1930s sought to break away from Judaism and the Diaspora to found a new Hebraic culture embedded in the Semitic culture of the Middle East. The aim was to establish a single state for Jews and Arabs. The myths and values of the Israeli *intelligentsia* until the early 1980s (notably its massive rejection of Judaism and Jewish history) were cast in the mold of Canaanite ideology.

78. Cf. the interview reprinted by Anita Shapira in "Politique et mémoire collective: Le débat sur les 'nouveaux historiens' en Israël," in *Les nouveaux enjeux de l'historiographie*, 148.

79. Dina Porat, "L'Historiographie israélienne sur le Yichouv à l'époque du génocide," in *Les nouveaux enjeux de l'historiographie israélienne*, ed. F. Heymann (Jerusalem: Centre de recherches français, 1998).

Chapter 4

1. See Shmuel Trigano, *Philosophie de la loi, l'origine de la politique dans la Tora* (Paris: Le Cerf, 1991), for an attempt to define the idea of a "Jewish people" philosophically, in particular, chapters 2 and 3.

2. Cf. Trigano, ed., *La Société juive à travers l'histoire* (Paris: Fayard, 1992–1994), a four-volume encyclopedic study of Jewish society throughout history, which I believe contributes to clarifying and analyzing the subject from a nonideological perspective.

3. Cf. Hegel, "The Spirit of Christianity and Its Fate [1798–1800]," in *Early Theological Writings*, trans. T. M. Knox, (Chicago, IL: University of Chicago Press, 1948).

4. Cf. D. Elazar, "Fondement de la politique juive," in *La Société juive*, vol. 2.

5. Cf. Shmuel Trigano, *La Demeure oubliée, genèse religieuse du politique* (Paris: Gallimard, 1985).

6. Cf. Trigano, "Espaces, ruptures, unités," in *La Société juive*, vol. 4.

7. Brossat, *L'Épreuve du désastre*, 285.

8. Gregoire, "Motion en Faveur des Juifs," 24.

9. Brossat, *L'Épreuve du désastre*, 205.

10. "The extermination killed millions of individuals who were left no chance to be anything other than Jewish, Gypsy, Communist, etc.," Jean-Luc Nancy in an interview published in *Le Monde* (March 29, 1994) and cited in Brossat, ibid., 314.

11. Ibid., 289.

12. Léon Poliakov, *La Causalité diabolique. Essai sur l'origine des persécutions* (Paris: Calmann-Lévy, 1980).

13. See the analysis in Trigano, *Philosophie de la loi*, and in "Sur le judaïsme comme force d'intervention dans la politique du retour," *Un exil sans retour? Lettres à un Juif égaré* (Paris: Stock, 1996).

14. Theodor Herzl, *The Jewish State*. Translation from the German by Sylvie D'Avigdor, available on the Internet. This edition was published in 1946 by the American Zionist Emergency Council.

15. "The Jews will leave as honored friends, and if some of them return, they will receive the same favorable welcome and treatment at the hands of civilized nations as is accorded to all foreign visitors," ibid.

16. I do not in any way underestimate the Palestinian problem that emerged in the wake of the creation of the Jewish State, knowing that the Arabs of this region were all part of "Greater Syria" until then and there never was a Palestinian people or a Palestinian state before that time. Palestinian identity, its national movement, and its structures are inextricably bound up with the existence of Israel, through force of circumstances, but also—which is less widely acknowledged—in terms of the model of

organization and system of values that the Palestinians found in the Zionist movement. If Israel disappeared, then so would Palestine. The first Zionists were so keenly aware of the problem that they accepted the different UN plans of partition that the Arabs rejected systematically. If the Israelis are now in the West Bank, then this is the result of their victory in a war that the Arabs started in 1967. But to see the "expulsion" of the Palestinians as a compensation for the Shoah is not objective. A semi-independent Jewish society (the Yishuv) existed in Palestine since the beginning of the twentieth century. There is no doubt, though, that the Palestinian drama—which is real—goes hand in hand with the existence of Israel. And the problem remains unresolved. What we see at work in it is the universal logic of the nation-state and its dramatic impact on peoples, and there is no reason to doubt for an instant that the Palestianians will put to work this selfsame logic in the construction of their own nation-state. Cf. Shmuel Trigano, "Lieu, projet pour une problématique juive de la Paix," in "La Paix maintenant," *Les Temps modernes* 398 (September 1979): 534.

17. Herzl, *The Jewish State*.

18. Emmanuel Lévinas, "Etre Juif," *Confluences* (1947): 260.

19. In addition to regulations peculiar to Jewish citizens, Arab Israelis can be active in parties of their choice, eventually in parties of their own; they are represented in the Knesset, have their own courts for personal law, and enjoy a higher standard of living than the Arabs in the region. Setting aside the conditions arising from a fragile peace and a potential for war, they are legally living in the *practical* condition of a minority group in a majority democracy. That does not make them "second-class citizens," but it does not necessarily preclude eventual slipups.

20. Cf. Trigano, "Qu'est-ce que l'École juive de Paris?"

21. Emmanuel Lévinas, "La Conscience juive face à l'histoire : le Pardon," closing speech at the conference 'Rencontre entre intellectuals juifs de France et intellectuals rapatriés d'Algérie," February 17, 1963, in *Colloque des intellectuals juifs de France* (Paris: PUF, 1965), 239.

Chapter 5

1. Rémy Brague, *Europe, la voie romaine* (Paris: Critérion, 1992), 99.

2. Cf. Shmuel Trigano, *La Demeure oubliée, genèse religieuse du politique* (Paris: Gallimard, 1985), in particular, the chapter "L'Homme à l'image du Dieu."

3. I am picking up here the analysis that I developed in "L'Apostasie du Messie. Le paradoxe de l'Emancipation," *Esprit* 5 (May 1979): 6, and "Européodicée? L'Éconimie symbolique du signe juif de l'Europe après la Shoa," in *La Sho'ah tra interpretazione e memoria*, ed. P. Amodio, R. de Maio, and G. Lissa, 799 (Naples: Vivarium, 1999).

4. Paul Ricœur, *Temps et récit* (Paris: Seuil, 1985).

5. Philippe Boyer, "Le Point de la question," *Collectif Change* 22, *L'Imprononçable, l'écriture nomade* (Paris: Seghers, February 1975), 44.

6. Ibid.

7. Ibid. The quote from Maurice Blanchot is taken from *The Infinite Conversation*, trans. Susan Hanson (Minneapolis: University of Minnesota Press, 1993), 125.

8. Boyer, "Le Point de la question," 42.

9. Jean-Pierre Faye, "Notes autour des migrations du récit sur le people juif," *Collectif Change*, 99. Jabès's quote comes from *The Book of Questions Volume II*, trans. Rosmarie Waldrop, 290.

10. Evgen Bavcar, "Mots pour Jabès," ibid., 217.

11. See part 3, chapter 3, "The Jew-of-the-Man."

12. Faye, *Collectif Change*, 98, emphasis added.

13. Boyer, "Le Point," 48–49. The quote is from Derrida, *La pharmacie de Platon*, in *La Dissémination* (Paris: Le Seuil, 1972), 142.

14. Boyer, "Le Point," 6.

15. Faye, *Collectif Change*, 88.

16. Boyer, "Le Point," 54.

17. Lévinas, *Otherwise Than Being or Beyond Essence*, trans. Alphonso Lingis (The Hague: Martinus Nijhoff, 1981), 48–49, cited in Boyer, "Le Point," 50.

18. Boyer, "Le Point," 50. Lévinas's comment is taken from *Autrement qu'être ou au délà de l'essance* (La Haye: Nijhoff, 1974), 58.

19. Jean-François Lyotard, *Heidegger and "the jews,"* trans. Andreas Michael and Mark Roberts (Minneapolis: University of Minnesota Press, 1990), 3. (In French upper case is used in reference to peoples, nations, and lower case is used in reference to religions, etc.)

20. Ibid., 80.

21. Ibid., 23.

22. Ibid., 81.

23. Ibid., 4.

24. Ibid., 3.

25. Ibid., 83–84.

26. Ibid., 94.

27. Ibid., 22.

28. Ibid., 93–94.

29. This is what Hannah Arendt describes so thoroughly in *Antisemitism* (New York: Harcourt, Brace & World, 1951), as we will see later.

30. Robert Faurisson, "Je cherche midi à midi," *Les Nouvelles Littéraires* (February 10–17, 1997).

31. Ibid.

32. "Universal creed" is Serge Thion's term; Nadine Fresco, "Les Redresseurs des morts. Chambres à gaz: la bonne nouvelle. Comment on révise l'histoire," *Les Temps Modernes* 407 (June 1980).

33. Brossat, *L'Épreuve du désastre*, 323.

34. This neo-Kantian morality, draped in the absolute truth of its categorical imperative, underpins the thinking of neoleftist circles. Incapable of confronting modern history philosophically, they have retreated to the position of moralizing preachers atop a romantic and solitary rock lambasting a world given over to evil, in the name of a morality that is, alas, all too abstract (because if the moral imperative is celebrated in it, this morality does not have commandments anymore nor words to express it).

Chapter 6

1. Jean-Paul Sartre, *Anti-Semite and Jew, an Exploration of the Etiology of Hate*, trans. George J. Becker (New York: Schocken Books, 1948; reprint 1995), 152. The page numbers of all further references to this book will be noted in parentheses in the main body of the text.

2. The impasse is the result, of course, of his difficulty in conceiving of the historicity of the Jewish condition.

3. Arendt refers to Sartre in the preface only to dismiss the "myth" of "Sartre's 'existentialist' interpretation of *the* Jew as someone who is regarded and defined as a Jew by others," and in so doing, she overlooks his extraordinary analysis of the system that produces the Jew, which clearly had more than a minor influence on her own thinking. Hannah Arendt, *Antisemitism* (New York: Harcourt, Brace & World, 1951; reprinted 1968). The page numbers of all further references to this book will be noted in parentheses in the main body of the text.

4. Hannah Arendt, *Eichmann in Jerusalem: A Report on the Banality of Evil* (New York: Penguin, 1994).

5. Lefort, *L'Invention démocratique. Les limites de la domination totalitaire* (Paris: Fayard, 1981), 57. Emphasis added.

6. [TN: The translation is slightly modified to render the idea, essential here and in the following paragraph, of a "legal subject"; the Shocken translation states that "the anti-Semite realizes that he has rights," which misses the point here.]

7. The emphasis here and in the following two passages, is added. [TN: Slightly modified translation].

8. One could hardly imagine a more Durkheimian definition of the social production of values: the gathering of men produces a representation of the collectivity, in which they recognize a god from whom they believe they have received their values and norms of conduct.

9. And here Sartre contradicts himself, because he presupposes the existence of a "principle of French conduct."

10. This parallel to sociology or ethnology is authorized by Sartre's own analogy between the anti-Semitic crisis and "the running amuck of the Malays" (43).

11. It is then the system that produces both of them that is at the origin of the syndrome analyzed.

12. To defend the Jew, the democrat needs him to embody "the principle of the Good" (73). As the embodiment of an abstract principle, the Jew is glorified and absent at once. After all, who could possible embody goodness? The democrat defends an abstract model, not a real Jew.

13. This would be a good definition of the New Left's position.

14. The question mark is there because it seems obvious, until further notice, that the Jew is spontaneously a man, and so it is senseless to speak of a relationship between the self and the self.

15. Sartre was to change his mind on the subject at the end of his life in his controversial conversations with Benny Lévy, when he remarked, "If there's a Jewish history, that changes everything."

16. For Sartre, there are two avenues of Jewish authenticity: accepting martyr-dom and its memory by (heroically) taking up the challenge of the anti-Semite, or opposing the anti-Semite through militant and determined autonomy (Zionism).

17. See the remarkable description he gives on pp. 73–76.

18. This is exactly the same typology as Turner's, just as the idea of "social warmth and energy" is typically Durkheimian.

19. This is basically Marx's and Engels' interpretation of anti-Semitism as a vestige of medieval archaism in capitalist society.

20. The quotations, as Arendt specifies in a footnote, are from Jacob Katz, *Exclusiveness and Tolerance, Jewish-Gentile Relations in Medieval and Modern Times* (New York: Schocken, 1962).

21. See also her discussion of the attitude of assimilated Jews, 7–8.

22. The quote, as Arendt specifies in the note, is from "the liberal Protestant theologian" H. E. G. Paulus, *Die jüdische Nationalabsonderung nach Ursprung, Folgen und Besserungsmitteln*, 1831.

23. The quotation is from Karl Kraus.

24. "Rapport édité par M. Vion, conseiller référendaire en la chancellerie du Palais et member du comité du district de Saint-Germain l'Auxerrois," *EDHIS*, vol. 6, 1.

25. Ibid., vol. 7.

26. "Rapport fait par Saladin au nom d'une commission spéciale composée des représentants Grégoire, Chappuy, Couvot, Beyts et Saladin, 7 fructidor, an VII," *EDHIS*, vol. 8.

27. "Observation pour les Juifs d'Avignon à la Convention nationale" (signed by Aaron Revel, *chargé de pouvoirs*, and A. David Milhaud), cited in "La Révolution française et l'émancipation des Juifs," *EDHIS*, vol. 5 (1968), 13.

28. "Rapport fait par Saladin," *EDHIS*, vol. 8.

Chapter 7

1. Avishai Margalit and Gabriel Motzkin, "The Uniqueness of the Holocaust," *Philosophy and Public Affairs* 25 (1996): 74.

2. Ibid., 75.

3. Ibid.

4. Brossat, *L'Épreuve du désastre*, 305.

5. Ibid., 306.

6. Aristotle, *The Nicomachean Ethics*, Book Ten, vii–viii.

7. Sartre, *Anti-Semite*, 58.

8. Abbé Grégoire, *Essai sur la régénération physique, morale and politique des Juifs* (1789). Reprinted in *La Révolution française et l'émancipation des Juifs*, vol. 3, 108 (Editions d'Histoire Sociale [EDHIS], 1968). The discussion here is based on my essay *La République et les Juifs* (Les Presses d'Aujourd'hui, 1982).

9. Mirabeau, *Chefs-d'œuvre oratoires* (Colin de Plancy, 1822,), vol. 1, 308–309.

10. Cited in Arendt, *Antisemitism*, 57.

11. Ibid., 57, note 7.

12. Ibid., 58.

13. Hannah Arendt, *Imperialism*, part 2 of *The Origins of Totalitarianism* (Harcourt, 1968, revised 1976), 291.

14. Mirabeau, *Réflexions impartiales d'un citoyen sur la question de l'éligibilité des Juifs*, EDHIS, vol. 7, 8.

15. Ibid., 88.

16. Grégoire, *Essai sur la régénération*, 84.

17. Ibid., 172.

18. Ibid., 178.

19. Ibid., 183.

20. Cf. Trigano, *La République et les Juifs*.

21. This is what Marx was saying when he maintained that if the Jews could be politically emancipated by the liberal democracy and remain religiously Jews, then the political emancipation that characterized the bourgeois state was fictive. Marx considered religion the height of alienation and Judaism but an example of "human degeneracy." Sartre pursued—if with more generosity—this typical avenue of revolutionary ideology with his idea that the Jew is a man that other men designate as Jewish.

22. Grégoire, *Essai sur la régénération*, 172.

23. "Rapport édité par M. Vion," vol. 6, 1.

24. "Dissertations . . . lues à l'Assemblée de la Commune de Paris par M. Vieillard, ancien consul de France à la curie, commissaire du comité de Saint-Roch," EDHIS, vol. 6, 12.

25. "Observations sur l'état civil des Juifs adressées à l'Assemblée nationale," par M. l'abbé L., 1790, EDHIS, vol. 8, 15.

26. "Lettre au Comité de constitution sur l'affaire des Juifs par M. de Bourge représentant de la commune de Paris," EDHIS, vol. 7, 20.

27. Zalkind-Hourwitz, "Apologie des Juifs," EDHIS, vol. 4, 77.

28. "Mémoire particulier pour la communauté des Juifs établis à Metz par Isaac Ber Bing, EDHIS, vol. 5, 5.

29. Grégoire, *Essai sur la régénération*, 108.

30. Ibid., 166.

31. Thiery, "Dissertation sur cette question : est-il des moyens pour rendre les Juifs plus heureux et plus utiles en France ?," 1788, EDHIS, vol. 2, 79.

32. Michel Berr, "Appel à la Justice des nations et des rois," Strasbourg, 1801, EDHIS, vol. 8, 15.

33. "Opinion de l'abbé Bertolio devant l'Assemblée générale des représentants de la Commune," January 30, 1790, EDHIS, vol. 7, 23.

34. Thiéry, "Dissertation," 37.

35. "Rapport édité par M. Vion," 1.

36. Grégoire, *Essai sur la régénération*, 70.

37. Thiéry, "Dissertation," 20.

38. Mirabeau, *Réflexions impartiales*, 37.

39. Abbé Grégoire, "Motion en faveur des Juifs," 1789, EDHIS, vol. 7, 24.

40. Hourwitz, "Apologie des Juifs," 82.

41. If not for the clear-sightedness—alas untimely—of political Zionism.
42. Ibid., 269.
43. Ibid., 300.
44. See her detailed analysis of these rights, ibid., 295.
45. Ibid., 269.
46. Ibid., 272.
47. Ibid.
48. Ibid., 275.
49. Ibid., 292.
50. Ibid., 286.
51. Ibid.
52. Ibid., 291.
53. Ibid.
54. Ibid., 269.
55. Ibid., 299.
56. Ibid., 300.
57. Ibid., 297.
58. Ibid., 298.
59. Ibid., 300.
60. Ibid., 298.
61. Ibid., 296.
62. Ibid., 297.
63. Ibid.
64. Ibid., 300.
65. Ibid., 301.
66. Ibid., 300.
67. Ibid., 301.
68. Ibid.
69. Sartre, *Anti-Semite and Jew*, 37.
70. Ibid., 54.
71. Ibid., 69.
72. Ibid., 66.
73. Ibid., 84.
74. Ibid., 55.
75. Ibid., 57.
76. Ibid., 56.
77. Ibid., 57.
78. Ibid.
79. Ibid., 60.
80. Ibid., 144–45.
81. Ibid., 77.
82. Ibid., 98.
83. Ibid., 134.
84. Ibid., 133–34.
85. Ibid., 134.
86. Ibid., 136.

87. Ibid., 150.

88. *Considerations on France* (1796). Cited in Bertrand Binoche, *Critiques des droits de l'homme* (Paris: PUF, 1989), 44. This book presents a broad spectrum of opinions on the revolution. See also the anthology, F. Worms, ed., *Droits de l'homme et philosophie* (Paris: Presses Pocket, 1993). Source of English translation of Maistre's text here and hereafter from Internet HTML text.

89. Edmund Burke, *Reflections on the Revolution in France* (1790); the quotations hereafter from Burke are all from the same online source.

90. Binoche, *Critiques*, 69.

91. Ibid., 81.

92. Ibid., 75.

93. Ibid., 76.

94. Ibid., 81.

95. Ibid.

96. Hegel, *Philosophy of Right*, §258 (English translation from Internet HTML text).

97. Ibid., §211.

98. Ibid., §209.

99. Binoche, *Critiques*, 102–103.

100. Marx, *The German Ideology* (online source).

101. Marx, *On the Jewish Question* (online source).

102. Binoche, *Critiques*, 112.

103. Marx, *The Jewish Question* (online source).

104. Ibid.

105. Ibid.

106. Annie Kriegel, in J. Droz, ed., *Histoire générale du socialism* (Paris: Presses Universituires de France, 1977), vol. 3, 574.

107. Ibid.

Chapter 8

1. Chapter 4, "The Unthought Singularity."

2. Brossat, *L' Épreuve du désastre.*

3. And these terms were self-contradictory. As noted in chapter 1, article 5 of the decree of November 14, 1935, of the Reich Citizenship Law states, "A Jew is an individual who is descended from at least three grandparents who were, racially, full Jews." And what qualifies a Jew as a full Jew? "Full-blooded Jewish grandparents are those who belonged to the Jewish religious community," according to article 2.

4. "Lettre au Comité de la Constitution par M. de Bourge, représentant de la Commune de Paris," *La Révolution Française* (EDHIS), vol. 7, 31.

5. Gregoire, "Apologie des Juifs," vol. 3, 59.

6. This was the subject of the 1787 essay contest for the Metz royal society of arts and sciences.

7. Grégoire, "Mention en faveur des Juifs," vol. 7 (1789), 38.

8. Thiéry, "Dissertation sur cette question : Est-il des moyens pour render les Juifs plus heureux et plus utiles en France," vol. 2 (1788), 98.

9. Ibid., 87.

10. Grégoire, *Essai sur la régénération*, 134.

11. "Assemblée des representants de la Commune de Paris," February 24, 1790, vol. 6, 11.

12. Arendt, *Antisemitism*, 54.

13. Ibid.

14. Ibid.

15. Ibid., 55.

16. Ibid.

17. Sartre, *Anti-Semite and Jew*, 119.

18. Ibid., 120–21.

19. Ibid., 119–20.

20. Ibid., 121.

21. Ibid., 122.

22. Ibid., 146–47.

23. Alexis De Tocqueville, *Democracy in America* (trans. Henry Reeve) (online source).

24. This overview draws heavily on Olivier Le Cour Grandmaison, *Les Citoyennetés en Révolution (1784–1794)* (Paris: PUF, 1992), and P. Pluchon, *Nègres et Juifs au XVIIIe siècle* (Paris: Taillandier, 1984). For the discourse on the Jews, I have picked up the main lines of my discussion in *La République et les Juifs*.

25. Le Cour Grandmaison, *Les Citoyennetés*, 199.

26. "Opinion de R. Ribes, deputé du département de l'Aude sur le régime des Colonies," in "Archives parlementaires de 1787 à 1860. Recueil complet des débats législatifs et politiques des Chambres françaises par MM. Madival et E. Laurent" (Paris: Dupont, 1867), January 1792 session.

27. Abbé Maury, Arch. parl., May 13, 1791 session.

28. Arch. parl. (February 18, 1794), vol. 85, 225.

29. Mirabeau, arch. parl. (March 8, 1790), vol. 12, 76.

30. Montesquieu, *Spirit of Laws*, bk. 15, CHS. 1, §7 (online source).

31. Cf. *Les Citoyennetés*, 205.

32. Cf. ibid., 207.

33. Voltaire, "Essais sur les mœurs et l'esprit des nations et sur les principaux faits de l'histoire depuis Charlemagne jusqu'à Louis XIV," in *Œuvres complètes* (Paris: Imprimerie de la Société littéraire et typographique, 1784–1789), vol. 16, 10.

34. Emmanuel Kant, *Observations on the Feeling of the Beautiful and the Sublime* (online source).

35. Ibid.

36. "Adresse à la Convention nationale, à tous les Clubs et sociétés patriotiques pour les nègres détenus en esclavage dans les Colonies françaises de l'Amérique sous le régime de la République" (May 27, 1793), cf. *Les Citoyennetés*, 212.

37. Ibid., 213.

38. Ibid., 218.

39. Ibid.

40. Condorcet, "Réflexions sur l'esclavage des nègres" (1788), in *Œuvres* (Paris: Firmin-Didot, 1847–1879), vol. 7, 79.

41. Ibid., 92.

42. *Les Citoyennetés*, 225.

43. At the National Convention on October 31, 1793, in Elisabeth Badinter (ed.), *Paroles d'hommes, 1790–1793* (Paris: P.O.L., 1989), 168.

44. Rousseau, *Émile or Education*, Book V, §1433 (online source).

45. Ibid., §1266.

46. E. Kant, "Anthropologie du point de vue pragmatique," in *Œuvres completes*, vol. 3, 1026.

47. *Les Citoyennetés*, 284

48. Condorcet, "Sur l'admission des femmes au droit de cité" (July 3, 1790), *Oeuvres*, vol. 10, 126.

49. Frank Maloy Anderson, ed., *The Constitution and Other Select Documents Illustrative of the History of France, 1789–1907* (New York: Russell and Russell, 1908), 59–61 (translation slightly modified).

50. Arendt, *Imperialism*, 293. Moreover, "people took refuge in statelessness after the First World War in order to remain where they were and avoid being deported to a 'homeland' where they would be strangers" (Arendt, *Imperialism*, 254).

51. Ibid., 280, note 27.

52. Cf. Sophie Wahnich, *L'Impossible citoyen: l'étranger dans le discours de la Révolution française* (Paris: Albin Michel, 1997).

53. André Frossard, *Le Crime d'être né* (Paris: Desclée de Brouwer, 1997).

54. Arendt, *Imperialism*, 291.

55. Jeremy Bentham, *Sophismes anarchiques*, in *Critiques des droits de l'homme*, 31.

56. Marx, *On the Jewish Question* (online source).

57. Burke, *Reflections on the Revolution in France* (online source).

58. Ibid.

59. Ibid.

60. Maistre, *Considerations on France* (online source).

61. Ibid.

62. Ibid.

63. Benjamin Constant, in *Critiques*, 41.

64. Maistre, *Considerations on France* (slightly modified translation; online source).

65. Maistre, *Du pape*, n. 13, §VIII, 112–13.

66. Savigny in *Critiques*, 81

67. Ibid.

68. Arendt, *The Origins of Totalitarianism*, 301.

69. Ibid.

70. Ibid.

71. Ibid.

72. Ibid., 302.

73. Ibid.

74. Ibid., 301–302.

75. Cf. Claude Lefort, *Essais sur le politique, XIXe–XXe siècles* (Paris: Le Seuil, 1986) 295.

76. Jacques Lacan translated Freud's *verwerfung* (rejection, excision, symbolic abolition) by the term *forclusion*. To "foreclose" originally means to exclude, to cut off, to prevent in a definitive way, whence the idea of cutting off from the law in the name of the law. What is outlawed is included in the framework of the law (take, for instance, an *"État d'exception,"* or "State of Emergency," which is provided for by the law, or the foreclosure by which the law suspends the validity of one of its rulings as of a certain date).

77. Solal Rabinovitch, *La Forclusion* (Toulouse: Erès, 1998), 87.

78. Ibid.

79. Ibid., 22.

80. Ibid.

81. It is through the agency of the physical "fetish" of the origin that the moderns got back in touch with the origin, in an exacerbated manner, of course. The best example thereof is the athletic competition. Sports has thus become a vehicle of contact with anteriority, hence a vehicle of religious experience.

82. Pierre Legendre, "Analecta" in *Filiation, Léçons IV, suite 2*, ed. Alexandra Papageorgiou-Legendre, 186–87 (Paris: Fayard, 1990).

83. Ibid. [TN: For Legendre's use of the term *Interdiction* and other concepts quoted below, such as the Third, see "An Abbreviated Glossary," in *Law and the Unconscious: A Legendre Reader*, ed. Peter Goodrich (New York: St. Martin's Press, 1997).]

84. Alexandra Papageorgiou-Legendre, ibid., 174.

85. Legendre, "Prologue," ibid., 16.

86. Ibid, 17. *Tiers*, or Third, is the outside element, the founding reference.

87. Ibid., 11.

88. Ibid., 17.

89. Ibid., 180.

90. Ibid., 187.

91. Ibid., 191–92.

92. Ibid., 196.

93. Ibid., 193.

94. Ibid., 192.

95. Ibid., 193.

96. Ibid., 200.

97. Ibid., 190.

98. Ibid., 191.

99. Legendre, "L'attaque nazie contre le principe de filiation," ibid., 205–21.

100. Ibid., 205.

101. Ibid., 206.

102. Ibid.

103. Ibid., 209.

104. Ibid.

105. Ibid., 208.

106. Ibid., 206.
107. Ibid., 208.
108. Ibid., 207.
109. Ibid., 208.
110. Ibid., 207–208.
111. According to Arendt, "The loss of a community willing and able to guarantee any rights whatsoever [. . .] cannot be expressed in the categories of the eighteenth century because they presume that rights spring immediately from the 'nature' of man." See *The Origins of Totalitarianism*, 297.
112. Legendre, "L'attaque," 205.

Chapter 9

1. Cf. my own work on the subject in *Philosophie de la loi*, and "La Fonction lévitique," in *Le Politique et le religieux*, ed. Alvarez-Pereyre (Centre de recherche français de Jérusalem: CNRS, 1995), and a shorter version of this article in the *M.A.U.S.S.* 8 (Paris: La Découverte, 2nd semester, 1996).
2. Cf. J.-C. Filloux, "Personne et sacré chez Durkheim," *Archives de Sciences Sociales des Religions* 69 (January–March 1990): 41.
3. Cf. José A. Prades, "La Religion de l'humanité. Notes sur l'anthropocentrisme durkheimien," *Arch. Sc. Soc. des Rel.*, ibid., 57.
4. Saint-Simon, *Système industriel* VI 53, cited in *Arch.*, ibid., 58.
5. Émile Durkheim, *La science sociale et l'action* (Paris: Presses Universitaires de France, 1970), 197.
6. Durkheim, *Suicide, A Study in Sociology*, trans. John Spaulding and George Simpson (London: Routledge & Kegan Paul, 1952), 334.
7. Durkheim, *Moral Education, A Study in the Theory & Application of the Sociology of Education*, trans. Everett Wilson and Herman Schnurer (New York: The Free Press, 1961), 107.
8. W. S. F. Pickering, "The Eternality of the Sacred: Durkheim's Error?" *Archives*, 100.
9. Durkheim, "Individualism and the Intellectuals," in *Émile Durkheim on Morality and Society: Selected Writings*, ed. Robert Bellah (Chicago: University of Chicago Press, 1973) (online source).
10. Durkheim, *Sociology and Philosophy*, trans. D. F. Pocock (Glencoe, IL: The Free Press, 1953), 37.
11. Durkheim, *Moral Education*, 107.
12. Durkheim, *Sociology and Philosophy*, 69.
13. Ibid., 36.
14. Ibid., 37.
15. Filloux, "Personne et sacré, 45.
16. Cf. Filloux, "Personne et sacré," 51: remarks and quotations taken from Durkheim, "Éducation sexuelle et santé social," in *Textes* 2 (Paris: Minuit), 241–51.
17. Filloux, ibid., 51.

18. Durkheim, *Sociology and Philosophy*, 58–59.
19. Ibid., 53.
20. Ibid.
21. Quoted by Filloux, "Personne et sacré," 45. Durkheim, *Suicide*, 337.
22. Filloux, ibid., 46.
23. Ibid., 48.
24. Durkheim, "Individualism and the Intellectuals" (online source).
25. Quoted in Filloux, "Personne et sacré," 47.
26. Ibid.
27. Durkheim, "Individualism and the Intellectuals" (online source).
28. Ibid.
29. Filloux, "Personne et sacré," 45.
30. Paul Ladrière, "Durkheim et le retour," 148.
31. Filloux, "Personne et sacré," 45.
32. Ladrière, "Durkheim," 148.
33. Durkheim, *Elementary Forms*, 270.
34. Ibid., 271.
35. Durkheim, "Individualism."
36. Ibid.
37. Ibid.
38. Durkheim, *Elementary Forms*, 270.
39. Ladrière, "Durkheim," 149.
40. Durkheim, *Elementary Forms*, 272.
41. Ibid., 270 (translation slightly altered).
42. Ibid., 272.
43. Filloux, "Personne et sacré," 49.
44. Durkheim, *Leçons de sociologie* (Paris: PUF, 1997), 123.
45. Claude Lefort, *The Political Forms of Modern Society: Bureaucracy, Democracy, Totalitarianism* (Boston, MA: MIT, 1986), 279.
46. Ibid., 66–67.
47. Lefort, *Democracy and Political Theory*, trans. David Macey (Oxford: Polity Press, 1988), 16 (translation altered).
48. Lefort, *The Political Forms*, 301.
49. Ibid., 287.
50. Ibid., 302.
51. Ibid., 303–304.
52. Lefort, *Democracy and Political Theory*, 232.
53. I have developed a political theory based on "foreignness" rather than autochtony in *Philosophie de la Loi*, and in *La Séparation d'amour* (Paris: Arléa, 1998).
54. Lefort, *Democracy*, 235.
55. Ibid., 251.
56. Ibid., 293.
57. "On the Irreducible Element" is the title of the chapter containing the essay "Permanence of the Theologico-Political?."
58. See Turner, *Le Phénomène rituel*.

59. Cf. Spinoza, *Tractatus Theologico-Politicus*, § XVI, and Jean-Jacques Rousseau, *The Social Contract*, Book IV, § 8.

60. For more on "political religions," see Robert Bellah, "Civil Religion in America," *Daedalus* (1967), and the overview by Danièle Hervieur-Léger in *La Religion pour mémoire* (Paris: Le Cerf, 1993), 162.

61. Cf. Jean-Pierre Vernant and Pierre Vidal-Naquet, *Myth and Tragedy in Ancient Greece*, trans. Janet Lloyd (New York: Zone, 1988); René Girard, *Violence and the Sacred*, trans. Patrick Gregory (Baltimore, MD: Johns Hopkins University Press, 1977). "Plato's Pharmacy," *Dissemination*, trans. Barbara Johnson (Chicago, IL: University of Chicago Press, 1981), 63–171.

62. Geza Roheim, *Animism, Magic and the Divine King* (London: Routledge and Kegan, 1930), 364.

63. Yves Chevalier, *L'Antisémitisme* (Paris: Cerf, 1998), 103.

64. Ibid., 106.

65. One desires what the other desires, or rather one desires the other person's desire more than the object of the other's desire, and the violence generated by this is expelled through the sacrifice of a scapegoat.

66. Girard, *Violence and the Sacred*, 79.

67. Ibid., 49.

68. Chevalier, *L'Antisémitisme*, 143.

69. Legendre, "Le Sujet du suicide," *Filiation*, 213.

70. Ibid., 214.

71. Ibid., 215.

72. Ibid., 216.

73. Ibid. [TN. For Legendre's particular use of the word "instance," see "Introduction to the Theory of the Image," in *Law and the Unconscious: A Legendre Reader*, ed. Peter Goodrich, 212 (New York: St. Martin's Press, 1997).]

74. Ibid., 219.

75. Ibid.

76. Ibid., 218.

77. Ibid., 216.

78. Ibid., 219.

79. Ibid., 220.

80. Ibid., 218.

81. Lefort, "Quinet and the Revolution that Failed," in *Democracy and Political Theory*, 123.

82. Ibid., 123.

83. Ibid., 124.

84. Ibid.

85. Ibid., 125.

86. Ibid., 126.

87. Ibid.

88. Ibid., 128.

89. This is the title of Book 16 in the first section of his work.

90. Ibid.

91. Ibid.

92. Ibid., 130.

93. Ibid., 127.

94. Ibid.

95. Ibid.

96. Sartre, *Anti-Semite and Jew*, 72–73.

97. Louis Moreau de Bellain, "Sacrifice et précarité, *La Revue du M.A.U.S.S.* 5 (First semester 1995): 158.

98. Jean-Pierre Dupuy, *Libéralisme et justice sociale* (Paris: Hachette), 145.

99. Caillé, "Sacrifice, don, utilitarisme," *La Revue du M.A.U.S.S.*, 276.

100. Guy Nicolas, "Résurgences contemporaines du don sacrificial," ibid., 147.

101. Ibid., 148.

102. Ibid.

103. Marcel Gauchet, *La Révolution des droits de l'homme* (Paris: Gallimard, 1989), 26.

104. Lefort, *The Political Forms of Modern Society*, 271–72 (slightly modified translation).

105. Dupuy, *Libéralism et justice sociale*, 44.

106. René Girard with Jean-Michel Oughourlian and Guy Lefort, *Things Hidden since the Foundation of the World* (Stanford, CA: Stanford University Press, 1978). Trans. Stephen Bann and Michael Metteer, Athlone Press, 1987.

107. J.-P. Dupuy, "John Rawls et la question du sacrifice," *La Revue du M.A.U.S.S.* 5 (Semester 1, 1995): 44.

108. Ibid., 46–47.

109. Cited by Caillé in "Sacrifice, don . . . ," 286.

110. Saint Augustine, *City of God*, X-6.

111. Caillé, "Sacrifice, don . . . ," 286.

112. Cf. Manent, "La Violence légitime," *Esprit*, 44.

113. Arendt, *Antisemitism*, 14.

114. Ibid., 4.

115. Ibid., 4–5.

116. Ibid., 22.

117. Sartre, *Anti-Semite and Jew*, 51.

118. Ibid., 136.

119. Ibid., 91.

120. Ibid., 89.

121. Ibid., 85.

122. Ibid., 87.

123. Ibid., 88.

124. Ibid., 135–36.

125. Ibid., 50.

126. Ibid., 136.

127. Ibid., 26.

128. Ibid., 29.

129. Ibid., 57.

130. Ibid.

131. Ibid., 69.
132. Ibid., 67–68.
133. Ibid.

Chapter 10

1. Henry Rousso, *The Vichy Syndrome: History and Memory in France since 1944*, trans. Arthur Goldhammer (Cambridge, MA/London: Harvard University Press, 1991), 132.
2. Ibid., 133.
3. Ibid., 137.
4. Ibid., 138. Where in this typology would he fit the crisis that Vichy represented for the Jews in France?
5. Ibid.
6. Cf. my "From Individual to Collectivity: The Rebirth of the Jewish Nation in France," in *The Jews in Modern France*, ed. F. Malino and B. Wasserstein (Hanover: University Press of New England, 1985).
7. Rousso, *The Vichy Syndrome*, 157.
8. Interview with Henry Rousso, "Le Tribunal de l'histoire a jugé Vichy depuis longtemps," *Le Monde* (April 7, 1997).
9. Rousso, *The Vichy Syndrome*, op. cit., 134.
10. Interview with Pierre Nora, "Tout concourt aujourd'hui au souvenir obsédant de Vichy," *Le Monde*, April 7, 1998.
11. See my article "Le concept de communauté comme categorie de définition du judaïsme français," *Archives européennes de sociologies* 35 (1994): 49.
12. Cf. Shmuel Trigano, ed., "L'École de pensée juive de Paris," *Pardès* 23 (editions In Press, 1997), which traces an outline of an intellectual history.
13. Sartre, *Anti-Semite and Jew*, 139.
14. Ibid., 81.
15. Ibid., 82.
16. Ibid., 91.
17. Ibid., 87.
18. Ibid., 91.
19. Ibid., 94–95.
20. Ibid., 97.
21. I am purposefully leaving aside the Machiavellian interpretation.
22. Jean-Michel Chaumont, *La Concurrence des victimes. Génocide, identité, reconnaissance* (Paris: La Découverte, 1997), 334.
23. Ibid., 39. Chaumont quotes Simon Veil's testimony on this subject: "Jewish deportees were [. . .] dispossessed of their experience," ibid., 36.
24. Ibid., 231.
25. Ibid., 28.
26. Ibid., 249.
27. Ibid., 95.
28. Ibid., 50.

29. Ibid., 349.
30. Ibid., 240.
31. Ibid., 10.
32. Ibid., 321.
33. Ibid., 209.
34. Ibid., 210.
35. Ibid., 94.
36. Ibid., 201.
37. Ibid., 348.
38. Ibid., 242.
39. Ibid., 315.
40. Ibid., 224. Chaumont cites here my analysis in Trigano, ed., "Penser Auschwitz."

Part 3

1. By "Jewishness" I am referring to the many ways of being Jewish, religious or secular, as if there were a global prism, an abstract continuum that could bring together all of the specific modes of being Jewish in a single framework.

Chapter 11

1. See chapter 5, "The Universal Narrative of Singularity."
2. Cf. "Comment on écrit l'histoire juive," *Pardès* 1 (Paris: Lattes, 1985), reprinted in Trigano, *La Demeure oubliée, genèse religieuse et politique*, and "Espaces, rupture, unités," in *La Société juive à travers l'histoire*, ed. Trigano (Paris: Fayard, 1992–1994), vol. 3, 15–73.
3. Cf. Trigano, *Le Récit de la disparue, essai sur l'identité juive* (Paris: Gallimard, 1977); *La Nouvelle question juive* (Paris: Gallimard, 1979); *Philosophie de la Loi, l'origine de la politique dans la Tora* (Paris: Le Cerf, 1991).
4. Cf. Trigano, "Le Désert de l'amour, commentaire de Jérémie II," *Dédale* 7 and 8 (Paris: Maisonneuve et Larose, Spring 1998).
5. Cf. Trigano, "Comment on écrit l'histoire juive."
6. Cf. Trigano, "Introduction à une épistémologie des études juives," *La demeure oubliée . . .* , 443.
7. Cf. Trigano, *Le Récit de la disparue*; *La Nouvelle question juive*; *Philosophie de la Loi*.
8. Paul Ricœur, *Time and Narrative*, vol. 3, trans. Kathleen Blarney and David Pellauer (Chicago, IL: University of Chicago Press, 1988), 246.
9. Ibid.
10. Ibid., 248.
11. The term Ricœur employs in French is *intrigue*, which he says corresponds to the English "plot." It is not without interest to note that this is the term that designates the imaginary narrative, the "international Jewish plot," that democracy unconsciously produced to account for the continuity of Jewish identity.

12. Ricœur, *Time and Narrative*, vol. 1, 34.

13. Ricœur, *Time and Narrative*, vol. 3, 248.

14. This is the subject of my *La Demeure oubliée*.

15. Spinoza, *A Theologico-Political Treatise*, part 1, trans. Elwes, chapter 5, §83 (online source).

16. Ricœur, *Time and Narrative*, vol. 3, 332, note 16.

17. For a philosophical approach to this void, see Trigano, *Philosophie de la Loi*.

18. Cf. ibid. for the politics of the biblical void.

19. Ahad HaAm, "Torah Shebalev," in *Al Parashat Haderackim*, first printed in *Pardes* 2 (Odessa, 1854).

20. Cf. Trigano, *La Nouvelle Question juive*.

21. Ibid.

22. Cf. Trigano, "Lévinas et le projet de la philosphie juive," *Revue Descartes* 19, special "Emmanuel Lévinas" issue (Paris: Collège international de philosophie, PUF, 1998).

23. "Our great task is to express in Greek those principles about which Greece knew nothing. Jewish singularity awaits its philosophy." Emmanuel Lévinas, *Beyond the Verse: Talmudic Readings and Lectures*, trans. (slightly modified) Gary D. Mole (London: The Athlone Press, 1994).

24. The question of Israel's particularism in the universal haunted Jewish philosophers. Cf. Trigano, *La Demeure oubliée*.

25. Emmanuel Levinas, *Otherwise Than Being or Beyond Essence*, trans. Alphonso Lingis (The Hague: Martinus Nijhoff, 1974), 117.

26. Levinas, *Nine Talmudic Readings*, trans. Annette Aronowicz (Bloomington: Indiana University Press, 1990), 98.

27. Naomi Seidman, "Elie Wiesel and the Scandal of Jewish Rage," *Jewish Social Studies* 3, 1 (Fall 1996): 1–19.

28. Cf. Trigano, *Un exil sans retour ? Lettres à un Juif égaré* (Paris: Stock, 1996).

Chapter 12

1. Benedict Anderson, *Imagined Communities: Reflections on the Origin and Spread of Nationalism* (London and New York: Verso, 1991), 5.

2. Eric Hobsbawm and Terence Ranger, eds., *The Invention of Tradition* (Cambridge: Cambridge University Press, 1983).

3. Cf. the earlier discussion of the concepts that Legendre develops in *Filiation*.

4. Danièle Hervieu-Léger, *La Religion pour mémoire* (Paris: Le Cerf, 1993), 250.

5. Ricœur, *Time and Narrative*, 259.

6. Joseph Albo, *Sefer Haikarim*, fifteenth century. Cf. David Novak's enlightening analysis in "The Image of the Non Jew in Judaism, an historical and constructive study of the Noahide Laws," *Toronto Studies in Theology* 14 (Toronto and New York: The Edwin Mellen Press, 1983), 319.

7. Ibid., I. 5.

8. Ibid, I. 6.

9. Ibid., I. 10.

10. Cf. Trigano, *La Séparation d'amour,* § "La Morale collective."

Chapter 13

1. Pierre Bourdieu, "Quelques questions sur la question gay et lesbienne," in *Les Études gay et lesbiennes,* ed. Didier Eribon, 48 (Paris: Centre Georges-Pompidou, 1998).

2. Bersani, "Trahisons gaies," ibid., 65.

3. Sylviane Agacinski, *Parity of the Sexes,* trans. Lisa Walsh (New York: Columbia University Press, 2000), 15.

4. Ibid., 64.

5. Sartre, *Anti-Semite and Jew,* 117.

6. Ibid., 153.

7. Dominique Schnapper, *La Communauté des citoyens* (Paris: Gallimard, 1994), 103.

8. Gracchus Babeuf, *La Guerre de Vendée et le système de depopulation,* with an introduction, presentation, chronology, bibliography, and notes by Reynald Secher and Jean-Joël Brégeon (Paris: Tallendier, 1987). I thank Yolain Dilas-Rocherieux for bringing this book to my attention.

9. In the conclusion to *La Communauté des citoyens* (Paris: Gallimard, 1994), Schapper states her regret that "modern thought [. . .] destroyed the sacredness first of religion than of politics," when all power derives "from the sacred." And she recognizes that this development is ascribable to "the horrors perpetrated in the twentieth century in the name of political values" (103).

10. "There is no power except that constituted by the will of individuals or by the general will. It is to preserve this principle, in all its purity, that the constitution has abolished all corporations and their intermediary interests, from one end of the state to another, and henceforth recognizes only society as a whole, and individuals," the revolution proclaimed with the Chapelier Law of June 14, 1791. But these intermediary interests were to come back with a vengeance in the form of parties, associations, labor unions, and the Napoleonic empire's nobility, until the adoption of the famous French law on associations in July 1901.

11. Arendt, *The Origins of Totalitarianism,* 54.

12. For a more elaborate discussion of this point, see my *Philosophie de la loi.*

13. Charles Taylor, *Multiculturalism and "The Politics of Recognition"* (Princeton, NJ: Princeton University Press, 1993).

14. Cf. Trigano, *La Séparation d'amour.*

15. Emmanuel Levinas, *Outside the Subject,* trans. Michael B. Smith (Stanford, CA: Stanford University Press, 1994), 124.

16. Ibid., 125.

17. Ibid.

18. Ibid., 123.

19. Ibid., 124

20. Ibid., 117.

21. Ibid., 118.

22. Cf. Trigano, *Philosophie de la Loi*, chapter 1, "La théorie de la part gardée."

23. Cf. Trigano, *La Séparation d'amour*.

24. Sartre, *The Anti-Semite and the Jew*, 150.

25. This is the thesis I developed in *Philosophie de la loi*.

26. Antonio Negri, *Insurgencies: Constituent Power and the Modern State*, trans. Maurizia Boscagli (Minneapolis: University of Minnesota Press, 1999).

27. Ibid., 12.

28. Ibid., 13.

29. Ibid., 24–32.

30. Online source.

31. Jean-Jacques Rousseau, "The General Society of the Human Race," in *Social Contract and Discourses*, ed. G. D. H. Cole, 172–74 (London: J. M. Dent, 1993).

32. Ibid., 174.

33. Ibid.

34. See also Machiavelli: "And as the observance of the ordinances of religion is the cause of the greatness of a State, so their neglect is the occasion of its decline." *Discourses on the First Decade of Titus Livius*. Online source.

35. Spinoza, *Tractatus Theologico-Politicus*, § II.

36. Ibid., § XIX.

37. Quoted by Mona Ozouf in "L'idée républicaine et l'interprétation du passé national," *Le Monde* (June 19, 1998).

Index

323

Rome, 20, 32, 47, 66, 86, 87, 126, 131, 144, 167, 173, 176, 187, 201, 231, 234, 239, 260, 271, 282, 289, 305, 317
Rothschild, 128, 143
Rousseau, Jean-Jacques, 184, 195, 218, 226, 227, 233, 285, 287–289, 291, 292, 311, 315, 321
Rousso, Henry, 23, 239–241, 297, 317
Rubenstein, R. L., 298
Rue Copernic, 43

Saint Augustine, 232, 316
Saint-Just, 184
Saint-Simon, 204, 313
Sartre, Jean-Paul, 22, 100, 101–120, 121, 122–124, 131, 144, 146, 151, 157, 161–163, 179, 227, 235, 236, 243–245, 250, 262, 272, 285, 297, 305–308, 310, 316, 317, 320, 321
Savigny, F. K. von, 165–167, 168, 192, 193, 311
Scapegoat, 45, 75, 118, 120, 121, 123, 142, 146, 220, 221, 234, 235, 315
Schnapper, Dominique, 272, 274, 320
Schoelcher, Victor, 181, 183
Second World War, 4, 28, 29, 49, 78, 90, 99, 248, 249, 274
Segev, Tom, 64
Seidman, Naomi, 260, 319
Shapira, Anita, 68, 301
Sieyès, 230, 231
Sirat, René Shmuel, 31
Six day war, 30, 33, 34, 63, 241, 245, 257, 258
Socialism, 7, 25, 45, 50, 62, 103, 212, 216, 228, 309
Societas, 109, 217
Solzhenitsyn, 212, 260
SOS Racisme, 44
Spinoza, 218, 226, 254, 288, 292, 315, 319, 321
Stalin, Joseph, 7, 49, 50, 53, 54, 56, 58–60, 296, 299
Steele, Shelby, 51, 299

Steg, Adi, 31
Steiner, Georges, 1, 295

Talmon, Jacob, 7, 173, 296
Taylor, Charles, 280, 320
Thiéry, 296, 307, 310
Tocqueville, Alexis de, 134, 135, 181, 214, 235, 292, 310
Todorov, Tzvetan, 2, 3, 9, 43, 51–54, 56, 58, 99, 239, 242, 245, 295, 296, 298–300
Torah, 73, 200, 319
Totalitarianism, 5–7, 9, 10, 50, 54, 59, 62, 75, 101, 104, 120, 133, 144, 146, 163, 171, 173, 187, 199, 211, 213–216, 224, 271, 282, 289, 307, 311, 313, 314, 320
Toussenel, 102
Transcendence, 4, 109, 168, 214, 216–219, 224, 230, 232, 233, 255, 272, 282–292
Tribalism, 53, 68, 72, 89, 112, 124, 125
Turner, Victor, 109, 217, 221, 306, 314

UGIF, 23
Uniqueness, 2, 3, 15, 28, 30, 51, 53, 128, 156, 238, 241, 246, 247, 281, 296, 300, 306
Universal suffrage, 172, 213, 218, 261, 272, 286
Universalism, 6, 11, 17, 25, 68, 83, 112, 113, 122, 127, 161, 163, 164, 167, 229, 258, 263, 271–282, 284, 292
Universality, 1, 3, 4, 8, 15, 26, 28, 30, 39, 52, 53, 57, 61, 65, 76, 79, 80, 83, 84, 86–89, 94, 96–100, 102, 108, 110, 111, 128, 134, 137, 139, 141, 142, 143, 153, 158, 160, 161–163, 165, 166–170, 171, 172, 176, 178, 179, 182, 188, 189, 191, 193, 194, 208, 210, 211–214, 218, 219, 220, 232, 233, 238, 242, 247, 249, 250, 253, 258, 259, 261, 268, 271, 272,